First World War
and Army of Occupation
War Diary
France, Belgium and Germany

11 DIVISION
Headquarters, Branches and Services
General Staff
1 September 1917 - 7 September 1917

WO95/1789

The Naval & Military Press Ltd
www.nmarchive.com
Published in association with The National Archives

Published by

The Naval & Military Press Ltd

Unit 10 Ridgewood Industrial Park,

Uckfield, East Sussex,

TN22 5QE England

Tel: +44 (0) 1825 749494

www.naval-military-press.com

www.nmarchive.com

This diary has been reprinted in facsimile from the original. Any imperfections are inevitably reproduced and the quality may fall short of modern type and cartographic standards.

© Crown Copyright
Images reproduced by permission of The National Archives, London, England, 2015.

Contents

Document type	Place/Title	Date From	Date To
Heading	11th Division General Staff Sep 1917		
Heading	War Diary, September 1917. General Staff. 11th. Division. Vol 16		
War Diary	X Camp. A.16.c.25	01/09/1917	04/09/1917
War Diary	Watou.	05/09/1917	11/09/1917
War Diary	D.17.d.0.0. (S.E. of Herzeele).	12/09/1917	18/09/1917
War Diary	Wormhoudt.	19/09/1917	24/09/1917
War Diary	Border Camp 28/A.30.Central.1/20,000	25/09/1917	30/09/1917
Miscellaneous	Appendix 1. Location Of Units.		
Miscellaneous	1st. August 1917. 11th Division. Location Of Units At 8 A.M. August 2nd.1917	01/08/1917	01/08/1917
Miscellaneous	2nd. August, 1917. 11th. Division. Location Of Units At 8 A.M. 3rd. August 1917	02/08/1917	02/08/1917
Miscellaneous	3rd. August, 1917. 11th. Division.	03/08/1917	03/08/1917
Miscellaneous	4th. August 1917. 11th. Division.	04/08/1917	04/08/1917
Miscellaneous	11th. Division No. G.S. 169	05/08/1917	05/08/1917
Miscellaneous	6th. August, 1917 11th. Division.	06/08/1917	06/08/1917
Miscellaneous	11th. Division. Location Of Units At 6 A.M. 8th. August. 1917	08/08/1917	08/08/1917
Miscellaneous	8th. August, 1917. 11th. Division. Location Of Units At 8 A.M. August 9th. 1917	08/08/1917	08/08/1917
Miscellaneous	9th. August, 1917. 11th. Division. Location Of Units At 8 A.M. August 10th. 1917	09/08/1917	09/08/1917
Miscellaneous	11th. Division No. G.S. 231. Location Of Units At 8 A.M. August 11th. 1917	11/08/1917	11/08/1917
Miscellaneous	11th. August 1917. 11th. Division. Location Of Units At 8 A.M. 12th. August 1917	11/08/1917	11/08/1917
Miscellaneous	12th. August 1917. 11th. Division. Location Of Units At 8 A.M. August 13th 1917	12/08/1917	12/08/1917
Miscellaneous	13th. August 1917. 11th. Division.	13/08/1917	13/08/1917
Miscellaneous	14th. August 1917. 11th. Division.	14/08/1917	14/08/1917
Miscellaneous	15th. August 1917. 11th. Division.	15/08/1917	15/08/1917
Miscellaneous	16th. August 1917. 11th. Division.	16/08/1917	16/08/1917
Miscellaneous	17th. August 1917. 11th. Division	17/08/1917	17/08/1917
Miscellaneous	18th. August 1917. 11th. Division.	18/08/1917	18/08/1917
Miscellaneous	11th. Division. No. G.S. 404. 11th. Division. Location Of Units At 8 A.M. August 20th. 1917	20/08/1917	20/08/1917
Miscellaneous	20th. August 1917. 11th. Division.	20/08/1917	20/08/1917
Miscellaneous	21st. August 1917. 11th. Division.	21/08/1917	21/08/1917
Miscellaneous	22nd. August 1917. 11th. Division No. G.S. 130	22/08/1917	22/08/1917
Miscellaneous	24th August, 1917. 11th Division.	24/08/1917	24/08/1917
Miscellaneous	23rd. August 1917. 11th. Division No. G.S. 454	23/08/1917	23/08/1917
Miscellaneous	25th. August 1917. 11th. Division No. G.S. 480	25/08/1917	25/08/1917
Miscellaneous	11th. Division.	27/08/1917	27/08/1917
Miscellaneous	27th August, 1917. 11th Division.	27/08/1917	27/08/1917
Miscellaneous	28th. August. 1917. 11th. Division.	28/08/1917	28/08/1917
Miscellaneous	29th. August. 1917. 11th. Division.	29/08/1917	29/08/1917
Miscellaneous	30th. August. 1917. 11th. Division.	30/08/1917	30/08/1917
Miscellaneous	11th. Division. Location Of Units At 8 A.M. September 1st. 1917	31/08/1917	31/08/1917

Heading	Appendix 4. Diary Of Messages Recieved And Despatched During Operations		
Heading	Diary of Messages Received During Operations 16th to 30th August 1917		
Heading	Diary of Messages Despatched During Operations 16th to 30th August, 1917		
Heading	Appendix 2. Divisional Orders.		
Miscellaneous	11th Division No. G.S. 127	01/08/1917	01/08/1917
Operation(al) Order(s)	11th Division Order No. 94. Appendix 2.a 23	05/08/1917	05/08/1917
Miscellaneous	Table Of Moves To Accompany 11th. Divisional Order No. 94		
Miscellaneous	Distribution 11th. Division 10 a.m. 8/8/1917	08/08/1917	08/08/1917
Miscellaneous	11th Division Order No. 95. Appendix 2.b.	09/08/1917	09/08/1917
Miscellaneous	11th. Division No. G.S. 246	10/08/1917	10/08/1917
Operation(al) Order(s)	Addendum No. 1 To 11th. Division Order No. 95. Divisional Cavalry & Liaison Work.		
Miscellaneous	11th. Division No. G.S. 237	10/08/1917	10/08/1917
Map	Poelcappelle		
Miscellaneous	11th Division No. G.S. 281	12/08/1917	12/08/1917
Operation(al) Order(s)	To Accompany 11th. Division Order No. 95. Machine Gun Programme & Barrage Map. Appendix 2		
Miscellaneous	Table 1		
Miscellaneous	Table 2		
Map	Poelcappelle		
Diagram etc			
Miscellaneous	11th. Division No. G.S. 307	13/08/1917	13/08/1917
Operation(al) Order(s)	To Accompany 11th. Division Order No. 95. Machine Gun Programme & Barrage Map. Appendix 2		
Miscellaneous	Table 1		
Miscellaneous	Table 2		
Diagram etc	Machine Gun Barrage Map To Accompany Appendix 2		
Miscellaneous	11th. Division No. G.S. 246	10/08/1917	10/08/1917
Map	Poelcappelle		
Map	Trenches Corrected To 5-8-17		
Operation(al) Order(s)	To Accompany 11th. Division Order No. 95. Machine Gun Programme & Barrage Map.		
Operation(al) Order(s)	To Accompany 11th. Division Order No. 95. R.E. Instructions.		
Operation(al) Order(s)	Administrative Instruction No. 19. (In Connection With 11th Division Order No 95).	08/08/1917	08/08/1917
Miscellaneous	11th Division. No. S/388	15/08/1917	15/08/1917
Diagram etc	Machine Gun Barrage Map To Accompany Appendix 2		
Operation(al) Order(s)	To Accompany 11th. Division Order No. 95. Medical Arrangements.		
Operation(al) Order(s)	To Accompany 11th. Division Order No. 95. Arrangements For "Contact" And "Infantry Protection" Aeroplanes.		
Miscellaneous	11th. Division No. G.S. 328	15/08/1917	15/08/1917
Operation(al) Order(s)	(To Accompany 11th. Division Order No. 95.) Arrangements For Inter-Communication. Appendix 7		
Diagram etc			
Map	11th Div. Map No 15		
Miscellaneous	(To Accompany 11th. Division Order No. 95.) Arrangements For Inter-Communication. Appendix 7		
Diagram etc			
Miscellaneous	11th. Division No. G.S. 237	10/08/1917	10/08/1917

Type	Description	Date 1	Date 2
Miscellaneous	11th. Division No. G.S. 274	12/08/1917	12/08/1917
Operation(al) Order(s)	11th Division Order No. 96. Appendix 2.c.	10/08/1917	10/08/1917
Operation(al) Order(s)	Movement Table To Accompany 11th. Division Order No. 96		
Miscellaneous			
Operation(al) Order(s)	11th Division Order No. 97. Appendix 2.d.	10/08/1917	10/08/1917
Map	Poelcappelle		
Operation(al) Order(s)	Appendix 1. (11th Divisional Artillery Order No. 57	12/08/1917	12/08/1917
Miscellaneous	Table "A" Artillery Instructions.		
Miscellaneous	Table "B" 11th Divisional Artillery Programme (To Accompany 11th D.A. Order No. 57.)18-Pdr Barrages.		
Miscellaneous	Table B 11th Divisional Artillery Programme (To Accompany 11th D.A. Order No. 57) 18-Pdr. Barrage.		
Miscellaneous	Table C 11th Divisional Artillery Programme (To Accompany 11th D.A. Order No. 57) 4.5" Hof. Barrages		
Miscellaneous	Table C 11th Divisional Artillery Programme (To Accompany 11th D.A. Order No. 57) 4.5" Howitzer Barrages.		
Miscellaneous	11th Divisional Artillery. Table D. (to Accompany 11th D.A Order No 57) Smoke Barrages.		
Miscellaneous	Table "E" Rates Of Fire		
Miscellaneous	Table "F". Artillery Liaison Officers.		
Miscellaneous	Table "G".		
Operation(al) Order(s)	Distribution of Order No. 57		
Miscellaneous	11th. Division No. G.S. 304	13/08/1917	13/08/1917
Miscellaneous	11th. Division No. G.S. 297	13/08/1917	13/08/1917
Miscellaneous	11th. Division No. G.S. 295	13/08/1917	13/08/1917
Miscellaneous	11th. Division No. G.S. 297	13/08/1917	13/08/1917
Miscellaneous	11th. Division No. G.S. 329	15/08/1917	15/08/1917
Operation(al) Order(s)	11th Division Order No. 98. Appendix 2.e.	13/08/1917	13/08/1917
Miscellaneous	11th Division No. G.S. 296	13/08/1917	13/08/1917
Operation(al) Order(s)	11th Division Order No. 99. Appendix 2F	14/08/1917	14/08/1917
Miscellaneous	11th. Division No. G.S. 328.	15/08/1917	15/08/1917
Miscellaneous	11th. Division No. S/388	15/08/1917	15/08/1917
Miscellaneous	C Form. Messages And Signals.		
Operation(al) Order(s)	11th Division Order No. 100. Appendix 2g	17/08/1917	17/08/1917
Miscellaneous	Table To Accompany 11th Division Order No. 100		
Miscellaneous	11th. Division No. G.S. 374	17/08/1917	17/08/1917
Miscellaneous	11th. Division Instructions No. 9	17/08/1917	17/08/1917
Operation(al) Order(s)	11th. Division Order No. 101. Reference Poelcappelle Map 1/10.000. Appendix 2R	18/08/1917	18/08/1917
Diagram etc			
Operation(al) Order(s)	11th Division Order No. 102. Appendix 2 J	19/08/1917	19/08/1917
Miscellaneous	11th. Division No. G.S. 373. 33rd. Inf. Bde. "G" Battn. Tanks. 11th. Division Warning Order.	17/08/1917	17/08/1917
Miscellaneous	C Form Messages And Signals.		
Operation(al) Order(s)	11th Division Order No. 103. Appendix 2.k.	20/08/1917	20/08/1917
Miscellaneous	11th. Division No. G.S.432	21/08/1917	21/08/1917
Miscellaneous	Machine Gun Programme.		
Diagram etc			
Miscellaneous	Table 1		
Operation(al) Order(s)	11th Division Order No. 104. Appendix 2.l.	22/08/1917	22/08/1917
Miscellaneous	11th. Division No. G.S. 469	23/08/1917	23/08/1917
Miscellaneous	Table To Accompany 11th. Division Order No. 104		
Miscellaneous	11th. Division No. G.S. 449	23/08/1917	23/08/1917

Type	Description	Date	Date
Operation(al) Order(s)	11th Division Order No. 105. Appendix 2.m.	25/08/1917	25/08/1917
Operation(al) Order(s)	Appendix 2. To Accompany 11th. Division Order No. 105. Machine Gun Programme.		
Miscellaneous	Table 1		
Diagram etc	Machine Gun Barrage Map		
Operation(al) Order(s)	Appendix 3. (To Accompany 11th. Division Order No. 105). R.E. Instructions.		
Operation(al) Order(s)	Appendix 4. To Accompany 11th. Division Order No. 105. Administrative Instructions.		
Operation(al) Order(s)	Appendix 5. To Accompany 11th. Division Order No. 105. Medical Arrangements.		
Operation(al) Order(s)	Appendix 6. (To Accompany 11th. Division Order No. 105). Inter-Communication.		
Operation(al) Order(s)	Appendix 7. (To Accompany 11th. Division Order No. 105). Liaison Arrangements.		
Operation(al) Order(s)	11th. Division No. G.S. 509. Reference 11th. Division Order No. 105 Dated	26/08/1917	26/08/1917
Miscellaneous	11th. Division No. G.S. 507	26/08/1917	26/08/1917
Miscellaneous	11th. Division No. G.S. 490. Herewith Appendix 6, "Inter-Communication To 11th. Division Order No. 105	25/08/1917	25/08/1917
Miscellaneous	11th. Division No. G.S. 500	25/08/1917	25/08/1917
Diagram etc	Diagram of Visual Stations.		
Diagram etc	Amplifier & Power Buzzer Communications All Stations Can Send Both Ways		
Diagram etc	Wore Less Communications All Stations Can Send Both Ways.		
Map	Poelcappelle		
Miscellaneous	11th. Division No. G.S. 469. 11th. Division Order No. 104 Dated 22/8/17. Para.	23/08/1917	23/08/1917
Miscellaneous	Table To Accompany 11th Division Order No. 104		
Miscellaneous	11th. Division No. G.S. 509. Reference 11th. Division Order No. 105 Dated 25/8/17	26/08/1917	26/08/1917
Miscellaneous	11th. Division No. G.S. 483	25/08/1917	25/08/1917
Miscellaneous	Machine Gun Programme.		
Miscellaneous	Table 1		
Diagram etc			
Miscellaneous	11th. Division No. G.S. 432	21/08/1917	21/08/1917
Miscellaneous	11th. Division No. G.S. 374	17/08/1917	17/08/1917
Miscellaneous	11th. Division Instruction No. 9	17/08/1917	17/08/1917
Miscellaneous	C Form (Original). Messages And Signals		
Operation(al) Order(s)	Provisional: To Be Brought Into Force By A Wire From B.H.Q. 11th. Division Order No. 106. Appendix 2.n. 22	27/08/1917	27/08/1917
Miscellaneous	Movement Table To Accompany 11th. Division Order No. 106		
Miscellaneous			
Miscellaneous	11th. Division No. G.S. 505	26/08/1917	26/08/1917
Operation(al) Order(s)	11th. Division Order No. 107	26/08/1917	26/08/1917
Miscellaneous	11th. Division No. G.S. 394	29/09/1917	29/09/1917
Miscellaneous	11th. Division Instructions No. 11. (Reference Special Map Issued To Commanders).	29/09/1917	29/09/1917
Map			
Map	Ref: 11th Div. G.S. 860		
Diagram etc	11th Div: Diagram No 17b		
Diagram etc	11th Div: Diagram No 17		
Map	Dispositions of 33rd Infantry Bde: at 8 A.M.		
Miscellaneous	11th. Division No. G.S. 394	18/08/1917	18/08/1917

Map	Poelcappelle		
Miscellaneous	11th. Division No. G.S.470	23/08/1917	23/08/1917
Map	Poelcappelle		
Miscellaneous	11th. Division No. G.S. 483	25/08/1917	25/08/1917
Heading	War Diary. Weekly Operation Reports. Appendix 5		
Miscellaneous	11th. Division Weekly Operation Report For Period 10 A.M. 8th August To Noon 10th. August.	08/08/1917	08/08/1917
Miscellaneous	11th. Division Weekly Operation Report For Period 10 A.M. 11th. August To 8 A.M. 16th. August.	11/08/1917	11/08/1917
Miscellaneous	11th. Division Weekly Operation Report From 8 A.M. 17/8/17 To 8 A.M. 24/8/17. (In Continuation Of G.S. 377 Dated 17/8/17).	17/08/1917	17/08/1917
Miscellaneous	11th. Division Weekly Operation Report. From 8 A.M. August 24th. To 8 A.M. August 31st. (In Continuation Of G.S. 473 Dated 24/8/17.)	24/08/1917	24/08/1917
Miscellaneous			
Heading	Appendix 1. Location Returns.		
Miscellaneous	11th. Division No. G.S. 921. 11th. Division.	30/09/1917	30/09/1917
Miscellaneous	11th. Division No. G.S. 884. Amendment To Location Return Dated 28/9/17	28/09/1917	28/09/1917
Miscellaneous	28th. Sept. 1917. 11th. Division. 11th. Division No. G.S. 885	28/09/1917	28/09/1917
Miscellaneous	11th. Division No. G.S. 866. 11th. Division.	28/09/1917	28/09/1917
Miscellaneous	11th. Division No. G.S. 851. 11th. Division.	26/09/1917	26/09/1917
Miscellaneous	25th Sept. 1917. 11th Division.	25/09/1917	25/09/1917
Miscellaneous	11th. Division. 11th. Division No. G.S. 819	24/09/1917	24/09/1917
Miscellaneous	22nd September, 1917. 11th Division.	22/09/1917	22/09/1917
Miscellaneous	20th. September, 1917.11th. Division. 11th. Division No. G.S.751	20/09/1917	20/09/1917
Miscellaneous	19th. September, 1917. 11th. Division. 11th. Division No. G.S.771	19/09/1917	19/09/1917
Miscellaneous	18th September, 1917, 11th. Division	18/09/1917	18/09/1917
Miscellaneous	17th. September, 1917. 11th. Division. 11th. Division No. G.S.749	17/09/1917	17/09/1917
Miscellaneous	16th September, 1917. 11th. Division.	16/09/1917	16/09/1917
Miscellaneous	11th Division. Location Of Units At 8 A.M. 16th Sept. 1917	16/09/1917	16/09/1917
Miscellaneous	11th Division. Location Of Units At 8 A.M. 15th Sept 1917	14/09/1917	14/09/1917
Miscellaneous	11th. Division. Location Of Units At 8 A.M. September 14th.	14/09/1917	14/09/1917
Miscellaneous	12th September, 1917. Location Of Units At 8 A.M. September 13th.	12/09/1917	12/09/1917
Miscellaneous	11th Division.	12/09/1917	12/09/1917
Miscellaneous	10th September, 1917. 11th Division Location Of Units At 8 A.M. September 11th	10/09/1917	10/09/1917
Miscellaneous	10th September 1917. 11th Division. Location Of Units At 8 A.M. September 11th.		
Miscellaneous	10th. September 1917. 11th. Division. Location Of Units At 8 A.M. September 11th.	09/09/1917	09/09/1917
Miscellaneous	8th September, 1917. 11th Division. Location Of Units At 8 A.M. 9th Sept. 1917	08/09/1917	08/09/1917
War Diary	7th September 1917. 11th Division. Location Of Units At 8 A.M. Sept. 8th. 1917	07/09/1917	07/09/1917
Miscellaneous	6th September, 1917. 11th Division. Location Of Units At 8 A.M. Sept. 7th.	06/09/1917	06/09/1917

Miscellaneous	5th. Sept. 1917. 11th. Division. Location Of Units At 8 A.M.	05/09/1917	05/09/1917
Miscellaneous	4th. Sept. 1917. 11th. Division. 11th. Division No. G.S. 654	04/09/1917	04/09/1917
Miscellaneous	3rd. September 1917. 11th. Division. 11th. Division No. G.S. 622	03/09/1917	03/09/1917
Miscellaneous	2nd. September 1917. 11th. Division 11th. Division No. G.S. 608	02/09/1917	02/09/1917
Miscellaneous	1/9/1917. 11th. Division. 11th. Division No. G.S. 597	01/09/1917	01/09/1917
Heading	Appendix 2. Operation Orders.		
Operation(al) Order(s)	Amendment To 11th. Division Order No. 106	28/08/1917	28/08/1917
Operation(al) Order(s)	11th Division Order No. 109. Reference 1/20,000 Map. Sheet 27 N.E.	09/09/1917	09/09/1917
Miscellaneous	Table To Accompany 11th. Division Order No. 109		
Operation(al) Order(s)	11th. Division Order No. 108. Reference Maps 1/40,000 Sheets 27 & 28	03/09/1917	03/09/1917
Miscellaneous	Table To Accompany 11th. Division Order No. 108		
Miscellaneous	Administrative Instructions No. 23. (Reference To 11th Divn. Order No. 109 Dated 9/9/17	09/09/1917	09/09/1917
Miscellaneous	11th Division Warning Order.	16/09/1917	16/09/1917
Operation(al) Order(s)	11th Division Order No. 110	18/09/1917	18/09/1917
Miscellaneous	Warning Order. (Provisional)		
Operation(al) Order(s)	11th Division No. G.S. 922. Reference 11th Division Order No. 111. Dated 22nd. September, 1917	24/09/1917	24/09/1917
Operation(al) Order(s)	11th Division Order No. 111. Ref. 1/40,000 Map Sheet 28	22/09/1917	22/09/1917
Miscellaneous	Table To Accompany 11th. Division Order No. 111		
Operation(al) Order(s)	11th Division Order No. 112		
Miscellaneous	11th. Division No. G.S. 860. 32nd. Inf. Bde.	28/09/1917	28/09/1917
Operation(al) Order(s)	11th Division Order No. 113. Reference Pilckem & Poelcappelle 1/10.000 Special Maps & Sheet 27 1/20,000	28/09/1917	28/09/1917
Operation(al) Order(s)	11th. Division Order No. 114.	28/09/1917	28/09/1917
Operation(al) Order(s)	Movement Table To Accompany 11th. Division Order No. 114		
Miscellaneous			
Operation(al) Order(s)	Appendix To 11th. Division Order No. 114. Embussing And Debussing Routine.		
Operation(al) Order(s)	11th Division Order No. 115. Reference Poelcappelle Map 1/10,000	30/09/1917	30/09/1917
Miscellaneous	11th. Division No. G.S. 940	01/10/1917	01/10/1917
Miscellaneous	11th. Division No. G.S. 910	30/09/1917	30/09/1917
Miscellaneous	Movement Table To Accompany 11th. Division Order No. 114		
Miscellaneous			
Miscellaneous	11th. Division No. G.S. 962. Ref. Map Poelcappelle 1/10,000 Edition. 3	03/10/1917	03/10/1917
Miscellaneous	11th. Division No. G.S. 923. G.O.C., H.A.	30/09/1917	30/09/1917
Heading	Appendix 3. Miscellaneous.		
Miscellaneous	11th. Division No. G.S. 549	29/08/1917	29/08/1917
Miscellaneous	11th. Division No. G.S. 624. Part I	03/09/1917	03/09/1917
Operation(al) Order(s)	Notes On The Operations.		
Miscellaneous	11th. Division No. G.S. 625	03/09/1917	03/09/1917
Miscellaneous	11th. Division No. G.S. 905	29/09/1917	29/09/1917
Miscellaneous	11th. Division Instructions No. 10. Preliminary Instructions.	23/09/1917	23/09/1917

Miscellaneous	11th. Division No. G.S. 860. 32nd. Inf. Bde.	27/09/1917	27/09/1917
Miscellaneous	11th. Division No. G.S. 894	29/09/1917	29/09/1917
Miscellaneous	11th. Division Instructions No. 11. (Reference Special Map Issued To Commanders).	29/09/1917	29/09/1917
Heading	Appendix 4. 11th Division Intelligence Summaries.		
Miscellaneous	11th. Division Intelligence Summary No. 1. For 24 Hours Ending 6 P.M. 25th. Sept. 1917. Not To Be Taken Beyond Battalion Or Battery Headquarters.	25/09/1917	25/09/1917
Miscellaneous	11th. Division Intelligence Summary No. 2. For 24 Hours Ending 6 P.M. September 26th.	26/09/1917	26/09/1917
Miscellaneous	Appendix To 11th. Division Intelligence Summary No. 2		
Miscellaneous	Appendix To 11th. Division Intelligence Summary No. 2. Field Company R.E.		
Miscellaneous	11th. Division Intelligence Summary No. 3. For 24 Hours Ending 6 P.M. 28th. September 1917	28/09/1917	28/09/1917
Miscellaneous	11th. Division Intelligence Summary No. 4. For 24 Hours Ending Noon September 29th.	29/09/1917	29/09/1917
Miscellaneous	11th. Division Intelligence Summary No. 5. 24 Hours Ending Noon 30th. September 1917	30/09/1917	30/09/1917
Heading	Appendix 5. Divisional Instructions And Miscellaneous.		
Miscellaneous	11th. Division No. G.S. 168. Appendix 3a	05/08/1917	05/08/1917
Miscellaneous	11th. Division No. G.S. 196. Appendix 3b	07/08/1917	07/08/1917
Miscellaneous	11th. Division Instructions No. 5. (General Staff).		
Miscellaneous	11th. Division No. G.S. 193. Appendix 3c	07/08/1917	07/08/1917
Miscellaneous	11th. Division Instructions No. 6. R.E. Instructions.		
Miscellaneous	Artillery And Infantry Cable Communication Scheme. Appendix 3.d.		
Miscellaneous	11th. Division No. G.S. 226. Appendix 3.e.	09/08/1917	09/08/1917
Miscellaneous	11th. Division Instructions For The Offensive No. 7. Anti-Aircraft Precautions.		
Miscellaneous	11th. Division No. G.S. 232. Appendix 3f	10/08/1917	10/08/1917
Miscellaneous	11th. Division Instructions For The Offensive No. 6. Co-Operation Of Infantry With Tanks.		
Miscellaneous	Forming Up 34th. Infantry Brigade. Appendix 3.g.	10/08/1917	10/08/1917
Map	Secret.		
Miscellaneous	11th. Division No. G.S 374. Appendix 2.h.	17/08/1917	17/08/1917
Miscellaneous	11th. Division Instructions No. 9	17/08/1917	17/08/1917
Miscellaneous	11th. Division No. G.S. 415	20/08/1917	20/08/1917
Miscellaneous	Special Order Of The Day. Appendix 3i	29/08/1917	29/08/1917
Miscellaneous	XVIII. Corps Left Sector. Handing Over Report. Reference Special Maps Attached: Appendix 2.j.	30/08/1917	30/08/1917
Miscellaneous	Reference. Roads Passable For Light Traffic.		
Heading	Appendix 6. 11th Division. Report On Operations. 8th To 30th August, 1917		
Miscellaneous	11th. Division. Report On Operation-8th. To 30th. August 1917. Index.	08/08/1917	08/08/1917
Miscellaneous	11th. Division Order Of Battn.		
Miscellaneous	11th. Division. Report On Operation From 8th. To 20th. August 1917	08/08/1917	08/08/1917
Miscellaneous	Notes On The Operations.		
Miscellaneous			
Miscellaneous	Appendix 1. Artillery Report.		
Miscellaneous	Impressions.		
Miscellaneous	Ammunition Expenditure. From 8th August 1917 To 30th August 1917	08/08/1917	08/08/1917

Miscellaneous	Appendix 2. Machine Gun Support. 8th.-30th. August 1917	08/08/1917	08/08/1917
Miscellaneous	Appendix 3. R.E. Work.		
Miscellaneous	Appendix 4. Administrative Arrangements.		
Miscellaneous	Operations 27th. August 1917	27/08/1917	27/08/1917
Miscellaneous	Appendix 5. Medical Arrangements.		
Miscellaneous	Appendix 6. Inter-Communications. Period August 8th.-August 28.1917	08/08/1917	08/08/1917
Miscellaneous	Appendix 7. Casualties. From Noon 7th. To Noon 30th. August 1917	07/08/1917	07/08/1917
Miscellaneous	Appendix 8. Prisoners Etc. Capture Captured From 8th. August To 30th. August 1917	08/08/1917	08/08/1917
Heading	Maps 1, 2, & 3		
Map	Poelcappelle		
Map	51 Div Disposition Map Pilckem.		
Map	Poelcappelle		

11TH DIVISION

GENERAL STAFF
SEP 1917

CONFIDENTIAL.

WAR DIARY.

September 1917.

GENERAL STAFF.

11th. DIVISION.

Army Form C. 2118

WAR DIARY

~~INTELLIGENCE SUMMARY~~

(Erase heading not required.)

GENERAL STAFF,
11th Division.

September 1917.

Instructions regarding War Diaries and Intelligence Summaries are contained in F.S. Regs., Part II. and the Staff Manual respectively. Title Pages will be prepared in manuscript.

Place	Date	Hour	Summary of Events and Information	Remarks and references to Appendices
"X" Camp. A.16.c.25.	1/9/17.		Training continued. Re-organization of Platoons. Quiet day. For location of Units see Appendix 1.	
do	2nd.		Training. Conference held at D.H.Q. at 3 p.m. Brigadiers, Staff Officers and Heads of Departments attended. Decisions arrived at on various points brought out in recent operations, issued to all concerned under G.S. 549.	Appendix No.3.
do	3rd.		Instructions received for 33rd: and 34th Brigades to move on 4th September to WORMHOUDT Area. Warning wire issued to all concerned.	
do	4th.		Move of two Brigades to WORMHOUDT cancelled. Two Brigades move instead to WATOU Area by March Route on 4th September; D.O. No. 108 issued accordingly. Much hostile aerial activity during night 2nd/3rd and many bombs dropped in back areas. Weather fine.	APP. 2.
do			Weather fine. Hostile aeroplanes again very active over back areas during night 2rd/4th and many bombs dropped. Bombs fell amongst Lancashire Fusiliers, forming up for their march to WATOU Area, about 4-30 a.m. in DIRTY BUCKET Camp and caused about 90 casualties. (15 killed, 78 wounded). Brigades marched to WATOU Area, march completed by 12 noon. 33rd. and 34th.	
WATOU.	5th.		Divl. H.Q. closed at "X" Camp at 12 noon and opened at WATOU the same hour. All Brigades on Company and Platoon Training.	
"	6th. to 8th.		Training continued.	
"	9th.		Orders received from Corps for 33rd. and 34th. Brigades to move to HOUTKERQUE and LE NOUVEAU MONDE Areas respectively and Divl. H.Q. to move out of WATOU, "G" Branch to new Training Area and remainder to POPERINGHE. Order 109 issued accordingly.	APP. 2.
"	10th.		Training continued.	

1875 Wt. W593/826 1,000,000 4/15 J.B.C. & A. A.D.S.S./Forms/C. 2118.

Army Form C. 2118

WAR DIARY

~~INTELLIGENCE SUMMARY~~

(Erase heading not required.)

GENERAL STAFF,
11th. Division.

September, 1917.

Instructions regarding War Diaries and Intelligence Summaries are contained in F.S. Regs, Part II. and the Staff Manual respectively. Title Pages will be prepared in manuscript.

Place	Date	Hour	Summary of Events and Information	Remarks and references to Appendices
WATOU.	11th.		33rd. and 34th. Brigades moved to HOUTKERQUE and LE NOUVEAU MONDE Areas respectively. D.H.Q. moved from WATOU, "G" Branch to D.17.d.0.0. (Sheet 27) and remainder to POPERINGHE.	
D.17.d.0.0. (S.E. of HERZEELE).	12th. to 18th.		Training continued. Divl. Order No. 110 issued on 18th. inst. for move of D.H.Q. from POPERINGHE and D.17.d.0.0. to WORMHOUDT.	APP. 2.
WORMHOUDT.	19th.		Divl. H.Q. opened at WORMHOUDT at 4 p.m. Training continued. Heavy rain after 3 p.m.	
do	20th.		Training continued.	
do	21st.		Training continued. (Provisional) warning order issued, stating that 11th Division would probably relieve 51st Division in the line on the night 24/25th September.	APP.2
do	22nd.		(Saturday) Training continued. Divnl order no 111 issued, ordering 32nd Inf Bde to relieve 152nd Inf Bde in the line, on the night 24/25th Sept.	App.2
do	23rd.		(Sunday) A conference was held at Divnl Headquarters, at 3 p.m., at which forthcoming operations were discussed, and proposals made as to methods of carrying out the attack on POELCAPPELLE. Instructions No. 10 were issued, giving the role of the 32nd Brigade in holding the line, and the probable course of events, in the near future.	APP.3.
-do-	24th.		Weather fine and warm. 32nd. Inf. Bde. relieving 152nd. Inf. Bde. of 51st. Division in front line – locations as shown in Appendix 1. 11th. Div. Order No. 112 issued – re M.G. assistance to attack of 58th. Division on AVIATIX RIDGE (Appx. 2).	APP. 2.

Army Form C. 2118.

WAR DIARY
or
INTELLIGENCE SUMMARY

(Erase heading not required.)

GENERAL STAFF.

11th. Division.

Instructions regarding War Diaries and Intelligence Summaries are contained in F.S. Regs., Part II. and the Staff Manual respectively. Title Pages will be prepared in manuscript.

Place	Date	Hour	Summary of Events and Information	Remarks and references to Appendices
BORDER CAMP. 28/A.30. central. 1/20,000	25th.		Weather fine. Divisional Headquarters moved to BORDER CAMP 9.30 a.m. and G.O.C. took over command of the line. 32nd. Inf. Bde. completed relief 2.20 a.m. No Infantry action; our artillery active; enemy's artillery shelled the area behind our front line. Hostile aeroplanes active all day. 33rd. and 34th. Brigades engaged in training for coming offensive. Location report attached.	Map "A" App. 1.
—do—	26th.		Weather fine, but poor visibility. 32nd. Inf. Bde. redistributed its units, so as to reduce casualties and simplify reliefs during the night 25th/26th. Assisted attack of 58th. Division on our right with Artillery and M.G. barrage. Cyclist Battn. of XVIII Corps worked dummies on our front. 33rd. and 34th. Inf. Brigades practices for coming offensive carried out.	
—do—	27th.		Weather fine visibility fair. Our artillery engaged in harassing fire throughout the day, and also put down a barrage in response to S.O.S. from 48th. Division on our right. Enemy's artillery carried out searching and counter-battery fire. No Infantry activity. No change in dispositions. 33rd. and 34th. Brigades engaged in practising for coming offensive.	
—do—	28th.		Weather fine and warm. Hostile artillery used gas shell in the night 28th/29th. Handed over to 48th. Division on our right the portion of front shown on attached map "B" completed 11.15 p.m. Operation Order No. 113 issued for forthcoming relief of 32nd. Inf. Bde. by 33rd. and 34th. Inf. Bdes. 33rd. and 34th. Inf. Bdes. practising for coming offensive. Dispositions as in Appendix 1. No Infantry action.	App. 2.
—do—	29th.		Weather fine. Visibility poor in forenoon, good in afternoon. Issued Operation Order No. 114 and Instructions No. 11 about coming offensive. Locations as in Appendix 1. Units engaged in preparation for the offensive. Artillery carried out harassing fire. No Infantry action.	App. 2. App. 1

Army Form C. 2118.

WAR DIARY
or
INTELLIGENCE SUMMARY

GENERAL STAFF.
11th. Division.

(Erase heading not required.)

Instructions regarding War Diaries and Intelligence Summaries are contained in F. S. Regs., Part II. and the Staff Manual respectively. Title Pages will be prepared in manuscript.

Place	Date	Hour	Summary of Events and Information	Remarks and references to Appendices
BORDER CAMP. 28/A.30 central. 1/20,000	30th.		Weather fine. Visibility good. Units engaged in preparation for the offensive. Locations as in Appendix 1. Artillery continued harassing fire. No Infantry action. Operation Orders No. 115, 116 with appendices xxxxxxxxxxxxxxxxxxxxxxx and revised Movement Table to order No. 114 issued.	App. 2.
			C A S U A L T I E S.	
			Killed. Wounded. Missing. O. O.R. O. O.R. O. O.R. 2 104 25 505 - 3	
			(signed) Major General, Commanding 11th. Division.	
3/10/1917.				

APPENDIX 1.

LOCATION OF UNITS.

S E C R E T.   1st. August 1917b   11th. Division No. G.S. 12?a

11th. DIVISION.

Location of Units at 8 a.m. August 2nd, 1917.

```
32nd. Infantry Brigade.  H.Q.)  "D" Camp.
    9th. W. Yorkshire Regt.    )
    6th. Yorkshire Regt.       ) "A" 30 Central.

    6th. W. Riding Regt.       )
    8th. Yorks & Lancs. Regt.  ) POPERINGHE.

    32nd. M.G. Company.           A.30.
    32nd. T.M. Battery.           A.30. Central "D" Camp.


    33rd. M.G. Company.           "N" Camp F.27.a. & c. Sheet 27.
```

OTHERWISE NO CHANGE.

S E C R E T.   2nd. August, 1917.   11th. Division No. B.S. 140.

11th. DIVISION.

Location of Units at 5 a.m. 3rd. August 1917.

6th. E. Yorks Regt. (Pioneers) H.Q.   B.29.d.7.1.

             1 Coy. B.30.b.3.2.
             1 Coy. C.20.a.4.1½
             2 Coys. C.28.a.8.9.

33rd. M.G. Company.   F.27.a. Sheet 27.

     OTHERWISE NO CHANGE.

S E C R E T.   3rd. August, 1917.   11th. Division No. G.S. 146.

11th. DIVISION.

Location of Units at 8 a.m. August 4th. 1917.

33rd. Field Ambulance.	A.23.c.2.9.	Sheet 28.
34th. " "	A.28.a.20.65.	-do-
35th. " "	B.29.d.5.9.	Sheet 27.

Divnl. Salvage Coy. and Dump. A.22.d.7.5 on POPERINGHE-ELVERDINGHE
                                            Road.

OTHERWISE NO CHANGE.

4th. August 1917.   11th. Division No. G.S. 15A.

11th. DIVISION.

Location of Units at 8 a.m. Sunday 5th. August.1917.

NO CHANGE.

11th. Division No. G.S. 169.

Location of Units at 8 a.m. August 6th. 1917.

NO CHANGE.

5/8/17.

S E C R E T.   8th. August, 1917   11th. Division No. G.S.199.

11th. DIVISION.

Location of Units at 8 a.m. August 8th. 1917.

Divisional Headquarters.	6 Rue Des Pots, POPERINGHE.
32nd. Infantry Brigade.	H.Q. A.30.Central.
9th. W. Yorks Regt.	CANAL BANK.
6th. Yorkshire Regt.	A.30.Central.
8th. W. Riding Regt.	CANAL BANK.
8th. York & Lancs. Regt.	POPERINGHE.
32nd. M.G. Company.	CANAL BANK.
32nd. T.M. Battery.	CANAL BANK.
33rd. Infantry Brigade. H.Q.)	
6th. Lincoln Regt.)	
6th. Border Regt.)	
7th. S. Staffs Regt.) ST. JAN TER BIEZEN.	
9th. S. Foresters.)	
33rd. M.G. Company.)	
33rd. T.M. Battery.)	
34th. Infantry Brigade. H.Q.	WINDMILL CAMP. A.17.d. Sheet 28.
8th. Northd. Fusiliers.)	
9th. Lancashire Fusiliers.)	
5th. Dorset Regt.)	
11th. Manchester Regt.)	-do-
34th. M.G. Company.)	
34th. T.M. Battery.)	
6th. E. Yorks Regt. (Pioneers).	B.29.d.7.1.
C.R.E., 11th. Division.	
67th. Field Company.)	POPERINGHE.
68th. " ")	
86th. " "	A.30.a.0.4.
C.R.A., 11th. Division. H.Q.	22 Rue des Pretre, POPERINGHE.
58th. F.A.B.	B.29.d.6.1.
59th.	B.28.a.6.1.
D.A.C.	B.20.c.8.5.
D.T.M.O.	B.28.a.2.3.
A.D.M.S., 11th. Division.	POPERINGHE.
33rd. Field Ambulance.	A.23.c.2.9.
34th. " "	A.28.a.20.65.
35th. " "	F.29.d.5.9.
A.P.M., 11th. Division.	POPERINGHE.
D.A.D.O.S., 11th. Division.	L.11.b.3.3.
D.A.D.V.S., 11th. Division.	POPERINGHE.
22nd. Mobile Vet. Section.	F.22.c.2.3.
11th. Divisional Train. H.Q.	POPERINGHE., 16, Rue de la Balance.
No. 1 Company.	F.27.b.8.5.
No. 2 "	F.22.a.2.2.
No. 3 "	F.22.c.5.4.
No. 4 "	F.28.a.2.2.
11th. Divisional Supply Column.	E.29.b.5.2.
11th. Divisional Laundry.	40 Rue de Furnes, POPERINGHE.
Salvage Company and Dump.	A.22.d.7.5 on POPERINGHE-ELVERDINGHE ROAD

11th. DIVISION.

Location of Units at 8 a.m. 8th. August, 1917.

Divisional Headquarters. 6 Rue de Pots, POPERINGHE. Moving on 8th.
to "X" Camp, A.16.c.2.5.

32nd. Infantry Brigade. H.Q. FOCH FARM.
  9th. W. Yorkshire Regt. Front Line. Right Sub-sector.
  6th. Yorkshire Regt. 3 Coys. on Move to CANAL BANK.
    1 Coy. BLUE LINE.
  8th. W. Riding Regt. Front Line. Left Sub-sector.
  6th. York & Lancs. Regt.) On Move to CANAL BANK.

  32nd. M.G. Company. Line.
  32nd. T.M. Battery. CANAL BANK.

33rd. Infantry Brigade. H.Q.)
  6th. Lincoln Regt.)
  6th. Border Regt.)
  7th. S. Staffs Regt.) ST. JAN TER BIEZEN.
  9th. S. Foresters.) Moving on 8th. to DIRTY BUCKET
  33rd. M.G. Company.) CAMP. A.30.central.
  33rd. T.M. Battery.)

34th. Infantry Brigade. H.Q. WINDMILL CAMP. A.17.d. Sheet 28.
  Moving on 8th. to SIEGE CAMP. B.21.c.

  8th. Northd. Fusiliers.)
  9th. Lancs. Fusiliers.)
  5th. Dorset Regt.)
  11th. Manchester Regt.) -do-
  34th. T.M. Battery.)
  34th. M.G. Company.)

6th. E. Yorks Regt. (Pioneers) H.Q., A.30.a.1.1.
  Advanced H.Q. CANAL BANK.
  1 Coy. A.22.Central.
  1 Coy. C.20.a.40.15.
  2 Coys. CANAL BANK.

C.R.E., 11th. Division. POPERINGHE. Moving to "X" Camp.A.16.c.2.5
  67th. Field Company. CANAL BANK.
  68th. " " B.23.a.5.1.
  86th. " " CANAL BANK.

C.R.A., 11th. Division. H.Q. POPERINGHE. Moving to "X" Camp.
A.16.c.10.25.
  58th. F.A.B. B.29.d.8.1.
  59th. " B.28.a.6.1.
  D.A.C. B.20.c.8.5.
  D.T.M.O. B.28.a.2.3.

A.D.M.S., 11th. Division. POPERINGHE. Moving to "X" Camp.
A.16.c.2.5.
  33rd. Field Ambulance. ESSEX FARM. C.19.c.4.1.
  34th. " " ESSEX FARM. C.19.c.4.1.
  35th. " " F.29.d.5.9.

A.P.M., 11th. Division. POPERINGHE.

D.A.D.O.S., 11th. Division. A.22.d.6.5. (Sheet 28)

D.A.D.V.S., 11th. Division. POPERINGHE.
  22nd. Mobile Vet. Section. F.20.c.2.3.

11th. Divisional Train. H.Q. A.28.c.7.7. Sheet 28.
  No. 1 Company. A.21.b.6.4. "
  No. 2 " A.21.b.6.4. "
  No. 3 " A.28.c.7.7. "
  No. 4 " A.28.c.7.7. "

S E C R E T.   8th. August, 1917.   11th. Division No. G.S. 203.

11th. DIVISION.

Location of Units at 8 a.m. August 9th. 1917.

Divisional Headquarters.   "X" Camp, A.16.c.2.5.

32nd. Infantry Brigade.   H.Q. FOCH FARM.
  9th. W. Yorkshire Regt.   Front Line. Right Sub-sector.
  6th. Yorkshire Regt.   3 Coys. CANAL BANK.
                                1 Coy. BLUE LINE.
  8th. W. Riding Regt.   Front Line. Left Sub-sector.
  8th. York & Lancs. Regt.   CANAL BANK.
  32nd. M.G. Company.   Line.
  32nd. T.M. Battery.   CANAL BANK.

33rd. Infantry Brigade.   H.Q.)
  6th. Lincoln Regt.   )
  6th. Border Regt.   )DIRTY BUCKET CAMP
  7th. S. Staffs Regt.   )
  9th. S. Foresters.   )   A.30. Central.
  33rd. M.G. Company.   )
  33rd. T.M. Battery.   )

34th. Infantry Brigade.   H.Q.)
  8th. Northd. Fusiliers.   )
  9th. Lancs. Fusiliers.   )
  5th. Dorset Regt.   ) SIEGE CAMP. B.21.c.
  11th. Manchester Regt.   )
  34th. M.G. Company.   )
  34th. T.M. Battery.   )

6th. E. Yorks Regt. (Pioneers). H.Q. A.30.a.1.1.
                Advanced H.Q. CANAL BANK.
                        1 Coy. A.22. Central.
                        1 Coy. C.20.a.40.15.
                        2 Coys. CANAL BANK.

C.R.E., 11th. Division.   "X" Camp. A.16.c.2.5.
  67th. Field Company.   CANAL BANK.
  68th.   "   "   B.23.a.5.1.
  86th.   "   "   CANAL BANK.

C.R.A., 11th. Division.   H.Q. "X" Camp. A.16.c.10.25.
  58th. F.A.B.   B.29.d.8.1.
  59th.   "   B.28.a.6.1.
  D.A.C.   B.20.c.8.5.
  D.T.M.O.   B.28.a.2.3.

A.D.M.S., 11th. Division.   "X" Camp. A.16.c.2.5.
  33rd. Field Ambulance.   ESSEX FARM. C.19.c.4.1.
  34th.   "   "   ESSEX FARM. C.19.c.4.1.
  35th.   "   "   F.29.d.5.9.

A.P.M., 11th. Division.   "X" Camp A.16.c.2.5.

D.A.D.O.S., 11th. Division.   A.22.d.6.5. (Sheet 28).

D.A.D.V.S., 11th. Division.   POPERINGHE.
  22nd. Mobile Vet. Section.   F.22.c.2.3.

11th. Divisional Train.   H.Q. A.28.c.7.7.
  Nos. 1 & 2 Companies.   A.31.b.6.4.
  Nos. 3 & 4   "   A.28.c.7.7.

11th. Divisional Supply Column. E.29.b.5.2.

S E C R E T.   9th. August, 1917.   11th. Division No.G.S.313.

11th. DIVISION.

Location of Units at 8 a.m. August 10th. 1917.

Divisional Headquarters.	"X" Camp. A.16.c.2.5.
32nd. Infantry Brigade.	H.Q. FOCH FARM.
9th. W. Yorkshire Regt.	H.Q. MONTY FARM.
	Bn. In Line.
6th. Yorkshire Regt.	CANAL BANK (E. Side).
8th. W. Riding Regt.	H.Q. GOURNIER FARM.
	Bn. In Line.
6th. York & Lancs. Regt.	CANAL BANK (W. Side).
	1 Coy. Old British front line about MORTELDJE EST.
32nd. M.G. Company.	H.Q. C.9.a.7.5.
32nd. T.M. Battery.	In Line.

33rd. Infantry Brigade.	H.Q. BORDER CAMP.	)
6th. Lincoln Regt.	"D" Camp.	)
6th. Border Regt.	"E" Camp.	) DIRTY BUCKET
7th. S. Staffs Regt.	"B" Camp.	)
9th. S. Foresters.	A.30.Central.	) &
33rd. M.G. Company.	"D" Camp.	)
33rd. T.M. Battery.	"D" Camp.	) A.30.Central Camps.

34th. Infantry Brigade.	H.Q.)
8th. Northd. Fusiliers.	)
9th. Lancs. Fusiliers.	)
5th. Dorset Regt.	) SIEGE CAMP. B.21.c.
11th. Manchester Regt.	)
34th. M.G. Company.	)
34th. T.M. Battery.	)

6th. E. Yorks Regt. (Pioneers).	H.Q. A.30.a.1.1.
	Advanced H.Q. CANAL BANK.

C.R.E., 11th. Division.	
67th. Field Company.	"X" Camp. A.16.c.2.5.
68th. " "	CANAL BANK. B.23.a.5.1.
86th. " "	CANAL BANK.

C.R.A., 11th. Division.	H.Q. "X" Camp. A.16.c.10.25.
58th. F.A.B.	B.29.d.8.1.
59th. "	B.28.a.5.1.
D.A.C.	B.20.c.8.5.
D.T.M.O.	B.29.a.2.3.

A.D.M.S., 11th. Division.	"X" Camp. A.16.c.2.5.
33rd. Field Ambulance.	ESSEX FARM. C.19.c.4.1.
34th. " "	ESSEX FARM. C.19.c.4.1.
35th. " "	F.29.d.5.9.

A.P.M. 11th. Division.	"X" Camp. A.16.c.2.5.
D.A.D.O.S. 11th. Division.	A.22.d.6.5. (Sheet 28)
D.A.D.V.S., 11th. Division.	POPERINGHE.
22nd. Mobile Vet. Section.	A.28.a.8.9.

11th. Divisional Train. H.Q.	A.28.c.7.7.
Nos. 1 & 2 Companies.	A.21.b.6.4.
Nos. 3 & 4 "	A.28.c.7.7.

11th. Divisional Supply Column.	E.29.b.5.2.
11th. Divisional _____.	_____ (Sheet 28).

11th. Division No. G.S. 831.

Location of Units at 8 a.m. August 11th. 1917.

NO CHANGE.

SECRET.   11th. August 1917.   11th. Division No. G.S.261

11th. DIVISION.

Location of Units at 8 a.m. 12th. August 1917.

9th. W. Yorkshire Regt.	1Coy.	CANAL BANK (W. Side). Old British Front line, about MORTELDJE EST.
8th. Yorkshire Regt.	H.Q.	GOURNIER FARM.
	Bn.	Line.
8th. W. Riding Regt.		CANAL BANK. (E. Side).
6th. York & Lancs. Regt.	H.Q.	MINTY FARM.
	Bn.	Line.
68th. Field Company.		B.29.d.8.8.
Salvage Company.		A.23.d.7.5. Sheet 28.

OTHERWISE NO CHANGE.

S E C R E T.   12th. August 1917.   11th. Division No. G.S. 877.

11th. DIVISION.

Location of Units at 8 a.m. August 13th. 1917.

NO CHANGE.

S E C R E T. 13th. August 1917. 11th. Division No.G.S.292.

11th. DIVISION.

Location of Units at 8 a.m. August 14th. 1917.

Divisional Headquarters. "X" Camp, A.16.c.8.5.

32nd. Infantry Brigade. H.Q. FOCH FARM.
  9th. W. Yorkshire Regt. DIRTY BUCKET CAMP.
  6th. Yorkshire Regt. In Line.
  8th. W. Riding Regt. DIRTY BUCKET CAMP.
  6th. York & Lancs. Regt. In Line.
  32nd. M.G. Company. In Line.
  32nd. T.M. Battery. CANAL BANK.

33rd. Infantry Brigade. BORDER CAMP. A.30.central.
  6th. Lincoln Regt.
  6th. Border Regt.
  7th. S. Staffs Regt.
  9th. S. Foresters -do-
  33rd. M.G. Company.
  33rd. T.M. Battery.

34th. Infantry Brigade. H.Q. SIEGE CAMP B.21.c.
  8th. Northd. Fusiliers. Moving to CANAL BANK on 14th.
  9th. Lancs. Fusiliers. SIEGE CAMP B.21.c.
  5th. Dorset Regt. Moving to CANAL BANK on 14th.
  11th. Manchester Regt. SIEGE CAMP B.21.c.
  34th. M.G. Company. Moving to CANAL BANK on 14th.
  34th. T.M. Battery. SIEGE CAMP B.21.c.

6th. E. Yorks Regt. (Pioneers) A.30.a.1.1.

C.R.E., 11th. Division. "X" Camp A.16.c.8.5.
  67th. Field Company. CANAL BANK.
  68th. " " B.29.d.8.8.
  86th. " " CANAL BANK.

C.R.A., 11th. Division. H.Q. "X" Camp A.16.c.8.5.
  58th. F.A.B. B.29.d.8.1.
  59th. " B.28.a.6.1.
  D.A.C. B.20.c.8.5.
  D.T.M.O. B.28.a.2.3.

A.D.M.S., 11th. Division. "X" Camp A.16.c.8.5.
  33rd. Field Ambulance. ESSEX FARM. C.19.c.4.1.
  34th. " " ESSEX FARM C.19.c.4.1.
  35th. " " F.29.d.5.9.

A.P.M., 11th. Division. "X" Camp A.16.c.8.5.

D.A.D.O.S., 11th. Division. A.22.d.6.5.

D.A.D.V.S., 11th. Division. POPERINGHE.
  22nd. Mobile Vet. Section. A.28.a.8.9.

11th. Divisional Train. H.Q. A.28.c.7.7.
  Nos. 1 & 2 Companies. A.21.b.6.4.
  Nos. 3 & 4. " A.28.c.7.7.

11th. Divisional Supply Column. B.29.b.5.2.

11th. Divisional Laundry. A.22.d.6.5.

Salvage Company. A.22.d.7.5.

S E C R E T.　　　　　　14th. August 1917.　　11th. Division No. G.S. 313.

11th. DIVISION.

Location of Units at 8 a.m. 15th. August 1917.

Divisional Headquarters.	"X" Camp, A.16.c.2.5.

32nd. Infantry Brigade. H.Q.)
  9th. W. Yorkshire Regt.)　　　　A.30. Central.
  6th. Yorkshire Regt.)
  8th. W. Riding Regt.)　　　　DIRTY BUCKET CAMP.
  6th. York & Lancs. Regt.)
32nd. M.G. Company.)
32nd. T.M. Battery.)

33rd. Infantry Brigade.　　H.Q. BORDER CAMP. A.30. Central. Moving to
                                                                                     SIEGE CAMP.
  6th. Lincoln Regt.　　　　　"　　"　　"　　"　　"　　"
  6th. Border Regt.　　　　　"　　"　　"　　"　　"　　"
  7th. S. Staffs Regt.)
  9th. S. Foresters.)　　　　SIEGE CAMP. B.21.c.
33rd. M.G. Company.　　　　SIEGE CAMP. Moving to Line.
33rd. T.M. Battery.　　　　BORDER CAMP. A.30. Central. Moving to
                                                                                     SIEGE CAMP.

34th. Infantry Brigade.　　H.Q. FOCH FARM.
  8th. Northd. Fusiliers.　　In Line.
  9th. Lancs. Fusiliers.　　CANAL BANK.
  5th. Dorset Regt.　　　　In Line.
  11th. Manchester Regt.　　CANAL BANK.
34th. M.G. Company.　　　　In Line.
34th. T.M. Battery.　　　　CANAL BANK.

6th. E. Yorks Regt. (Pioneers). A.30.a.1.1.

C.R.E., 11th. Division.　　　　"X" Camp. A.16.c.2.5.
  67th. Field Company.　　　　CANAL BANK.
  68th.　"　　"　　　　　　　B.29.d.8.3.
  86th.　"　　"　　　　　　　CANAL BANK.

C.R.A., 11th. Division. H.Q.　"X" Camp. A.16.c.2.5.
  58th. F.A.B.　　　　　　　B.29.d.80.97.
  59th.　"　　　　　　　　　B.28.a.6.1.
  D.A.C.　　　　　　　　　　B.20.c.8.5.
  D.T.M.O.　　　　　　　　　B.20.a.2.3.

A.D.M.S., 11th. Division.　　"X" Camp. A.16.c.2.5.
  33rd. Field Ambulance.　　ESSEX FARM. C.19.c.4.1.
  34th.　"　　"　　　　　　ESSEX FARM. C.19.c.4.1.
  35th.　"　　"　　　　　　F.29.d.5.9.

A.P.M., 11th. Division.　　　"X" Camp. A.16.c.2.5.

D.A.D.O.S., 11th. Division.　A.22.d.6.5.

D.A.D.V.S., 11th. Division.　POPERINGHE.
  22nd. Mobile Vet. Section.　A.28.a.8.9.

11th. Divisional Train. H.Q.　A.28.c.7.7.
  Nos. 1 & 2 Companies.　　A.21.b.6.4.
  Nos. 3 & 4　"　　　　　　A.28.c.7.7.

11th. Divisional Supply Column. E.29.b.5.2.

11th. Divisional Laundry.　　A.22.d.6.5.

Salvage Company.　　　　　　A.22.d.7.5.

S E C R E T.   15th. August 1917.   11th. Division No. G.S.357.

11th. DIVISION.

Location of Units at 8 a.m. August 16th. 1917.

32nd. Infantry Brigade.
    H.Q. and Units.   A.30. Central.

33rd. Infantry Brigade. H.Q.   HINDENBURG FARM.
  6th. Lincoln Regt.   ) SIEGE CAMP.
  6th. Border Regt.   ) B.21.c.
  7th. S. Staffs Regt.   ) GOUANIER FARM.
  9th. S. Foresters.   )
33rd. M.G. Company.   In Line.
33rd. T.M. Battery.   CANAL BANK.

34th. Infantry Brigade. H.Q.   FOCH FARM.
                 Units.   In Line.

OTHERWISE NO CHANGE.

SECRET.   16th. August 1917.   11th. Division No. G.S. 356.

11th. DIVISION.

Location of Units at 8 a.m. August 17th. 1917

32nd. Infantry Brigade. H.Q.) and Units.)	A.30. Central. DIRTY BUCKET CAMP.
32nd. M.G. Company.	In Line.
33rd. Infantry Brigade.	In the Line.
34th. Infantry Brigade.	In the Line.

OTHERWISE NO CHANGE.

SECRET.   17th. August 1917.   11th. Division No. G.S. 368.

11th. DIVISION

Location of Units at 8 a.m. August 18th. 1917.

32nd. Infantry Brigade. less 2 Bns. & 32nd. M.G. Coy.)	CANAL BANK.
2 Bns. 32nd. Inf. Bde.	MURAT CAMP.
32nd. M.G. Company.	MURAT CAMP.
33rd. Infantry Brigade.	In Line.
34th. Infantry Brigade.	SIEGE CAMP. B.21.c.
34th. M.G. Company.	Attd. 33rd. Brigade.

OTHERWISE NO CHANGE.

SECRET.   18th. August 1917.   11th. Division No. G.S. 383.

11th. DIVISION.

Location of Units at 8 a.m. 19th. August 1917.

32nd. Infantry Brigade. H.Q.	MURAT CAMP.
2 Bns. & 32nd. M.G. Coy.	CANAL BANK.
2 Bns. 32nd. Inf. Bde.	MURAT CAMP.
33rd. Infantry Brigade. H.Q. at	In Line with HINDENBURG FARM.
34th. Infantry Brigade.	SIEGE CAMP B.21.c.
34th. M.G. Company.	Attd. 33rd. Brigade.

OTHERWISE NO CHANGE.

S E C R E T.   11th. Division No. G.S. 404.

11th. DIVISION.

Location of Units at 8 a.m. August 20th. 1917.

32nd. Infantry Brigade. H.Q.)
   6th. Yorkshire Regt.   )MURAT CAMP.
   6th. York & Lancs. Regt.)
   32nd. M.G. Company.   )

   9th. W. Yorkshire Regt.)
   8th. W. Riding Regt.   )CANAL BANK.
   32nd. L.T.M. Battery.   )

33rd. Infantry Brigade.   In Line.
                      H.Q. at CANE POST. C.9.a.6.3.

Advanced Dressing Station. Moving to MINTY FARM.

OTHERWISE NO CHANGE.

SECRET.   20th. August 1917.   11th. Division No. G.S. 411.

11th. DIVISION.

Location of Units at 8 a.m. August 21st. 1917.

Divisional Headquarters.   "X" Camp, A.16.c.2.5.

32nd. Infantry Brigade.   H.Q.)
  6th. Yorkshire Regt.   ) MURAT CAMP.
  6th. York & Lancs. Regt.   )
  32nd. M.G. Company.   )

  9th. W. Yorkshire Regt.   )
  8th. W. Riding Regt.   ) CANAL BANK.
  32nd. T.M. Battery.   )

33rd. Infantry Brigade.   In Line
      H.Q. at CANE POST C.9.a.6.3. Sheet 28.

34th. Infantry Brigade. H.Q.   )
  8th. Northd. Fusiliers.   )
  9th. Lancs. Fusiliers.   )
  5th. Dorset Regt.   ) SIEGE CAMP B.21.c.
  11th. Manchester Regt.   )
  34th. M.G. Company.   )
  34th. T.M. Battery.   )

6th. E. Yorks Regt. (Pioneers).   A.30.a.1.1.

C.R.E., 11th. Division.   "X" Camp. A.16.c.2.5.
  67th. Field Company.   CANAL BANK.
  68th.   "   "   B.29.d.8.9.
  86th.   "   "   CANAL BANK.

C.R.A., 11th. Division.   H.Q.   "X" Camp, A.16.c.2.5.
  58th. F.A.B.   B.29.d.80.97.
  59th.   "   B.28.a.6.1.
  D.A.C.   B.20.c.8.5.
  D.T.M.O.   B.28.a.2.3.

A.D.M.S., 11th. Division.   "X" Camp, A.16.c.2.5.
  33rd. Field Ambulance.   ESSEX FARM. C.19.c.4.1.
  34th.   "   "   ESSEX FARM. C.19.c.4.1.
  35th.   "   "   F.29.d.5.9.

A.P.M., 11th. Division.   "X" Camp. A.16.c.2.5.

D.A.D.O.S., 11th. Division.   A.22.d.6.5.

A.D.V.S., 11th. Division.   POPERINGHE.
  22nd. Mobile Vet. Section.   A.28.a.8.9.

11th. Divisional Train.   H.Q.   A.28.c.7.7.
  Nos. 1 & 2 Companies.   A.21.b.6.4.
  No. 3 & 4.   "   A.28.c.7.7.

11th. Divisional Supply Column.   E.29.b.5.2

Laundry.   A.22.d.6.5.

Salvage Company.   A.22.d.7.5.

S E C R E T.   21st. August 1917.   11th. Division No. G.S.487

11th. DIVISION.

Location of Units at 8 a.m. August 22nd. 1917.

32nd. M.G. Company.   In Line.

OTHERWISE NO CHANGE.

22nd. August 1917.   11th. Division No. G.S. 439.

Location of Units at 8 a.m. August 23rd. 1917.

NO CHANGE.

SECRET   24th August, 1917.   11th Div. No. G.S. 754.

11th Division.

Location of Units at 8 a.m. 25th August.

NO CHANGE.

23rd. August 1917.   11th. Division No. G.S. 454.

Location of Units at 6 a.m. August 24th. 1917.

NO CHANGE.

S E C R E T.   25th. August 1917.   11th.Division No.G.S. 480

11th. DIVISION.

Location of Units at 8 a.m. August 26th. 1917.

Divisional Headquarters.   BORDER CAMP. A.30.b.2.3.

32nd. Infantry Brigade.   H.Q. CANE POST. C.9.a.6.3.
  9th. W. Yorkshire Regt.   MURAT CAMP.
  6th. Yorkshire   Regt. H.Q. GOURNIER FARM.
  8th. W. Riding Regt.   MURAT CAMP
  6th. York & Lancs. Regt.H.Q. LANCASHIRE FARM.
  32nd. M.G. Company.   Line.
  32nd. T.M. Battery.   Line.

33rd. Infantry Brigade.   H.Q. TROIS TOURS CHATEAU.

  2 Battalions.   CANAL BANK.
  2 Battalions.   In Line.

34th. Infantry Brigade. H.Q,)
  8th. Northd. Fusiliers.   )
  9th. Lancs. Fusiliers.   ) SIEGE CAMP B.21.c.
  5th. Dorset Regt.   )
  11th. Manchester Regt.   )
  34th. T.M.Battery.   )
  34th. M.G. Company.   LINE.

6th. E. Yorks Regt. (Pioneers).   A.30.a.1.1.

C.R.E., 11th. Division.   BORDER CAMP.
  67th. Field Company.   CANAL BANK.
  68th.   "   "   B.29.d.8.9.
  86th.   "   "   CANAL BANK.

C.R.A., 11th .Division.   H.Q.   BORDER CAMP.
  58th. F.A.B.   B.29.d.80.97.
  59th. "   B.28.a.6.1.
  D.A.C.   B.20.c.8.5.
  D.T.M.C.   B.28.a.2.3.

A.D.M.S., 11th. Division.   BORDER CAMP.
  33rd. & 34th. Fd. Ambulances. ESSEX FARM. C.19.c.4.1.
  35th. Field Ambulance.   L'EBBE FARM F.29.d.5.9. Sheet 27.

A.P.M., 11th. Division.   BORDER CAMP.

D.A.D.O.S., 11th. Division.   A.22.d.6.5.

D.A.D.V.S., 11th. Division.   BORDER CAMP.

11th. Divisional Train.   A.28.c.7.7.
  Nos. 1 & 2 Companies.   A.21.b.6.4.
  Nos. 3 & 4   "   A.28.c.7.7.

11th. Divisional Supply Column.   E.29.b.5.2.

11th. Division.

Location of Units at 8 a.m. August 27th. 1917.

32nd. Infantry Brigade. H.Q. CANE POST C.9.a.8.3.
  9th. W. Yorkshire Regt. Line.
  6th. Yorkshire Regt. HINDENBURG FARM.
  8th. W. Riding Regt. Line.
  6th. York & Lancs. Regt. GOURNIER FARM.
32nd. M.G. Company. In Line.
32nd. T.M. Battery. In Line.

2 Battalions 33rd. Inf. Bde. CANAL BANK.
2 Battalions " " " MURAT CAMP.

      OTHERWISE NO CHANGE.

SECRET	27th August, 1917.	11th Div. No. G.S.763.

11th Division.

Location of Units at 8 a.m. August 28th.

NO CHANGE.

SECRET.   28th. August 1917.   11th. Divn. No. G.S. 537.

11th. DIVISION.

Location of Units at 6 a.m. August 29th. 1917.

Divisional Headquarters.	CANAL WEST BANK.	
Rear H.Q.	BORDER CAMP. A.30.b.2.3.	

32nd. Infantry Brigade.	H.Q. CANE POST. C.9.a.6.3.	} Moving to
9th. W. Yorkshire Regt.	Line.	
6th. Yorkshire Regt.	HINDENBURG FARM.	} BRAKE CAMP
8th. W. Riding Regt.	Line.	
6th. York & Lancs. Regt.	GOURNIER FARM.	} from line.
32nd. M.G. Company.	In Line.	
32nd. T.M. Battery.	In Line.	

33rd. Infantry Brigade.	H.Q. BRAKE CAMP.
6th. Lincoln Regt.)	
6th. Border Regt.)	
7th. S. Staffs.)	
9th. S. Foresters.)	-do-
33rd. M.G. Company.)	
33rd. T.M. Battery.)	

34th. Infantry Brigade.	H.Q. SIEGE CAMP. B.21.c.
8th. Northd. Fusiliers.)	
9th. Lancs. Fusiliers.)	
5th. Dorset Regt.)	-do-
11th. Manchester Regt.)	
34th. T.M. Battery.)	
34th. M.G. Company.	In Line.

6th. E. Yorks Regt. (Pioneers).	CANAL WEST BANK.

C.R.A., 11th. Division. H.Q.	CANAL WEST BANK.
58th. F.A.B.	B.29.d.80.97.
59th. "	B.28.a.6.1.
D.A.C.	B.20.c.8.5.
D.T.M.O.	B.28.a.2.3.

C.R.E., 11th. Division.	BORDER CAMP. A.30.b.2.3.
67th. Field Company.	CANAL BANK.
68th. " "	B.29.d.8.9.
68th. " "	CANAL BANK.

A.D.M.S., 11th. Division.	BORDER CAMP. A.30.b.2.3.
33rd. and 34th. Fd. Amb.	ESSEX FARM. C.19.c.4.1.
35th. Field Ambulance.	L'EBBE FARM. F.29.d.5.9.

A.P.M., 11th. Division.	BORDER CAMP. A.30.b.2.3.
D.A.D.O.S., 11th. Division.	A.22.d.6.5.
11th. Divisional Train. H.Q.	A.28.c.8.7.
11th. Divisional Supply Column.	E.29.b.5.2.
Salvage Company.	No.3 CANAL BANK EAST.

War Diary

SECRET.   29th. August 1917.   11th. Division No. G.S. 550.

11th. DIVISION.

Location of Units at 8 a.m. August 30th. 1917.

<u>Divisional Headquarters.</u>   CANAL WEST BANK. Moving to "X" Camp.
              Rear H.Q. "X" Camp. A.16.c.2.5.

<u>32nd. Infantry Brigade.</u> H.Q. 8 Rue des Pots, POPERINGHE.
   9th. W. Yorkshire Regt.   )
   6th. Yorkshire Regt.   )
   8th. W. Riding Regt.   )   POPERINGHE.
   6th. York & Lancs. Regt.   )
   32nd. M.G. Company.   )
   32nd. T.M. Battery.   )

<u>33rd. Infantry Brigade.</u> H.Q. BRAKE CAMP.
   6th. Lincoln Regt.   )
   6th. Border Regt.   )
   7th. S. Staffs. Regt.   )
   9th. S. Foresters.   )   -do-
   33rd. M.G. Company.   )
   33rd. T.M. Battery.   )

<u>34th. Infantry Brigade.</u> H.Q. DIRTY BUCKET CAMP.
   8th. Northd. Fusiliers.   )
   9th. Lancs. Fusiliers.   )
   8th. Dorset Regt.   )
   11th. Manchester Regt.   )   -do-
   34th. M.G. Company.   )
   34th. T.M. Battery.   )

<u>6th. E. Yorks Regt.</u> (Pioneers) CANAL WEST BANK.

<u>C.R.A., 11th. Division.</u>   CANAL WEST BANK.
   58th. F.A.B.   B.29.d.80.97.
   59th. "   B.28.a.6.1.
   D.A.C.   B.20.c.8.5.
   D.T.M.O.   B.28.a.2.3.

<u>C.R.E., 11th. Division.</u>   "X" Camp.
   67th. Field Company.   CANAL BANK.
   68th.   "   "   B.29.d.8.9.
   86th.   "   "   CANAL BANK.

<u>A.D.M.S., 11th. Division.</u>   "X" Camp.

<u>A.P.M., 11th. Division.</u>   "X" Camp.

<u>D.A.D.O.S., 11th. Division.</u> A.22.d.6.5.

<u>11th. Divisional Train.</u> H.Q. A.28.c.7.7.

<u>11th. Divisional Supply Column.</u> E.29.b.5.2.

<u>Salvage Company.</u>   No. 3 CANAL WEST BANK.

WAR DIARY

SECRET.   30th. August 1917.   11th. Division No. G.S. 559.

11th. DIVISION.

Location of Units at 8 a.m. August 31st. 1917.

Divisional Headquarters.	"X" Camp. A.16.c.2.3.
32nd. Infantry Brigade.	H.Q. 6 Rue Des Pots, POPERINGHE.
9th. W. Yorkshire Regt.)	
6th. Yorkshire Regt.)	
8th. W. Riding Regt.)	
6th. York & Lancs. Regt.)	POPERINGHE.
32nd. M.G. Company)	
32nd. T.M. Battery.)	
33rd. Infantry Brigade.	H.Q. BRAKE CAMP.
6th. Lincoln Regt.)	
6th. Border Regt.)	
7th. S. Staffs. Regt.)	
9th. S. Foresters.)	-do-
33rd. M.G. Company.)	
33rd. T.M. Battery)	
34th. Infantry Brigade.	H.Q. DIRTY BUCKET CAMP.
8th. Northd. Fusiliers.)	
9th. Lancs. Fusiliers.)	
5th. Dorset Regt.)	
11th. Manchester Regt.)	-do-
34th. M.G. Company.)	
34th. T.M. Battery.)	
6th. E. Yorks Regt.(Pioneers).	A.30.a.1.1.
C.R.E. 11th. Division.	"X" Camp. A.16.c.2.3.
67th. Field Company.	CANAL BANK.
68th. " "	B.29.d.8.9.
86th. " "	CANAL BANK.
C.R.A. 11th. Division.	"X" Camp. A.16.c.2.3.
58th. F.A.B.	B.29.d.80.97.
59th. "	B.28.a.6.1.
D.A.C.	B.20.c.8.5.
D.T.M.O.	B.28.a.2.3.
A.D.M.S., 11th. Division.	"X" Camp. A.16.c.2.3.
33rd. Field Ambulance.	A.23.c.5.9.
34th. " "	GHENT FARM. A.28.a.20.65.
35th. " "	L'EBBE FARM. F.29.d.5.9.
A.P.M., 11th. Division.	"X" Camp. A.16.c.2.3.
D.A.D.O.S., 11th. Division.	A.22.d.6.5.
11th. Divisional Train. H.Q.	A.28.c.7.7.
No. 1 Company.	A.21.b.6.4.
Nos. 2 and 3 Coys.	F.29.c.3.6.
No. 4 Company.	F.27.b.9.4.
11th. Divisional Supply Col.	B.29.d.5.2.
D.A.D.V.S., 11th. Division.	"X" Camp. A.16.c.2.3.
Salvage Company.	No. 5. CANAL BANK WEST.

"War Diary"

31/8/17.

11th. Division No. G.S. 586.

11th. Division.

Location of Units at 8 a.m. September 1st. 1917.

NO CHANGE.

APPENDIX 4.

Diary of Messages received and despatched
during Operations

DIARY OF MESSAGES RECEIVED DURING OPERATIONS

16th to 30th August, 1917.

	Date	How received or sent.	Time of despatch or receipt.	From or To.	Sender's Number.	Text of Message.
(1)	16/8/17.	Recd. by wire	6.45 a.m.	20th.Div.	G.B. 77.	F.O.O. reports first objective taken all going well. Prisoners coming in.
(2)	"	"	6.19 a.m.	"	G.B. 78.	Prisoners passing STRAY FM. aaa F.O.O. states some of our men passing ALOUETTE farm.
(3)	"	"	6.15 a.m.	48th. "	G.A. 15.	145 Bde. report 5.30 a.m. aaa Enemy barrage weak at first aaa From ST. JULIEN to CORNER COT road has been barraged during the night No further information.
(4)	"	Pigeon.	6.25 a.m.	O.C. "C" Coy 5 Dorsets.		Reports his position at U.29.central.
(5)	"	Recd. by wire.	6.35 a.m.	48 Divn.	G.A. 16.	Officer wounded just before Zero aaa reports assembly successfully carried outz
(6)	"	"	6.45 a.m.	20 Divn.	G.B. 81.	F.O.O. reports our troops in artillery formation moving from U.29.central.
(7)	"	"	6.48 a.m.	34th.Bde.	B.M. 385	Prisoners have passed MINTY HO. Reported taken on LANGEMARCK ROAD by 8th. Northd.Fus.
(8)	"	By 'phone.	6 a.m.	Maj.Harrison at 34th. Bde.		Signal message picked up that enemy barrage came down 5 minutes after Zero. Wire was received from Dorsets that their forming up was complete.
(9)	"	"	6.55 a.m.	34th. Bde.		Wounded report :- Manchesters are formed up in good time for further advance. Dorsets reported by runner at 5.45 a.m. strong point U.29.c.1.2 taken with prisoners.
(10)	"	Contact Aero.	6.50 a.m.			Few casualties reported aaa Flares seen at U.29.d.5.5, U.29.d.9.2 and at C.6.a.5.0.
(11)	"	By Wire.	7.15 a.m.	20 Divn.	G.B. 80.	Aeros.report BLUE LINE taken all along our front.

Date.		How received or sent.	Time of despatch or receipt.	From or To.	Sender's Number.	Text of Message.
16/8/17.	(12)	Contact Aero.	7.9 a.m.	For 48th.Div recd. by 11th.Div.		Flares seen at D.7.a.8.1 - D.7.a.4.2 - C.12.b.9.5 - C.12.d.8.5 - 6.8 - 4.9 - C.6.d.2.1 - 0.5.
"	(13)	Recd. by wire.	7.15 am.	34th.Bde.	G.O. 3.	First objective reported by 33rd. Bde. scouyts to have been taken fairly easy aaa. Number of prisoners coming through aaa. Manchesters reported by wounded to have been formed up in good time for their advance aaa.
"	(14)	Recd. by wire.	7.27 a.m.	48 Divn.	G.A. 18.	F.O.O. reports flares at C.12.b.35 at 5.10 a.m. aaa. Contact aeroplane reports flares at C.6.a.5.0 at 5.55 a.m. aaa. Green lights at 5.52 a.m. at C.S.c.4.6 aaa. Bde. reports 6.34 a.m. cannot get communication into ST. JULIEN owing to barrage fire aaa. Wounded N.C.O. reports progress was satisfactory at 5.15 a.m.
"	(15)	Recd. by 'phone	7.40 a.m.	Capt.White.		145 Bde. at 6.45 report SPRING-FIELD taken and right of right Battalion well on but northern Houses of ST. JULIEN not taken when they left.
"	(16)	" wire.	7.41 a.m.	18 Corps.		14 Corps very happy in their GREEN LINE.
"	(17)	" "	7.40 a.m.	48 Divn.	G.O. 323.	Contact patrol message reads some enemy shelling in U.25. Flares at 5.50 a.m. at 29.d. 62.58 - d.71.40 - d.8.3 - d.91.14 One flare at 5.55 a.m. at 6.a.5.0. GReen lights at 5.52 a.m. at C.6.c.4.6 aaa.

	Date.	How received or sent.	Time of despatch or receipt.	From or To.	Sender's Number.	Text of Message.
(18)	16/8/17.	Recd. by wire.	7.46 a.m.	20 Divn.	G.B. 88.	F.O.O. saw runners from forward Bn. which was stated to be about to reach GREEN LINE at 6.55 a.m.
(19)	"	"	7.49 a.m.	48 Divn.	G.A. 19.	Report from Brigade at 6.45 a.m. aaa Wounded state SPRINGFIELD taken and right of right Bn. got on well aaa Northern houses of ST. JULIEN not taken when they left aaa About 50 prisoners reported coming down through ST. JULIEN aaa O.P. reports 6.45 a.m. aaa Barrage on STEENBEEK listed aaaTRIANGLE FARM and vicinity heavily shelled.
(20)	"	" pigeon.	7.58 a.m.	F.O.O., "B" Coy. 5 Dorsets.		Objective taken informed 34th. Brigade.
(21)	"	" wire.	7.58 a.m.	Liaison 20 Divn.	M.3.	20th. Division report 6.40 a.m. all BLUE LINE taken aaa Aeroplanes report flares seen at 6.42 a.m. on GREEN LINE 29th. Divn. front.
(22)	"	" 'Phone.	8.4 a.m.	"		F.O.O. report GREEN LINE taken.
(23)	"	" wire.	8.15 a.m.	20 Divn.	G.B. 89.	F.O.O's orderly reports GREEN LINE taken. F.O.O. wounded on way to Bde. H.Q.
(24)	"	" 'Phone.	8.19 a.m.	Adv. R.O.		I and III Bns. 184 I.R. relieved 2 Battns.268 I.R. last night. Relief not completed at time of attack. Prisoners state 440 I.R. in OOSTNIEUKERKE and 418 I.R. in LANGEMARCK Line.
(25)	"	" "	8.25 a.m.	54th.Bde.		(1) Dorsets say Lancs. Fus. prisoners report attack going well. (2) Dorsets say casualties very few. 60 prisoners taken by 1 Platoon. (3) Adv. Battn. report centre reports consolidation can be seen taking place. R.E. working parties of 33rd.Bde. have passed at 7.35 a.m. Runners coming direct from Dorsets but nothing from L.F's direct.

Date.	How received or sent.	Time of despatch or receipt.	From or To.	Sender's Number.	Text of Message.
(26) 16/8/17.	Recd. by wire.	8.25 a.m.	20 Divn.	G.B. 90.	F.O.O. reports GREEN LINE taken but view much obscured by smoke and dust aaa Not yet confirmed by air.
(27) "	"	8.28 a.m.	34th.Bde.	B.M. 378.	Following message from 5th. Dorsets timed 6.38 a.m. begins aaa 9th. L.F. escort to prisoners reports attack going well aaa. 15 Prisoners at least have passed our H.Q. aaa. Ends aaa. Later message timed 6.40 a.m. from Dorsets states casualties very few 60 prisoners taken by a platoon aaa.
(28) "	"	8.45 a.m.	33rd.Bde.	B.M. 433.	Staffords and Sherwoods on BLUE LINE 7.43 a.m. Whole of Staffords pushing forward to Line VON WERDER HO - FRANCOIS FM. three coys. well on way and last. Coy. first leaving BLUE LINE at 7.45 a.m. aaa.
(29) "	"	8.53 a.m.	18 Corps.	G.I. 54.	14th. Corps report aaa Prisoners taken 50 I.R. 261, 262 R.I.R. aaa Order of battle North to South 50 I.R., 214 Divn. 261 and 262 R.I.R. 79 Res. Dn.
(30) "	" 'Phone.	8.55 a.m.	Capt.White.		Prisoners 1 Officer and 30 O.R. of 184 I.R. and 262 R.I.R. action following.
(31) "	" Wire.	9 a.m.	48 Divn.		Bde. reports 7.7 a.m. enemy who had been giving trouble with M.G's at C.12.c.3.6 surrendered about 40 strong aaa BORDER HO. captured 6 a.m. aaa. ends. O.P. report 7.20 a.m. our troops have reached LANGEMARCK line at d.7.8. aaa More seen to be moving on ridge aaa Ends aaa E.A. crashed 1.30 a.m. in 11.d. aaa
(32) "	" wire.	9.5 a.m.	"	A.W. 1.	1 and 3 Bns. 184 I.R. relieved 2 Bns. of 263 I.R. last night aaa Relief not complete at time of attack aaa Prisoners state 440 I.R. in OOSTNIEUKERKE line aaaOrder of battle N. to S. 1st, 4th. 9th. Coys. /184....

Date.	How received or sent.	Time of despatch or receipt.	From or To.	Sender's Number.	Text of Message.
(32) contd.	Recd. by wire.	9.5 a.m.	Capt. White.	A.W. 1.	184 I.R. aaa Whole Division to be relieved aaa Prisoners through Divisional Cage so far 1 Officer 30 O.R.
(33) 16/8/17	"	9.8 a.m.	18 Corps.	G.S. 55.	Prisoners of 2nd. M.G. Coy. 7th. Bav. Regt. aaa First and 3rd. Coys. in line aaa Order of Battle North to South 213 R.I.R. 7th. Bav. 19th. Bav. aaa 2nd. M.G. Coy. in line, been in about 3 days aaa Right Coy. Dorsets report at least 100 prisoners sent back aaa Our casualties 20 (over-estimated if anything) In touch with right and left.
(34) "	'Phone	9.5 a.m.	34th. Bde.		Artillery officer with Bde. is positive enemy now shelling LANGEMARCK LINE on our front aaa
(35) "	Wire	9.18 a.m.	48 Divn.	G.A. 21.	
(36) "	Pigeon.	9.25 a.m.	"Z" Coy. 8th. N.F.		Have gained my objective which is at C.5.p 7.9. Hostile M.G. about C.6.c.1.7. Companies on left front digging in at C.6.a.2.3.
(37) "	Runner.	9.20 a.m.	20th. Divn.	G.S.O. I	20th. Division report: GREEN LINE definitely taken and troops moving forward to attack of RED LINE aaa Some of 20th. Div. have been seen at WINDMILL U.23.d.6.9 but this wants confirmation aaa whole of enemy 79th. Div. has been engaged also prisoners of 184th. R.I.R. including C.O. captured but prisoners statements say, this is the only Regt. that has come forward of 183rd. Div. Aeroplane map message now show 20th. Div. line (still advancing) U.23.d.5.0 - 23 central - Rly. 23.a.4.7. This message dropped about 8 a.m.
(38) "	'Phone.	9.25 a.m.	Capt. White.	gap ?	Message from Adv. Report Centre 34th. Bde. to 34th. Bde. O.C. Manchesters, afraid my men are going too far to left. Gap on right. No sign of Print. Casualties considerable, line thinned. Two platoons being sent up from O.C. Manchesters. He doesn't say if the two platoons are to be re-inforced or fill gap.

Date.	How received or sent.	Time of despatch or receipt.	From or To.	Sender's Number.	Text of Message.
(39) 18/8/17.	Recd. by 'phone	9.25 a.m.	Capt. White.		Message from N.F's. Position gained and am consolidating. Estimated casualties 4 Officers and 50 O.R. LANGEMARCK road being barraged by enemy.
(40) "	wire	9.26 a.m.	"	A.W. 2.	Prisoners so far 3 Officers 89 O.R. aaa 1 - 3, 4 & 9 Coys. 194 I.R. identified aaa Prisoners state men of 5 Coy. sent to reinforce 9th. Coy. aaa casualties very heavy.
(41) "	"	9.27 a.m.	20th. Div.	G.B. 91.	Brigadier 60th. Bde. can see our troops on RED LINE near Mill U.24.c.O.6./ 2 Sections of 67th.Fd. Coy. and 2 Platoons Inf. started work on track GOURNIER FARM to MILITARY ROAD at 7 a.m. Work started at C.10.a.3.5, track is now being taped as far as MILITARY ROAD. So far work on track has not been interfered with. Total strength of Infantry 36 men 2 Sections R.E. under Lieut. Fox and DaVies left GOURNIER FARM for work on bridge at 5.25 a.m.
(42) "	'Phone.	9.30 a.m.	O.C., 67th. Fd. Coy. GOURNIER FM.		
(43) "	"	9.45 a.m.	18 Corps"g"		R.F.C. report one of their machines fallen at U.21.d.9.1. Anxious to know what has happened to it and personnel.
(44) "	wire.	9.57 a.m.	"	G.I. 57.	19th. Corps wires aaa Prisoners of 7th. Bav. I.R. taken N. of WIELTJE STERAVENSTAFEL road aaa State N. of WIELTJE STERAVENSTAFEL road aaa State 19th. Bav. I.R. on their left aaa Prisoners Regt. unknown on their right aaa 7th. Bav. I.R. relieved 21st.Bav. I.R. two days ago aaa 21st. Bav. I.R. in reserve.
(45) "	"	10.4 a.m.	18 Corps.	G. 325.	French airman reports a German Division concentrating at POELCAPPELLE.
(46) "	"				

	Date.	How received or sent.	Time of despatch or receipt.	From or To.	Sender's Number.	Text of Message.
(46)	16/8/17.	Recd. by wire.	10 a.m.	34th.Bde.	B.M. 379.	Message from Northd.Fusiliers states:- Objectives gained and being consolidated aaa Estimated casualties 5 officers 50 O.R. aaa Enemy barraging LANGEMARCK road aaa Message from Manchesters states :- Afraid my men going too far to the left, gap on right no sign of 1/4 Oxford and Bucks. 145 Bde. Casualties considerable and line mow thin. Two platoons being sent up.
(47)	"	'Phone.	10 a.m.	Maj.Harrison.		From Adv. Bde. Station Arty. Officer reports we have reached our second objective and many prisoners coming down 33rd. Bde. scouts report Arty. fire more concentrated on right than on left.
(48)	"	Wire.	10.40 a.m.	Capt.White.		Prisoner of 12th. Coy. 263 R.I.R. states they were relieved by 12th. Coy. 184 I.R. this morning. 21st. Bav. I.R. was on left, and this Regt. was relieved the evening before last. Their Coy. Commander warned then that he would probably attack to-day z Prisoner of 3rd. Coy. 184 I.R. states his Coy. relieved 3 Coy. 263 I.R. The Regt. has been attached to 79th. Res. Div. for several days and was in rest. They had orders to counter attack early yesterday morning but it was postponed at the last moment and relief ordered. Nothing seen of 440 I.R. 418 I.R. seen yesterday at OOSTNIWKERKE.
(49)	"	'Phone.	11.5 a.m.	Maj.Harrison.		Col.Hannay has been up to his Regt. and the Dorsets have gained the objectives and are digging in. In touch on right and left. States that Northd.Fus. are digging in just S.W. of LANGEMARCK - ZONNEBEKE Road.

Date.	How received or sent.	Time of despatch or receipt.	From or To.	Sender's Number.	Text of Message.
(50) 16/8/17.	Recd. by wire.	11.7 a.m.	33rd.Bde.	B.M.436.	33rd. Bde. disposed as follows :- 3 Coys. of 7th. S. Staffs. digging in 200 yards West of the VON WERDER HOUSE - FRANCOIS FM. One Coy. of 7th.S.Staffs. E. of the STEENBEEK where it went to avoid barrage. 3 Coys. of 9th.S.Foresters between line CANE-CANNISTER-CANNON Trench and line VONWERDER HO. - FRANCOIS Fm. Bn. H.Q., 7th. S. Staffs. and 9th. S. Foresters GOURNIER Fm. 6th. Borders in position on BLUE LINE. Bde. H.Q. FOCH FARM.
(51) "	" 'Phone.	11.15 a.m.	48th.Divn.		No news from their left Bde. either on GREEN LINE or RED LINE. The last report from the left stated they had passed the TRIANGLE.
(52) "	Runner for 20th.Div. H.Q.	10.55 a.m.	Major Meugens our Liaison Offr. with 20th. Div.		(1) Left Bde: 20th.Div. say that D.C.L.I.(left Bn) have been seen by telescope definitely from Bde.H.Q. This report reached me here at 8.40 a.m. (2) Aeroplane message map dropped about 8 a.m. showed 29th.Div. troops definitely in RED LINE. (3) During the Advance from STEENBEEK at 5 a.m.- 15 mins. late. Barrage light and died down about 7.30 a.m. LANGEMARCK was shelled by enemy after its capture. Our casualties at present appear to be light. (4) Have not yet heard definitely from Maj.Welsh that our GREEN LINE is captured but XVIII Corps just reported here, alright on RED line from Corps H.Q. (5) C.O. of 184 R.I.R. reports another Div (name not mentioned) E. of POELCAPPELLE but no troops reported W. of it. (6).I think it can be safely said 20th.Div. are on RED line but will 'phone confirmation as soon as received.
(53) "	Recd. by 'phone.	11.28 a.m.	33rd.Bde.		4th.Coy. of Sherwoods is in BLACK line in centre of Divnl.Sector. The Coy.of S.Staffs. E. of STEENBEEK crossed over bridge about C.5.8.2.2 and is in touch with 1/7 Words. on right.

	Date.	How received or sent.	Time of despatch or receipt.	From or To.	Sender's Number.	Text of Message.
(54)	16/8/17.	Recd. by wire.	11.40 a.m.	20th.Div.	G.B. 98.	F.O.O. reports our Infantry have occupied RED Line. 1 Section prisoners captured. and more
(55)	"	'Phone.	11.40 a.m.	Capt.White.		2 Wounded men of Manchesters :- 1 States he reached PHEASANT FARM and the other said he got to PHEASANT TRENCH. Their statements may be taken as fairly reliable. The COCKCROFT appears to have given trouble with M.G. fire. Enemy barrage may have caught rear of Bns. attacking 2nd. objective. Casualties at Adv. Dressing Station up to 10.30 a.m. 7 Officers and 152 O.R. Prisoners 4 officers and 171 O.R. The Shropshires (58th.Bde.) 20th.Division) have Bn .H.Q. at ALOUETTE FARM.
(56)	"	"	11.48 a.m.	"		61st.Bde.has captured RED Line on whole front and consolidating and in touch on right and left.
(57)	"	"	11.50 a.m.	Maj.Harrison.		L.F's have reached RED line. Men lining up about BULOW FARM. Both men and N.C.Os still report M.G. fire from MON DU HIBOU.
(58)	"	Runner from 20 Divn.	12 noon.	Our Liaison Offr.with 20 Divn.	M. 9.	F.O.O. continues to report 20th. Division in whole of RED line but aeroplane message timed 10.45 a.m. shows line held by 20th.Div. as follows :- U.23.d.8.0 - 15 - 75.50 - 52.98 - U.23.b.30.30 - 00.15 then gap between then U.23.a.85.95 -48.18. Message then says troops on right not actually holding the trench but seem to have withdrawn,as ground is very wet, for a little way. 6 Oxford & Bucks. report in touch with 5th. Dorsets on GREEN LINE at 7.40 a.m. No touch yet reported at WHITE HOUSE. Message by runner just received says :-

Date.	How received or sent.	Time of despatch or receipt.	From or To.	Sender's Number.	Text of Message.
(58) contd.					Shropshires report troops established at 9.5 are in WINDMILL 23.d.95.10 and have got in touch with 9th.Lancs. Fus. on right but does not say where. Shropshires are consolidating 150 yards in front of WINDMILL with their H.Q. at ALOUETTE Fm.
(59) 16/8/17.	Recd. by wire.	12.18 p.m.	20th.Divn.		8th.Bde. report Shropshires in WINDMILL U.24.c.1½, and consolidating line 150 yards E. of Salient in enemy line. H.Q. ALOUETTE Fm. Bn. in touch with 9th. Lanc. Fus.
(60)	"	12.10 p.m.	34th.Bde.	B.M. 381.	Report from 8th. Northd. Fus. timed 9.30 a.m. begins Front line established on GREEN LINE in touch with 5th. Dorsets on left but left of 48th.Division held up at MONT DU HIBOU. Am consolidating second line from C.5.b.6.1, C.5.d.6.9 – 5.8 – 8.6 – 6.5. M.G. at MONT DU HIBOU holding up our right. My H.Q. at C.5.d.15.15. Report from 11th.Manchesters at MON BULGARE timed 9.55 a.m. begins From reports received front line held just E. of GREEN LINE. M.G. at HIBOU still active on my flank. Right Coy. holding line from C.6.a.5.8 – C.6.a.6.2.
(61)	"	12.45 p.m.	48th.Divn.	G.B. 25.	Bde. reports 10.25 a.m. Right Bn. line BORDER HO. Gun pit C.12.d.2.3 – 1.5. W of JANET FM. Held up by M.G. at WINNIPEG and gun pit C.12.d.7.3. Centre Bns hold SPRINGFIELD with L.G. and small party. Flanking parties from C.12.a.6.6 – 8.5 also about 40 men of Left Bn. Situation very obscure. Another report says enemy in MON DU HIBOU and HILLOCK FM. and our men on line 200 yards to W. Div. O.P. reports our men can be seen LANGEMARCK Line.

Date.	How received or sent.	Time of despatch or receipt.	From or To.	Sender's Number.	Text of Message.
(62) 16/8/17.	Recd. by wire.	12.45 p.m.	33rd.Bde.	B.M. 437.	9th.Sherwood Foresters disposed as follows :- 1 Coy. CANE TRENCH 2 Coys. C.9.b. 1 Coy. C.3.d.
(63) "	"	1 p.m.	20 Divn.	G.A. 126.	Confirming telephone conversation 60th. Bde. will take steps to form WM if necessary a defensive flank on both RED and GREEN lines in case of counter attack from east. Strong points ordered at U.29.a.9₤.20 to be pushed on well. Brigadiers to consider defensive measures for holding captured line in accordance with para. 17 amended instructions No. 8 reversed.
(64) "	"	1.25 p.m.	18thCorps.	G 329.	14 Corps wire 11.55 a.m. begins aaa We hold WINDMILL at U.24.c.1.1 and approx. RED DOTTED line on entire Corps front though not quite clear if actually in RED line between U.23.d. 8.3 and U.23.b.0.6 aaa Estimated 500xpxixexexxx captures 4 o₤ 5 guns and howitzers over 500 prisoners and several M.G's.
(65) "	"	1.47 p.m.	18 Corps.	G. 330.	14 Corps wire 12.50 p.m. begins aaa Right Division report 8th. Shropshire L.I. established in WINDMILL U.24.c.1.1 and consolidating line 150 yards east of Salient in enemy lines aaa H.Q. ALOUETTE FARM aaa Bn. in touch with 9th. Lancs. Fusiliers.
(66) "	"	2.30 p.m.	P.F. Paterson.	Pigeon Service.	Please put barrage on PHEASANT TRENCH at once this trench has never been occupied enemy reported massing for counter attack.

Date.	How received or sent.	Time of despatch or receipt.	From or To.	Sender's Number.	Text of Message.
(67) 18/8/17.	Recd. by wire.	2.40 p.m.	58th.F.A.B.	W.Q.	The position is as follows :- Left Battalion hold a line 300 yards on the North side of the LANGEMARCK Road aaa The Right battalion have been held up by M.G. fire from C.6.b.0.4 but are now consolidating a line on the LANGEMARCK road aaa Left battalion are pushing forward posts but movement is impossible owing to sniping and M.G. fire being carried on constantly aaa German barrage is on a line C.5.a.central and C.5.b central also on RED FARM aaa Most of the firing was from 5.9 batteries attrue bearing of 71 degrees from HAANIXBEEK FARM aaa Enemy were reported massing between WHITE HOUSE and PHEASANT FARM at 11 a.m. aaa The ground is very muddy pack transport would at present be impossible aaa PHEASANT TRENCH is chiefly manned by M.G's aaa F.O.O. 58 Bde. 12.15 p.m.
(68) "	"	2.45 p.m.	33rd.Bde.	B.M.439.	OBVIATE report British aeroplane brought down in flames at JOLIE FM. aaa Lt. Mason Observer and Lieut. Luxton pilot taken to CANE AVENUE dressing station aaa Luxton wounded in face Mason badly shaken aaa Please inform 7th. Squad. R.F.C.
(69) "	"	2.35p.m.	Adv.48th. Division.		Artillery officer sent to Div. O.P. Confirms O.P. officer's statement that our men are in LANGEMARCK Line aaa No definite reports yet but enemy is in WINNIPEG aaa Left Flank Coy. 7th. Worcesters in touch with right Coy. of S.Staffs. at C.11.a. central. Two coys.went at 12.30 p.m. to fill gap on right.
(70) "	"	2.30 p.m.		G.A. 29.	
(71) "	" Contact Plane.	2.10 p.m.			Reports no flares seen, although called for.

Date.	How received or sent.	Time of despatch or receipt.	From or To.	Sender's Number.	Text of Message.
(69ᴬ) 16/8/17.	Recd. by 'Phone.	2.10 p.m.	34th. Bde.		Lancs. Fus. have retired from Red on to GREEN LINE. 10.25 a.m. Sergt. Hopkins X Coy. has just returned saying there are only about 20 men left in the Coy. They are held up approx. at U.30.c.2.8. He reports all officers wounded and is not in touch on his left. I have sent a patrol to find out situation. Have no news of other Coys. Only means of communication are runners, who are trying to find the Coys. now. Lt. Hornby Z Coy. just come back and reports that they are having a very bad time from snipers and M.G's. Lt. Hornby's platoon is on Right front of X Coy. He can see left post of Manchesters. ORIGIN informs me that they cannot hold on to where they are. I am therefore instructing him to withdraw quietly to line held by ORIENT.

Date.	How received or sent.	Time of despatch or receipt.	From or To.	Sender's Number.	Text of Message.
(72) 16/8/17.	Recd. by 'phone.	3 p.m.	C.R.A.		Report F.O.O. – RAT HOUSE.
(73) "	" "	3.5 p.m.	48 Divn.		Pigeon messages from 4th.Oxfords timed 12.50 p.m. shows line running from C.6.c.0.8 to SPRINGFIELD running W. of the TRIANGLE. This line is held by both Divisions, boundary being C.6.c.4.3.
(74) "	" "	3.5 p.m.	Maj.Harrison.		Report from Dorsets timed 1.14 p.m. Captain Wilston "B" Coy. on right is not in touch with N.F. on his right. Echeloned D Coy.(Reserve) to a line U.29.d.7.3 – C.5.b.7.7. Message from Manchesters timed 11.50 a.m. O.C. R. supporting Coy. reported 100 enemy attacking them they were driven off by rifle and Lewis Gun fire. Enemy digging 50 yards S.W. of LANGEMARCK – WINNIPEG ROAD C.6.c.c. People on right are retiring.
(75) "	" wire.	3.15 p.m.	"		With regard to 7th. S. Staffs. Col. Carter considers he can made right flank quite secure with 2 Coys. after personal reconnaissances. 1 Coy. is already over and the other started at 2.28 p.m. The other 2 Coys. he is moving up on the W. side and is getting into touch with Col.Jackson. Enemy massing for counter attack 50 yards E. of LANGEMARCK – WINNIPEG ROAD.
(76) "	Pigeon.	3.25 p.m.	2/Lt.WINKLEY Adjt. Manchesters		
(77) "	" by wire.	3.35 p.m.	48 Divn.	G.A. 32.	Pigeon message timed 12.50 p.m. shows Bn. in touch with 11th. Division W. of TRIANGLE FARM.
(78) "	" "	3.30 p.m.	OBLIGE.	B.M. 443.	OBEY are moving one Coy. east of STEENBEEK and remaining 2 coys. close to and west of STEENBEEK (1 Coy. already east of STEENBEEK) aaa OBJECT will move forward two coys. to position vacated by OBEY at once aaa Commdrs.of these coys. will get touch with OBEY and the situation in front of them and on their flanks aaa

Date.	How received or sent.	Time of despatch or receipt.	From or To.	Sender's Number.	Text of Message.
(79) 16/8/17.	Recd. by wire.	4.20 p.m.	20th. Div.	I.G. 730.	From latest aeroplane report timed 2.5 p.m. Our line now runs U.24.c.35.00 - U.24.c.00.40 - U.23.b.55.00 - U.23.b.33.25 - U.23.b.00.55 - U.23.a.45.82 - U.16.d.75.15 aaa ELOPE H.Q. at U.23.c. central aaa
(80) "	" "	5.20 p.m.	20th. Divn.	I.G.B. 106a.	Evening report aaa Situation unchanged consolidation proceeding aaa Prisoners unwounded 14 officers 138 O.R. and others not yet counted aaa Captured material 2 - 10 cm hows. 2 M.G's.
(81) "	'phone.	4.35 p.m.	Capt.White.		L/Cpl. of Lancs. Fus. wounded states :- About 1.30 p.m. L.F's 300 yards short of PHEASANT FARM as it appears strongly held. At this time Manchesters were in line with them. Shropshires succeeded in entering PHEASANT TRENCH - L.F's in shell holes since the Boch has counter attacked. F.O.O. 255th. Bde. with Col. Thurston, says :- 1 Coy. L.F's got in PHEASANT TRENCH centre of opposition. Big dug-outs 30.c.20.75. This man sent back by Col. Thurston.
(82) "	" "	"	"		20th. Division wire they are sending out special officers to ascertain whether CHINESE HOUSE - GOEDTERVERTEN FARM are occupied by enemy. Also nature of the BROEMBEEK just E. of Railway. ENCORE is to ascertain whether BLUE HOUSE and houses U.24.c.4.8 are occupied by the enemy.
(83) "	" "	4.45 p.m.	Maj.Townsend.		48th.Divn. are in parts of GREEN LINE but the enemy still hold portion of it. They are sending two ½ coys. to stalk the enemy out of these strong points. Should this method not succeed an operation on a larger scale with a barrage will be carried out to-night. The enemy 48th.Divn. are not in touch with us. They still hold MON DU HIBOU but we are still in SPRINGFIELD.

Date.	How received or sent.	Time of despatch or receipt.	From or To.	Sender's Number.	Text of Message.
(84) 16/8/17.	Recd. by 'phone.	4.50 p.m.	Capt.White.		26 more prisoners have arrived Total to date 203.
(85) "	"	5 p.m.	"		48th. Division are attacking each of the following strong points with 1 platoon in about 2½ hours. WINNIPEG - SHOT FARM TRIANGLE - VANCOUVER.
(86) "	"	6 p.m.	ORANGE.	B.M.385.	Line according to latest reports now runs :- C.5.d.65.70 - C.5.b.6.0 C.5.b.8.8 - C.5.b.9.7 - U.29.d.95.35 - RAT HOUSE - Exclusive to WHITE HOUSE (doubtful) aaa In touch with post about C.6.c.1.2 on our right aaa MON DU HIBOU held by enemy aaa ORIENT have a post about C.29.central in touch with ENCORE aaa
(87) "	"	6.10 p.m.	48 Divn.		The 48th. Division say their troops are in RED Line. They are sending 2 battalions forward, to mop up the posts in our lines held by the enemy and eventually form the post on the BLUE DOTTED LINE.

Date.	How received or sent.	Time of despatch or receipt.	From or To.	Sender's Number.	Text of Message.
(88) 16/8/17.	Recd. by 'phone	7.30 p.m.	33 Bde.		O.C. Commanding 2 Coys. 7th. S. Staffs. beyond E. of STEENBEEK reports I have reported to Lt.Col.Jackson at 3.45 P.m. at MON BULGARE. He informs me that he already has a defensive flank I have placed my two companies at the disposal of Lt.Col. Jackson if he should require them. Disposition of Manchesters - 2 Coys. strength 170 rifles at C.5.b.9.7 in cemetery. 2 Coys. in U.29.d.9.2 - 2 platoons C.5.b.6.0 - gun pits C.5.d.6.6. Dispositions 7th.Worcfester as follows - 1 Coy. E. of STEENBEEK at C.5.d.6.1. 1 Coy. REGINA CROSS. 1 Coy. round ALBERTA 1 Coy. Northern part of C.17.a. Batt. H.Q. C.10.a.6.5.
(89)	" wire.	6.50 p.m.	20th.Divn.	G.A. 128.	Dispositions for the night aaa. Right aaa. Sector aaa. ENGAGE and ENJOY in RED Line aaa. ENDURE and two coys. ENLIST GREEN AND BLUE LINES ENLIST less two Coys. about BON GITE aaa Left Bde. sector aaa. ELOPE and ELBOW in depth on RED and GREEN LINES ELOPE being on right aaa. ERECT & BRIDGE on BLUE LINE aaa. ELASTIC and ELIXIR will be relieved during the night and march to Camps in MALAKOF Area aaa. HOOD now under orders B.G.C. ENCORE will pass under command of B.G.C. ELSIE it will be held in reserve and be used for defensive purposes only aaa. HORSE will be at disposal of B.G.C. ENCORE for carrying tonight aaa
(90)	" "	7 10 p.m.	18 Corps.	G. 336.	11th. and 48th. Divisions will detail special parties to mop out all strong points still holding out in Rear of their present line aaa Operations will then continue until Original objectives are captured and consolidated aaa Special steps will be taken to guard flank aaa Schemes to be submitted to CorpsH.Q. by Divns. but Divs. will not wait for Corps approval aaa Concerted action where required will be arranged between Divisions direct aaa G.Os O. 11th. and 48th Divisions will remain in command of their sectors /until....

Date.	How received or sent.	Time of despatch or receipt.	From or To.	Sender's Number.	Text of Message.
(90) contd. 16/8/17.					until further orders aaa Schemes A and B issued under 18th. Corps No. G.S. 1/150 dated 11th. August are hereby cancelled aaa Acknowledge.
(91) "	Recd. by 'phone	7.45 p.m.	18 Corps.		Report from 14th. Corps that our men were been at WHITE HOUSE by a Staff Officer.
(92) "	" wire	8.19 p.m.	48 Divn.	G.A. 35.	Scheme aaa Special platoons of leading line 143 and 144 Bdes. have been ordered forward at 7.30 p.m. to STALK known enemy strong points aaa. After mopping up leading Bns. will establish line as far forward as possible up to BLUE line aaa 145 Bde. being withdrawn tonight to reform in OB and O.G. 1 after 143 and 144 have gone forward aaa Defensive flanks BORDER HO. JEW HILL, JANET FM, and will be advanced to include WINNIPEG when taken aaa Until further information no bombardment W. of LANGEMARCK line but barrage and searching fire beyond blue line aaa Wll arrangements made with flank Divs. aaa
(93) "	" "	9.1 pm.	48 Divn.	G.A. 36.	Situation still obscure aaa No further reports yet received aaa Party of enemy just W. of WINNIPEG fired on by Arty. with direct observation aaa
(94) "	" "	9.16 p.m.	18 Corps.	G. 340.	Following received from 14th. Corps 8.16 p.m. aaa 20th. Division report Germans have pressed back their right flank between WHITE HOUSE and RAT HOUSE. aaa
(95) "	" "	10.29 p.m.	33rd.Bde.	B.M. 448.	Following are now dispositions of OBILGE. aaa 3 Coy. S. Staffs. East of STEENBEEK in close supprt of Manchesters aaa These companies together number 290 and are commanded by Captain CHARLTON who has been given careful /instructions...

Date.	How received or sent.	Time of despatch or receipt.	From or To.	Sender's Number.	Text of Message.
(95) continued. 16/8/17.					instructions aaa 1 Coy. S.Staffs.dug in 200 yards behind line VON WERDER HO, FRANCOIS FM. aaa 2 Coys. 6th. Borders in C.9.d.and C.10.c. aaa 2 Coys. 6th. Borders om BLUE LINE aaa Whole of 6th. Lincolns at SIEGE CAMP aaa 33rd. M.G. Coy. in line, 33rd.T.M.B. in CANAL BANK aaa B.G.C. and B.M. FOCH FARM until 5 p.m. to-morrow then CANAL BANK aaa In touch with GOURNIER FM by wire thence practically to front line by lamp aaa S.Staffs. report right post of 11th.Manchesters at C.5.d.6.3 left post of 48th. Division at C.5.d.5.1 aaa Only a gap of 150 yards well covered by fire.
(96)	Recd. by wire.	10.38 p.m.	18 Corps.	G. 342.	A/contact aeroplane will call for flares tomorrow morning at about 8 a.m. in the area between the LANGEMARCK GHELUVELT line and the LANGEMARCK - WINNIPEG Road aaa Troops will specially be warned to be on the look out for calls at that hour aaa Ensure that sufficient flares are issued aaa
(97)	"	10.50 p.m.	Adv 48th. Divn.	G.A. 36.	7th. Worc. Regt. report about 8.37 p.m. aaa Attack on MON DU HIBOU held up aaa 143 Bde. report 8th. Warwicks trying to push forward towards WINNIPEG on a three Company front aaa

Date.	How received or sent.	Time of despatch or receipt.	From or To.	Sender's number.	Text of Message
(98) 17/78/18.	Recd. by wire.	1.30 a.m.	60th.Bde.	B.M.248.	Evening disposition aaa ENGAGE WHITE HOUSE U.24.c.0.4 3 Coys. aaa Just East of ALLOUETTE FARM 1 Coy aaa ENJOY C.23.d.0.95.50 - C.23.b.8.1 aaa H.Q. ENJOY U.23.d.2.2 HQ. ENGAGE ALLOUETTE FARM ENDURE 1 Coy. assisting ENJOY to join up with ELSIE on left flank 1 Coy. with 2 platoons ENLIST attached in GREEN LINE 2 Coys. with 2 platoons ENLIST one Coy. BLUE LINE and H.Q. about U.28.b.8.1 ENLIST one Coy. as above 1½ coys. at and above GREEN LINE 2 platoons ordered to fill gap on right flank aaa H.Q. U.28.d. 2.6 aaa HORSE 1 Coy. AU BON GITE H.Q. and 3 Coys. CANDLE trench employed carrying aaa.
(99)	"	2.42 a.m.	Adv. 48 Divn.	G.O. 336.	Enemy's artillery has now quietened considerably aaa. No reports as yet received from front aaa.
(100)	"	5.12 a.m.	20th.Divn.	G.B. 116.	Morning report aaa Situation quiet aaa Hostile artillery active during night aaa.
(101)	"	5.36 a.m.	48th.Divn.	G.O. 338.	No further reports as yet received as to position of leading troops aaa. Hostile shelling fairly heavy but not concentrated aaa
(102)	"	7.20 a.m.	34th.Bde.	B.M. 393.	Situation is now as follows :- Two Coys. of ORDEAL and two platoons of ORIGIN hold works C.5.d.7.8 and C.5.d.6.9 aaa. Two Coys. ORDEAL supporting in and behind Cemetery at C.5.b.8.8 aaa Three and a half Coys. of ORIGIN holding posts from Cemetery C.5.b.8.8 to U.30.c.10.46 aaa. BULOW FARM and COCKCROFT not held by us aaa. ORGAN hold U.29.d.99.50 9.7, 8.8, U.29.b.7.0, 65.20, 60.30, 80.50 N.E. to U.24.c.45.10, 40.20 aaa Gap at U.29.b.8.4 filled by post of ORIENT aaa ORGAN in touch with both flanks aaa. Rest of ORIENT disposed as follows aaa One Coy. in posts C.5.b.2.7 5.8, U.29.d.5.2 aaa Another Coy U.29.d.5.5, 4.6, 3.7, 25.85 aaa Another Coy. U.29.b.20.15 4.2, 1.3, with post mentioned above at U.29.b.8.4 aaa Another Coy. supporting in four posts round U.29.central aaa WHITE HOUSE and RAT HOUSE not held by us. aaa

Date.	How received or sent.	Time of despatch or receipt.	From or To.	Sender's number.	Text of Message
(103) 16/8/17.	Recd. by wire.	7.41 a.m.	48 Divn.	G.C. 339.	Patrol to HILLOCK FARM found enemy 40 yards W. of Farm aaa. POPE in touch with PLAIN post at C.12.a.5.2 where enemy hold strongly held line of posts about 400 yards E. of STEENBEEK with bend towards MON DU HIBOU aaa. This is still thought held by the enemy but reports from Coy. Comndrs attacking not yet received aaa Shelling heavy all night aaa Much rifle fire 400 yards W. of STEENBEEK aaa
(104) "	"	7.50 a.m.	34th. Bde.	B.M.395.	ORIENT reports prisoner from 440 I.R. brought to right support coy supposed to have been captured in front of our line.
(105) "	"	8.55 a.m.	Adv. 48 Div.	G.A. 43.	Left Brigade reports got into MON DU HIBOU last night and were bombed out aaa Coy. now dug in with leading platoon about C.6.c.0.1.
(106) "	"	9.50 a.m.	"	H.A. 44.	Line now runs BORDER HO, JEW HILL, line of gun pits C.12.c.9.6 A.5.2. in front of MON DU HIBOU aaa Enemy hold HILLOCK FM aaa Contact aeroplane message shows flares C.12.b.9.3, 6.d.5.3 and VIEILLES MAISONS aaa No report yet received from patrols sent to get touch with SPRING-FIELD.
(107) "	"	10.20 a.m.	18th. Corps.	G.I. 58.	14th. Corps report prisoner of 3rd. Bav. Res. Regt. 9th. Bav. Res. Divn. taken North of STADEN Railway exact location unknown aaa. Indicated relief of 214th. Div. by 9th. Bav. Res Div. aaa
(108) "	"	10.25 a.m.	I.O. 11th. Div.	I.W. 2.	Prisoner of 1st. M.G. R. 51st.. R.I.R. captured states 1st. and 2nd. Bns. of Regt. moved to PASSCHENDAELE Area yesterday afternoon aaa. No definite orders were given but prisoner believes they were to reinforce the line should we attack aaa. Prisoner was sent forward alone to look for some machine guns but lost his way and ran into our men aaa
(109) "	"	12.5 p.m.	I.O. 11 Divn.	I.W. 6.	Our left Bn. reports prisoner of 440 I.R. taken in front of their line this morning aaa Further details not available as yet aaa

	Date.	How received or sent.	Time of despatch or receipt.	From or To.	Sender's number.	Text of Message
(110)	17/8/17.	Recd. by wire	1.8 p.m.	34th. Bde.	B.M. 401.	ORIENT report two field guns were captured by them yesterday at HAANIXBEEKE Farm.
(111)	"	" "	2.15 p.m.	34th. Bde.	B.M. 403.	ORIGIN report 12.35 p.m. begins aaa Enemy lining up as if for counter attack east of LEKKERBOTERBEEK about 300 yards in front of LANGEMARCK WINNIPEG road aaa
(112)	"	" "	2.40 p.m.	34th. Bde.	B.M. 405.	Right support Coy. of ORIENT reports two enemy have come into posts and surrendered.
(113)	"	" "	1.35 p.m.	18 Corps.	G. 353.	14th. Corps report timed 12.5 0 p.m. enemy put up a smoke screen from about U.24.central to U.17.central aaa It is thought that they may be massing for counter attack behind this screen aaa
(114)	"	" "	2.7 p.m.	34th. Bde.	B.M. 402.	Ref. my 393 of today aaa ORGAN reports two posts between U.30.b.30.50 and U.24.c.45.10 at U.30.a.39.50 astride PHEASANT TRENCH and at U.30.a.1.7 aaa Strength of these four posts 2 officers and 86 O.R. aaa. Also Liaison officer with PRISM wires contact aeroplane reports flares U.30.a.17.50 to U.30.a.20.73 also U.24.c.25.00 to U.24.c.00.50 also U.23.d.50.70 to U23.d.35.90 aaa First three map references obviously ORGANS men aaa Lieut. Hayes states his Coy. lit flares at 7.40 a.m. aaa
(115)	"	" "	2.50 p.m.	18 Corps.	G. 354.	In continuation of my G.350 of today aaa Aeroplane reconnaissance 1.25 p.m. reports no more smoke screen visible and no enemy movements. aaa
(116)	"	" "	5.2 p.m.	34th. Bde.	B.M. 409.	Situation unchanged aaa. Enemy has line of posts West of LANGEMARCK between COOKCROFT and C.6.c.5.8 aaa Enemy movements also seen in COCKCROFT MONT DU HIBOU aaa Hostile artillery and aircraft not so active as yesterday aaa 2 prisoners and 2 field guns captured aaa Wind S.W. aaa

Date.	How received or sent.	Time of despatch or receipt.	From or To.	Sender's number.	Text of Message
(116) 17/8/17	Recd. by wire.	5.27 p.m.	18 Corps.	G.I. 62.	Prisoner of 1st. Bn. Bn. M.G. Coy. 51 R.I.R. 12 R.D. captured on left Divs. front this morning states aaa 1st. and 3rd. Bns. came up yesterday afternoon to counter attack LANGEMARCK but became disorganised by artillery fire aaa Prisoner had lost his way aaa Prisoner is rather unreliable aaa
(117) "	"	5.50 p.m.	18 Corps "I".	H.I. 61.	Prisoner of 7th. Coy. 440 R.I.R. taken on left Corps front this morning aaa Regt. were ordered to reinforce line last night aaa States 418 R.R. were alarmed tx morning of 16th. for counter attack aaa States all three Regts. in line on Regts. front aaa Prisoner is rather unreliable.
(118) "	"	7.27 p.m.	20th Divn.	G.B. 132.	Evening report aaa Situation unchanged aaa Artillery activity normal aaa Enemy aircraft very active flying low over our lines aaa Unwounded prisoners 1 officer 48 O.R. captured aaa Material Nil aaa

	Date.	How received or sent.	Time of despatch or receipt.	From or To.	Sender's number.	Text of Message
(119)	18/8/17.	Recd. by wire.	8.20 a.m.	I.O., 11th. Division.		1st. and 3rd. Battns. 184 I.R. withdrawn owing to casualties aaa H.Q. of both these Battalions were in PHEASANT FARM aaa No order of battle available aaa. Prisoners were sent forward to clear up situation aaa.
(120)	"	"	8.20 a.m.	"	I.W. 15.	Two prisoners of the 8th. Company 184 I.R. taken last night state that 2nd. Bn. moved up from WESTROOSEBEEK on night of 15th/16th. occupying the LANGEMARCK line and shell holes in front of it aaa 6th. and 7th. Coys. in front line and 5 and 8 in reserve aaa LANGEMARCK with elements line appears to be held with elements of 418 I.R. 440 I.R. and 51 R.I.R. aaa. Prisoners both state that the regiments are disorganised and mixed up together owing to our shell fire. aaa
(121)	"	"	1.40 p.m.	33rd. Bde.	M. 232.	Following wire from OBEY begins aaa British single seater biplane crashed 11.25 a.m. at C.6.a.3.7 aaa No signs of pilot aaa.
(122)	"	"	3.8 p.m.	Adv. 48 Divn.	G.C. 358.	Situation quiet aaa. In touch with OCEAN at C.5.d.7.3 sheet 28 aaa.
(123)	"	"	5.26 p.m.	20th. Divn.	G.B. 155.	Evening report aaa Situation unchanged aaa Prisoners one unwounded O.R. 262 R.I.R. one woundede 440 I.R. aaa Captured material aaa Add to my evening report of 16th. one 77 mm. gun less breach block and minimum of 10 machine guns aaa.
(124)	"	"	5.35 p.m.	33rd. Bde.	M. 234.	Situation quiet aaa With west aaa Some sniping from direction of COCKCROFT aaa
(125)	"	"	6.4 p.m.	Adv. 48 Divn.	G.B. 366.	Situation unchanged aaa. Considerable hostile shelling at 4 p.m. when our smoke barrage was put down aaa Captures 2 O.R. aaa
(126)	"	"	11.45 p.m.	33rd. Bde.	B.M. 474.	COUTTS. aaa

	Date.	How received or sent.	Time of despatch or receipt.	From or To.	Sender's number.	Text of Message
(127)	19/8/17.	Recd. by wire.	10.20 a.m.	48 Divn.	GO. 381.	One Co. POWER hold MON DU HIBOU cross roads C.6.c.8.5 and positions between above and CORNER FARM along E. of POELCAPPELLE ST. JULIEN Road corner farm only a heap of bricks shelling and M.G. fire lively.
(128)	"	"	10.21 a.m.	A.G.BAKER.		Our infantry have taken HIBOU aaa and are consolidating along ST. JULIEN POELCAPPELLE Road aaa Enemy Infantry only 20 O.R. 30 seen all running out of HIBOU after my 6 pdr. had fired aaa Enemy artillery not too bad aaa Tanks visible just spoken to MORGAN who has several men wounded and is going to ST. JULIEN aaa. My tank hopelessly ditched I have taken guns out and helped Warwicks under Wennington aaa When Warwicks are fully dug in I am returning to Chedder if possible.
(129)	"	"	10.25 a.m.	2/Lt.CLOSE.	2.	Our infantry not insight aaa Enemy infantry holding strong posts on left and right aaa Enemy artillery negligible aaa Tanks visible none aaa My tank hopelessly ditched and in near proximity to enemy aaa Ground wet on edge of road 5 guns out of action aaa Ground wet on edge of road
(130)	"	"	10.48 a.m.	33rd.Bde.	B.M. 481.	COCKCROFT in our hands 10 a.m. Further details follow aaa Trying join hands with POPE.
(131)	"	"	11.4 a.m.	18 Corps.	G.I. 65.	Fifth Army reports prisoner of 60 I.R. 121 Div. traced S. of YPRES - ROULERS Rly. Station 121 Div. from line at BOURSIES is relieving 54 Div.
(132)	"	"	11.22 a.m.	48 Divn.	G,B. 382.	Left. Battalion reports established C.6.c.75.20 C.6.c.8.4 C.6.c.7.5 C.6.c.5.7 Coy. H.Q. MON DU HIBOU casualties to date about 12 aaa Situation thoroughly cleared up aaa Posts all consolidated junction with OCEAN established W. of HIBOU aaa OCEAN not reached objective yet aaa Inflicted considerable casualties aaa
(133)	"	"	11.25 a.m.	33rd.Bde.	B.M.483.	Established posts at Gun pit C.6.a.20.65 Dugouts C.6.a.56.75 alsp on Road at C.6.a.30.05 and at C.6.a.30.75 and C.6.a.2.6 at 18.34 a.m

Date.	How received or sent.	Time of despatch or receipt.	From or To.	Sender's number.	Text of Message
(134) 19/8/17.	Recd. by wire.	11.29 a.m.	18 Corps.	G.I. 66.	Captured German map of recent date shows southern boundary of 7th. Bavarian Regt. 5th. Bav. Divn. BORDER HO. WINNIPEG CROSS Rds. D7.b.central aaa Northern boundary HILLOCK FM to D.1.a.central aaa H.Q. shown as follows aaa Fighting troops YETTA HUBNER FARM D.1.c.5.6 aaa Support troops YETTA HOUSE D.3.d.4.7 aaa Regtl. H.Q. V.28.c.7.1 aaa Photographs taken recently all shew signs of activity and tracks at these points aaa
(135)	"	2 p.m.	18 Corps "I".	G.I. 67.	10 prisoners of 185 Bn. 125 I.R. 26th. Divn. taken in C.6.c. came up to relieve 51 R.I.R. night 17th/18th. but could not find them and occupied post aaa 2nd. Coy. is North of them aaa Order of battle unknown aaa
(136) 19/8/17z	"	4.20 p.m.	"	G.68.	Reference our G.I. 66 BORDER HOUSE to WINNIPEG is battalion boundary aaa Southern boundary of Regt. is C.18.a.central to D.9.c.central aaa Another map of recent date shows troops in reserve three battalions in STADEN LINE and V.9.a,V.10.c, V.15.b, V.16.a, and two battalions in STADEN LINE and U.27.b & d. & V.20.a &c.aaa
(137)	"	6.10 p.m.	38th Divn.	G. 862.	IN continuation of evening report aaa. Enemy arty. activity intermittent aaa. Bursts of fire on LANGEMARCK, AU BON GITE, STEENBEEK and PILCKEM Ridge aaa
(138)	"	7.18 p.m.	33rd. Bde.	F.I. 109.	Prisoners taken by OBEY at 2.30 p.m. this afternoon wounded in cheek aaa. Belonged to 2nd. Coy. 3rd. Bn. 184 I.R. aaa Place of capture
(139)	"	8.44 p.m.	48th.Divn.	G.A. 61.	Reconnoitre remainder of TRIANGLE to-night and occupy VANCOUVER if not occupied by enemy aaa Adds. POPE reptd. Plain and OCEAN.

	Date. How received or sent.	Time of despatch or receipt.	From or To.	Sender's number.	Text of Message
(140)	22/8/17. Recd. by wire.		48 Divn.	G.B.431.	All twelve foxes left starting point at Zero going well.
(141)	" Pigeon.	7.1 a.m.	J.T.CLARK. D.48.		Our infantry have not yet established contact with Infantry aaa Enemy artillery heavy fire on Wend of WINNIPEG ROST.JULIEN Road aaa On the whole heavy retaliation aaa Tanks visible D.50 knocked out D.47 ditched Mr.MacDonald ditched Mc.Shaws ditched my Tank held up by ditched Tanks in front and by impassable ground aaa Ground impassable aaa Wire none encountered.
(142)	"	7.51 a.m.	A.J.ENOCK, D.45.	1.	Our infantry in strength on East side of TRIANGLE aaa Enemy infantry seem to be a minus quantity aaa Enemy Artillery barraging E. of WINNIPEG Road and Vancouver aaa Tanks visible on WINNIPEG - VANCOUVER Line aaa My Tank going strong on east side of TRIANGLE aaa Ground rather bad, Wire, none to be seen
(143)	" Aeroplane.	7.45 a.m.	Lt.N.SHARPLES.		Nine tanks observed near ST. JULIEN as per map between 7.15 and 7.30 only one on the ST. JULIEN - POELCAPPELLE Road observed moving Two on ST. JULIEN - WINNIPEG Road apparently ditched. Smoke barrage very effective Observations from 1000 feet. No movement of troops seen Only five flares seen as per map. E.A. active.
(144)	" wire	8.5 a.m.	144 Bde.	B.M.182.	PONY report time 6.30 a.m states within 50 yards of right objective and in touch with PLAIN who are in SPRINGFIELD aaa Tank dealing with VANCOUVER which was then still held by M.G's. Casualties reported slight aa One prisoner 23rd.Regt: aaa
(145)	"	8.20 a.m.	Symonds. D.44.		Enemy artillery getting my range. My tank covering BULOW and VIEILLES MAISONS and returning.
(146)	"	8.33 a.m.	OBLIGE.	B.M. 9	OBTAIN report all objectives gained and in touch with troops on right and left aaa troops of PANAMA on our right not got so far as expected and we have formed a defensive flank aaa OBJECT digging in on line through U.30.a.4.0.5—U.30.a.40.0 and in touch with troops on left aaa

Date.	How received or sent.	Time of despatch or receipt.	From or To.	Sender's number.	Text of Message
(147) 22/8/17.	Recd. by wire.	8.41 a.m.	OBLIGE.	B.M. 10.	Enemy barrage found on LANGEMARCK Road and their side of it aaa Our casualties few aaa No prisoners yet aaa Female tanks knocked out in POELCAPPELLE road and Officer and Sergt. killed aaa Infantry reached objective long before tanks aaa OBTAINS right firmly established aaa.
(148) "	"	8.42 a.m.	48 Divn.	G.A. 71.	All objectives gained on whole of OBLIGE front aaa Army consolidating.
(149) "	"	8.55 a.m.	48 Divn.	E.A. 14.	Report from Left.Bn. timed 6.30 a.m. aaa Tank dealing with VANCOUVER which was then still held by M.G's aaa. Right within 50 yards of objective C.12.b.35.75 and in touch with next Bn. which was in SPRINGFIELD aaa.
(150) "	"	6.30 a.m.	Capt.H.B. Montmorency. OBLIGE.		51 prisoners of 23rd. R.I.R. 12th. Res. Divn. taken this morning at WINNIPEG aaa. Objectives all captured and posts established at 6 a.m. Artillery barrage very short at present on our line of work. Estimated casualties one and ten majority from our own barrage.
(151) "	"	9.10 a.m.	OBLIGE.	B.M. 12.	Enemy shelling against Battn. on right between MON DU HIBOU and STEENBEEK. Left troops of Battn. on our right falling back so have lost touch with them and am endeavouring to establish touch again. Our right quite firm. Four prisoners seen coming down in distance. Number of enemy seen moving away as we reached objective.
(152) "	"	9.30 a.m.	I.O. 11th.Div.	T.W. 10.	Prisoners of 9th. Coy. 23rd.R.I.R. state relieved by 7th. Bav. I.R. night 18/19. 1st. and 3rd. Bns. in front with 3 Coys. in front and one in support. Second batta. in reserve. Order of battle North to South appears to be 31st. R.I.R. 1st. Bn. and 3rd. Bn. 23rd. R.I.R., 39th. R.I.R. 9th. Coy. was in touch with 3rd. Coy. 9th. Bn. Many casualties inflicted this morning by our aircraft Willingall officers appear to the Coy. Prisoners appear to have been taken at JURY FM.

Date.	How received or sent.	Time of despatch or receipt.	From or To.	Sender's number.	Text of Message
(153) 22/8/17	Recd. by wire.	3.16 p.m.	33rd Bde.	B.M. 21.	Situation quiet aaa OBTAIN joins hands with PONY at C.6.c.70.65 and line runs approximately as follows C.6.c.70.65 to main road at C.6.c.99 along main road to C.6.b.1.5 east of BULOW FM to U.30.d.1.2 to U.30.c.5.7 which is junction of OBTAIN and ONJECT aaa Thence along 'track thro' U.30.43.08 to U.30.a.2.5 where it joins old line aaa OBLIGE right post only 30 yards from PONY left post aaa Many concrete dugouts at BULOW FM which will be explored to-night aaa 2 M.G's captured by OBTAIN aaa Remaining two prisoners reported are wounded and will be sent down later aaa They are of same Regt. aaa No opposition encountered at BULOW FARM enemy fled before our arrival aaa POPE situation unknown for certain they appear to be slightly in advance of original line aaa
(154) "	"	9.30 a.m.	18 Corps "I"	G.I. 73.	50 prisoners of 23rd. R.I.R. 12 Res.Divn. taken at WINNIPEG this morning.
(155) "	"	8.30 a.m.	48th. Divn.	E.A. 14.	51 prisoners of 23rd. R.I.R. 12 Res. Divn. taken this morning at WINNIPEG aaa
(156) "	"	8.47 a.m.	48th Divn.	G.A. 71.	Report from left Battalion 6.30 a.m. aaa Tank dealing with VANCOUVER which was then still held by M.G's aaa Right battalion 50 yards of objective C.12.b.35 75 and in touch with next bn which was in SPRINGFIELD aaa
(157) "	"	9 a.m.	33rd. Bde.	B.M. 9.	OBTAIN reports all objectives gained and in touch with troops on right and left aaa Troops of PANAMA on our right not got so far as we expected and we have formed a defensive flank aaa OBJECT digging in on line through U.30.a.2.5 - U.30.a.43.08 and in touch with troops on left aaa Enemy barrage fell in LANGEMARCK road and this s side of it aaa Our casualties few aaa No prisoners yet aaa Female tank knocked out and officer and Sergt. killed Infantry reached objective long before Tanks aaa OBTAINS right firmly established.

Date.	How received or sent.	Time of despatch or receipt.	From or To.	Sender's number.	Text of Message
(158) 22/8/17	Recd. by wire.	8.57 a.m.	144 Bde.	B.M. 182.	PONY report time 6.30 a.m. States within 50 yards of right objective and in touch with PLIAN who are in SPRINGFIELD aaa Tank dealing with VANCOUVER which was still held by M.G's casualties reported slight aaa One prisoner 23rd. Regt.
(159) "	"	10.4 a.m.	33rd. Bde.	B.M. 12.	Enemy shelling hard against battalion on right between MON DU HIBOU and STEENBEEK aaa Left troops of battalion on our right falling back and so have lost touch with them and are endeavouring to establish touch again aaa Our right quite firm aaa Four prisoners seen coming in aaa Number of enemy seen running away as we reached the objective.
(160) "	"	10.40 a.m.	38th. Divn.	G. 912.	144 Bde. report considerable activity during night and especially on STEENBEEK and area S.W. aaa HOLD relieved HORSE in right sub-sector aaa
(161) "	"	12 a.m.	48th. Divn.	G.A. 72.	Right Bde. reports 11 a.m. aaa Gun pits C.12.d.7.3 captured after severe fight aaa Gun pits C.10.d.8.8 not captured aaa Leading wave digging in on line 150 yards W. of WINNIPEG SPRINGFIELD road aaa Tanks failed to pass JANET FARM and tank waves did not pass through owing to tanks failing aaa In touch with 61 Div. about C.12.d.7.3 aaa Enemy holding CEMETERY and SPRINGFIELD aaa Ends aaa Left bde. reports 11.30 a.m. Situation on right not clear aaa VANCOUVER not captured aaa Post reported digging in at C.6.central but not known if they have retired in view of 11th. Division report aaa

Date.	Low received or sent.	Time of despatch or receipt.	From or To.	Sender's number.	Text of Message
(162) 22/8/17	Recd. by wire.	11.19 a.m.	33rd. Bde.	B.M. 14.	OBTAIN line now runs from U.30.c.5.7 where it joins right of OBJECT to U.30.d.1.2 aaa. Thence down POELCAPPELLE road to C.6.c.9.9 aaa Patrol gone at t to get touch with PONY aaa Very little M.G. fire from VIEILLES MAISONS aaa Some sniping from shell holes while wounded were being brought in aaa Our right dug in and firm aaa A Lot of BOCHE Hills in aaa. Two prisoners of ERSTAZ Bn. O.R. 125 arrived OBTAIN H.Q. and two more on way aaa More prisoners expected from shell holes in front aaa Casualties estimated 2 officers wounded one O.R. killed 30 very slightly wounded aaa
(163) "	"	1.27 p.m.	I.O. 11 Div.	G.A. 14.	Prisoner of 9th. Coy. 23rd. R.I.R. States that they relieved the 7th. and 21st. Bav. night 18/19 aaa Order of battle North to South 125 I.R. 1st. 2nd. and 3rd. Coys. of 1st. Bn. 23rd. R.I.R. 9th. Coy. 3rd. Bn. of 23rd. R.I.R. company made up of remnants of 10th. 11th. and 12th. Coys 3rd. Bn. 23rd. R.I.R. and 51st. R.I.R. wnet back to rest on night 19/20 aaa Suffered severe casualties this morning aaa Prisoners taken near JURY FM aaa.
(164) "	"	2.23 p.m.	48th.Divn.	G.A. 74.	143 Bde. in addition to maintaining all its forward positions will before or after dark today capture any additional ground in or about WINNIPEG Cemetery - SPRINGFIELD necessary to secure the left flank of 61st. Divn. and our own point of junction aaaaxxxx with that Division at the road junction about 290 yards S.E. of WINNIPEG Cross roads aaa. 144 bde. holding all its present positions will before or after dark today establish its post at C.6.central and will capture any additional ground necessary to maintain its junction with 143 Bde. at or near SPRINGFIELD aaaAnys special artillery preparation will be arranged if asked for aaa
(165) "	"	2.31 p.m.	48th.Divn.	G.A. 75.	Right bde. now reports enemy counter attack about 9 a.m. drove us back from gunpits C.12.d.7.3 aaa Line on right now uncertain but aft Bn. in same place 150 yards from WINNIPEG SPRINGFIELD Road aaa Left Bfe. from C.12.8.8.4 9.6 TRIANGLE FM. C.6.d.9.0 C.8.7 aaa Tank seen moving forward in 61 Div. front apparently in direction of SCHULER FM aaa.

Date.	How received or sent.	Time of despatch or receipt.	From or To.	Sender's number.	Text of Message
(166) 22/8/18	Recd. by wire.	2.17 p.m.	18 Corps	G.I. 77.	14th. Corps reports wounded prisoner of 119 R.I.R. gives order of battle North to South 119 R.I.R. 119 I.R. aaa 119 R.I.R. 1st. Bn. has two coys in front line two coys. in immediate support 2nd. Coy Bn. is in support echeloned in depth all in krankken shell holes and elements in trenches aaa Has seen no other Regts. of his Div. but has heard they are in this Area aaa Saw men of 414 I.R. in VYFWEGEN on 20th. inst. aaa. Losses in 1st. Bn. 119 R.I.R. have been heavy from shell fire aaa
"	"	4.49 p.m.	33rd.Bde.	F.I.127.	Situation quiet aaa Heavy shelling of STEENBEEK at midday aaa Everything quiet now aaa Captured 2 M.G's and 4 prisoners two wounded 125 I.R. aaa A few more prisoners believed to have been taken but not sent down yet aaa
"	"	5.59 p.m.	48th.Divn.	G.A. 76.	Right Bn. reports doubtful if enemy have gunpits E.12.d.7.3 aaa. Probably some of our men in or near them and leaving line of right Bn. thence along line about 150 yards W. of WINNIPEG SPRINGFIELD Road aaa Orders have been issued to clear up situation and occupy forward line after dark aaa No further attack tonight aaa No change on remainder of front aaa.

Date.	How received or sent.	Time of despatch or receipt.	From or To.	Sender's Number.	Text of Message.
27/8/17.	Wire.	8 p.m.	48 Divn.	H.A. 98.	Left Brigade 5.50 p.m. Situation at Springfield still obscure but one M.G. emplacement captured. Right Bn. holding line 200 yards to 250 yards in front of original line. M.G. emplacements C.6.d.8.2. holding up advance. Situation of Left Bn. not clear.
"	Wire.	8-16 p.m.	48 Divn.	G.A. 99.	Right Bde. reports 7-45 p.m. Our Infantry now in part of SPRINGFIELD and captured some prisoners there.
"	"	8-25 p.m.	32nd. Bde.	B.M.354.	8th W.Ridings holds line WHITE HOUSE to U.30.c.66. thence 100 to 150 yards in front of our orginal line of posts. Casualties heavy from M.G. fire. Strong German posts with M.G,s unaffected by barrage at U.30.a.7.6. U.30.a.80.45. & U.30.central. Mud very bad Lewis Guns difficult to use owing to mud. Situation on right not yet cleared up. Portion of VIEILLES MAISONS believed to be taken.
"	Wire.	8-53 p.m.	48 Divn.	G.A. 101.	Left Bde. reports 8-5 p.m. SPRINGFIELD taken and being consolidated.
"	"	10-38 p.m.	32nd. Bde.	B.M. 358.	No further reports received. Units ordered to consolidate on present gains and to establish touch on flanks.
"	"	10-40 p.m.	POPE.	B.M. 219.	POTENT estimates from patrol reports to have advanced 300 yards. Position still obscure held up by M.G.s and snipers.
"	"	10-52 p.m.	48 Divn.	G.A. 103.	VANCOUVER reported captured. Left Brigade believed to be 300 yards W. of LANGEMARK Line.

Date.	How received or sent.	Time of despatch or receipt.	From or To.	Sender's Number.	Text of Message.
27/8/17.	Wire.	11-25 p.m.	48 Divn.	G.O.539.	One Officer twenty three O.R. 1st Battn. 414 Z.R. 204 Divn. taken. 15 and Officer were garrison of SPRINGFIELD with two M.G. inside concrete dug-out and several light M.G. in shell holes outside.
28/8/17.	"	12-44 a.m.	32nd.Bde.	B.M. 360.	Prisoner of 413 I.R. captured by 9th W.Yorks.. He is wounded and is being sent to dressing station.
"	"	12-34 a.m.	HUSK.	B.M. 229.	Situation EAGLE TR. still obscure. Patrols are clearing up situation. All gained is being consolidated.
"	"	12-35 a.m.	POPE	POPE B.M. 226.	Left of POTENT reported consolidated at C.6.d.4.7. Report M.G. fire from VIEILLES MAISONS.
"	"	12-58 a.m.	48 Divn.	G.O. 542.	Three more prisoners 1st Battn. 414 I.R. 204 Divn. Corpl. and Private state that they were to be relieved tonight by another Battalion same Regiment.
"	"	3-35 a.m.	32nd.Bde.	B.M. 362.	Situation report. Line now reported to run C.6.b.8.3. in PHEASANT TR. one house in VIEILLES MAISONS - Derilect Tank on Road at C.6.6.0.2. - E. of BULOW FM. - thence both battalions in touch at U.30.C.6.7. - U.30.a.45.10. - U.30.a.5.5. - U.30.a.50.55. PHEASANT TR. held from U.30.a.48. to U.30.a.29. also 4 posts on line U.30.a.4.5. to U.30.a.7.5. In touch with HUZ but not with POZ. Patrol sent out to C.6. central to find POZ. Patrols sent to WHITE HOUSE but result not yet reported. Casualties heavy due to M.G.s. Untouched by barrage. 9th W.Yorks. have one Officer per Coy. left. Two platoon O.B.s have been sent to 8th W.Ridings for purposes of Counter Attack.

Date.	How received or sent.	Time of despatch or receipt.	From or To.	Sender's Number.	Text of Message.
28/8/17.	Wire.	4-45 am.	32nd.Bde.	B.M. 363.	No further situation reports received. Information difficult to obtain to darkness and heavy going. Further reconnaissances will be carried out at dawn.
"	"	5-53 a.m.	48 Divn.	G.B. 545.	Situation unchanged.
"	"	6-25 a.m.	PRISM.	B.M. 252.	Situation. Fairly quiet. Dispositions of right Battn. Right Coy. 1 Platoon gunpits C.2.d.22. - 23. 2 1 Platoon round C.17.b.95.70. Right centre Coy. 1 Platoon gunpit W. of JANE FM. C.12.d.15.40. 10.60., 1 Platoon 100 yards W. in area of gunpits. Left centre Coy. gunpits C.12.d.07. - C.12.c. 90.85. Left Coy. 2 Platoons in and around SPRINGFIELD, 1 Platoon gunpit C.12.a.95.25. - 80.45. Ground round SPRINGFIELD waist deep in places. Disposition left not yet received but in touch with flank Bde. at KEERSELARE.
"	Pigeon.	7-17 a.m.	"X" Coy. 9/W.Yorks.	-	"Z" Coy. have captured PHEASANT FM.Trench in front of PHEASANT FM. and advance is held up about 100 yards from it. The Germans are strong by the dug-outs in the trench and have several M.G.s. I have not seen any of "Z" Coy Officers but have taken command of all the men. I can find. Casualties of the men I have seen pretty heavy. "X" Coy. MARRIOTT wounded and about 30 others. Am trying to push forward but not much luck.
"	Wire.	6-5 a.m.	HYTHE.	G.1023.	Situation report. 11th S.W.B. and 17th R.W.F. hold orginal line. 16 Welsh is reorganising in rear of orginal front line. Intermittent shelling. Generally quiet. Heavy enemy barrage was put down on lines in front of and behind LANGEMARCK 7 p.m. to 8-30 p.m. Wind S. Prisoners and war material NIL.

Date.	How received or sent.	Time of despatch or receipt.	From or To.	Sender's Number.	Text of Message.
28/8/17.	Wire.	7 a.m.	32nd.Bde.	B.M.364.	9th W.Yorks. report we hold one house of VIEILLES MAISONS and command entrance to the other so hope to get it also. They are also in touch with POZ. near VIEILLES MAISONS. Enemy barrage died down at 11-30 pm last night.and practically no shelling since.
"	"	10-51 a.m.	48 Divn.	G.B.549.	PRISM now on line H.Q. CHEDDAR VILLA with 1/4 R.BERKSR right front 1/4 OXFORD & BUCKS. L.I. left front. 1/5 GLOUCESTER R. right reserve, 1/ BUCKS left reserve. Elements of 1/7 and 1/8 WORCS. still in line. Front line now reported GUN PITS C.12.d.7.3. - JANET FM. - C.12.d.19. - SPRINGFIELD - E. of VANCOUVER C.6.d.44 - 47. where in touch with 11th Divn. and at KEERSELARE.
"	"	5-26 a.m.	HYTHE.	G.1040.	Situation report. All quiet. Intermittent enemy shelling. Captured. War material NIL. Prisoners TWO
"	"	6-8 p.m.	48 Divn.	G.B.559.	Situation unchanged. Hostile Artillery fairly quiet our guns shelling enemy strong points. Captured since 1-55 p.m. yesterday 2 OFFRS. 52 O.R. 1 M.G.
"	"	5-10p.m.	32nd.Bde.	B.M.367.	Evening report. Situation quiet. Line now reported to run PHEASANT TR. from left boundary to U.30.a.4.8. thence to U.30.a.30.25. - U.30.a.5.1. - U.30.c.65.50. - BULOW FM. inclusive C.66.05.25. - VIEILLES MAISONS one building inclusive - C.6.b.4.1. Wind. S.W. Captures NIL.
"	"	5-19 p.m.	HUSK.	B.M.255.	Quiet. Intermittent shelling. Captured war material NIL. Prisoners 2 O.R. last night.

DIARY OF MESSAGES DESPATCHED DURING OPERATIONS

16th to 30th August, 1917.

Date.	How received or sent.	Time of despatch or receipt.	From or To.	Sender's Number.	Text of Message.
16/8/17.	Sent by wire.	6.35 a.m.	18 Corps Flank Divs and Units.	G.505.	Contact aeroplane reports flares seen at U.29.d.5.5 to U.29.d.9.2 and at O.6.a.5.0 at 5.52 a.m. aaa Pigeon message timed 5.42 a.m. reports ORIENT at U.29.central aaa
"	"	7.15 a.m.	-do-	G.506.	Pigeon message timed 5.42 a.m. report U.29.central reached by ORIENT aaa Contact aeroplanes reports flares seen at U.29.d.5.5 to U.29.d.9.2 and at O.6.a.5.0 at 5.52 a.m. aaa Pigeon message timed 5.42 a.m. reports ORIENT at U.29.central aaa Left Division report aeroplanes report BLUE LINE taken all along our front aaa
"	"	9 a.m.	"	G.507.	Situation report aaa Left Battalion ORIENT has reached GREEN LINE and is consolidating aaa Casualties slight aaa ORDEAL on right believed to have reached GREEN LINE but requires confirmation. aaa ORIGIN and ORGAN for attack on Red Dotted Line advanced on time aaa No report on progress yet received aaa View much obscured by smoke aaa Prisoners 1 Officer 300.R. of 184 I.R. and 262 I.R. have crossed bridge and more coming.
"	"	10.47 a.m.	"	G.508.	The 5th. Dorsets and 8th. Northd.Fus. have definitely got the GREEN LINE and are consolidating aaa Dorsets say casualties are few. Northd. Fus. 3 Offrs and 50 O.R. aaa Prisoners passed through Div. cage 3 Officers and 130 O.R. more coming down aaa One platoon Dorsets say captured 60 aaa The 20th. and 48th. Divisions have also definitely got GREEN LINE aaa Our attack appears to be going well.
"	"	10.52 a.m.	32nd.Bde. H̶r̶k̶x̶B̶d̶e̶x̶ C.R.A. Corps & Divns. & Units.	G.509.	Situation report aaa Unconfirmed report that ORIGIN have reached final objective aaa No news of ORGAN aaa ORIENT and ORDEAL consolidating aaa Prisoners 3 Officers and 132 O.R.

Date.	How received or sent.	Time of despatch or receipt.	From or To.	Sender's Number.	Text of Message.
16/8/17.	Sent by wire.	12.10 p.m.	34th.Bde.	G.510.	ENGAGE report they have troops established at 9.5 a.m. in WINDMILL at U.23.d.95.10 and are in touch with ORGAN but they do not say where aaa. ENGAGE are consolidating 100 yards in front of WINDMILL with Hd Qrs. at ALOUETTE FARM.
"	"	12.40 p.m.	Corps & Flank Divs. & all concerned.	G.511.	Situation report aaa ORGAN appear to have reached RED Line and are in touch with ENGAGE on their left aaa. ORIGIN are reported to be hung up about BULOW FARM aaa. Prisoners captured 4 officers and 171 O.R.
"	'phone.	1.5 p.m.	34th.Bde.		Asked Major Harrison what steps are being taken to clear up the situation on right flank. 33rd. Bde. Scouts told to get in touch with 2 front Bns. The G.O.C. orders the 34th. Bde. to send an officer up to obtain information regarding the situation of the front Bns.
"	"	2.20 p.m.	WAIST. OBLIGE. ORANGE. EAGLE. PALAMA	G.512.	In confirmation of telephone conversation aaa. Unconfirmed report from Artillery F.O.O. that our Infantry have been seen withdrawing from RED line towards GREEN line on OCEAN front and that PALAMA are not in RED line and that MON DU HIBOU is still held by the enemy aaa. If this is the case and RED Line on our front has been given up GREEN Line must be held on to and a flank formed from GREEN line running forward in front of RAT HOUSE to RED line on our side of junction with EAGLE aaa In any case OBLIGE will send one battalion across the STEENBEEK at once as a support to ORANGE to be used at the discretion of the O.C. this battalion aaa Added.OBLIGE & ORANGE who will Acknowledge rept. WAIST, EAGLE and PALAMA.

Date.	How received or sent.	Time of despatch or receipt.	From or To.	Sender's Number.	Text of Message.
16/8/17.	Sent by 'phone.	1.15 p.m.	33rd.& 34th.Bdes. by G.O.C.		Verbal order by G.O.C. to 33rd. Bde. to send 1 Batt. across STEENBEEK the C.O. to be given power to act as the situation demands. 34th.Bde. ordered to hold the GREEN LINE, to keep touch with 20th.Divn. on RED line, RAT HOUSE to be held.
"	"	2.45 p.m.	34th.Bde. by G.O.C.		Left battalion hold a line 300 yards N. of LANGEMARCK road. Right Bn. held up by M.G. fire from C.6.b.0.4 and are consolidating on LANGEMARCK Road.- ZONNEBEKE Road. Left Bn. pushing forward posts but movement difficult owing to sniping and M.G. fire. German barrage on C.5.a.central - C.5.b.central - and on RED Farm. Ground too muddy for pack transport. PHEASANT TRENCH chiefly manned by M.G's.
"	" wire.	6.25 p.m.	32nd. & 33rd.Bdes. Flank Divs & Locals.	G.515.	Line according to latest reports now runs :- C.5.d.65.70 - C.5.b.6.0 C.5.b.8.8 - C.5.b.9.7 U.29.d.95.35 - RAT HOUSE exclusive to WHITE HOUSE (doubtful) aaa. In touch on our right with post about C.6.c.1.2 aaa MON DU HIBOU held by enemy aaa ORIENT have a post about C.29.central in touch with ENCORE aaa
"	" wire.	7.45 p.m.	Corps & Flank Divs	G.517.	Night situation report aaa. ORDEAL 2 Coys. C.5.d.8.7 2 Coys. C.5.d.6.9 in touch with PRISM about C.6.c.1.1 aaa ORIGIN at C.5.b.9.7 in cemetery U.29.d.9.2 and at C.5.b.6.0 aaa ORIENT on btch sides LANGEMARCK ROAD from U.29.d.6.2 to U.29.central and are in touch with ENCORE aaa. ORGAN at U.30.c.0.6 - U.30.a.7.5 - WHITE HOUSE in touch with ENCORE aaa. 2 Coys OBEY at C.5.central and 2 Coys in line RED BARM - FERDINAND FARM.

Date.	How received or sent.	Time of despatch or receipt.	From or To.	Sender's Number.	Text of Message.
16/8/17.	Sent by wire	2.53 p.m.	7th.Squad R.F.C.	G.513.	Following wire OBLIGE begins aaa OBVIATE report British aeroplane brought down in flames at JOLIE Fm. aaa Lt.Mason Observer and Lt. Luxton pilot taken to CANE AVENUE dressing Station aaa Luxton wounded face Mason badly shaken aaa.
"	"	11.16 p.m.	ORANGE WAIST EAGLE. OATEN.	G.521.	In confirmation of verbal instructions already issued aaa You will order ORGAN to take up a defensive line during the night with their right in touch with ORIGIN and their left with ENCORE in the LANGEMARCK Line aaa If ORGAN are unable to carry out this you will push in portions of ORIENT until gap is filled aaa. It is most important that right of ENCORE is not turned aaa.

Date.	How received or sent.	Time of despatch or receipt.	From or To.	Sender's Number.	Text of Message.
17/8/17.	Sent by wire.	9.5 a.m.	All Units.	G.527.	Wire from 48th.Division begins aaa Left Bde. reports got into MON DU HIBOU last night and were bombed out aaa Coy. now dug in with leading platoon about C.6.c.0.1.
"	"	1.55 a.m.	ORANGE.	G.528.	Wire from 60th. Brigade begins aaa Evening disposition aaa ENGAGE WHITE HOUSE U.24.c.0.4 3 Coys. aaa Just East of ALLOUETTE FARM 1 Coy. aaa ENJOY C.23.d.95.50 - C.23.b.8.1 aaa H.Q. ENJOY U.23.d.2.2 H.Q. ENGAGE ALLOUETT FARM ENDURE 1 Coy. assisting ENJOY to join up with ELSIE FARM ENDURE 1 Coy. eith 2 platoons ENLIST attached to on left flank 1 Coy. with 2 platoons ENLIST in on GREEN LINE 2 Coys. with 2 platoons wikk ENLIST 1 Coy. as BLUE LINE and H.Q. about U.28.b.8.1 ENLIST 1 Coy. as above 1½ Coys. at and above GREEN LINE 2 Platoons ordered to fill up gap on right flank aaa H.Q. U.28.d.26 aaa HORSE 1 Coy.AU.BON GITE HQ. and 3 Coys. CANDLE trench employed carrying aaa
"	"	10.25 a.m.	48th.Div.	G.528.	Line now runs C.5.d.7.8 d.65.95 C.5.b.7.8 U.30.c.1.5 29.d.99.50 b.53, 64, 84, U.24.c.4.1 35.20.
"	"	11.18 a.m.	34th.Bde.	G.529	Ref. G.365 aeroplane flew as stated no flares were seen Please furnish explanation.
"	"	11.48 a.m.	18 Corps.	G.530.	Wire from OBEY timed 10.15 a.m. begins aaa Single seater biplane A.92 c.9 crashed engine trouble 300 yards E. of GOURNIER FARM pilot unhurt 9.45 a.m. Ends.
"	"	1.35 p.m.	33rd.Bde. 34th. "	G.532.	14th. Corps reports at 12.50 p.m. enemy put up a smoke screen from about U.24.central to U.17 central aaa It is thought that they may be massing for counter attack behind this screen aaa
"	"	5.15 p.m.	18 Corps Flank Divs.	G.539	Situation unchanged aaa. Enemy has line of posts between COOKCROFT and C.6.c.5.8 aaa Enemy movement also seen in COOKCROFT and MON DU HIBOU aaa. Hostile artillery & aircraft not so active as yesterday aaa 2 prisoners & 2 field guns captured aaa Wind S.W.

Date.	How received or sent.	Time of despatch or receipt.	From or To.	Sender's number.	Text of Message
19/8/17.	Sent by wire	7.45 a.m.	18 Corps & 48 Divn.	G.564.	Message dropped from aeroplane 3411 7.40 a.m. states Tank at C.6.c.8.7 aaa Tank at C.6.c.5.8 aaa Tank at C.6.c.6.8 aaa From 6.45 a.m. to 7.20 a.m., all stationery and emitting smoke.
"	"	8.2 a.m.	33rd.Bde. 48th. Divn.	G. 565.	—do—
"	"	10.55 a.m.	18 Corps & Flank Divs.	G.567.	COCKCROFT in our hands 10.0 a.m. no details yet to hand aaa
"	"	11.40 a.m.	"Q". Units.	G. 568.	Posts established at gun pits C.6.a.20.65 and dugouts C.6.a.5.6 also on road at C.6.a.30.05 and at C.6.a.30.75 at 10.34 a.m.
"	"	12.15 p.m.	C.R.A.	G.569.	Wire from 18 Corps begins aaa Captured German map of recent date shows southern boundary of 7th. Bav. Regt. 5th. Bav. Div. BORDER HOUSE WINNIPEG CROSS Rds. D.78 central aaa Northern boundar HILLOCK FM. to D.1.a central aaa H.Qrs. shown as follows aaa Fighting troops HUBNER FARM D.1.c.5.6 aaa Support troops YETTA HOUSE D.3.d.4.7 aaa Regt. H.Q. U.28.c.7.1 aaa Photos. taken recently all show signs of activity and tracks aaa ends.

Date received or sent.	Time of despatch or receipt.	From or To.	Sender's number.	Text of Message
22/8/17. Sent by wire.	9 a.m.	18th. Corps Flank Divns.	G.619.	Wire from OBLIGE begins aaa OBTAIN reports all objectives gained and in touch with troops on right and left aaa. Troops of PANAMA on our right not got so far as we expected and we have formed a defensive flank aaa. OBJECT digging in on line through U.30.a.2.5 U.30.a.4.8 0.8 and in touch with troops on left aaa. Enemy barrage put down on LANGEMARCK Road and their side of it aaa. Our casualties few aaa. No prisoners yet aaa Females tanks knocked out in POELCAPPELLE road and officer and sergt. killed. Infantry reached objective long before tanks aaa OBTAINS right firmly established aaa
"	10.40 a.m.	3 Bdes.CRA	G.620.	12 Res. Divn. appears to have been relieved 5th.Bav. Divn. night 18/19 inst aaa. Order of Battle North to South appears to be 51st. R.I.R. 1 and 3rd. Bns. 23rd. R.I.R. 38 R.I.R. aaa Div. boundaries not known aaa.
"	3.15 p.m.	Units.	G.624.	Line now runs approx. as follows C.6.c.70.65 - C.6.c.7.9 along road to C.6.b.1.5 - east of BULOW FM U.30.d.1.2 - U.30.b.5.7 (Battalion junction) thence along road - track to U.30.a.43.08 - U.30.a.2.5 aaa Post at C.6.c.70.65 in touch with PONYS left post which is 30. yards distant aaa Many concrete dugouts at BULOW FM aaa 2 M.G's captured aaa Situation now quiet aaa.
"	5.5 p.m.	Corps & Flank Divs.	G.625.	Situation quiet aaa Heavy shelling of STEENBEEK at midday aaa Everything quiet now aaa Captured 2 M.G's and 4 prisoners two wounded 125 I.R. aaa A few more prisoners prisoners believed to have been taken but not sent down yet aaa.

Date.	How received or sent.	Time of despatch or receipt.	From or To.	Sender's number.	Text of Message
22/8/1917.	Sent.by wire.		48 Divn.	G.616.	Symonds D.44. 6.B.35 wires Our Infantry digging in at point 6 centre aaa. Enemy Infantry not in sight aaa Enemy artillery have disabled D.41 (Lt.Lansel and Sergt.Week killed) aaa Tanks visible abandoned and blocking all round my tank O.K. aaa Ground bad aaa Wire, none visible.
"	"		48th. Divn.	G.617.	A.Jl.Enoch D.43 C.694 wires Our Infantry in strength on East side of TRIANGLE aaa. Enemy Infantry seem to be a. minus quantity aaa Enemy artillery barraging E. of WINNIPEG Road) and VANCOUVER Line aaa My Tank going strong on East side of TRIANGLE aaa Ground rather bad wire none to be seen.
"	"		"	G.618.	2/Lt. J.T.Clark D.48 C.12.d.0.4 wires out infantry have not yet established contact with infantry aaa. Enemy artillery heavy fire on bend of WINNIPEG ST. JULIEN Road aaa. On the whole heavy retaliation aaa Tanks visible D.50 knocked knocked out D.47 ditched Mb.Mc.Donalds ditched Mc.Shaws ditched my Tank held up by ditched Tanks in front and by impassable ground aaa. Ground impassable aaa Wire none encountered.

APPENDIX 2.

DIVISIONAL ORDERS.

SECRET   11th Division No. G.S. 127.

32nd Inf. Bde.
33rd Inf. Bde.
34th Inf. Bde.
C.R.A.
C.R.E.
48th Division. ✓ (for information).

      The attached Instructions 48th Division No. 5. are forwarded for information.

      B.G's C. 32nd and 34th Brigades should get in touch with the B.G.C. 144th Brigade and the C.R.A. with the C.R.A. 48th Division.

      Definite instructions will not be issued until the situation is clearer, but, if possible, the original plan of proposed operations will be strictly adhered to: i.e. The 34th Brigade will attack trenches in front of PHEASANT FARM and ROSE HOUSE. The 32nd Brigade will pass through the 34th Brigade, capture POELCAPPELLE and establish itself North East of the village.

      The 33rd Brigade will be in Divisional Reserve.

ACKNOWLEDGE.

                                       J. D. Coleridge.

H.Q. 11th Division.   Lieut-Colonel,
1st August, 1917.   General Staff. 11th Division.

SECRET

APPENDIX 2.a.

Copy No. 23

11th Division Order No. 94.

Reference 1/20,000 Map.
Sheet 28. N.W.

August 5th. 1917.

1. (a) The 11th Division (less Artillery) will relieve the 51st Division (less Artillery) in the Left Sector of the XVIII Corps front by the morning of the 8th instant.

   (b) Movements will take place in accordance with attached Table 1.

   (c) Details of the actual relief of the line will be arranged direct between the G.O's C. 32nd and 154th Inf. Bdes.

   (d) Units of the 32nd Inf. Bde. on arrival at the CANAL BANK will come under the orders of the G.O.C. 51st Division until the command passes on the 8th August.

2. On completion of the relief the Division will be disposed in accordance with Table 2.

3. The 51st Divisional Artillery will remain in the line under the orders of the C.R.A. 11th Division.

4. Field Companies and Pioneer Battalion of the 11th Division will take over the duties now carried out by the R.E. and Pioneers of the 51st Division: Details to be arranged by the C.R.E.'s of the two Divisions.

5. (a) Units not mentioned in Tables 1 and 2. will move under orders of A.A. & Q.M.G. 11th Division.

   (b) Administrative Instructions will be issued later

6. Divisional Headquarters will close at 6 RUE DE POTS, POPERINGHE at 10 a.m. on 8th inst. and will reopen at X Camp. A.18.c.2.5. at the same hour, at which time the Command of the Sector will pass to G.O.C. 11th Division.

7. ACKNOWLEDGE.

J. D. Coleridge
Lieut-Colonel,
General Staff. 11th Division.

Issued at 5-45 p.m.

Copy No. 1. A.D.C. for G.O.C.
   2. C.R.A.
   3. C.R.E.
   4. 32nd Inf.Bde.
   5. 33rd Inf.Bde.
   6. 34th Inf.Bde.
   7. 6th E. Yorks R.
   8. Q.
   9. Signals.
   10. Train.
   11. A.D.M.S.
   12. A.P.M.
   13. XVIII Corps G.
   14. XVIII Corps Q.

Copy. No. 15. 20th Division.
   16. 39th "
   17. 48th "
   18. 51st "
   19. Area Comdt. DIRTY BUCKET CAMP.
   20. " " SIEGE CAMP.
   21. " " CANAL BANK.
   22 & 23. War Diary.
   24 - 25. File.

Table of Moves to Accompany 11th. Divisional Order No. 94.   TABLE 1.

Serial No.	Date.	Unit.	From.	To.	Route.	Remarks.
1.	August 6th.	2 Battalions 32nd.Inf.Bde. 32nd.M.G.Co. 32nd.L.T.M.B.	DIRTY BUCKET CAMP. (1 Bn. from POPERINGHE)	CANAL BANK.	DIRTY BUCKET CORNER-HOSPITAL FARM-BRIDGE JUNCTION-X Roads B.22.c.6.9-B.29.d.7.5-ESSEX FARM. (Bn. from POPERINGHE to move via ELVER-DINGHE Road and A.30.central under Bde. arrangements.)	Time to be arranged by Brigadiers concerned. To take over accommo-dation of 2 Bns.154th. Bde., 1 154th.M.G.Co. 1 232nd.M.G.Co. and of 154th.L.T.M.Bty.
2.	Aug.7th/8th.	2 Bns.32nd. Inf.Bde. & 32nd.M.G.Co.	CANAL BANK.	Front line.	-	Times and details to be arranged between Brigadiers concerned.
3.	August 8th.	2 Bns.32nd. Inf. Bde. & 32nd.Bde.H.Q.	DIRTY BUCKET CAMP. (1 Bn. from POPERINGHE)	CANAL BANK.	Same route as Serial No.1.	Head of Battalions to reach CANAL BANK at 9 a.m. Time of Bde. H.Q. taking over to be arranged by Brigadiers concerned.
4.	August 8th.	34th. Inf. Bde.	WINDMILL CAMP.	SIEGE CAMP.	Via DROMORE CORNER-HOSPITAL FARM.	To pass STEENTJE Windmill at 8 a.m. March to be completed by 10 a.m.

/Table 1 continued......

TABLE 1. continued.

Serial No.	Date.	Unit.	From.	To.	Route.	Remarks.
5.	August 8th.	33rd.Inf.Bde.	TUNNELLING CAMP. ST.JAN TER BIEZEN.	DIRTY BUCKET CAMP.	POPERINGHE - POPERINGHE - VLAMERTINGHE - Road - Road junction G.5.d.0.2 - A.30.central.	March to be completed by 10 a.m.

NOTE : All units will be preceded at sufficient distance by a mounted officer to give warning to Traffic Control Posts of the approach of a column.

The following distances will be maintained :-

East of the RENINGHELST - POPERINGHE - PROVEN Road, 200 yards between Companies.

TABLE 2.

DISTRIBUTION 11th. DIVISION 10 a.m. 8/8/1917.

Divisional H.Q.	X Camp. A.16.c.2.5.
C.R.A. H.Q.	X Camp. A.16.c.2.5.
11th. D.A.	In action.
C.R.E. H.Q.	X Camp. A.16.c.2.5.
11th. Divnl. R.E.) 6th. E. Yorks (Pioneers).)	At work in forward area under orders of C.E., XVIII Corps. Located in CANAL BANK.
32nd. Inf. Brigade. H.Q.	FOCH FARM. C.20.d.2.8.

2 Battalions.
    2 Battalions.
    M.G. Company.
    L.T.M. Battery.
	In line.) After
	 CANAL BANK.)relieving
	 In Line.)154th.Inf.
	 CANAL BANK.)Brigade.

33rd. Inf. Brigade.	A.30.Central. DIRTY BUCKET CAMP.
34th. Inf. Brigade.	B.21.d. SIEGE CAMP.
A.D.M.S.	X.Camp. A.16.c.2.5.
33rd. Field Amb. H.Q.	A.23.c.2.9.
34th. " " H.Q.	C.19.d.4.1.
35th. " " H.Q.	L'EBBE FARM. F.29.d.5.9.

APPENDIX 2.G.

Copy No. 26

SECRET

11th Division Order No. 95.

9th August, 1917.

Reference 1/20,000 Map
Sheets 28 N.W. & 20. S.W.
& Special POELCAPPELLE
Map 1/10,000.

1.   On a date and at an hour to be detailed later the Fifth Army will attack the enemy on its front. All preparations will be completed by August 12th.

2.   The 11th Division will attack on the Left of the XVIII Corps with the 145th Brigade (48th Division) on its right and the 60th Brigade (20th Division) on its left.

3.   The 11th Division attack will be carried out by the 34th Brigade.

4.   The objectives and boundaries between Divisions are shown on the attached Map "A".

The 1st Objective will be the GREEN LINE.
The 2nd Objective will be the RED DOTTED LINE.

The Right portion of the 145th Brigade will pause for 20 minutes on the GREEN LINE and assault the RED DOTTED LINE as far to the left as C.12.b.8.9. simultaneously with the XIXth Corps on its right.
The 34th Brigade will pause for one hour and 55 minutes on the GREEN LINE and assault the RED DOTTED LINE simultaneously with the 60th Brigade on its left and the left portion of the 145th Brigade on its right.
On arrival on the GREEN LINE and until such time as the 60th Brigade has captured ALOUETTE FARM   the left flank of the 34th Brigade will be refused as shown on the attached Map "A", care being taken that house at U.29.d.1.9. is held.

5.   The main objective is the capture of the LANGEMARCK - GHELUVELT LINE.
After the capture of this line, outposts will be established on a general line through FLORA COTTAGE (to 145th Brigade) PHEASANT FARM - WHITE HOUSE (to 34th Brigade).
The G.O.C. 34th Brigade will detail distinct and complete units for this purpose beforehand.
Under cover of these outposts patrols will be sent out to discover the enemy's dispositions and seize any points of tactical importance vacated by the enemy.

6.   The 34th Brigade will form up on both sides of the STEENBEEK.
Forming up places will be marked by tapes and discs.
The approaches from the BLACK LINE to the STEENBEEK will be marked with tapes and direction posts. Especially trained guides will assist in leading troops to their places of assembly.

7.   Assaulting troops will follow the barrage closely; and especial units, detailed beforehand, will deal with the various farms and concrete shelters included in the Divisional area.

Direction will be kept by compass bearings.

/8...........

8.	On the main objective being gained consolidation will be carried out on the following lines (for approximate positions of posts Vide Map "A").

(a)	The outpost line and 1st. line of resistance consisting of eight posts Nos. 1 - 8.

(b)	The 2nd. line of resistance consisting of eight posts Nos. 9 - 16.

(c)	The LANGEMARCK - WINNEPEG ROAD Line consisting of eight posts Nos. 17 - 24 and including RAT HOUSE.

(d)	A support line to (c) of eight posts Nos. 25 - 32 including strong points at enclosure C.5.b.6.0 - the COCKCROFT - House U.29.d.1.9 - HANNIXBEEKE FARM.

Work on (c) and (d) to commence directly the GREEN LINE is taken.
The object in view will be to consolidate the RED DOTTED and GREEN LINES so that they can eventually be held by two battalions disposed in depth.
The outpost line will be especially sited and prepared with a view to a further advance.
R.E. personnel will assist in the consolidation Vide Appendix No. 3.

9.	In order to ensure close touch with the flanking Divisions the G.O.C., 34th. Brigade will detail 1 section to meet similar parties of 145th. and 60th. Brigades at each of the following places :-

60th. Brigade.		145th. Brigade.	
Place.	Time.	Place.	Time.
X Roads U.29.c.3.8.	Zero plus 20 minutes.	MON DU HIBOU.	Zero plus 30 mi
		The COCKCROFT.	Zero plus 50 mi
X Roads U.29.b.0.2.	Zero plus 1 hr. 15 minutes.	X Roads C.6.b.1.5.	Zero plus 2 hr 50 minutes.
WHITE HOUSE.	Zero plus 3 hrs. 40 minutes.	New Houses.	Zero plus 3 hr 10 minutes.

10.	The attack will be made under :-

(a)	An Artillery barrage. - Vide Appendix 1.

(b)	A Machine Gun Barrage. - Vide Appendix 2.

The Artillery barrage will come down 300 yards Eas of the STEENBEEK on the right and 250 yards East of it on the left.   It will lift at Zero plus 5 minutes and advanc at a rate of 100 yards in 5 minutes.
There will be a smoke barrage during the pause on the GREEN LINE.   Details will follow.

- 3 -

11. Eight Tanks have been allotted to assist the 11th Division in the attack.
Four will be allotted to the Right of the attack and four to the Left.
The Tanks will assemble in the STEENBEEK Valley by ZERO minus 2 hours.
The Tanks will move as far forward as possible in the advance, and will assist the Infantry in capturing strong points.
Tanks and Infantry will work together for the reduction of strong points, especial Tanks being detailed for particular strong points beforehand in the same way as the Infantry.
Detailed instructions regarding co-operation with Tanks will be issued later.

12. A contact aeroplane will be in the air during the attack on each objective.
The leading troops <u>only</u> will mark their positions by flares to contact aeroplanes when asked for by either :-

      (a) KLAXON HORN.
or (b) A series of white lights.

13. Situation reports will be rendered by 34th Brigade every two hours after ZERO.

14. The 33rd Brigade less 2 Battalions will assemble in the CANAL BANK by Zero minus six hours, and will form the Divisional Reserve.
The G.O.C. 33rd Infantry Brigade will report at Divisional Headquarters at Zero plus 2 hours.
Two Battalions 33rd Brigade will be located at SIEGE CAMP and the 32nd Brigade at DIRTY BUCKET CAMP at Zero.

15. Orders detailing the relief of the 32nd Brigade by the 34th Brigade in the line, and other moves will be issued later.

16. Headquarters at Zero will be as under :-

H.Q. 11th Division.	'X' Camp. A.16.c.1.6.
Advanced Report Centre.	CANAL BANK. (GORDON TERRACE).
H.Q. 20th Division.	ELVERDINGHE CHATEAU.
H.Q. 48th Division.	REIGERSBURG CHATEAU.
H.Q. 33rd Brigade.	CANAL BANK. (GORDON TERRACE).
H.Q. 34th Brigade.	FOCH FARM. C.20.d.2.8.
Advanced Report Centre 34th Brigade.	GOURNIER FARM. C.9.d.2.7.
H.Q. 60th Brigade.	STRAY FARM. C.3.c.2.7.
H.Q. 145th Brigade.	VAN HEULE FARM. C.17.d.2.6.
H.Q. 20th Coy. Tanks.	CANAL BANK. (GORDON TERRACE).

17. The following Appendices will be issued with this order, Nos. 2 to 6 are forwarded herewith, No. 1. will be issued later.

    1. R.A. Programme and Barrage Map.
    2. Machine Gun Programme and Barrage Map.
    3. R.E. Instructions.
    4. Administrative Instructions.
    5. Medical Instructions.
    6. Arrangements for 'Contact' and 'Infantry Protection' Aeroplanes.

- 4 -

18. Attention is drawn to Battle Standing Orders and Instructions for the Offensive No. 1 (as far as it is applicable) and Nos. 2 to 8. (Nos. 7 and 8 are being issued to-day).

19. An Officer from Divisional Headquarters will call at Infantry Brigade Headquarters about 11 a.m. and 8 p.m. on "X" and "Y" days for the purpose of synchronization of watches.
Watches will be synchronised with 11th. D.A. at Divisional Headquarters at 10 a.m. and 7 p.m. on "X" and "Y" days.

20. ACKNOWLEDGE.

T. D. Coleridge
Lieut.Colonel,
General Staff, 11th. Division.

Issued at 7-30 p.m.

```
Copy No.  1.  A.D.C. for G.O.C.
          2.  C.R.A.
          3.  C.R.E.
          4.  32nd. Inf. Bde.
          5.  33rd.   "    "
          6.  34th.   "    "
          7.  6th. E. Yorks Regt.
          8.  "Q".
          9.  Signals.
         10.  A.D.M.S.
         11.  A.P.M.
         12.  Train.
         13.  XVIII Corps "G".
         14.  XVIII Corps "Q".
         15.  20th. Division.
         16.  23rd. Division.
         17.  48th. Division.
         18.  51st. Division.
         19.  XVIII Corps R.A.
         20.    "     "   H.A.
         21.  20th. Coy. "G" Bn. Tanks.
      22 - 25  Liaison Officers.
      26 - 27  War Diary.
      28 - 29  File.
         30.  Area Comdt. CANAL BANK.
```

SECRET.   11th. Division No. G.S 246

To:- 48' Div

Reference Para. 16, 11th. Division Order No. 95
dated 9/8/1917.

1.   The following amendment will be made :-
        For " H.Q. 48th. Division, REIGERSBURG CHATEAU"
        read " On West CANAL BANK at C.25.d.2.4 (old
                Right Brigade H.Q.)".

Amended

2.   Please note that Appendix 2 is in process of
        amendment.   Details follow.

3.   ACKNOWLEDGE.

                        G5227.
                          m

                              T. L. Colridge
                                         Lieut. Colonel,
10th. August, 1917.   General Staff, 11th. Division.

To all recipients of D.O. 95.

SECRET.

ADDENDUM No. 1 to 11th. DIVISION ORDER No.95.

DIVISIONAL CAVALRY & LIAISON WORK.

With reference to 11th. Division Order No. 95, the following arrangements will be made :-

1. (a) 1 Troop, "B" Squadron King Edward's Horse is allotted as Divisional Cavalry.

   (b) This troop is employed as under :-

   (i) 2 N.C.O's and 6 men (dismounted) to act as guides in leading Battalions to their forming up places on Y/Z night.

   (ii) 1 N.C.O. and 12 men are allotted as mounted orderlies to the 11th. Signal Company, and are distributed as needed by Brigades.

2. The 34th. Brigade will attack as follows :-

   (a) For attack on GREEN LINE.

Left Battalion.	Right Battalion.
5th. Dorset Regt.	8th. Northd. Fusiliers.
O.C., Lt.Col. C.C.HANNAY.	O.C., Lt.Col. V.R. FORD.

   (b) For attack on RED DOTTED LINE.

Left Battalion.	Right Battalion.
9th. Lancs. Fusiliers.	11th. Manchester Regt.
O.C., Lt.Col. V.B.THURSTON.	O.C., Lt.Col. Sir T.JACKSON, M.V.O., D.S.O.

3. The following officers of the 11th. Division are detailed for Liaison work:-

   (a) With XVIII Corps.   Capt. C.B.MAY, 6th. Border Regt.

   (b) With 48th. Division. Major F.TOUNSEND, 9th.W.Yorks Regt.

   (c) With 20th. Division. Major G.E.MEUGENS, 11th. Manchester Regt.

4. The G.O.C., 34th. Brigade will arrange for liaison with the 145th. Brigade on his right and the 60th. Brigade on his left.

/2..........

- 2 -

2. (a)   The G.S.O. 2, 11th. Division will join H.Q. 34th. Brigade at Zero minus 3 hours.

(b)   The G.S.O. 3, 11th. Division will proceed to Advanced Divisional Report Centre so as to arrive there at Zero minus 3 hours.

(c)   Captain K.J. MARTIN, D.S.O., Brigade Major 32nd. Brigade will report for duty at 11th. Divisional Headquarters at Zero minus 6 hours.

3.   The G.O.C., 32nd. Brigade will detail 2 officers to proceed to the Advanced Dressing Station (C.19.c.4.1, (ESSEX FARM)), so as to arrive there at Zero for the purpose of interrogating lightly wounded officers and men.
    These officers will be provided with a number of especial questions forms, and a Despatch Rider will be placed at their disposal for communication with Divisional Headquarters.

=:=*=*=*=*=*=:=

SECRET.

ADDENDUM No. 1 to 11th. DIVISION ORDER No. 95.

DIVISIONAL CAVALRY & LIAISON WORK.
==================================

With reference to 11th. Division Order No. 95, the following arrangements will be made :-

1. (a)   1 Troop, "B" Squadron King Edward's Horse is allotted as Divisional Cavalry.

   (b)   This troop is employed as under :-

   (i)   2 N.C.O's and 6 men (dismounted) to act as guides in leading Battalions to their forming up places on Y/Z night.

   (ii)   1 N.C.O. and 12 men are allotted as mounted orderlies to the 11th. Signal Company, and are distributed as needed by Brigades.

2.   The 34th. Brigade will attack as follows :-

   (a) For attack on GREEN LINE.

Left Battalion.	Right Battalion.
5th. Dorset Regt.	8th. Northd. Fusiliers.
O.C., Lt.Col. C.C.HANNAY.	O.C., Lt.Col. V.R. FORD.

   (b) For attack on RED DOTTED LINE.

Left Battalion.	Right Battalion.
9th. Lancs. Fusiliers.	11th. Manchester Regt.
O.C., Lt.Col. V.B. THURSTON.	O.C., Lt.Col. Sir T. JACKSON, M.V.O., D.S.O.

3.   The following officers of the 11th. Division are detailed for Liaison work:-

   (a) With XVIII Corps.   Capt. C.B.MAY, 6th. Border Regt.

   (b) With 48th. Division. Major F. TOUNSEND, 9th. W. Yorks Regt.

   (c) With 20th. Division. Major G.E. MEUGENS, 11th. Manchester Regt.

4.   The G.O.C., 34th. Brigade will arrange for liaison with the 145th. Brigade on his right and the 60th. Brigade on his left.

/5..........

5. (a) The G.S.O. 2, 11th. Division will join H.Q. 34th. Brigade at Zero minus 3 hours.

(b) The G.S.O. 3, 11th. Division will proceed to Advanced Divisional Report Centre so as to arrive there at Zero minus 3 hours.

(c) Captain K.J. MARTIN, D.S.O., Brigade Major 32nd. Brigade will report for duty at 11th. Divisional Headquarters at Zero minus 6 hours.

6. The G.O.C., 32nd. Brigade will detail 2 officers to proceed to the Advanced Dressing Station (C.19.c.4.1, (ESSEX FARM)), so as to arrive there at Zero for the purpose of interrogating lightly wounded officers and men.
These officers will be provided with a number of especial questions forms, and a Despatch Rider will be placed at their disposal for communication with Divisional Headquarters.

S E C R E T.   11th. Division No. G.S. 237.

To:- ....

   ....

         Herewith   copies of Addendum No. 1 to
11th. Division Order No. 95 - " DIVISIONAL CAVALRY AND LIAISON
WORK".

         Please acknowledge receipt.

                         J. D. Coleridge, Lieut. Colonel,
                           General Staff, 11th. Division.

10th. August, 1917.

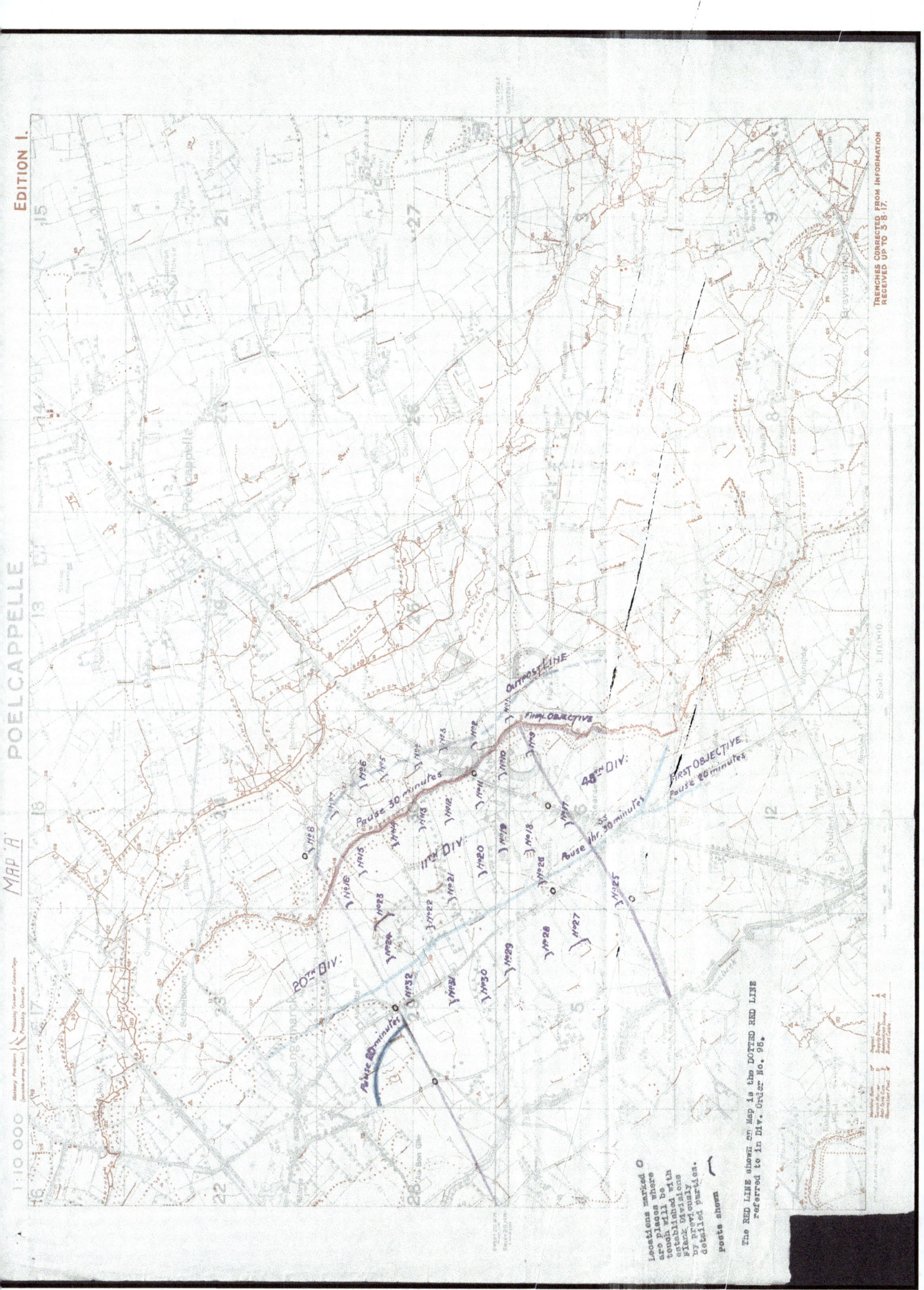

SECRET   11th Division No. G.S. 281.

To War Diary

1.   Herewith copy copies of Artillery Barrage Map (portion of Appendix 1 to 11th Div. Order No. 95 dated 9th August, 1917).   Artillery Programmes will follow.

2.   It should be noted that

(a) The Artillery Barrage lifts off the LANGEMARCK-ZONNEBEKE ROAD at 35 minutes after Zero.

(b) The Barrage protecting the GREEN Line moves forward again at 2 hours and 35 minutes after ZERO.

(c) The Artillery Barrage lifts off PHEASANT Trench at 3 hours after ZERO.

3.   Barrage Maps will not be taken into action.

4.   Please acknowledge.

H.Q. 11th Division.   Lieut-Colonel,
12th August, 1917.   General Staff.11th Division.

APPENDIX 2.

To Accompany 11th. Division Order No. 95.

MACHINE GUN PROGRAMME & BARRAGE MAP.

1. The advance of the 11th. Division will be covered by a M.G. Barrage vide Map "C" and attached tables, consisting of 32 guns of the 32nd. and 33rd. M.G. Coys.

2. These guns will be organised into groups of two batteries. Each battery will consist of eight guns. An officer will be in command of each group.

3. The personnel of each battery will consist of 2 officers, 40 O.R. machine gunners and 32 attached Infantry men.

4. Groups will be lettered A and B, and batteries c.d.e.f.

5. The approximate positions of the guns and their barrage lines will be as shown on attached tracing.

6. Headquarters of group commanders will be at CANE AVENUE.

7. These Headquarters will be in telephonic communication with the 34th. Brigade Headquarters.

8. The Officer commanding "A" group will be responsible for maintaining a line from his battery positions to VANACKERT FARM, and the Officer Commanding "B" Group from his battery positions to FRANCOIS FARM.

9. The 34th. M.G. Company will be disposed of as under :-

    (a) Eight guns to assist in consolidation.

    These guns will not move with the assaulting waves, but behind them and when possible they should be allotted definite objectives beforehand. These objectives should be chosen so that the guns are distributed in depth.

    (b) The remaining eight guns should be kept in Reserve.

10. After 12 midnight night X/Y, all the machine guns with the exception of the following four, holding defensive positions in the line, may be withdrawn.

    Guns at (i)   U.4.a.6.5.
            (ii) U.4.a.6.4.
            (iii) U.4.d.9.7.
            (iv) U.5.c.2.4.

11. The guns at the above-mentioned four positions may be withdrawn on Y/Z night.

12. On Z minus 2 days the 32nd. and 33rd. M.G. Coys. will come under the orders of the Divisional Machine Gun Officer.

13. Officers Commanding Groups will forward copies of their calculations for fire to the D.M.G.O. by 12 noon 14th. instant.

TABLE 1.

Group.	Battery.	Personnel.	Task.	Rate of fire.	Remarks.
A	c, d.	32nd M.G. Coy.	Zero plus 30 minutes open fire on BLUE Barrage line	1000 rounds per hour, except on receipt of S.O.S. Call.	Battery commanders will take the necessary precautions to prevent hitting men moving near the guns.
B	e, f.	33rd M.G. Coy.	Zero plus 40 minutes lift and search forward at the rate of 100 yards in 10 minutes.		
			Zero plus 1-30 fire on RED Barrage lines.		
			Zero plus 4-30 cease fire fire.		
			After Zero plus 4 hrs. 30 mins. fire will be opened at once on Red Barrage lines, on receipt of an S.O.S. call.		

TABLE 2.

Location of Dump.	Amount of S.A.A. in Dump.	TOTAL.
HURST PARK.	160,000.	160,000.
Each gun position	8,000	256,000

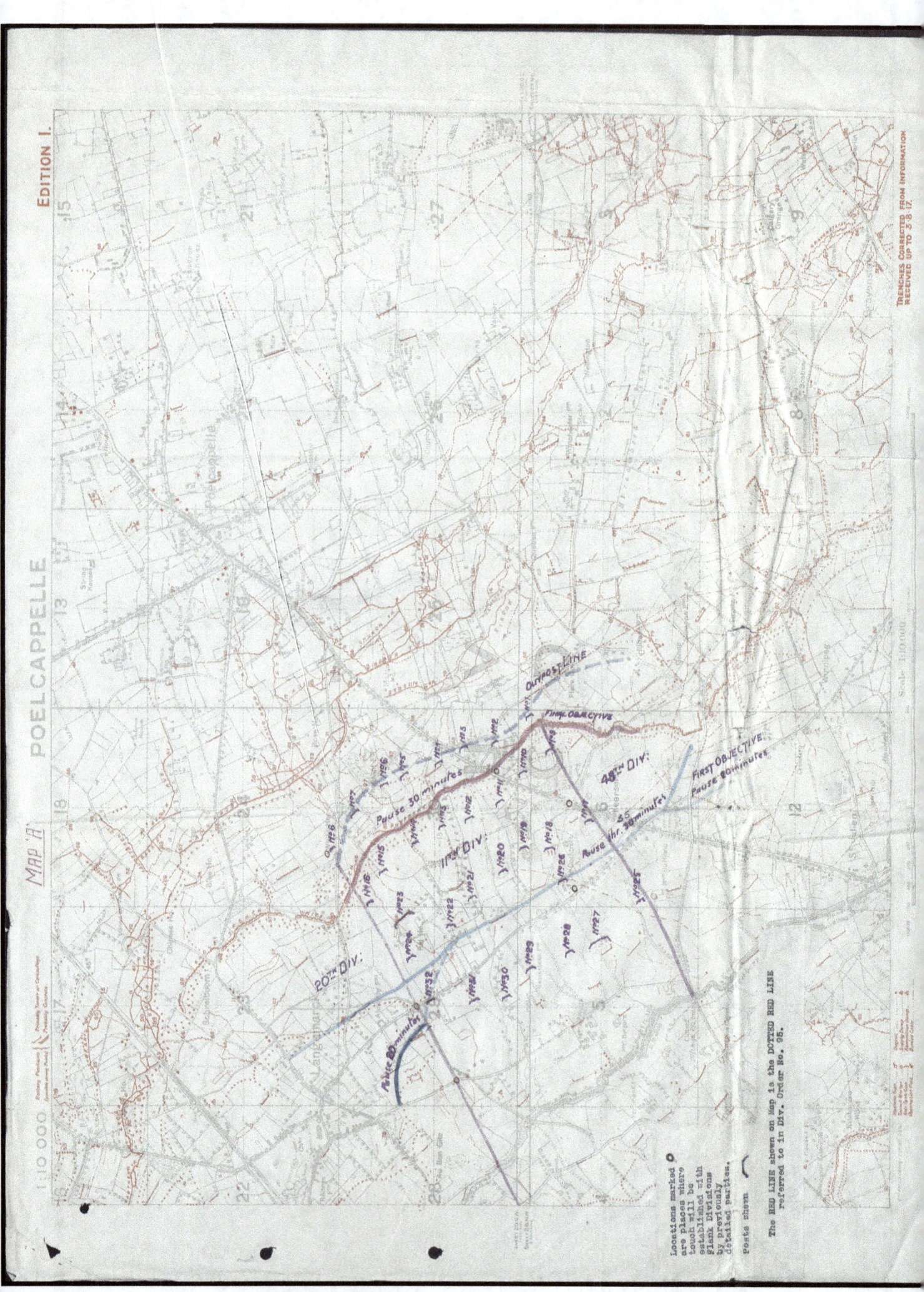

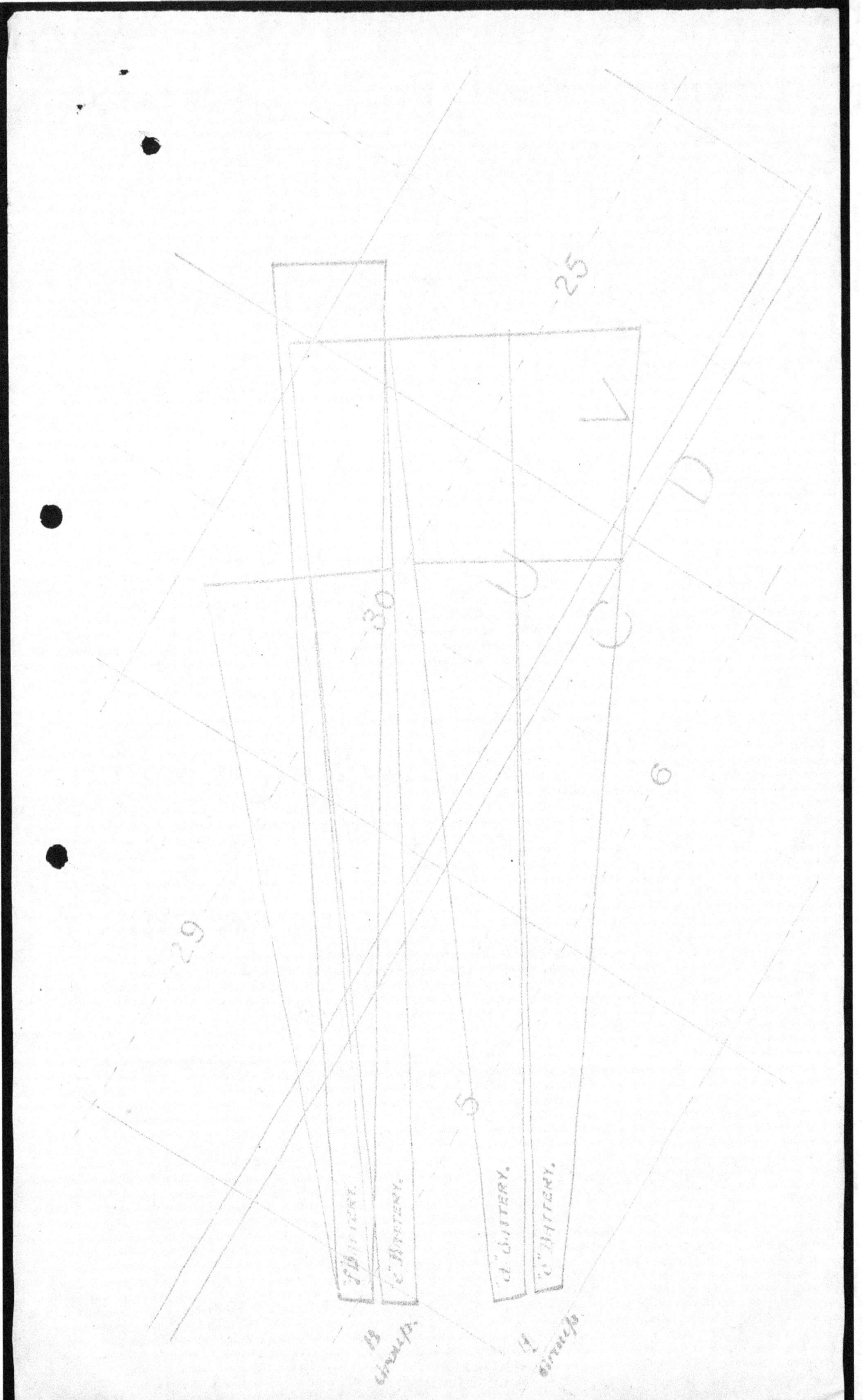

SECRET.   11th. Division No. G.S. 307.

TO:............48th Division............

(A).   Para. 14 of 11th. Division Order No. 95 is cancelled and the following substituted :-

   "14.   The 33rd. Infantry Brigade less 2 companies will act in support of the 34th. Infantry Brigade as under :-

      1 (a)   At Zero, 33rd. Inf. Bde. less 2 battalions and 33rd. M.G. Coy. will be located on the CANAL BANK.
              Brigade H.Q. on the CANAL BANK (11th. Division Advanced Report Centre).

        (b)   1½ Battalions will be at SIEGE CAMP.

      2.(a)   At Zero plus 2 hours the Brigade less 2 Battalions and 33rd. M.G. Coy. will advance from the CANAL BANK to previously reconnoitred positions in C.15.a. and C.14.c. and d.
              Brigade H.Q. will join 34th. Bde. H.Q. at FOCH FARM at Zero plus 2¼ hours.

        (b)   At Zero plus 4 hours 1½ battalions from SIEGE CAMP will reach the CANAL BANK and halt there.

        (c)   From Zero onwards Advanced Report Centres of both 33rd. and 34th. Inf. Brigades will be at MINTY FARM. C.10.c.1.5.

      3.   At Zero plus 1 hour, the remaining two companies of the 33rd. Brigade will reach the CANAL BANK and come under the orders of the C.R.E. for the work detailed in Appendix 3.

(B).   Para 16 should be amended as follows :-

              Advanced Report Centre)   For "GOURNIER FARM C.9.d.3.7"
              34th Brigade.   )   read "MINTY FARM. C.10.c.1.5".

          ACKNOWLEDGE.
   13th August, 1917.   Harrison, Major,
                                             General Staff, 11th Division.

APPENDIX 2.

To accompany 11th. Division Order No. 95.

MACHINE GUN PROGRAMME & BARRAGE MAP.

1. The advance of the 11th. Division will be covered by M.G. barrages vide Map "C" and attached tables, consisting of 32 guns of the 32nd. and 33rd. M.G. Coys.

2. These guns will be organised into groups of two batteries. Each battery will consist of eight guns. An officer will be in command of each group.

3. The personnel of each battery will consist of 3 officers (battery Commander and two section officers) 40 O.R., machine gunners and 32 attached Infantry men.

4. Groups will be lettered A and B. and batteries c,d,e,f.

5. The approximate positions of the guns and their barrage lines will be as shown on attached tracing.

6. The 34th. M.G. Company will be disposed of as under :-

   (a) Eight guns to assist in consolidation.

   These guns will not move with the assaulting waves, but behind them and when possible they should be allotted definite objectives beforehand. These objectives should be chosen so that the guns are distributed in depth.

   (b) The remaining eight guns should be kept in Reserve.

8. After 12 midnight night X/Y, all the machine guns with the exception of the following four, holding defensive positions in the line, may be withdrawn.

   Guns at   (i)   U.4.a.6.5.
              (ii) U.4.a.8.4.
              (iii) U.4.d.9.7.
              (iv) U.5.c.2.4.

9. The guns at the above-mentioned four positions may be withdrawn on Y/Z night.

10. On Z minus 2 days the 32nd. and 33rd. M.G. Coys. will come under the orders of the Divisional Machine Gun Officer.

11. Officers Commanding Groups will forward copies of their calculations for fire to the D.M.G.O., by 12 noon 11th. instant.

TABLE 1.

No. of Barrage.	Group.	Battery.	Personnel.	Task.	Rate of fire.	Remarks.
1st.Barrage.	A. B.	c. d. e. f.	32nd.M.G.Co. 33rd.M.G.Co.	Zero. Open fire on GREEN barrage lines. 0 plus 10 mins. lift on to GREEN DOTTED barrage lines. 0 plus 30 mins. lift on to BLUE Barrage lines. 0 plus 2 hrs. 35 mins. cease fire.	3000 rounds per hour.	Prior to Zero hour battery commanders and section Officers will reconnoitre their advanced positions and the routes to them.
2nd.Barrage.	A. B.	c.d. e.f.	32nd.M.G.Co. 33rd.M.G.Co.	0 plus 2 hrs. 45 mins. c. battery. 0 plus 3 hrs. d. battery. 0 plus 3 hrs. 15 mins. e. battery. 0 plus 5 hrs.30 mins. f. battery. (These Move forward to advanced positions as shown on Map "G".) Supplement the artillery protective barrage by keeping a barrage on RED barrage line, and firing on selected targets. Put down an intensive barrage on RED barrage line on receipt of the S.O.S. Signal.	3000 rounds per hour except on receipt of an S.O.S. call when fire will be intensive.	

TABLE 2.

Location of Dump.	Amount of S.A.A. in Dump.	Total.
HURST FARM.	160,000	160,000
Each gun position in first positions.	10,000	320,000
Each forward battery position.	15,000	60,000

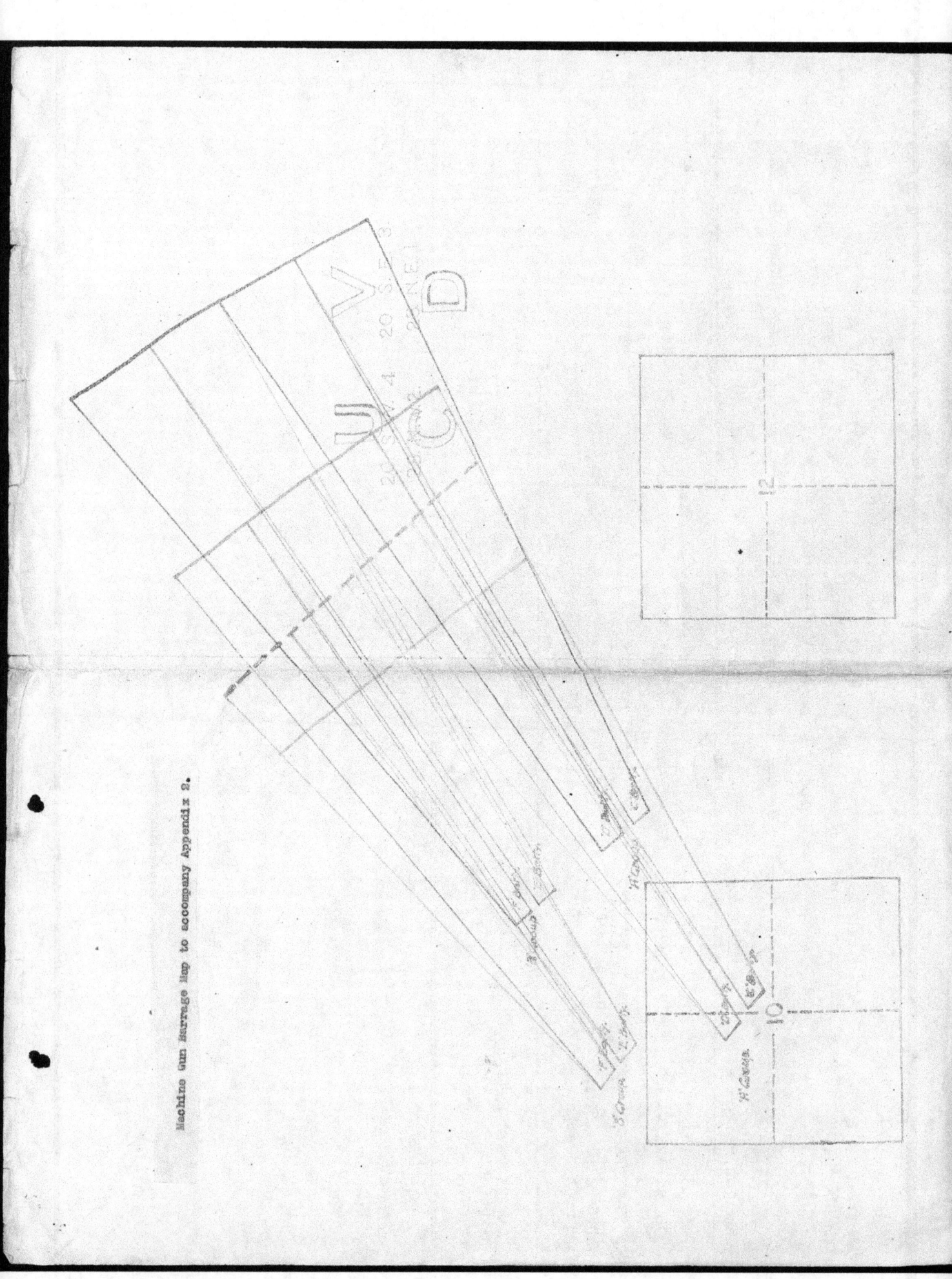

Machine Gun Barrage Map to accompany Appendix 2.

```
S E C R E T.
```
11th. Division No. G.S 246

TO:- ....

....

Reference Para. 16, 11th. Division Order No. 95 dated 9/8/1917.

1.   The following amendment will be made :-
         For " H.Q. 48th. Division, REIGERSBURG CHATEAU"
         read " On West CANAL BANK at C.25.d.2.4 (old
              Right Brigade H.Q.)".

2.   Please note that Appendix 2 is in process of
         amendment.   Details follow.

3.   ACKNOWLEDGE.

                                  T. L. Colridge
                                          Lieut. Colonel,
10th. August, 1917.   General Staff, 11th. Division.

To all recipients of D.O. 95.

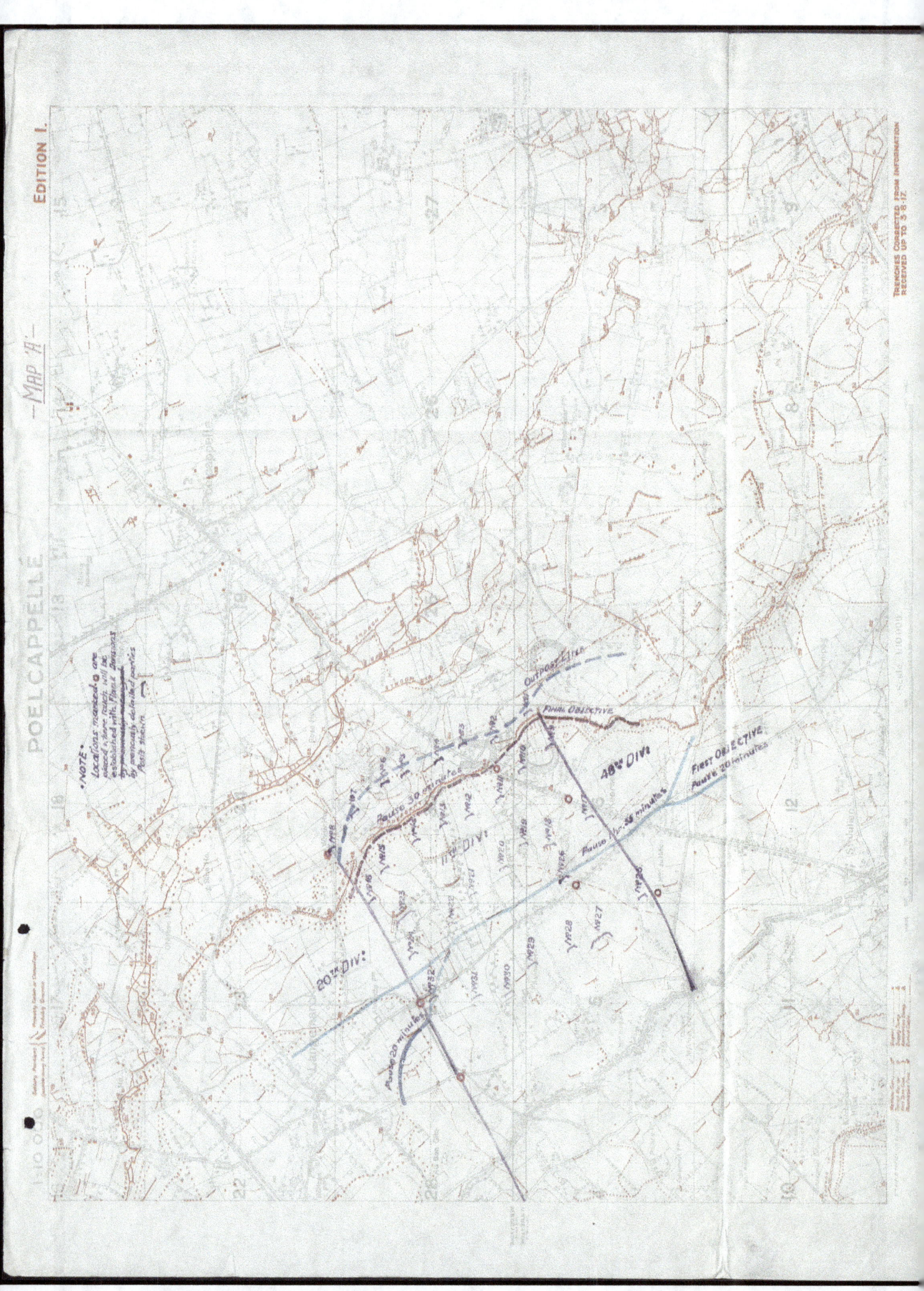

APPENDIX 2.

To accompany 11th. Division Order No. 95.

MACHINE GUN PROGRAMME & BARRAGE MAP.

1. The advance of the 11th. Division will be covered by M.G. barrages vide Map "C" and attached tables, consisting of 32 guns of the 32nd. and 33rd. M.G. Coys.

2. These guns will be organised into groups of two batteries. Each battery will consist of eight guns. An officer will be in command of each group.

3. The personnel of each battery will consist of 3 officers (battery Commander and two section commanders) 40 O.R., machine gunners and 32 attached Infantry men.

4. Groups will be lettered A and B. and batteries c, d, e, f.

5. The approximate positions of the guns and their barrage lines will be as shown on attached tracing.

6. The 34th. M.G. Company will be disposed of as under :-

    (a) Eight guns to assist in consolidation.

    These guns will not move with the assaulting waves, but behind them and where possible they should be allotted definite objectives beforehand. These objectives should be chosen so that the guns are distributed in depth.

    (b) The remaining eight guns should be kept in Reserve.

8. After 12 midnight night X/Y, all the machine guns with the exception of the following four, holding defensive positions in the line, may be withdrawn.

    Guns at (i)   U.4.a.6.5.
            (ii) U.4.a.8.4.
            (iii) U.4.d.9.7.
            (iv) U.5.c.2.4.

9. The guns at the above-mentioned four positions may be withdrawn on Y/Z night.

10. On Z minus 2 days the 32nd. and 33rd. M.G. Coys. will come under the orders of the Divisional Machine Gun Officer.

11. Officers Commanding Groups will forward copies of their calculations for fire to the D.M.G.O., by 12 noon 11th. instant.

APPENDIX 3.

To Accompany 11th. Division Order No. 95.

R.E. INSTRUCTIONS.

1. To assist in the consolidation of the strong points vide para. 8.(d) of the above order, the O.C., 86th. Field Company will detail two sections as under :-

> One section to work on points C.5.b.6.0 and the COCKCROFT.
>
> One section to work on points U.29.d.1.9 and HANNIXBEEKE FARM.

The above parties will assemble in the BLACK LINE at Zero and will push forward to their objectives as soon as the enemy's barrage permits.

One platoon of infantry has been told off for each of these points. These platoons will advance with the assaulting waves.

2. Roads and tracks will be pushed forward as under, parties to be ready to commence work at Zero plus 2 hours.

(a) Overland track HURST PARK towards FERDINAND FARM.
     86th. Field Company (less 2 Sections) and
     2 Platoons Infantry.

(b) Overland track from GOURNIER FARM to join up with MILITARY ROAD at C.4.b.5.0.
     87th. Field Company (less 2 Sections) and
     2 Platoons Infantry.

(c) GOURNIER FARM - VARNA FARM ROAD.
     68th. Field Company and 2 Platoons Infantry.

(d) HURST PARK - REGINA CROSS ROAD.
     6th. E. Yorks Regt. (Pioneers).

Oc.C. Field Companies will arrange direct with O's C Infantry parties, time and place for meeting.

3. Light foot-bridges capable of being carried by 2 men, for making crossings over the STEENBEEK are being prepared and will be available as under :-

> 10 ft. bridges. 20
> 15 ft. bridges. 10

4. The O.C. 87th. Field Company will detail 2 sections for work on repairing bridges on the Divisional front to be prepared to start work at Zero plus 2 hours.

5. A dump of R.E. materials is being established at BURNT FARM.

SECRET.

APPENDIX 4.

ADMINISTRATIVE INSTRUCTION No. 19.
(In connection with 11th Division Order No. 95).

1. **BATTLE STANDING ORDERS.** Battle Standing Orders will be read in conjunction with these instructions.
Appendices 1 and 2 of Divisional Battle Standing Orders contain instructions as to Ammunition - Rations - Tools which will be carried on the soldier.

2. **STRAGGLERS' POSTS.** Straggler Posts will be established at :-

    Bridge 4   -   C.25.a.5.9.
    Bridge 4a. -   C.19.c.4.3.
    Bridge 5. -   C.19.c.3.6.
    Bridge 6. -   C.19.a.2.9.
    Causeway 1.-   C.25.a.4.8.
    Causeway 2.-   C.25.a.6.7.

Each post will consist of 1 N.C.O. and 3 men to be found from the T.M. Batteries.
The Posts collect all stragglers (viz. men who ought to be with their units) in the vicinity and pass them to the Straggler Collecting Station.
Those requiring Medical aid should be sent on as soon as possible to Dressing Station at BRIDGE 4.
Each Straggler Post will be provided with :-

  (a). Orders for Battle Straggler Posts.
  (b). Note Book and pencils.
  (c). Spare gas helmets and field dressings.
  (d). 12 empty grenade and S.A.A. boxes.
  (e). A lamp.
  (f). Rations for post for 2 days and water in 4 petrol tins.

3. **STRAGGLER COLLECTING STATION.** Situated at Bridge 4 (C.25.a.5.9.) 1 Officer and 6 N.C.Os., 1 Sergt. and 1 Corporal M.M.P. will be at the Straggler Collecting Station for the purpose of sorting out stragglers and either returning them to their respective Brigade Headquarters or seeing that those requiring medical aid are taken before a Medical Officer. All men fit to return are to be conducted back to their Brigade Headquarters.

4. **PRISONER OF WAR CAGE.** The Divisional P.O.W. Cage is situated at B.28.a.4.2. Chateau TROIS TOURS.
All Prisoners of War will be marched down to Bridge 4 (C.25.a.5.9.) under escort which will be as small as feasible. Here they will be taken over by Officer in charge P.O.W. Collecting Station.

5. **CASUALTIES.** Estimated casualties must be reported early. The actual numbers will be sent as soon as verified. Names of officer casualties will be carefully checked before report is made.

6. **BURIALS.** The dead should be buried in recognised cemeteries only. It is however often necessary for sanitary reasons that they should be buried by troops practically in the firing line - when this is done care should be taken that all details of men so buried, and the exact sites, are reported by Brigades to the Divisional Burial Officer.

7. AMMUNITION.

7. AMMUNITION.

(a). Divisional Dump. S.A.A., grenades, stokes bombs, flares, rockets, etc. can be drawn from Advanced Divisional Dump situated at C.19.d.3.8 under Brigade arrangements during an action. This dump will be on charge of the D.A.C. and maintained by them at the establishment laid down by D.H.Q.

For normal requirements requisitions should continue to be made on the D.A.C. which is situated at B.20.c.7.5. D.A.C. can be got on the telephone through K.O.A.

(b) BRIGADE DUMPS. Will be drawn upon before recourse is made to the Divisional Dumps.
All dumps must be protected as far as possible from hostile shell fire.

(c) FUZING. Fuzing will be carried out at Brigade Dumps under Brigade arrangements.

Ammunition dumps will not be utilized for the storage of rations or water.

(d) AMMUNITION RAILHEADS.

For Artillery - K.O.A. (B.26.c.6.8.) also to a certain extent ESSEX FARM (C.25.a.3.9.)

For S.A.A.,)
Grenades, etc.) - A.23.a.

(e) AMMUNITION REFILLING POINT.

For Artillery - ESSEX FARM (C.25.a.3.9.)

8. HOT MEALS. G.Os. C. Brigades will ensure that the troops under their command are provided with a hot meal before the attack.

9. RATIONS. The supply of rations as far as can be estimated will be normal but to guard against any contingency that may arise 8,000 preserved rations will be dumped at MARENGO HOUSE (B.24.d.9.5.). This can be drawn on by Brigades on a written demand by a C.O. on the Supply Officer in charge.

A further 4,000 are held on Advanced Brigade charge.
The solidified alcohol should be carefully husbanded and only used when no other means of obtaining a hot meal exists.

10. WATER. A second water bottle will be carried by troops taking part in the attack.

The petrol tins on charge of battalions will be filled and water stored under Brigade supervision. In addition 1,500 two gallon tins are held on charge of the O.C. Train to whom application should be made for any more that may be required to augment those in battalions.

Every effort will be made to return empty tins with stoppers complete.

80 Kajawahs to hold 4 two gallon tins are on charge of Brigade Groups.

300 two gallon petrol tins filled with water will be stored with the Brigade Ration Dumps.

No water in the German lines will be drunk by the troops until it has been passed as fit for drinking by a Medical Officer.

The locality of all water supplies discovered in the German lines should be reported early so that action can be taken to bring them into use.

11. WATER POINTS.

-3-

11. **WATER POINTS.** Water Points in our lines are at :-

    A.30.Central.
    H. 3.a.7.5.
    0.14.c.2.3.

In addition 2 water lorries one of 500 gallons and one of 400 gallons are attached to the Advanced Brigade. These can operate as far forward as motor transport can go.

12. **TRANSPORT.** Attention is directed to the Divisional Pack Transport Scheme. (Appendix 10 of Divisional Battle Standing Orders).

Wheeled transport will be used as far as feasible but pack will probably be found the safest means of transport.

YUKON PACKS are being issued at the rate of 20 per Battalion and 10 per Machine Gun Coy. and L.T.M. Battery for each Brigade taking part in the attack.

13. **SALVAGE.** Every effort will be made to salvage Arms, Equipment, Ammunition, Shrapnel shell bodies, and Shell cases. Each unit will establish a salvage dump of its own to which all individuals or parties returning should bring some article for salvage.

Brigades will establish Brigade Salvage Dumps to which, under Brigade arrangements, the salvage in units dumps will be brought. The Divisional Salvage Officer will be informed of the locality of Brigade Dumps, the salvage of which will be collected by him and brought in to the Divisional Salvage Dump.

All dumps should be situated on transport routes and should be clearly marked as SALVAGE.

14. **SPARE KIT.** Great coats and spare kit will be stacked and stored in the most forward camps which Brigades may occupy. Small caretaking parties will be left behind to take charge of them.

                                                                Lieut. Colonel,

8th August, 1917.   A.A. & Q.M.G., 11th Division.

S E C R E T.   11th Division. No. S/388.

Reference Appendix 4 of 11th Division Order No. 93.

A. Para 11 is cancelled and the following substituted :-

WATER POINTS.   Water Points in our lines are at :-

    A.30.Central.) Pipe line supply.
    H. 3.a.7.5.   )
    C.14.c.8.8.   (LANCASHIRE FARM). Well supply, 400 gallons a day.
    C.21.c.3.5.   (near HAMMONDS CORNER). 2,300 gallon tank filled under Corps arrangements.
                  To be ready by 8 a.m. Zero day.
    C.19.c.1.6.   (On W. side of YPRES-BOESINGHE Road). A 400 gallon tank, with arrangement for filling petrol tins.
                  33rd Bde. are responsible for filling this tank at 7 a.m., and 34th Bde. for filling it at 3 p.m. daily, starting on Y day.

    400 filled petrol tins are kept at Divl. Reserve Ration Dump at C.19.d.3.1. These will be issued on the signature of an officer. A similar number of empty tins must be handed in to replace full ones drawn.

    A number of empty tins are also kept at this point.
    The Train is responsible for keeping 400 tins filled.

    Water Lorries have been attached to Brigades as follows :-
        33rd Brigade -   1 300 gallon lorry.
        34th Brigade -   2 400 gallon lorries.

B. Para 13 is cancelled and the following substituted :-

SALVAGE.   Every effort will be made to salvage arms, equipment, ammunition, shrapnel shell bodies, and shell cases. Each unit will establish a Salvage Dump of its own to which all individuals or parties returning should bring some article for salvage.

    Brigade Salvage Dumps will be established at FOCH FARM and at ADMIRAL'S ROAD SIDING on the Light Railway (C.15.d.2.2)

    Units should establish their Salvage Dumps close to transport routes. These should be clearly marked SALVAGE.

    Brigades will be responsible for moving the salvage from unit's dumps to the nearest Brigade Dump.

    The Divisional Salvage Officer will take over the salvage at the two Brigade Dumps as above and arrange to evacuate it on the empty trucks of the light railway.

    Divisional Salvage Dumps are at ESSEX FARM and at GHENT COTTAGES (B.22.d.7.0).

    Divisional Salvage Coy. H.Q. will be established at GHENT COTTAGES on 16th inst.

    Divisional Salvage Officer will be responsible for collecting from Regtl. Stragglers' Posts and Adv. Dressing Stations, equipment, Grenades, and S.A.A., which have been collected from wounded men and which are not required for re-equipping stragglers being sent forward again.

                                                     P.T.O.

SALVAGE Continued.

He will collect from Adv. Dressing Stations the clothing of gassed men. A.D.M.S. will arrange to have this clothing dipped in a solution of soda crystals, dried, and packed in sacks before handing it over to Salvage.

Divisional Laundry Officer will collect from Salvage Coy. such underclothing as is serviceable and fit for re-issue.

D.A.D.O.S. will detail an Armourer Sergt. to report to Divisional Salvage Officer on Zero day for repairing arms etc.

ACKNOWLEDGE.

15th August, 1917.

E.Briey Captain.
D.A.Q.M.G., 11th Division.

Copies to all recipients of Divisional Order No. 95.

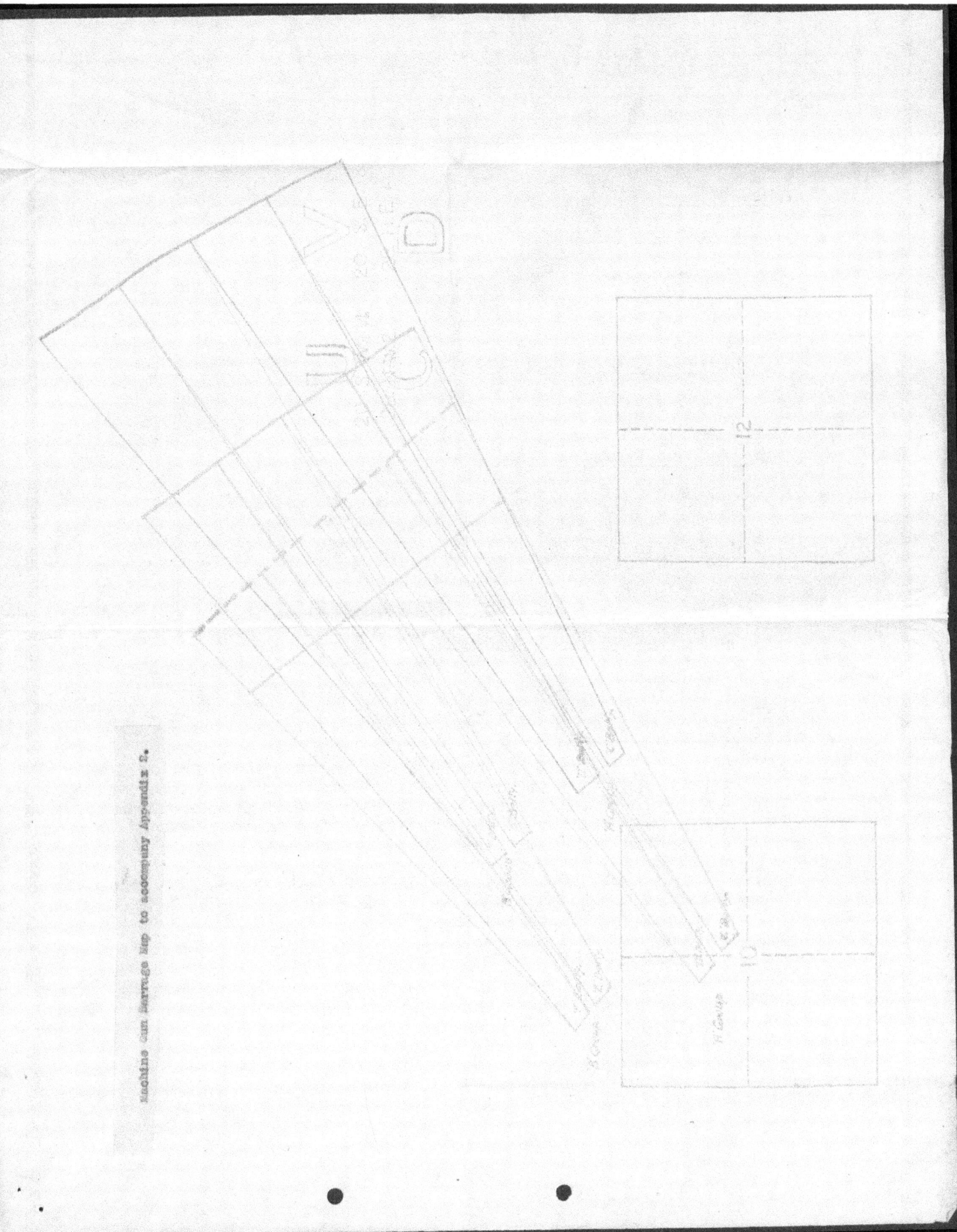

APPENDIX 5.

To accompany 11th. Division Order No. 95.

MEDICAL ARRANGEMENTS.

1. POSITION OF MEDICAL INSTITUTIONS.

    A. Regimental Aid Posts.

    C.5.c.4.5.   RED FARM.

    C.4.b.15.40.   COMEDY FARM.

    B. Divisional Collecting Post.

    C.15.c.5.1.

    C. Advanced Dressing Station.

    C.19.c.4.1.   ESSEX FARM.

    D. Corps Main Dressing Station.

    A.23.c.2.9.

    E. Corps Walking Wounded Collecting Post.

    H.3.d.5.6.

2. SCHEME OF EVACUATION.

    A.   All sick and wounded who are able to walk, will be sent to the Divisional Collecting Post, from where they will be directed along sign-posted routes to ESSEX FARM. From there they will be conveyed to the Corps Walking Wounded Collecting Posts in motor lorries or busses.

    B.   All other sick and wounded will be conveyed by Regimental Stretcher Bearers to Regimental Aid Posts from whence they will be taken to the Advanced Dressing Station by hand-carriage by R.A.M.C. bearers assisted by light railways and motor ambulances where possible.

    C.   Sick and wounded from Advanced Dressing Station will be conveyed to Corps Main Dressing Station in Motor Ambulance cars under Corps arrangements.

APPENDIX 6.

To Accompany 11th. Division Order No. 95.

ARRANGEMENTS FOR "CONTACT" AND "INFANTRY PROTECTION" AEROPLANES.

1. Marking of Contact Aeroplanes.

   Each Contact Aeroplane will be marked with two black rectangular flags (2 ft. by 1 ft. 3 ins) attached to an projecting from the lower plane, on each side of the fuselage.

2. Lighting of Flares.

   Contact aeroplanes will be in the air, at approximately the following times :-

   Zero plus 1 hour.
   Zero plus 1 hour 45 mins.
   Zero plus 3 hours 15 mins.
   Zero plus 4 hours 15 mins.

   At these hours, Infantry will be particularly on the look out for a call to light flares, although calls may come at other times as well.

   Flares will only be lit when actually called for by a contact aeroplane, and then only by the foremost Infantry.
   RED flares will be used.

3. Markings of Headquarters etc.

   Each Brigade and Battalion Headquarters will be marked by ground sheets of the authorised shape, with the code letters of the unit laid out with white strips alongside.

4. Dropping Stations.

Corps Dropping Station	-	Corps Headquarters.
48th. Division "	-	Parade Ground A.30.c.6.4.
11th. Division. "	-	Open space in front of Div. H.Q. at A.16.c.3.4.

   Sheet 28

   All Dropping Stations will be clearly marked with a large white X made from strips. Signallers will be in attendance to acknowledge the receipt of a message by waving flags.

5. An Infantry Protection Machine will work continuously throughout Z day on the Corps front.

   The principal duty of this machine is to discover and report to the artillery any hostile Infantry targets, particularly any bodies of enemy which appear to be concentrating for counter-attack.

   This Infantry Protection Machine will be relieved about every three hours from Zero. On its way back to the aerodrome, it will drop a message at 11th. and 48th. Division Headquarters, giving the position of our front line troops and any enemy troops which are in contact with them. This will be in addition to reports dropped by contact aeroplanes.

S E C R E T.   11th. Division No. G.S. 328.

To:- *War Diary*

     Owing to the state of the ground, Tanks will not take part in the next phase of operations.

     Para 11 of 11th. Division Order No. 95 and all other references to Tanks in the afore-mentioned order or attached Appendices are therefore cancelled.

     ACKNOWLEDGE.

15th. August 1917.　　　　　　　*J.M.R. Harrison* Major,
　　　　　　　　　　　　　　　　General Staff, 11th. Division.

To all recipients of D.O. 95.

APPENDIX 7.

(To accompany 11th. Division Order No. 95.)

ARRANGEMENTS FOR INTER-COMMUNICATION.

LOCATION H.Q. etc. 1.   Divisional Report Centre (call O Z Z R) will be in CANAL BANK at C.25.b.10.45.
    34th. Infantry Brigade Headquarters will be at FOCH FARM, and Report Centre at MINTY FARM.
    Direct telephonic communication will be maintained between Brigade Headquarters, O Z Z and O Z Z R.

WIRELESS. 2.   Wireless sets are installed at FOCH FARM and MINTY FARM, working to each other and Corps Directing Station, (C.25.d.0.6).
    Corps Directing Station is in direct telephonic communication with O Z Z R.
    A third Wireless Set will be installed at FERDINAND FARM at Zero minus 2 hours, and will work to Wireless sets at :-

       MINTY FARM
       FOCH FARM and
       CORPS DIRECTING STATION.

As soon as possible after the first attack it will proceed to BULOW FARM.

POWER BUZZERS & AMPLIFIERS. 3. (a)   Power Buzzers and Amplifiers will be installed, and working by Zero minus 6 hours at :-

       MINTY FARM
       FRANCOIS FARM.
       FERDINAND FARM.

    1 Power Buzzer and Amplifier will be at RED HOUSE in reserve to go forward at earliest moment to HAANIXBEEK FARM.
    2 Power Buzzers will be in front line with selected companies.
    When HAANIXBEEK FARM amplifier is installed a third Power Buzzer will be installed in the front line.

(b)   Power Buzzer and Amplifier at FRANCOIS FARM will, as soon as possible after the first objective is taken, dismantle and proceed to RAT HOUSE, this should be about Zero plus 2 hours.
    When the Power Buzzer and Amplifier at RAT HOUSE is established and <u>working satisfactorily,</u> <u>but not before</u>, HAANIXBEEK FARM set will dismantle and proceed to BULOW FARM.
    A fourth Power Buzzer will then go into the front line.

AEROPLANES. 4.   Divisional Dropping Station will be at A.16.c.6.4.
    Battalions will be prepared to work to aeroplanes with Ground Sheets and Lucas Lamps.

/5........

- 2 -

				CALL
VISUAL.	5.	Divnl. Visual Station will be at C.25.b.1.3.		A V
		Advanced -do- -do- C.14.b.5.3		K V

Both Stations will be permanently "manned"

MINTY FARM and FOCH FARM are both visible from Forward Station.
    Brigade Advanced Visual Station will be at C.14.b.5.3. This station will send "forwards" and "rearwards".

BALLOONS.   6.   The following units will work to Balloon if necessary:-

Advanced Divisional Visual Station.

                                                                         CALL.

From Zero to Zero plus 2.	5th. Dorsets. (FRANCOIS FARM)		O R K
	8th. Northd. Fus. (FERDINAND FARM)		O R H
Zero plus 2 onwards.	9th. Lancs. Fus. (RAT HOUSE).		O R I
	11th. Manchesters (BULOW FARM).		O R L

Advanced Divisional Visual Station will work continuously.

DOGS.   7.   Four dogs will be available, one for each Battalion.
    Instructions as to treatment will be given by the man bringing up the dogs, these should be very carefully followed, the chief point to remember is, do not allow anyone to pat or make friends with the dogs.

PIGEONS.   8.   Pigeons will be issued to all units from IRISH FARM.
    2 Pairs of Pigeons will be issued to 2 selected companies of each Battalion for release only on capture of objective, and to intimate the capture of the objective to the rear.
    2 Pairs will be available for each Battalion for general purposes.
    2 Pairs will be available for Brigade Headquarters and 1 pair for Brigade Forward Station.
    The 10 pairs of pigeons held in reserve at IRISH FARM will be at the disposal of the 33rd. Brigade if necessary.

CABLE ROUTES.   9.   "Lineman Posts" are established at :-

LEFT ROUTE.	C.14.d.50.75.	CALL.....	L T.
	C.14.a.7.4.	"	L A
	C.14.b.5.5.	"	L B
	C.8.d.9.3.	"	L C
	C.9.a.65.20.	"	L D
	C.9.b.9.8.	"	L E
RIGHT ROUTE	C.14.b.70.25	"	B W
	C.15.a.15.70	"	R A
	C.9.d.85.25	"	R B
	C.10.c.05.50	"	R C

/In each.......

In each route pairs 1, 2 and 5 are allotted for use of R.F.A.
    -do-   3 and 4   -do-   for Inf. Brigades.
    -do-   6.   -do-   for Lineman Pilot Line.

Communication diagram attached.

=*=*=*=*=*=

Diagram: Communication layout showing Front Line with Power Buzzer positions connected to Rat House, Bulow Farm, Ferdinand Farm, Minty Farm, Foch Farm, and Corps direct Set.

Key:
- W — Wireless
- ⊕ — Power Buzzer
- A — Amplifier.

At the taking of the final objective the above will be the arrangement of Wireless, Amplifiers, and Power Buzzers.

All sets mentioned above will remain in position and will continue to work as directed until ordered to dismantle.

Personnel will be relieved when possible.

APPENDIX 7.

(To accompany 11th. Division Order No. 95.)

ARRANGEMENTS FOR INTER-COMMUNICATION.

LOCATION H.Q. etc. 1. Divisional Report Centre (call O Z Z R) will be in CANAL BANK at C.25.b.10.45.
34th. Infantry Brigade Headquarters will be at FOCH FARM, and Report Centre at MINTY FARM.
Direct telephonic communication will be maintained between Brigade Headquarters, O Z Z and O Z Z R.

WIRELESS. 2. Wireless sets are installed at FOCH FARM and MINTY FARM, working to each other and Corps Directing Station, (C.25.d.0.6).
Corps Directing Station is in direct telephonic communication with O Z Z R.
A third Wireless Set will be installed at FERDINAND FARM at Zero minus 2 hours, and will work to Wireless sets at :-

MINTY FARM
FOCH FARM and
CORPS DIRECTING STATION.

As soon as possible after the first attack it will proceed to BULOW FARM.

POWER BUZZERS & AMPLIFIERS. 3. (a) Power Buzzers and Amplifiers will be installed, and working by Zero minus 6 hours at :-

MINTY FARM
FRANCOIS FARM.
FERDINAND FARM.

1 Power Buzzer and Amplifier will be at RED HOUSE in reserve to go forward at earliest moment to HAANIXBEEK FARM.
2 Power Buzzers will be in front line with selected companies.
When HAANIXBEEK FARM amplifier is installed a third Power Buzzer will be installed in the front line.

(b) Power Buzzer and Amplifier at FRANCOIS FARM will, as soon as possible after the first objective is taken, dismantle and proceed to RAT HOUSE, this should be about Zero plus 2 hours.
When the Power Buzzer and Amplifier at RAT HOUSE is established and <u>working satisfactorily</u>, <u>but not before</u>, HAANIXBEEK FARM set will dismantle and proceed to BULOW FARM.
A fourth Power Buzzer will then go into the front line.

AEROPLANES. 4. Divisional Dropping Station will be at A.16.c.6.4.
Battalions will be prepared to work to aeroplanes with Ground Sheets and Lucas Lamps.

/5........

- 2 -

				CALL
VISUAL	5.	Divnl. Visual Station will be at C.25.b.1.3.		A V
		Advanced -do- -do- C.14.b.5.3		K V

Both Stations will be permanently "manned"

MINTY FARM and FOCH FARM are both visible from Forward Station.
Brigade Advanced Visual Station will be at C.14.b.5.3. This station will send "forwards" and "rearwards".

BALLOONS. 6. The following units will work to Balloon if necessary:-

Advanced Divisional Visual Station.

CALL.

From Zero to Zero plus 2.	5th. Dorsets. (FRANCOIS FARM)	O R K
	8th. Northd. Fus. (FERDINAND FARM)	O R H
Zero plus 2 onwards.	9th. Lancs. Fus. (RAT HOUSE).	O R I
	11th. Manchesters (BULOW FARM).	O R L

Advanced Divisional Visual Station will work continuously.

DOGS. 7. Four dogs will be available, one for each Battalion.
Instructions as to treatment will be given by the man bringing up the dogs, these should be very carefully followed, the chief point to remember is, do not allow anyone to pat or make friends with the dogs.

PIGEONS. 8. Pigeons will be issued to all units from IRISH FARM.
2 Pairs of Pigeons will be issued to 2 selected companies of each Battalion for release only on capture of objective, and to intimate the capture of the objective to the rear.
2 Pairs will be available for each Battalion for general purposes.
2 Pairs will be available for Brigade Headquarters and 1 pair for Brigade Forward Station.
The 10 pairs of pigeons held in reserve at IRISH FARM will be at the disposal of the 33rd. Brigade if necessary.

CABLE ROUTES. 9. "Lineman Posts" are established at :-

LEFT ROUTE.	C.14.d.50.75.	CALL......	L T.
	C.14.a.7.4.	"	L A
	C.14.b.5.5.	"	L B
	C.8.d.9.3.	"	L C
	C.9.a.65.20.	"	L D
	C.9.b.9.8.	"	L E
RIGHT ROUTE	C.14.b.70.25	"	B W
	C.15.a.15.70	"	R A
	C.9.d.25.25	"	R B
	C.10.c.05.50	"	R C

/In each.......

- 3 -

In each route pairs 1, 2 and 5 are allotted for use of R.F.A.
    -do-   3 and 4   -do-   for Inf. Brigades.
    -do-   6.   -do-   for Lineman Pilot Line.

Communication diagram attached.

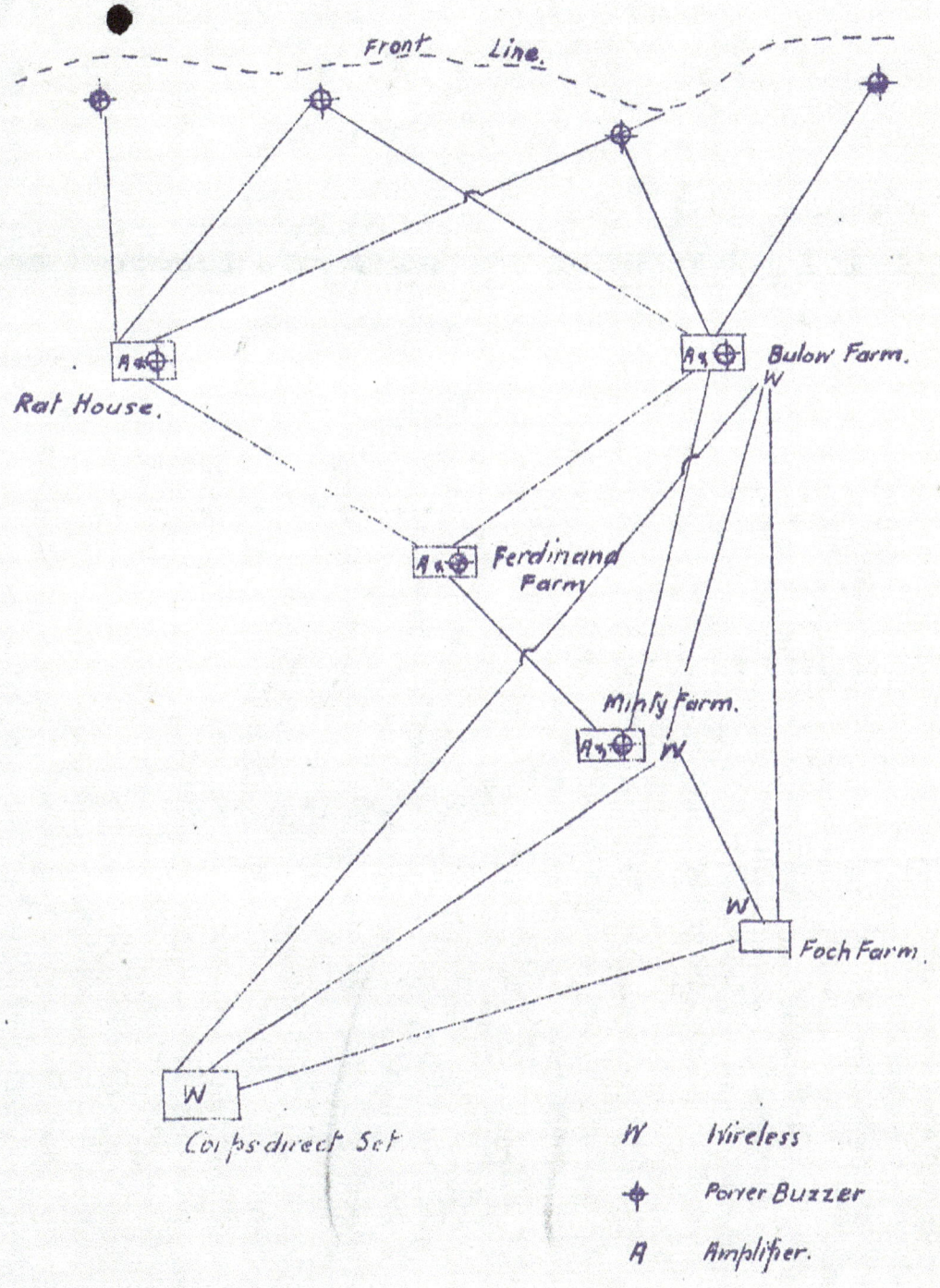

At the taking of the final objective the following (above) will be the arrangement of Wireless, Amplifiers, and Power Buzzers.

All sets mentioned above will remain in position and will continue to work as directed until ordered to dismantle. Personnel will be relieved when possible.

SECRET.   11th. Division No. G.S. 237.

To:- 48 DIV

Herewith   copies of Addendum No. 1 to
11th. Division Order No. 95 - " DIVISIONAL CAVALRY AND LIAISON
WORK".

Please acknowledge receipt.

J. D. Coleridge Lieut. Colonel,

10th. August, 1917.   General Staff, 11th. Division.

(G.B.227.)

S E C R E T.   11th. Division No. G.S. 274.

TO:- 48d Div

Reference Para. 2, No. G.S. 246 dated 10/8/17.

Herewith / copies of Appendix 2 (MACHINE GUN PROGRAMME AND BARRAGE MAP) to accompany 11th. Division Order No. 95 dated 9/8/17. This replaces Appendix 2 already issued which should be destroyed.

ACKNOWLEDGE.

12th. August, 1917.

J.M.R. Harrison Major,
General Staff, 11th. Division.

SECRET.

War Diary

APPENDIX 2.C.

Copy No. 26

10th. August 1917.

11th. Division Order No. 96.

Reference 1/20,000 Map
Sheets 28 N.W. & 20 S.W.
& Special POELCAPPELLE
Map 1/10,000.

1. With reference to 11th. Division Order No. 95 paras. 6, 14 & 15, moves therein referred to will be carried out in accordance with the attached table.

2. All details will be arranged direct between Brigades concerned.

3. On relief G.O.C., 32nd. Brigade will hand over all necessary trench maps, photographs, stores and appliances connected with the defence of the line to G.O.C., 34th. Brigade.

4. (a) The 3 Lewis Guns with personnel detailed by the 32nd. Brigade for the Anti-Aircraft defence of the BLACK LINE will remain in position and come under orders of the G.O.C., 34th. Brigade.

   (b) The Artillery, R.E. and Pioneers remain in action.

5. (a) Completion of the concentration of 34th. Brigade in its battle position will be reported by the code sentence - " NO BISCUIT REQUIRED".

   (b) Brigades will report completion of all moves (quoting Serial No.) to this office.

6. Reconnaissances of the tracks from the CANAL to the STEENBEEK by Officers and N.C.O's of the 33rd. and 34th. Brigades will be carried out daily.

7. Administrative instructions will be issued later.

8. ACKNOWLEDGE.

J. D. Coleridge
Lieut.Colonel,
General Staff, 11th. Division.

Issued at 6.45 p.m.

For distribution P.T.O.

Copy No. 1. A.D.C. for G.O.C.
2. C.R.A.
3. C.R.E.
4. 32nd. Inf. Bde.
5. 33rd.   "   "
6. 34th.   "   "
7. 6th. E. Yorks Regt.
8. "Q".
9. Signals.
10. A.D.M.S.
11. A.P.M.
12. Train.
13. XVIII Corps "G".
14. XVIII Corps "Q".
15. 20th. Division.
16. 23rd. Division.
17. 48th. Division.
18. 51st. Division.
19. XVIII Corps R.A.
20.   "   "   H.A.
21. 20th. Coy. "G" Bn. Tanks.
22 - 25 Liaison Officers.
26 - 27 War Diary.
28 - 29 File.
30. Area Commandant, CANAL BANK.

MOVEMENT TABLE TO ACCOMPANY 11th.DIVISION ORDER No. 96.

Date.	Serial No.	Unit.	From.	To.	Route.	Remarks.
X Day.	1	2 Bns.34th.Bde. 34th.M.G.Coy.	SIEGE CAMP.	CANAL BANK.	BRIELEN - B.29.d.7.5 - ESSEX FARM (or RUM ROAD if dry).	To come under orders of G.O.C. 33rd.Bde. on arrival at 8 a.m.
"	2.	2 Bns.33rd.Bde. 33rd.M.G.Coy.	DIRTY BUCKET CAMP.	SIEGE CAMP.	DIRTY BUCKET CORNER - HOSPITAL FARM - BRIDGE JUNCTION - SIEGE JUNCTION.	To be clear of DIRTY BUCKET CAMP at 8.0 a.m.
"	3	2 Bns. 32nd.Bde.	CANAL BANK.	DIRTY BUCKET CAMP.	B.29.d.7.5 - BRIELEN - SIEGE JUNCTION - HOSPITAL FARM (or RUM ROAD if dry).	To be clear of CANAL BANK at 8 a.m. and head of column not to reach SIEGE JUNCTION before 9 a.m. to come under orders of G.O.C. 33rd.Bde. on arrival.
Night X/Y.	4	2 Battalions 34th.Brigade. & 34th.M.G.Co.	CANAL BANK.	LINE.		} Under orders of G.O.C.
	5	32nd Brigade less 2 Bns. & 32nd M.G.Co.	Line.	CANAL BANK.		} 32nd Brigade.
	6.	33rd M.G.Coy.	SIEGE CAMP.	LINE.	As in No. 1 to CANAL BANK thence to line.	Under orders of G.O.C. 32nd. Brigade.

/Y Day-......

2.

Date.	Serial No.	Unit.	From.	To.	Route.	Remarks.
Y Day.	7.	34th.Bde. less 2 Battalions and 34th.M.G.Co.	SIEGE CAMP.	CANAL BANK.	As in No. 1.	To arrive CANAL BANK at 8 a.m. When G.O.C. 34th.Bde. takes over command of the line.
	8.	33rd.Bde. less 2 Bns. & 33rd. M.G. Company.	DIRTY BUCKET CAMP.	SIEGE CAMP.	As in No. 2.	To be clear of DIRTY BUCKET CAMP at 9 a.m.
	9.	32nd.Bde. less 2 Bns. & 32nd. M.G. Company.	CANAL BANK.	DIRTY BUCKET CAMP.	Supply Trains.	32nd. M.G. Company remain in action under D.M.G.O.
Night Y/Z.	10.	2 Bns.34th. Brigade.	CANAL BANK.	Position.		
	11.	33rd.Bde. less 2 Battalions.	SIEGE CAMP.	CANAL BANK.	As in No. 2.	Not to arrive CANAL BANK before 10.15 p.m. Y night.

NOTES: (1) Dates will be communicated Secretly.

(2) The following distances will be maintained :-

East of the RENINGHELST - POPERINGHE - PROVEN Road, 200 yards between Companies.

SECRET.

War Diary APPENDIX 2d.

Copy No. 12

11th. Division Order No. 97.   10th. August 1917.

Reference 1/10,000
Special Map, POELCAPPELLE.

1.   The XIVth. Corps are establishing a line of posts East of the STEENBEEK on the morning of the 11th. inst.
   The capture of AU BON GITE by the 20th. Division is included in the objectives.

2.   The 11th. Division will co-operate, by placing a barrage some 250 yards East of the STEENBEEK along the Divisional front.

3.   The 32nd. Brigade will take advantage of this barrage, and push forward their posts and consolidate them on a line between MON DU RASTA on the Right and the new advanced line of the 20th. Division, (200 yards East of the STEENBEEK) on the left.

4.   The Field Artillery covering the 11th. Division front will put down a barrage from Zero to Zero plus 14 as shown on the attached map.
   The barrage will lift at Zero plus 14 at the rate of 100 yards in 5 minutes for 10 minutes, and will then remain stationery till Zero plus 29 when it will cease.

5.   The 32nd. Brigade will withdraw their posts on the Eastern Bank of the STEENBEEK, to a safe distance on the Western Bank, by Zero minus 15 minutes.
   At Zero they will commence to move forward so as to be close up to the barrage by Zero plus 14.

6.   Zero hour will be 4.15 a.m. on the 11th. instant.

7.   Watches will be synchronised with 32nd. Brigade and C.R.A. by an Officer from Divisional Headquarters at 8 p.m. August 10th.

8.   ACKNOWLEDGE.

Issued at 5.30 p.m.

J. D. Coleridge Lieut.Colonel,
General Staff, 11th. Division.

Copy No. 1. 32nd. Inf. Bde.
       2. 33rd.   "   "
       3. 34th.   "   "
       4. C.R.A.
       5. C.R.E.
       6. A.D.M.S.
       7. "Q".
       8. XVIII Corps.
       9. 20th. Division.
      10. 48th. Division.
      11)
      12) War Diary.
      13)
      14) File.

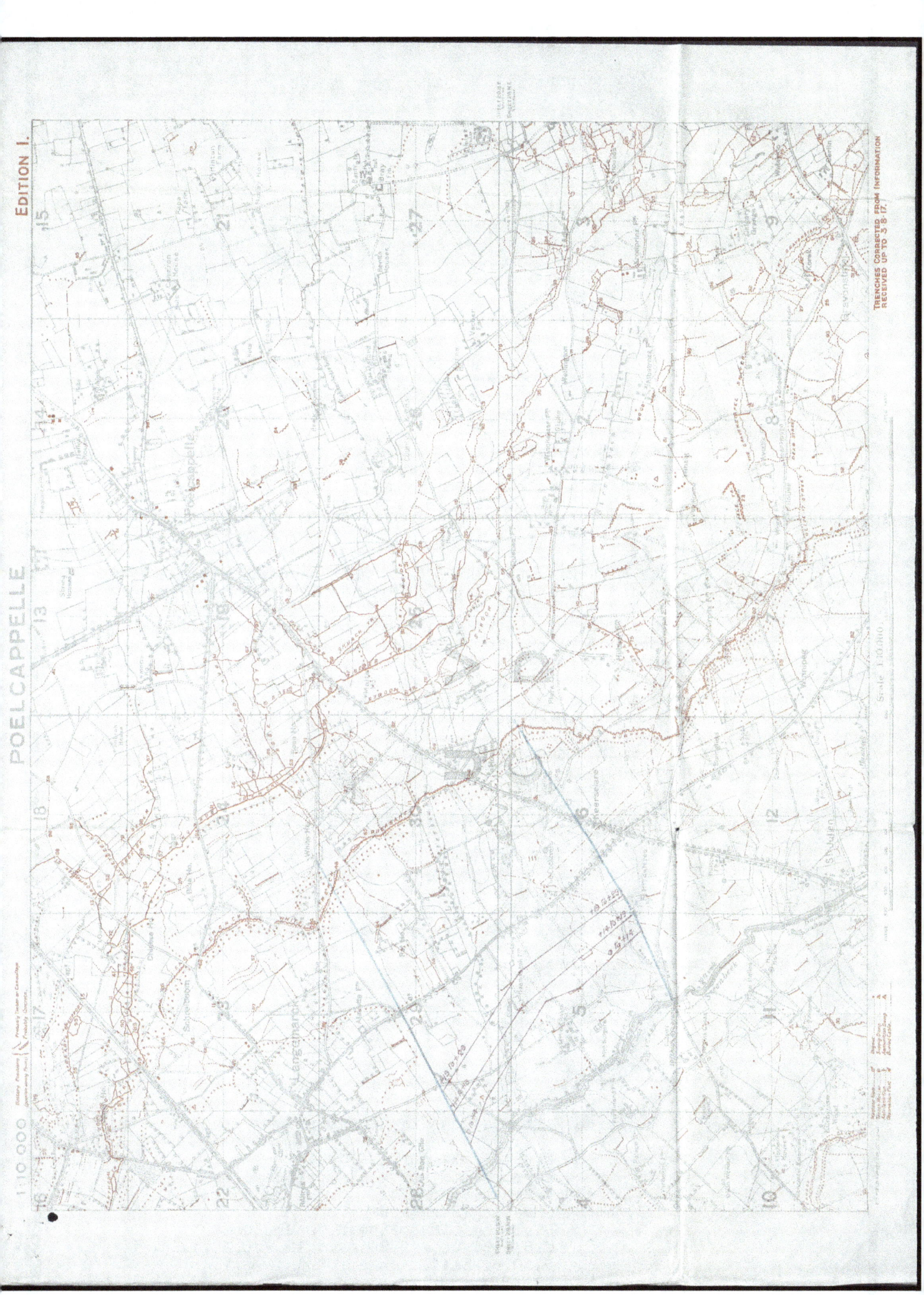

APPENDIX 1.

(to accompany 11th Div. Order No.95).

XVIII CORPS.
"O."
No. GS 66/32/12
Date. 14.8.17

SECRET   Copy No.

11th DIVISIONAL ARTILLERY ORDER NO.57.

Reference   August 12th, 1917.
  BELGIUM Sheet 28.

(1). On a date and at an hour to be notified later the Fifth Army will resume the Offensive.

(2). The 11th Division will be the Left attacking Division of the XVIIIth Corps.
   The 48th Division (145th Infantry Brigade) will be the Right attacking Division of the XVIIIth Corps.
   On the Left of the 11th Division the XIVth Corps will attack with the 20th Division (60th Infantry Brigade).

(3). The 11th Division attack will be carried out by 34th Infantry Brigade.
   The attack of the GREEN Line will be carried out by 8th Northumberland Fusiliers on the Right and 5th Dorsets on the Left.
   The attack of the Final Objective will be carried out by 11th Manchesters on the Right and 9th Lancashire Fusiliers on the Left.

(4) Objectives and Boundaries are shown on attached Barrage Map B.

(5). The main Objective is the capture of the LANGEMARCK - GHELUVELT Line (i.e. PHEASANT TRENCH).
   After the capture of this line Outposts will be established on a general Line through FLORA COTTAGE (to 145th Infantry Brigade) PHEASANT FARM - WHITE HOUSE (to 34th Infantry Brigade).

(6). The attack will be supported by the Divisional Artillery shewn in Table A (attached).

(7). The Divisional Artillery will be disposed as follows :-

   Eighteen Pounders.
       In each Group
           Five Batteries on Creeping Barrages.
           Two Batteries on Standing Barrages.
           Two Batteries on Searching Barrage.

   4.5" HOWITZERS.

       In each Group.
           Three Batteries on Standing Barrages.

(8). Table B. shews programme for 18-Pdrs.
   Table C. shews programme for 4.5" Howitzers.
   Table D. shews Smoke Barrages.
   Map B. shews Creeping Barrages
       Dividing Line between Group Zones
       C.5.d.60.20 - U.29.d.75.15 - U.30.d.13.97 - U.30.b.85.40.

(9). Barrages will be tested by Brigade Commanders and report rendered to this office to that effect.

Officers Commanding Right and Left Groups will arrange to test the junction of the flanks of their Barrages.

Arrangements are being made for testing the junctions of flank Barrages on the Divisional Front with the flank Barrages of neighbouring Divisions.

(10). Any Strong Points, M.G.emplacements etc. which are revealed by Aeroplane Photographs will be dealt with during the attack by special guns drawn from the Batteries forming the searching Barrages vide remark Column Table B.

(11). Rates of Fire and Natures of ammunition are shewn in Table E.

(12). During Protective Barrages one superimposed Battery in each Brigade will be detailed for the purpose of answering Zone calls.

(Instructions issued by R.A.XVIIIth Corps "Divisional Artillery in co-operation with R.F.C." are in possession of all Batteries).

(13). Table G. shews distribution of Artillery Liaison Officers.

(14). Table H. shews Headquarters of Units and Formations.

(15) Eight Tanks will assist the 34th Infantry Brigade in the attack.

(16) ACKNOWLEDGE.

Major. R.A.

Brigade Major. R.A.,11th Division.

Issued at :- 6pm.

TABLE "A" ARTILLERY DISPOSITIONS.

RIGHT GROUP.

Group Commander Lt.Colonel, O.de L'Epee "INTER
C.M.G. D.S.O. R.F.A.
Commanding 58th Brigade R.F.A.

	18-Pdr.	4.5" How.
58th Brigade R.F.A.	18	6
256th " "	18	6
282nd " "	18	6
	54	18

LEFT GROUP.

Group Commander Lt.Colonel T.M.ARCHDALE. D.S.O. R.F.A.
Commanding 77th Army Brigade R.F.A.

	18-Pdr.	4.5" How.
59th Brigade R.F.A.	18	6
77th " "	18	6
256th " "	18	6
	54	18

TOTAL 108 Eighteen Pounders.
       36   4.5" Howitzers.

TABLE "B"   11th DIVISIONAL ARTILLERY PROGRAMME   (to accompany 11th D.A. ORDER NO.57) 18-Pdr Barrages.

PHASE.	LEFT GROUP				RIGHT GROUP			REMARKS.
	CREEPING BARRAGE.	STANDING BARRAGE.	SEARCHING BARRAGE.	CREEPING BARRAGE.	STANDING BARRAGE.	SEARCHING BARRAGE.		
(A)	(B)	(C)	(D)	(E)	(F)	(G)		(H)
PHASE I 00 to +05 minutes.	5 Batteries C.5.d.91.38 to U.29.c.30. 25 to U.28.d.90.40.	2 Batteries WINNIPEG - LANGEMARCK Rd. U.29.d.75.15 to U.29.b.05.15.	2 Batteries Searches and sweeps within Group Zone to a depth of 1000 yards beyond creeping barrage Two guns on BULOW FARM	5 Batteries C.5.d.71.40 to C.5.a.91.58	2 Batteries WINNIPEG - LANGEMARCK Rd. C.6.c.50.85 to U.29.d.75.15 Two guns on the COCKCROFT	2 Batteries Searches and sweeps within Group Zone to a depth of 1000 yards beyond Creeping Barrage. Two guns on RAT HOUSE. Two guns on HANIXBEEK Farm		CREEPING Barrages will follow the lines shown on Barrage Map B. Points which require special attention will be notified later and guns from the "Searching" Barrage will be our marked to deal with them.
PHASE II +05 minutes to +20 minutes.	Rolls back at the rate of 100 yards in 5 minutes on to the line C.5.b.30.60 to U.29.c.45.80	Same as Phase I.	As for Phase I.	Rolls back at the rate of 100 yards in 5 minutes to the line. C.6.c.08.60 to C.5.b.30.60	Same as Phase I.	As for Phase I.		

TABLE B. 11th DIVISIONAL ARTILLERY PROGRAMME (to accompany 11th D.A. ORDER NO.57) 18-Pdr Barrages.

PHASE	LEFT GROUP				RIGHT GROUP			REMARKS
(A)	(B)	(C)	(D)		(E)	(F)	(G)	H
PHASE III +20 mins to +1 Hour.	Rolls back at the rate of 100 yards in 5 minutes to the line. U.30.c.25.43 to U.29.b.85.00 to U.29.b.58.45	As for Phase II. Lifts at +35 minutes to PHEASANT Trenches and WHITE HOUSE. U.30.d.13.97 to U.30.c.25.86 Two guns on PHEASANT Farm Two guns on WHITE HOUSE.	As for Phase II. Two guns on RAT HOUSE.		Rolls back at the rate of 100 yards in 5 minutes to the line. C.6.c.95.10 to U.30.c.25.43.	As for Phase II. Lifts at +35 to PHEASANT Trench. C.6.b.90.63 to U.30.d.13.97 Two guns on BULOW FARM Two guns on NEW HOUSES.	As for Phase II.	
PHASE IV +1 Hour to +2 Hours 35 minutes.	Swings at the rate of 100 yards in 5 minutes and rests on the line. U.30.c.25.43 to U.29.b.85.00 to U.29.b.58.45	As for Phase III	Searches and sweeps to a depth of 1000 yards beyond the line U.30.c.25.43 to U.29.b.85.00 to U.29.b.58.45 Two guns on RAT HOUSE.		Rests on the line C.6.c.95.10 to U.30.c.25.43	As for Phase III	Searches and sweeps to a depth of 1000 yards beyond the line C.6.c.95.10 to U.30.c.25.43	

TABLE B. 11th DIVISIONAL ARTILLERY PROGRAMME (to accompany 11th D.A. ORDER NO.57) 18-Pdr Barrages.

PHASE	LEFT GROUP				RIGHT GROUP			REMARKS.
(A)	(B)	(C)		(D)	(E)	(F)	(G)	(H)
PHASE V. 2 Hours 35 minutes to 3 Hours.	Rolls back at the rate of 100 yards in 5 minutes to PHEASANT TRENCH U.30.d.13.96 to U.30.a.23.86.	As Phase IV		Searches and sweeps to a depth of 1000 yards beyond PHEASANT Trench. Two guns on ROSE HOUSE.	Rolls back at the rate of 100 yards in 5 minutes to PHEASANT Trench C.6.b.90.62 to U.30.d.13.96	As for Phase IV (less 2 guns on BULO FARM).	Searches and sweeps within Group Zone to a depth of 1000 yards beyond PHEASANT Trench.	
PHASE VI 3 Hours to 3 Hours 30 minutes	Rolls back at the rate of 100 yards in 5 minutes and settles on the line U.30.b.50.20 to U.30.b.10.75 to U.24.c.61.10	Lifts on to KANGAROO Trench V.25.c.25.85 to U.24.d.25.50 two guns on PHEASANT FARM 2 guns on WHITE HOUSE		Searches and sweeps within Group Zone to a depth of 1000 yards beyond the line U.30.b.50.20 to U.30.b.10.75 to U.24.c.61.10 2 guns on ROSE HOUSE.	Rolls back at the rate of 100 yards in 5 minutes and settles on the line V.25.c.30.11 to U.30.b.50.20	Lifts on to the line V.25.a.00.50 to V.25.a.40.70.	Searches and sweeps within Group Zone to a depth of 1000 yards beyond the line V.25.c.30.11 to U.30.b.50.20. Two guns on BAVAROISE House V.25.c.82.56 Two guns on MALTA HOUSE V.25.a.15.51.	

TABLE B 11TH DIVISIONAL ARTILLERY PROGRAMME (to accompany 11th D.A. Order No.57) 18-pdr. Barrages.

PHASE.	LEFT GROUP.			RIGHT GROUP.			REMARKS.
	A	B	C	D	E	F. G	H
Phase VII + 5 hours 30 mins to + 5 hours 35 mins.	Rolls back at the rate of 100 yds in 5 mins. and settles on Protective Barrage. U.30.b.85.40 to U.30.b.45.90 to U.24.c.85.30.		Kangaroo Trench V.25.a.25.85 to U.24.d.25.50	Searches within Group Zone to a depth of 1000 yds beyond protective barrage. 2 guns on ROSE HOUSE. One Battery to search the following roads. U.24.d.70.10 to V.19.a.60.20 & V.24. 25.85 to V.19.c.60.20.	Rolls back at the rate of 100 yds in 5 minutes and settles on Protective Barrage V.25.c.65.30 to U.30.b.85.40.	As for Phase VI	Searches within Group Zone to a depth of 1000 yds beyond Protective Barrage. Two guns on BAUARTSE HOUSE Two guns on MALTA HOUSE.
+ 5 Hours 35 Minutes.	BARRAGE CLOSES.						

TABLE C 11th DIVISIONAL ARTILLERY PROGRAMME (to accompany 11th D.A.Order No.57) 4.5" HOW. BARRAGES.

PHASE	LEFT GROUP				RIGHT GROUP				REMARKS
	....Bty B	....Bty C	....Bty D	....Bty E	....Bty F	....Bty G	H
A 00 to +05 minutes	HAANEBEEK FARM	WINNIPEG-LANGEMARCK Road	WINNIPEG-LANGEMARCK Road U.29.d.75.15 to U.29.b.05.15	The COCKCROFT	WINNIPEG-Langemarck Road C.6.c.50.85 to U.29.d.75.15	WINNIPEG-LANGEMARCK Road	Vide Table D "Smoke Barrages.
+05 to +20 mins.	RAT HOUSE	do	do	do	do	do	
+20 to 1 hour 10 minutes	RAT HOUSE	Pheasant Trench U.30.d.13.97 to U.30.a.25.86	Pheasant Trench U.30.d.13.97 to U.30.a.25.86	Cross Roads C.6.b.05.35	BULOW FARM	Walks up the ST. JULIEN-POELCAPP-ELLE Road from Cross Roads C.5.b.05.35 to U.30.d.40.40.	
+1 Hour 10 mins. to 2 hours 45 mins.	WHITE HOUSE	PHEASANT FARM	do	Pheasant Trench C.6.b.90.63 to U.30.d.13.97.	BULOW FARM but lifts at +2 hours 20 mins. to Pheasant Trench C.6.b.90.63 to U.30.d.13.97	NEW HOUSES U.30.d.45.32 and POELCAPPELLE Road U.30.d.45.40	

TABLE C. 11TH DIVISION ARTILLERY BARRAGES (to accompany 11th D.A. ORDER No.57) 4.5 Howitzer Barrages.

PHASE	LEFT GROUP.			RIGHT GROUP.			REMARKS
	A	B	C	D	E	F	G	H
-2 hours 45 mins. to 2 hours 55 mins.	WHITE HOUSE	PLEASANT FARM.	ROSE HOUSE	DELTA HOUSE.	Lifts on to area V.25.c.70.40 70.80, 90.80, 90.40.	Houses at V.25.c.17.75 and BAVAROISE House V.25.c.82.56	
+2 hours 55 mins to +3 hours 35 mins.	Walks up road from WHITE HOUSE to U.24.c.60.10	KANGAROO and BEER TRENCH V.25.c.25. 85 to U.24.c.25 50.	ROSE HOUSE	do	do	POELCAPELLE	
+3 hours 35 mins. to 5 hours 35 mins.	DELTA HOUSE and DELTA Road Junction.	do	do	Rocas Area V.25.a 20.30 to V.19.c 70.20 to V.25.c. 95.70	V.25.c.90.40 to 70.80 to 90.30	do	

11TH DIVISIONAL ARTILLERY.

TABLE D. (to accompany 11th D.A. ORDER 57) SMOKE BARRAGES.

TIME	LEFT GROUP. One Section from each Howitzer Battery.	RIGHT GROUP. One Section from each Howitzer Battery	RATE OF FIRE IN ROUNDS PER GUN PER MINUTE.
+35 minutes to +39 mins	U.30.c.80.75 to U.30.a.10.75	C.6.b.50.40 to U.30.c.80.75	3
+39 minutes to +2 hours 20 minutes	-ditto-	-ditto-	1
+2 hours to +3 hours 4 minutes	V.25.c.40.60 to U.24.d.9.3.	One Section Area V.25.c.70.40 - 70.80 to 90.80 to 90.40 C.C.C. Two Sections V.25.c.90.80 to V.25.c.40.60	3
+3 hours 4 minutes to +3 hours 15 minutes	-ditto-	-ditto-	1

TABLE "E"

RATES OF FIRE

18-POUNDERS

00 - .05	4 Rounds per gun per minute.
.05 - .34	3 Rounds per gun per minute.
.34 - .40	4 Rounds per gun per minute.
.40 -1.10	3 Rounds per gun per minute.
1.10 - 2.30	1 Round per gun per minute.
2.30-2.57	3 Rounds per gun per minute.
2.57-3.03	4 Rounds per gun per minute.
3.03-3.10	3 Rounds per gun per minute.
3.10-3.25	1 Round per gun per minute.
3.25-3.30	4 Rounds per gun per minute.
3.30-3.40	3 Rounds per gun per minute.
3.40-5.35	1 Round per gun per minute.

4.5" HOWITZERS

Half the rate of 18-POUNDERS.

AMMUNITION.

CREEPING BARRAGES	- All Shrapnel, 50% on graze
STANDING BARRAGES	- 50% H.E. 50% Shrapnel.
SEARCHING BARRAGES	- Shrapnel, except when definite guns are on Houses or Strong Points when 50% H.E. will be used.
PROTECTIVE BARRAGES	- Shrapnel, except when length of range necessitates the use of H.E.

TABLE " F ".

ARTILLERY LIAISON OFFICERS.

One Senior Officer: 58th Brigade R.F.A. at Headquarters,

34th Infantry Brigade. FOCH FARM.

HEADQUARTERS OF BATTALION ATTACKING GREEN LINE.

One Officer Right Group, 11th D.A; Headquarters, Right Battalion
(8th N. F's). FERDINAND FARM.

One Officer Left Group. 11th D.A: Headquarters. Left Battalion

(5th DORSETS.) FRANCOIS Farm.

HEADQUARTERS OF BATTALION ATTACKING FINAL OBJECTIVE.

One Officer, Right Group. 11th D..; Headquarters. Right Battalion.

(11th MANCHESTERS.) RED FARM

One Officer Left Group. 11th D.A; Headquarters. Left Battalion,

(9th L.F's.) FRANCOIS Farm.

Artillery Liaison Officers will join their respective
Headquarters by noon (Z - 1) day.

T A B L E "G".

Headquarters. 11th Division. - "X" Camp. A.16.c.1.3.

Headquarters. 11th Divisional Artillery. "X" Camp. A.16.c.1.6.

Headquarters. 34th Infantry Brigade. - FOCH Farm. C.20.d.2.8.

Advanced Report Centre. 34th Infantry Brigade. GOURNIER Farm. C.9.d.2.7.

Headquarters. 33rd Infantry Brigade. CANAL BANK. (Gordon Terrace)

Headquarters. Right Group. 11th D.A. - BRUBANT FARM.

Headquarters. Left Group. 11th D.A. - LANCASHIRE FARM.

Headquarters. 58th Brigade.R.F.A. - BRUBANT FARM.

Headquarters. 59th Brigade. R.F.A. - LANCASHIRE FARM.

Headquarters. 255 Brigade R.F.A. - HINDENBURG FARM.

Headquarters. 256 Brigade R.F.A. - THE CANAL.

Headquarters. 77 (Army) Brigade R.F.A. - LANCASHIRE FARM.

Headquarters. 282 (Army) Brigade R.F.A.= H.6.a.5.8.

Headquarters. 8th Northumberland Fusiliers. / FERDINAND Farm.

Headquarters. 11th Manchesters. - RED Farm (to HAANIXBEEK FARM after capture of GREEN LINE.)

Headquarters. 5th Dorsets. - FRANÇOIS FARM.

Headquarters. 9th Lancashire Fusiliers. FRANÇOIS FARM (To HAANIXBEEK Farm after capture of GREEN Line.)

Headquarters. 60th Infantry Brigade. - STRAY Farm. C.3.c.2.7.

Headquarters. 145th Infantry Brigade. - VAN HEULE Farm. C.17.d.2.6.

Headquarters. Left Group. 48th Divisional Artillery. - LA BELLE ALLIANCE.

Headquarters. Right Group. 20th Divisional Artillery. -

DISTRIBUTION OF ORDER NO. 57.

```
Copy No  1.    11th Division.
         2.    R.A. XVlllth Corps.
         3.    XVlllth Corps Heavy Artillery.
         4.    32nd Infantry Brigade.
         5.    33rd ......do.........
         6.    34th ......do.........
         7.    20th Divisional Artillery.
         8.    48th .........do..........
         9.    51st .........do..........
        10.    O.C. Right Group, 11th Divisional Artillery.
     11-15.         .....do...., for 58th Brigade, R.F.A.
     16-20.         .....do...., "  256th .....do......
     20-24.         .....do...., "  282 (A) ...do......
        25.         .....do...., " Liaison Officer at Inf.Bde.R.W.
     26-27.         .....do...., "  .......do......., Battl.H.Q.
        28.    O.C. Left Group,  11th Divisional Artillery.
     29-33.         .....do...., for 59th Brigade, R.F.A.
     34-38.         .....do...., "  77th .....do......
     39-43.         .....do...., "  255th .....do......
     44-45.         .....do...., " Liaison Officers at Battl.H.Q.
     46-48.    46th Group R.G.A.
        49.    11th Divisional Ammunition Column.
        50.    51st ........do.................
        51.    11th Divisional Trench Mortar Officer.
        52.    No.7 Squadron R.F.C.
        53.    No.38 Kite Balloon Company.
        54.    XVlllth Corps Counter Battery Staff Officer.
        55.    Staff Captain, 11th Divisional Artillery.
     56-57.    War Diary.
     58-59.    Office.
```

S E C R E T.   11th. Division No. G.S. 304.

To:- 18th Corps G

        11th. Division No. G.S. 293 of to-day's date should be amended to read as follows :-

1.   " Reference para. 17 of 11th. Division Order No. 95, Add, "Appendix 8, TANK ARRANGEMENTS," (forwarded herewith").

2.   In the above Appendix, line 7, opposite "GEYSER" delete "ALOUETTE HOUSE".

                                          J.M.R. Harrison, Major,
13th. August, 1917.   General Staff, 11th Division.

SECRET.   11th. Division No. G.S. 897.

To:- 18th Corps 'G'   XVIII CORPS
                                                     "Q"
                                                   GS 66/32/14
                                                   13.8.17

Reference Appendix 5 (MEDICAL ARRANGEMENTS) to 11th. Division Order No. 95, the following new Sub-para will be added :-

"(3)   The 32nd. Infantry Brigade will detail two
"   companies (total strength 200 O.R.) to act as
"   stretcher bearers.
"   These will be placed at the disposal of the
"   A.D.M.S. and will report to Lt.Col.FAWCETT, D.S.O.
"   R.A.M.C., at the Advanced Dressing Station C.19.c.4.1
"   at Zero plus 4¼ hours. A Haversack ration will be
"   taken. This party will only be used if the R.A.M.C.
"   bearers cannot cope with the clearing of the battle-
"   field, they will be accommodated by the 33rd. Brigade
"   (by arrangements with the CANAL Commandant) in the
"   CANAL BANK North".

Acknowledged. G.E.P.

                                                      Major,
13th. August 1917.   General Staff, 11th. Division.

Copies to All Recipients of D.O. 95, and Commandant, CANAL BANK.

SECRET.

11th. Division No. G.S. 295.

To:- 42F Division

1. Reference Appendix 6, to 11th. Division Order No. 95, Para. 2 will be amended to read as follows :-

Lighting of Flares.

Flares will be lit at the following hours irrespective of whether they are called for by contact aeroplane or not :-

   Zero plus 1 hour.
   " " 1 hour 45 minutes.
   " " 3 hours 15 minutes.
   " " 4 hours 15 minutes.

The 7th. Squadron R.F.C. will arrange that an aeroplane is in the air at the above hours, to mark the positions where flares are lit.

At other times flares will only be lit when actually called for by an aeroplane.

Under all circumstances only the foremost Infantry will light flares.

RED flares will be used.

2. ACKNOWLEDGE.

                Major,
13th. August 1917.   General Staff, 11th. Division.

To all recipients of D.O. 95.

SECRET.  11th. Division No. G.S. 297.

To:- 48th Division

Reference Appendix 5 (MEDICAL ARRANGEMENTS) to 11th. Division Order No. 95, the following new Sub-para will be added :-

"(3)   The 32nd. Infantry Brigade will detail two
"   companies (total strength 200 O.R.) to act as
"   stretcher bearers.
"   These will be placed at the disposal of the
"   A.D.M.S. and will report to Lt.Col.FAWCETT, D.S.O.
"   R.A.M.C., at the Advanced Dressing Station C.19.c.4.1
"   at Zero plus 4½ hours.   A Haversack ration will be
"   taken.   This party will only be used if the R.A.M.C.
"   bearers cannot cope with the clearing of the battle-
"   field, they will be accommodated by the 33rd. Brigade
"   (by arrangements with the CANAL Commandant) in the
"   CANAL BANK North".

Major,

13th. August 1917.   General Staff, 11th. Division.

Copies to All Recipients of D.O. 95, and Commandant, CANAL BANK.

S E C R E T.   11th. Division No. G.S. 329.

To:- 18th Corps G

[Stamp: XVIII CORPS. "O." No. GS66/1/20 Date 15.8.17]

Herewith new Appendix 7, "ARRANGEMENTS FOR INTER-COMMUNICATION", to accompany 11th. Division Order No. 95.

Appendix 7, issued under G.S. 328 dated 7th. August should be destroyed.

ACKNOWLEDGE *done*

JmR. Harrison, Major,
General Staff, 11th. Division.

15th. August 1917.

To all recipients of D.O. 95.

SECRET.   Copy No. 12

APPENDIX 2.e.

11th. Division Order No. 98.

13th. Aug. 1917.

Reference 1/10,000 Map
POELCAPPELLE.

1. The 30th. Division on our Left are advancing their posts on their Divnl. Front under cover of an Artillery barrage to the East side of the STEENBEEK and 200 yards approximately from it, on the morning of the 14th. inst.

2. The 32nd. Brigade will co-operate and advance their left Battalion posts to a line U.28.d.80.50 - House at U.29.c.10.35 - MON DU RASTA.

3. * The advance will be carried out under an Artillery barrage as per attached Table.

4. Zero hour will be at 4.25 a.m.

5. A contact aeroplane will be in the air and will call for flares at 6.30 a.m.

ACKNOWLEDGE.

J. D. Coleridge Lieut. Colonel,
General Staff, 11th. Division.

Issued at 3-15 p.m.

Copy No. 1. 32nd. Inf. Bde.
2. 33rd. "
3. 34th. "
4. C.R.A.
5. C.R.E.
6. A.D.M.S.
7. "Q".
8. XVIII Corps.
9. 20th. Division.
10. 48th. Division.
11-12 War Diary.
13-14 File.
15 7th. Squadron R.F.C.
16 XVIII Corps H.A.
17 XVIII Corps R.A.

* Table not attached but handed personally to 32nd. Bde. by R.A.

S E C R E T.   11th. Division No. G.S. 296.

TO:- ....48th Div........

....

Reference 11th. Division Order No. 98 of to-day's date, Para. 4 will be amended to read as follows :-

"Zero hour will be at 4 a.m."

ACKNOWLEDGE.

                                                    Major,
13th. August 1917.   General Staff, 11th. Division.

Copies to all recipients of D.O. 98.

APPENDIX 2f

SECRET   Copy No. 10

11th. Division Order No. 99.   14th. August 1917.

Reference 1/10,000 Map
POELCAPPELLE.

1.   The 32nd. Infantry Brigade will before dawn on the 15th. instant withdraw all their posts on the East bank of the STEENBEEK, as far South as MON DU RASTA (exclusive), to a safe distance on the West bank of the STEENBEEK in order to allow strong points about C.5.a.25.75, C.5.a.23.68, C.5.a.65.65 and C.5.a.75.70 to be bombarded by Divisional and Heavy Artillery during 15th.inst.

2.   This bombardment will not be continued after 6 p.m. on the 15th.inst.

3.   As soon as it is sufficiently dark/the 34th. Brigade will occupy the posts East of the STEENBEEK previously occupied by the 32nd. Brigade and vacated by them as detailed in para. 1 above.
    on the 15th.inst.

4.   The greatest care will taken that the position of these posts is accurately pointed out to 34th. Brigade by the 32nd. Brigade during the night of the 14th/15th. to enable the former to occupy them without delay on the night of the 15th/16th.

5.   ACKNOWLEDGE.

                                            J. D. Coleridge
                                            ————— Lieut. Colonel,
                                            General Staff, 11th. Division.

Issued at 9 p.m.

Copy No. 1.   A.D.C. for G.O.C.
         2.   32nd. Inf. Bde.
         3.   34th.   "   "
         4.   C.R.A.
         5.   XVIII Corps "G".
         6.   "   "   R.A.
         7.   "   "   H.A.
         8.   20th. Division.
      9-10.   War Diary.
     11-12.   File.

SECRET. 11th. Division No. G.S. 328.

To:- 18th Corps "G"

> XVIII CORPS.
> "O."
> No. GS 66/32/21
> Date 15.8.17

Owing to the state of the ground, Tanks will not take part in the next phase of operations.

Para 11 of 11th. Division Order No. 95 and all other references to Tanks in the afore-mentioned order or attached Appendices are therefore cancelled.

ACKNOWLEDGE.

J.M.R. Harrison Major,
15th. August 1917. General Staff, 11th. Division.

To all recipients of D.O. 95.

SECRET.

XVIII CORPS.
"O."
No. ~~PS 66/3?/24~~
Date 15.8.17

11th Division. No. S/388.

XVIII Corps G

Reference Appendix 4 of 11th Division Order No. 95.

A. Para 11 is cancelled and the following substituted :-

WATER POINTS. Water Points in our lines are at :-

    A.30.Central.   } Pipe line supply.
    H. 3.a.7.5.   }
    C.14.c.2.2.   (LANCASHIRE FARM). Well supply, 400 gallons a day.
    C.21.c.3.5.   (near HAMMONDS CORNER) 2,300 gallon tank filled under Corps arrangements.
                           To be ready by 8 a.m. on Zero day.
    C.19.c.1.6.   (On W. side of YPRES-BOESINGHE Road). A 400 gallon tank, with arrangement for filling petrol tins.
                           33rd Bde. are responsible for filling this tank at 7 a.m., and 34th Bde. for filling it at 3 p.m. daily, starting on Y day.

    400 filled petrol tins are kept at Divl. Reserve Ration Dump at C.19.d.3.1. These will be issued on the signature of an officer. A similar number of empty tins must be handed in to replace full ones drawn.
    A number of empty tins are also kept at this point.
    The Train is responsible for keeping 400 tins filled.

    Water Lorries have been attached to Brigades as follows :-
        33rd Brigade - 1 300 gallon lorry.
        34th Brigade - 2 400 gallon lorries.

B. Para 13 is cancelled and the following substituted :-

SALVAGE. Every effort will be made to salvage arms, equipment, ammunition, shrapnel shell bodies, and shell cases. Each unit will establish a Salvage Dump of its own to which all individuals or parties returning should bring some article for salvage.
    Brigade Salvage Dumps will be established at FOCH FARM and at ADMIRAL'S ROAD SIDING on the Light Railway (C.15.d.2.2)
    Units should establish their Salvage Dumps close to transport routes. These should be clearly marked SALVAGE.
    Brigades will be responsible for moving the salvage from unit's dumps to the nearest Brigade Dump.
    The Divisional Salvage Officer will take over the salvage at the two Brigade Dumps as above and arrange to evacuate it on the empty trucks of the light railway.
    Divisional Salvage Dumps are at ESSEX FARM and at GHENT COTTAGES (B.29.d.7.0).
    Divisional Salvage Coy. H.Q. will be established at GHENT COTTAGES on 16th inst.
    Divisional Salvage Officer will be responsible for collecting from Regtl. Stragglers' Posts and Adv. Dressing Stations, equipment, Grenades, and S.A.A., which have been collected from wounded men and which are not required for re-equipping stragglers being sent forward again.

                                                            P.T.O.

SALVAGE Continued.

He will collect from Adv. Dressing Stations the clothing of gassed men. A.D.M.S. will arrange to have this clothing dipped in a solution of soda crystals, dried, and packed in sacks before handing it over to Salvage.
Divisional Laundry Officer will collect from Salvage Coy. such underclothing as is serviceable and fit for re-issue.
D.A.D.O.S. will detail an Armourer Sergt. to report to Divisional Salvage Officer on Zero day for repairing arms etc.

ACKNOWLEDGE. *done*

15th August, 1917.

[signature] Captain.
D.A.Q.M.G., 11th Division.

Copies to all recipients of Divisional Order No. 95.

"C" Form.
MESSAGES AND SIGNALS.

Army Form C. 2123.
(In books of 100.)

Prefix .... Code .... Words 31

Handed in at .... Office 8.0 a.m. Received 8.30 a.m.

TO: 48th Divn

*Sender's Number	Day of Month	In reply to Number	AAA
G 525	17		
Ref	11th	Division	order
100	march	table	serial
no	1	red (: read)	moves
to	be	completed	by
6.30	pm	and	not
6.30	am		

amended
0.0
100 not yet Read
by
9.30 p

FROM: 11 Div
PLACE & TIME: 8.0 am

SECRET

War Diary APPENDIX 2 g

Copy No. 25

11th Division Order No. 100.

17th August, 1917.

Reference Special Map
POELCAPPELLE 1/10,000.

1. The 33rd Brigade will relieve the 34th Brigade in the Line on the night 17th/18th. The 32nd Brigade will be in support to the 33rd Brigade.

2. (a) Moves will take place in accordance with the attached Table.

(b) All carrying parties etc., will rejoin their units by 12 noon, to-day.

3. All details of relief etc., will be arranged direct between Brigadiers concerned.

4. During the 17th: the 34th Brigade will adjust the Line, organize a proper system of defence and gain touch with flanking units.

5. The 34th M.G. Coy. will be attached to the 33rd Brigade for the defence of the line, and will be relieved on a date to be arranged later.

6. All Lewis Guns detailed for Anti-Aircraft Defence will remain in position.

7. The Artillery, R.E. and Pioneers remain in action.

8. The completion of each move will be reported to Divl. H.Q. by a wire quoting the Serial Number.

9. Completion of relief will be reported by Code Word

"MUSTARD"

10. Administrative Instructions will be issued later.

11. ACKNOWLEDGE.

Issued at 5-30 am

T. D. Coleridge
Lieut-Colonel,
General Staff, 11th Division.

Copy No.
1. G.O.C.
2. C.R.A.
3. C.R.E.
4. 32nd Inf. Bde.
5. 33rd Inf. Bde.
6. 34th Inf. Bde.
7. 6th E. Yorks Regt.
8. "Q"
9. Signals.
10. A.D.M.S.
11. A.P.M.
12. Train.
13. XVIII Corps "G"
14. XVIII Corps "Q"
15. 20th Division.
16. 23rd Division.
17. 48th Division.
18. 51st Division.
19. XVIII Corps R.A.
20. XVIII Corps H.A.
21-24. Liaison Officers.
25-26. War Diary.
27-28. File.
29. Area Comdt. CANAL BANK.

Table to accompany 11th Division Order No. 100.

Date.	Serial No.	Unit.	From.	To.	Route.	Remarks.
Aug.17th.	1.	32nd Brigade less } 2 Bns. & M.G. Coy. }	DIRTY BUCKET CAMP	CANAL BANK.	RUM and PERTH ROADS.	Moves to be completed by 6-30 p.m.
"	2.	2 Bns. 32nd Brigade	DIRTY BUCKET CAMP.	MURAT CAMP.	As in No. 1.	
"	3.	1 Bn. 33rd Brigade.	SIEGE CAMP.	BLACK LINE.	As in No. 1.	Not to arrive at CANAL before 7 p.m.
Night 17/18.	4	33rd M.G. Coy.	LINE.	MURAT CAMP.	"	On rejoining Brigade.
"	5	33rd Brigade.	BLACK LINE etc.	LINE.	"	The 33rd M.G. Coy. will rejoin the 33rd Bde. under orders to be issued by B.G.C.
"	6.	34th Bde. less } 34th M.G. Coy. }	LINE.	SIEGE CAMP.	By lorries from neighbourhood of CANAL.	Hour of leaving CANAL will be communicated later.

NOTES: 1. All accommodation on CANAL BANK will be allotted on application to Area Commandant.

2. If RUM and PERTH ROADS are too muddy for use, units will use BRIELEN – DAWSONS CORNER – SIEGE JUNCTION – HOSPITAL FARM ROADS.

SECRET.   11th. Division No. G.S. 374.

Rec'd 3.45 p.m.

TO:- 48. DIV.

....

      Herewith / copies 11th. Division Instructions No. 9.

      Please acknowledge receipt.

                                                         J.M.R. Harrison
                                                          Major,

17th. August, 1917.   General Staff, 11th. Division.

======================
S E C R E T.
======================

11th. DIVISION INSTRUCTIONS NO. 9.

GENERAL.

1. By the morning of the 18th. August the 33rd. Brigade will have relieved the 34th. Brigade in the Left Sector of the XVIII Corps front, and the Division will then be disposed as detailed in the Table attached to 11th. Division Order No. 100.

METHOD OF HOLDING THE LINE.

2. (a) The 33rd. Brigade will at first hold the sector.

(b) The consolidation and wiring of existing line will be pressed on with vigour, and it will be straightened out and re-organised without delay.

(c) The Front line will be lightly held and the troops disposed in depth. Should the enemy enter our lines he will be immediately counter-attacked by special troops detailed for the purpose.

(d) The Front will be protected by artillery and machine gun barrages, especial attention being given to the DELTA HOUSE - WHITE HOUSE and the POELCAPPELLE - ST. JULIEN ROADS along which the enemy are most likely to counter attack. The flanks of the barrages should be so arranged that they over-lap those of Divisions on either flank.

(e) The closest touch will be maintained with adjoining Units of Flanking Divisions, and a plan showing defensive arrangements submitted.

HOSTILE MACHINE GUNS & SNIPERS.

3. Every effort will be made to check the activity of hostile machine guns and snipers, who may be located in the neighbourhood of our lines. Plans must be made for the capture of machine gun posts and snipers must be counter-sniped or stalked. On no account is the enemy to be permitted to gain the upper hand in this direction, otherwise his moral will be increased to the detriment of ours.

FUTURE OPERATIONS.

4. On a date and at an hour to be detailed later the 11th. Division in conjunction with the Division on our Right will capture those parts of the RED DOTTED LINE not taken yesterday; and with this end in view the following preparations will be made without delay.

A. Positions likely to be held by the enemy, such as :-

1. The COCKCROFT.
2. Gun emplacements C.6.a.2.7.
3. Gun emplacements U.30.c.3.7.
4. RAT HOUSE enclosure.
5. Gun emplacement U.29.b.9.3.
6. House at C.6.a.6.5.
7. BULOW FARM.

will be reconnoitred and occupied if found vacated.

/If.....

- 2 -

If occupied by the enemy plans will at once be made for their capture. It has been found, that the concrete emplacements constructed by the enemy in this area are practically shell-proof against even the largest shells, so that the guns must not be expected to demolish them. Resort must be made, therefore, to other means. The entrance to the building must be screened by :-

(1) Smoke (either from shells or smoke bombs),

(2) Frequent bursts of shrapnel.

(3) Rapid L.T.M. fire.

(4) Machine and Lewis Gun fire.

Number (1) is designed to blind the enemy; Nos. (2), (3) and (4) are designed to force the enemy to keep inside the building until the attacking platoons are close enough to rush the building when the covering fire lifts.

B. On these positions being captured a line as parallel as possible to the RED DOTTED LINE will be taken up as the Divisional Front Line to enable an attack to be made on the RED DOTTED LINE in conjunction with the Division on our right.

WORKS. 5. The C.R.E. will press on work on communications East of the Corps Control; and Infantry parties will be allotted him when required from the supporting Brigade.

T. D. Coleridge
Lieut. Colonel,
General Staff, 11th. Division.

17th. August 1917.

APPENDIX 2 R.

SECRET.

Copy No. 15

11th. Division Order No. 101.   18th. August 1917.

Reference POELCAPPELLE
Map 1/10,000.

1. In confirmation of Warning Order issued to 33rd. Brigade, the 11th. and 48th. Divisions will capture the DOTTED GREEN LINE shown on attached tracing to-morrow 19th. inst. (if not already in their possession).
Zero hour will be notified later.

2. Objectives and boundary between Divisions are shown on attached tracing.

3. One Company Tanks (12 Tanks) is allotted to the 48th. Division for this operation. Each Tank will be given a definite objective. Two Tanks after completing the capture of the objectives allotted them by the 48th. Division, will move towards the COCKCROFT.

4. In the event of the above Tanks reaching the COCKCROFT, troops of the 33rd. Brigade, previously detailed for this operation, will immediately assault this place in co-operation with the Tanks. Should the Tanks not arrive however, the attack will not be carried out to-morrow and other arrangements for the capture of this objective, at a later time, will be made.

5. Artillery. At Zero, all high ground from which the enemy can observe the ST. JULIEN - POELCAPPELEE Road will be kept under a smoke, shrapnel, and lachrymatory barrage for two hours.
Other artillery arrangements will be made by G.O.C. 33rd.Bde. in consultation with C.R.A. 11th. Divn. and O.C., "G" Battn. Tanks.

6. A Contact Aeroplane will fly over the objective and call for flares at the following hours :-

Zero plus 1 hour.
Zero plus 2 hours.

At these hours, Red flares will be lighted by the front line of the attacking troops whether called for or not.

7. Watches will be synchronized at 7-0 p.m. to-day.

8. ACKNOWLEDGE.

T. D. Coleridge.
Lieut. Colonel
General Staff, 11th. Division.

Issued at......6-20 p.m.

For distribution P.T.O.

Distribution.

```
Copy No. 1.    A.D.C. for G.O.C.
         2.    32nd. Inf. Bde.
         3.    33rd.  "    "
         4.    34th.  "    "
         5.    C.R.A.
         6.    C.R.E.
         7.    "Q".
         8.    A.D.M.S.
         9.    20th. Division.
        10     48th. Division.
     11-12     XVIII Corps.
        13     "G" Battn. Tanks.
     14-15     War Diary.
     16-17     File.
```

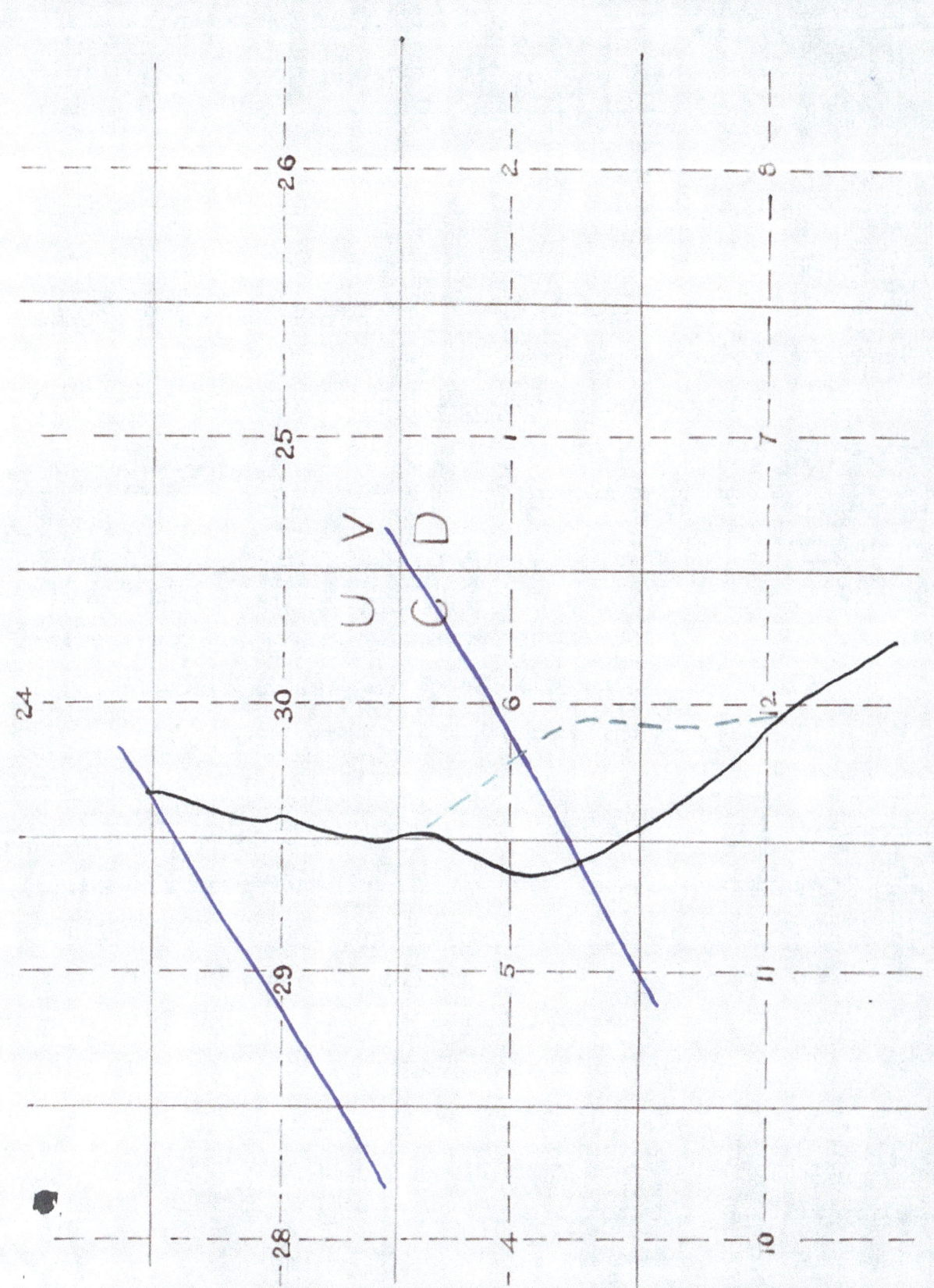

APPENDIX 2.j

====================
S E C R E T.   Copy No...15...
====================

11th. Division Order No. 102.   19th. August 1917.
_____

Reference 1/20,000
Sheet 28 N.W.
_____

1.   The 32nd. M.G. Company will relieve the 34th.
        M.G. Company in the line on the night of the 20th/21st.

2.   Details of relief to be arranged direct between
        G.Os.C. Brigades concerned.

3.   Completion of relief to be reported to 33rd. Brigade
        and D.M.G.O.

4.   The eight guns and teams of the 33rd. M.G. Company
        at present in the line, will remain there and will come
        under the orders of the O.C. 32nd. M.G. Company on
        completion of relief.

5.   The remainder of the personnel of the 33rd. M.G.
        Company exclusive of transport will move back to MURAT
        CAMP on the afternoon of the 20th. inst.

6.   ACKNOWLEDGE.

                                         T. D. Coleridge Lieut.Colonel,
Issued at 5. P.M   General Staff, 11th. Division.

Copy No. 1.   A.D.C. for G.O.C.
        2.   32nd. Inf. Bde.
        3.   33rd. "   "
        4.   34th. "   "
        5.   C.R.A.
        6.   C.R.E.
        7.   A.D.M.S.
        8.   "Q".
        9.   Train.
        10.   XVIII Corps.
        11.   "   " M.G.O.
        12.   38th. D.M.G.O.
        13.   48th. D.M.G.O.
    14-15   War Diary.
    16-17.   File.

SECRET.   11th. Division No. G.S. 373.

33rd. Inf. Bde.
"G" Battn. Tanks.

11th. DIVISION WARNING ORDER.

1. On an early date and at an hour to be detailed later the 48th. Division will reduce a number of hostile strong points situated in the vicinity of their front line.

2. A number of Tanks (probably 12) will assist, and will move along the ST. JULIEN - KEERSELARE Road, under cover of a smoke screen.

3. On the same date, and at the same hour the 11th. Division will occupy the COCKCROFT, if not previously taken.
   It is hoped, that 1 Tank will co-operate in this enterprise. This Tank will leave the main road at C.6.c.8.5 and approach the COCKCROFT from the South-east.

4. In preparation for this enterprise the G.O.C.,33rd. Brigade will :-

   Reconnoitre the COCKCROFT, which if found unoccupied by the enemy will be occupied. If it is found to be occupied, however, the following arrangements will be made :-

   (a) The O.C. party detailed for the enterprise will get into touch with the O.C. Tank mentioned in para. 3 above and make a combined plan with him.
   The name of this Officer will be communicated to O.C. Tanks and arrangements made for rendezvous.

   (b) Smoke bombs will be used to form a screen at various times prior to Zero followed by no action. This, it is hoped, will mystify the enemy, so that at Zero, when the Tanks move under the Smoke screen, the enemy will not realize that anything is afoot, and will take no action until the Tanks are near their objective.

5. Detailed orders follow.

6. ACKNOWLEDGE.

                                    T. D. Coleridge   Lieut. Colonel,
                                                General Staff, 11th. Division.
17th. August 1917.

"C" Form
MESSAGES AND SIGNALS.   No. of Message..........
                              Army Form C. 2123.
                              (In books of 100.)

Prefix....... Code....... Words. 10   Received Sent, or sent out   Office Stamp.
                                  From YK   At.............m.
  £ s. d.   By Anderson
Charges to collect   To.............
Service Instructions.   By.............

Handed in at 11 Div   Office 2-42 p.m. Received 2-55 p.m.

TO   18 Corps G.

*Sender's Number | Day of Month | In reply to Number | AAA
   G 598 | 21 | |

Ref   11th   Division   order   103
para   3   for   11 30 A 5 2   read
11 3 D A 2-5   aaa   acknowledge

Amended acknowledged

FROM
PLACE & TIME   11 Div
                2-15 pm

SECRET. Map not attached.

APPENDIX 2 K

Copy No. 19

11th. Division Order No. 103.

20th. Aug. 1917.

Reference: POELCAPPELLE
Map 1/10,000.

1. The 11th. and 48th. Divisions will capture the GREEN LINE as shown on attached map in conjunction with XIXth. Corps.

2. Date and Zero hour will be notified later.

3. The line held by the 11th. Division will be advanced to the line C.6.b.1.1 - X Roads C.6.b.05.34 - BULOW FARM C.6.a.9.9 (inclusive) - track running N.W. to U.30.a.43.08 - U.30.a.5.2.
Boundaries between Corps and Divisions are shown on the attached map.

4. The 33rd. Brigade will carry out the attack on the 11th. Division front, other Units will remain in their present positions.

5. Artillery.
The attack will be made under an Artillery barrage.
The barrage will come down 200 yards in front of our present line and will move forward at the rate of 100 yards in 8 minutes.
At Zero hour all high ground from which the enemy can observe the ST. JULIEN - WINNIPEG and the ST. JULIEN - POELCAPPELLE Roads will be kept under a smoke, shrapnel and lachrymatory barrage.
Artillery programme and barrage Lifts will be issued later.

6. Machine Guns.
Programme for machine gun co-operation will be issued later.

7. Tanks.
Two Tanks are detailed to assist the Division.
Tanks will be given a definite objective, and definite, distinct and complete Units will be detailed for the capture of each Tank objective.
At Zero hour Tanks will be as close to our front line as possible.
Arrangements will be made for the Tank and Infantry Officers concerned to meet beforehand and discuss co-operation.

/8.......

- 2 -

8. **Contact Aeroplanes.**

7th. Squadron R.F.C. will detail a Contact Aeroplane to fly over the objective at Zero plus 1 hour and Zero plus 2 hours, at both of which hours the front line of Infantry will light RED flares, whether called for or not.

At all other times flares will only be lit when called for by the aeroplanes.

9. The GREEN LINE will be consolidated with a view to a further advance to the BLUE DOTTED LINE in the near future.

10. **Liaison.**

The 33rd. Brigade will detail a special party to meet a similar party of the 48th. Division at Road junction C.6.c.9.9.

Close touch must be maintained with the 38th. Division on the left flank of the Divisional front.

11. Watches will be synchronized about 6 p.m. on August 21st.

12. ACKNOWLEDGE.

J. D. Coleridge
Lieut.Colonel,
General Staff, 11th. Division.

Issued at 11-45/a.m.

```
Copy No.  1      A.D.C. for G.O.C.
          2      32nd. Inf. Bde.
          3      33rd.  "    "
          4      34th.  "    "
          5      6th. E. Yorks Regt.
          6      C.R.A.
          7      C.R.E.
          8      A.D.M.S.
          9      Train.
         10      A.P.M.
         11      "Q"
         12      XVIII Corps "G"
         13        "     "   "Q"
         14      38th. Division.
         15      48th. Division.
         16      51st. Division.
         17      1st. Bde. Tank Corps.
      18-19      War Diary.
      20-21      File.
```

S E C R E T.   11th. Division No.G.S.432.

TO:- *War Diary*

        Reference Para. 6 of 11th. Division Order No. 103,
of the 20th. inst. Herewith Programme of Machine Gun
co-operation.

        ACKNOWLEDGE.

                                                J.M.R. Harrison. Major,

21st. August 1917.   General Staff, 11th. Division.

MACHINE GUN PROGRAMME.

1. During the attack by the 11th. Division on the GREEN LINE, the Machine Guns will assist by forming a M.G. Barrage vide Table 1, and attached tracing.

2. The approximate positions of the guns and the barrage lines will be as shown on attached tracing.

3. The 16 guns forming the barrage will be organised into a group consisting of two batteries, each of eight guns; batteries are allotted the letters "b" and "c".

4. O.C., 32nd. M.G. Company will be in command of the group.

5. Watches will be synchronized and the Zero hour communicated to O.C. 32nd. M.G. Company by the 33rd. Brigade.

6. The remaining eight guns of the 32nd. M.G. Company will remain under the direct orders of the G.O.C., 33rd. Brigade.

7. The guns forming the barrage will move into their barrage positions under the orders of the O.C., 32nd. M.G. Company.

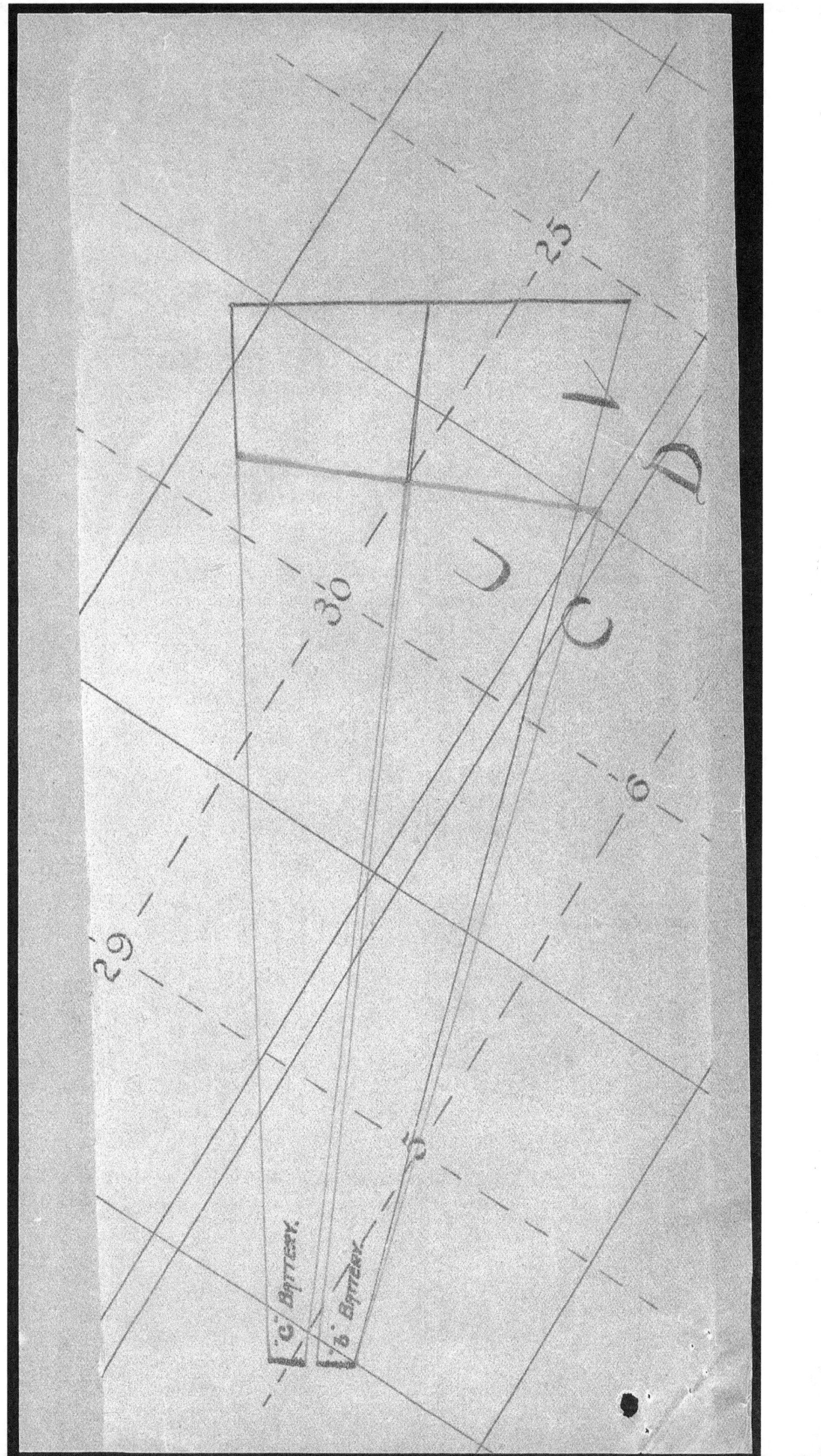

TABLE 1.

Battery.	Personnel.	Task.	Rate of Fire.	Remarks.
b.	32nd. M.G. Coy.	Zero, open fire on BLUE barrage lines.	1000 rounds per hour.	Battery Commanders will take the necessary precautions to prevent hitting men moving near the guns.
c.	33rd. M.G. Coy.	0 plus 42 minutes, increase rate of fire on BLUE barrage lines.	3000 rounds per hour.	
		0 plus 58 minutes lift to RED barrage lines.	" "	
		0 plus 1 hr.45 minutes cease fire except on receipt of an S.O.S. Call, when fire will be intensive on RED barrage lines.		

SECRET.   Copy No. 26

11th. Division Order No. 104.   22nd. August 1917.

Reference POELCAPPELLE.
Map 1/10,000.

1. (a)   On a date to be detailed later the 32nd.
           Brigade will relieve the 33rd. Brigade in the Line
           captured this morning.

   (b)   The 33rd. Brigade after relief will be in
           support of the 32nd. Brigade and will have 2 Battalions
           located on the CANAL BANK, and 2 at MURAT CAMP.

   (c)   The 34th. Brigade will remain at SIEGE CAMP
           as Divisional Reserve.

2.   All details of relief etc., will be arranged
           direct between Brigadiers concerned.

3.   The D.M.G.O. will arrange all details
           connected with Machine Gun defence, including Anti-
           Aircraft Defences, with G.O.C., 32nd. Brigade.

4.   The Artillery, R.E., and Pioneers remain in
           action.

5.   The completion of the relief will be reported
           by Code Word "PEPPER".

6.   Brigade Headquarters will be as under :-

   32nd. Brigade Advanced H.Q.   CANE POST C.9.a.6.3.
                 Rear   H.Q.   FOCH FARM.

   33rd. Brigade   TROIS TOURS CHATEAU.

7.   Administrative instructions will be issued
           later.

8.   ACKNOWLEDGE.
                              J. D. Coleridge Lieut. Colonel,
Issued at 2 p.m.   General Staff, 11th. Division.

For distribution P.T.O.

Distribution.

Copy No. 1 A.D.C. for G.O.C.
       2. C.R.A.
       3. C.R.E.
       4   32nd. Inf. Bde.
       5. 33rd. "   "
       6   34th. "   "
       7. 6th. E. Yorks Regt.
       8. "Q"
       9   Signals.
      10   A.D.M.S.
      11. A.P.M.
      12   Train.
      13   XVIII Corps "G".
      14   XVIII Corps "Q"
      15   38th. Division.
      16   23rd. Division.
      17   48th. Division.
      18   51st. Division.
      19   XVIII Corps R.A.
      20   XVIII Corps H.A.
   21-24   Liaison Officers.
   25-26   War Diary.
   27-28   File.
      29   Area Commandant, CANAL BANK.
      30   1st. Bde. Tanks

SECRET.   11th. Division No. G.S. 469.

To:- ...WAR DIARY...

....

    11th. Division Order No. 104 dated 22/8/17, para. 1 (a), and G.S. No. 449 dated 23/8/17, are amended in accordance with attached Table.

    Please acknowledge.

23rd. August 1917.   *J.M.R. Harrison* Major,
                                        General Staff, 11th. Division.

To all recipients of D.O. 104.

TABLE TO ACCOMPANY 11th. Division Order No. 104.

Serial No.	Unit.	Date.	From.	To.	Route.	Remarks.
1	2 Bns. 32nd. Brigade.	Night 24th/25th. August.	MURAT CAMP.	Support.	Under orders of G.O.C., 32nd. Brigade.	In relief of 2 Battns. 33rd.Bde. Coms under orders of G.O.C. 33rd. Brigade.
2.	2 Bns. 33rd. Brigade.	Night 24th/25th. August.	Support.	CANAL BANK.	Under orders of G.O.C., 33rd. Bde.	Remain under orders of G.O.C., 33rd. Brigade.
3.	2 Bns. 32nd. Brigade.	Night 24th/25th. August.	CANAL BANK.	MURAT CAMP.	Under orders of G.O.C., 32nd. Brigade.	
4.	2 Bns. 32nd. Brigade.	Night 26th/27th. August.	MURAT CAMP.	Line.	Under orders of G.O.C., 32nd. Brigade.	
5.	2 Bns. 33rd. Brigade.	Night 26th/27th. August.	Line.	MURAT CAMP.	Under orders of G.O.C., 33rd. Brigade.	
6.	32nd.Bde. H.Q.	Night 26th/27th. Aug.	MURAT CAMP.	CANE POST.		
7.	33rd.Bde.H.Q.	Night 26th/27th. Aug.	CANE POST.	TROIS TOURS CHATEAU.		Takes over Command of 32nd. Bde. and Line.

S E C R E T   11th Division No. G.S. 449.

To. *Wartwig*

1.   Reference 11th Division Order No. 104 dated
22nd August, 1917. Para 1 (a) :-
        The Relief therein mentioned will take place
on the night 24th/25th August.

2.   ACKNOWLEDGE.

                                    J.M.R. Harrison
H.Q. 11th Division.   Major,
23rd August 1917.   General Staff. 11th Division.

To all recipients of 11th Div. Order No. 104.

War Diary — APPENDIX 2 m.

SECRET   Copy No. 28

11th Division Order No. 105.

Reference 1/10,000   25th August, 1917.
Map POELCAPPELLE.

1.   On a date and at an hour to be detailed later the XVIII Corps in co-operation with the XIXth Corps on the Right and the XIVth Corps on the Left will resume the offensive, and establish itself on the BLUE DOTTED LINE.

2.   The 11th Division will attack on the Left of the XVIII Corps with the 48th Division on their Right and the 38th Division on their Left.

3.   The 11th Division attack will be carried out by the 32nd Brigade. The 144th Brigade will be attacking on the Right and the 115th Brigade on the Left.

4.   The boundaries will be as under :-

        Right Boundary 11th Division :-
            C.6.a.97.12 - C.6.b.20.23 - C.6.b.67.04 -
            D.1.a.0.2 - D.1.a.35.24 - D.1.a.65.20 -
            (VIEILLES MAISONS and FLORA COT inclusive to
            11th Division).

        Left Boundary 11th Division :-
            U.30.a.13.90 - U.24.d.00.44 (WHITE HOUSE
            inclusive to 11th Division).

5.   Objectives will be as under :-

   (a) 1st Objective. The GHELUVELT - LANGEMARCK Line (RED
        DOTTED LINE from C.6.b.87.14 to WHITE HOUSE
        inclusive) on which there will be a pause of
        30 minutes.

   (b) 2nd Objective. The Solid RED Line from D.1.a.0.2 to
        C.6.b.9.6 and the BLUE DOTTED LINE from C.6.b.9.6
        to WHITE HOUSE inclusive. There will be a pause
        of approximately 4 hours on this line.

   (c) 3rd. Objective. The 3rd. Objective of the 11th. Division
        will be the BLUE DOTTED LINE between D.1.a.65.20
        and C.6.b.9.6, and will include the capture of
        FLORA COT. Otherwise there will be no further
        advance from the 2nd. Objective.

6.   On a date to be communicated later the 48th. Division will resume their normal boundary (shewn Dotted Yellow on map) and relieve all troops of the 11th. Division South of the normal boundary.
        G.O.C., 32nd. Brigade will furnish a map before Zero shewing posts it is proposed to establish in this area.

/7........

- 2 -

7.　　　　After capture, each objective will be consolidated by means of a system of posts. The exact siting of these posts is left to local commanders, but the G.O.C., 32nd. Brigade will indicate the approximate positions of these posts, and definite parties will be detailed for the consolidation of each post beforehand.

FLORA COT, NEW HOUSES, PHEASANT FARM and WHITE HOUSE will be included in the system of defence. Posts at U.30.d.1.5 and U.30.a.0.5 will be constructed with R.E. assistance vide Appendix 3.

All posts will be constructed with a view to a further advance.

8.　　　　Under cover of the foremost posts patrols will be pushed forward as far as the protecting barrage permits to discover the enemy's dispositions.

9.　　　　The 32nd. Brigade will form up N.E. of the ST.JULIEN-LANGEMARCK Road with the rearmost troops at least 150 yards in advance of it. Every effort will be made to render the forming up inconspicuous; assaulting troops will shelter in trenches and shell holes, etc. and all movement will be reduced to a minimum.

10. (a)　　Assaulting troops will follow the barrage closely and especial units detailed beforehand will deal with the various farms and concrete shelters included in the Divisional area.

(b)　　Especial supporting troops will be detailed, whose duty it will be to attack or mask hostile strong points, which may be holding out on the flanks of the assaulting troops and hampering the advance by rifle and machine gun fire. Such posts will be engaged provided they are adjacent, whether they are within the Divisional area or not.

(c)　　The direction of the advance will be kept by compass bearings.

11.　　　　In order to ensure close touch with the flanking Divisions the following arrangements will be made :-

(a) With 48th. Division.

An especially detailed section from the 32nd. Brigade will meet a similar party of the 144th. Brigade at
　　　　(i) Road junction C.6.b.8.2
　　　　(ii) Cross Roads D.1.a.7.2.

(b) With 38th. Division.

One platoon from 115th. Brigade has been detailed to keep liaison with the left of the 11th. Division and to fill any gaps between the flanks of the Divisions. The 32nd. Brigade will get into touch with this platoon and arrange for a meeting at WHITE HOUSE.

(c)　　The meetings of these liaison parties will be especially reported.

/12.....

12.   The attack will be made under :-

(a) An Artillery barrage (for details see Appendix 1).

(b) A Machine Gun Barrage (for details see Appendix 2).

   (a) Artillery.
      (i)   For the capture of the 1st. and 2nd. Objectives :-
         The Artillery barrage will come down 200 yards in front of our present line. It will lift at Zero plus 12 minutes, and move forward at the rate of 100 yards in 8 minutes; at Zero plus 36 minutes it will lift off the RED DOTTED LINE and moving forward at the same rate will form a protective barrage, approximately 200 yards beyond the RED DOTTED LINE, on which it will pause until Zero plus 72 minutes when it will again lift and the Infantry will complete the occupation of the BLUE DOTTED LINE. The barrage will eventually become protective and remain so, on a line 200 yards in front of the BLUE DOTTED LINE until Zero plus 3 hours and 26 minutes.

      (ii)   For the capture of the 3rd. Objective :-
         From Zero plus 5 hours to Zero plus 5 hours and 5 minutes a quick rate of fire will be opened on the protective barrage line. The barrage on the right will then swing and move forward at the rate of 100 yards in 8 minutes. At Zero plus 5 hours and 21 minutes a protective barrage will be formed 200 yards beyond the whole of the BLUE DOTTED LINE where it will remain until Zero plus 7 hours and 21 minutes.

      (iii) Smoke.
         At Zero all high ground, from which the enemy can observe the area from our present line to the STEENBEEK, will be kept under a smoke, shrapnel, and gas barrage for 3 hours under Corps arrangements.

   (b) Machine Guns.
         The Machine Gun barrage for the capture of all objectives will precede the artillery barrage by 200 yards and will lift in accordance with it.

13.   Tanks will not co-operate with the 11th. Division.

14.   A Contact aeroplane will fly over the objectives at :-
   Zero plus 40 minutes.
   Zero plus 2 hours.
   8 p.m.
and when ordered by Corps Headquarters.
   Infantry will be ready to light RED flares at those hours, but will not do so unless called for by Klaxon horn or by dropping white lights.

15.   Situation reports will be rendered by the 32nd. Brigade every two hours after Zero.

/16......

16. Two Battalions of the 33rd. Brigade located in the CANAL BANK will be in support of the 32nd. Brigade, and ready to move at half an hour's notice.

17. Headquarters at Zero will be as under :-

Battle H.Q., 11th. Division.	CANAL West Bank. C.19.c.
Rear H.Q., 11th. Division.	BORDER CAMP.
Battle H.Q., 48th. Division.	CANAL West Bank. C.25.d.2.4.
H.Q., 38th. Division.	ELVERDINGHE CHATEAU.
Battle H.Q., 32nd. Brigade.	CANE POST. C.9.a.6.3.
Rear H.Q., 32nd. Brigade.	FOCH FARM.
H.Q., 33rd. Brigade.	TROIS TOURS CHATEAU.
H.Q., 34th. Brigade.	SIEGE CAMP.
H.Q. 144th. Brigade.	C.16.d.3.3.
H.Q. 115th. Brigade.	STRAY FARM.

18. The following Appendices are issued in connection with this order :-

    1. R.A. Programme and Barrage Map.

    2. Machine Gun Programme and Barrage Map.

    3. R.E. Instructions.

    4. Administrative Instructions.

    5. Medical Instructions.

    6. Inter-communication.

19. Attention is drawn to :-

  (a) Standing Battle Orders.

  (b) Instructions for the offensive with amendments.

20. Watches will be synchronised at 8 p.m. on Y day and 8 a.m. on Z day, by an officer from 11th. Division H.Q.

21. ACKNOWLEDGE.

J. D. Coleridge
Lieut. Colonel,
General Staff, 11th. Division.

Issued at 7.0 a.m.

Copy No. 1. A.D.C. for G.O.C.
    2. C.R.A.
    3. C.R.E.
    4. 32nd. Inf. Bde.
    5. 33rd. Inf. Bde.
    6. 34th. Inf. Bde.
    7. 6th. E. Yorks.
    8. "Q"
    9. Signals.
  10. A.D.M.S.
  11. A.P.M.
  12. Train.
  13. XVIII Corps "G"
  14.   "   " "Q".

Copy No. 15. XVIII Corps R.A.
  16.   "   " H.A.
  17. 38th. Division.
  18. 48th. Division.
  19. 51st. Division.
  20. 58th. Division.
  21. 7th. Squadron R.F.C.
  22. 1st. Bde. Tanks.
  23-26 Liaison Officers.
  27-28 War Diary.
  29-30 File.

APPENDIX 2.

To accompany 11th. Division Order No. 105.

MACHINE GUN PROGRAMME.

1. The attack of the 11th. Division on the RED LINE will be assisted by a M.G. barrage of 32 guns of the 33rd. and 34th. M.G. Companies Vide Table 1 and attached tracing.

2. These guns will organised into groups of two batteries. Each battery will consist of eight guns. An Officer will command each group.

3. There will be two officers with each battery, the Senior being in command of the battery.

4. Groups will be letter A. and B. and batteries c.d.e.f.

5. The approximate positions of the guns and the accurate positions of the barrage lines will be as shewn on the attached tracing.

6. Headquarters of Group Commanders will be at CANE AVENUE.

7. 33rd. and 34th. M.G. Companies will move into dug-outs close to their barrage positions on the night of 25th/26th. under the orders of their respective Company Commanders.

8. Eight guns of the 33rd. M.G. Company will relieve eight guns of the 32nd. M.G. Company in barrage positions West of the STEENBEEK.

9. All guns will be in their barrage positions ready to fire on their respective barrage lines by 4 a.m. on Zero day.

10. Only the minimum personnel required will be left with each gun. Every precaution must be taken to conceal the guns and men, and no movement whatever must take place around the guns between dawn and Zero hour.

11. Arrival in position to be wired to the D.M.G.O.

12. On relief the eight guns and teams of the 32nd. M.G. Company will return to MURAT CAMP.

13. On the night of the 25th/26th. two guns of the 32nd. M.G. Company will move into the two posts near WHITE HOUSE about V.30.d.9.5 under orders of Officer Commanding 32nd. M.G. Company.

14. These guns will not fire or disclose their positions before Zero unless there is an attack.

15. The remainder of the guns of the 32nd. M.G. Company will be under the direct orders of the G.O.C., 32nd. Brigade.

16. Watches will be synchronised and the hour of Zero communicated to the Officers Commanding 33rd. and 34th. M.G. Companies by the 32nd. Brigade.

TABLE 1.

Group.	Battery.	Personnel.	Task.	Rate of Fire.	Remarks.
A.	e. & d.	34th.M.G.Coy.	Zero - open fire on BLUE barrage lines.	4000 rounds per hour.	Officers Commanding batteries will take the necessary precautions to prevent hitting troops moving about near the guns.
B.	c. & f.	33rd.M.G.Coy.	Zero plus 8 minutes lift and search back to RED barrage lines at rate of 100 yards in 8 minutes. Zero plus 1 hour 20 minutes cease fire. Zero plus 5 hours re-open fire on RED barrage lines. Zero plus 5 hours 45 minutes cease fire. Guns will remain in their positions ready to open intense fire on RED barrage lines on receipt of an S.O.S. as long as the G.O.C. 32nd. Brigade may require. When no longer required they will return to their respective Brigades under the orders of the G.O.C. 32nd. Brigade.		
Two guns in posts near WHITE HOUSE.		32nd.M.G.Coy.	Zero - open fire on PHEASANT TRENCH for five minutes. Zero plus 5 minutes onwards fire at all visible targets paying special attention to enemy M.G's, PHEASANT FARM, MALTA HOUSE and ground round BAVAROISE HOUSE in U.25.d.		

Machine Gun Barrage Map
– To accompany Table 1. –

'f' Bath   'e' Bath   'd' Bath   'c' Bath

'B' GROUP   'A GROUP.

APPENDIX 3.

(To accompany 11th Division Order No.105).

R.E. INSTRUCTIONS.

CONSOLIDATION.

The O.C. 67th Field Coy. R.E. will detail one Section to assist in the consolidation of each of the following supporting points :-

    One point about   U.30.d.1.3.
    " " "   U.30.a.0.5.

Working parties for each of these points will be detailed by 32nd Brigade.

Work will not be commenced until after dark on ZERO day.

Reconnaissance of the ground to be carried out beforehand.

COMMUNICATIONS.

The 68th and 86th Field Coys. R.E. and the 6th East Yorks. (Pioneers) will continue the work on communications at present in hand.

The 67th Field Coy. R.E. less 2 Sections will be in Reserve.

APPENDIX 4.

To accompany 11th. Division Order No. 105.

ADMINISTRATIVE INSTRUCTIONS.

1. **STANDING BATTLE ORDERS.** Standing Battle Orders will be read in conjunction with these Instructions.

    Appendices 1 and 2 of Divisional Standing Battle Orders contain instructions as to Ammunition - Rations - Tools which will be carried on the soldier.

2. **STRAGGLERS' POSTS.** Straggler Posts will be established at:-

    Bridge 4 - C.25.a.5.9.
    Bridge 4a - C.19.c.4.3.
    Bridge 5 - C.19.c.3.6.
    Bridge 6 - C.19.a.2.9.
    Causeway 1 - C.25.a.4.8.
    Causeway 2 - C.25.a.6.7.

    Each post will consist of 1 N.C.O. and 3 men to be found from the T.M. Batteries.

    The Posts collect all stragglers (viz. men who ought to be with their units) in the vicinity and pass them to the Straggler Collecting Station.

    Those requiring Medical Aid should be sent on as soon as possible to Dressing Station at BRIDGE 4.

    Each Straggler post will be provided with :-

    (a) Orders for Battle Straggler Posts.
    (b) Note book and pencils.
    (c) Spare gas helmets and field dressings.
    (d) 12 empty grenade and S.A.A. boxes.
    (e) A Lamp.
    (f) Rations for post for 2 days and water in 4 petrol tins.

3. **STRAGGLER COLLECTING STATION.** Situated at Bridge 4 (C.25.a.5.9) 1 Officer and 6 N.C.O's., 1 Sergt. and 1 Corporal M.M.P. will be at the Straggler Collecting Station for the purpose of sorting out stragglers and either returning them to their respective Brigade Headquarters or seeing that those requiring medical aid are taken before a Medical Officer. All men fit to return are to be conducted back to their Brigade Headquarters.

4. **PRISONER OF WAR CAGE.** The Divisional P.O.W. Cage is situated at B.28.a.4.2 Chateau TROIS TOURS.

    All prisoners of war will be marched down to Bridge 4 (C.25.a.5.9) under escort which will be as small as is feasible. Here they will be taken over by Officer in charge P.O.W. Collecting Station.

5. **CASUALTIES.** Estimated casualties must be reported early. The actual numbers will be sent as soon as verified. Names of Officer casualties will be carefully checked before report is made.

/6.......

- 2 -

6. **BURIALS.**

The dead should be buried in recognised cemeteries only. It is however, often necessary for sanitary reasons that they should be buried by troops practically in the firing line - when this is done care should be taken that all details of men so buried, and the exact sites, are reported by Brigades to the Divisional Burial Officer.

7. **AMMUNITION.**
   (a) <u>Divisional Dump</u>.
   S.A.A., grenades, stokesbombs, flares, rockets, etc., can be drawn from Advanced Divisional Dump situated at C.19.d.1.1 under Brigade arrangements during an action. This dump will be on charge of the D.A.C. and maintained by them at the establishment laid down by D.H.Q.
   For normal requirements requisitions should continue to be made on the D.A.C. which is situated at B.20.c.7.5. D.A.C. can be got on the telephone.

   (b) <u>Brigade Dumps</u>. Will be drawn upon before resourse is made to Divisional Dumps.
   All dumps must be protected as far as possible from hostile shell fire.

   (c) <u>Fuzing</u>. Fuzing will be carried out at Brigade Dumps under Brigade arrangements.
   Ammunition dumps will **not** be utilised for the storage of rations or water.

   (d) <u>Ammunition Railheads</u>.

   For Artillery   -   XOB (A.21.a).

   For S.A.A.   )
   Grenades etc.) -   A.25.a.

   (e) <u>Ammunition Refilling Point</u>.

   For Artillery   -   REIGERSBURG.
                       ARRIVAL FARM (B.28.d.).

8. **HOT MEALS.**

G.Os C. Brigades will ensure that the troops under their command are provided with a hot meal before the attack.

9. **RATIONS.**

80% of Preserved Meat and Biscuit will be issued to 32nd. Brigade, to 33rd. and 34th. M.G. Companies for consumption on Z and Z plus 1 days, and 60% of Preserved Meat and biscuit to 33rd. Brigade for consumption on Z plus 1 day.

A Divisional Reserve of 7,000 Iron Rations has been dumped at POND COTTAGE (C.19.d.3.2) These rations can be drawn on by Units of Brigades on a written demand by a C.O. on the S.O. in charge.

3,000 Iron Rations on Advd. Bde. charge have been dumped at OUSE DUMP (C.5.c.4.9)

600 tons of solidified alcohol, for use during the operations for heating up tea etc., have been issued to 32nd.Bde.

/10. WATER POINTS.....

10. WATER POINTS.

Water points in our lines are at :-

A.30.Central	} Pipe Line Supply
H.3.a.7.5	
C.14.c.2.2.	(LANCASHIRE FARM). Well supply, 400 gallons a day.
C.21.c.3.5	(near HAMMONDS CORNER) 2,300 gallon tank filled under Corps arrangements.
C.19.c.1.6.	(On W. side of YPRES-BOESINGHE Road) A 400 gallon tank, with arrangement for filling petrol tins. 33rd. Bde. are responsible for filling this tank at 7 a.m. and 32nd. Bde. for filling it at 3 p.m. daily.

400 filled petrol tins are kept at Divisional Reserve Ration Dump at C.19.d.3.1. These will be issued on the signature of an officer. A similar number of empty tins must be handed in to replace full ones drawn.

A number of empty tins are also kept at this point.

The Train is responsible for keeping 400 tins filled.

Water lorries have been attached to Brigades as follows :-

33rd.Brigade - 1 300 gallon lorry.
32nd. Brigade- 1 400 gallon lorry.

500 filled petrol tins have been dumped at OUSE DUMP (C.5.c.4.9)

A second water bottle will be carried by troops taking part in the attack.

No water in the German lines will be drunk by the troops until it has been passed as fit for drinking by a M.O.

The locality of all water supplies discovered in the German lines should be reported early so that action can be taken to bring them into use.

11. TRANSPORT.

Attention is directed to the Divisional Pack Transport Scheme. (Appendix 10 of Divisional Standing Battle Orders).

Wheeled transport will be used as far as feasible but pack will probably be found the safest means of transport.

YUKON PACKS are being issued at the rate of 20 per Battalion and 10 per Machine gun Company and L.T.M.Btty. for each Brigade taking part in the attack.

12. SALVAGE.

Every effort will be made to salvage arms equipment, ammunition, shrapnel shell bodies, and shell cases. Each unit will establish a Salvage Dump of its own to which all individuals or parties returning should bring some article for salvage.

Brigade Salvage Dumps will be established at HURST PARK and at GOURNIER FARM.

Units should establish their Salvage Dumps close to transport routes. These should be clearly marked SALVAGE.

/Brigades.......

Brigades will be responsible for moving the salvage from unit's dumps to the nearest Brigade dump.

The Divisional Salvage Officer will take over the salvage at the two Brigade Dumps as above and arrange to evacuate it on the empty trucks of the light Railway.

Divisional Salvage Dumps are at ADMIRALS ROAD SIDING (C.15.c.8.4), ESSEX FARM and at GHENT COTTAGES (B.22.d.7.0).

Divisional Salvage Coy. H.Q. are established at GHENT COTTAGES.

Divisional Salvage Officer will be responsible for collecting from Regtl. Stragglers' Posts and Adv. Dressing Stations, equipment, Grenades, and S.A.A. which have been collected from wounded men and which are not required for re-equipping stragglers being sent forward again.

He will collect from Adv. Dressing Stations the clothing of gassed men. A.D.M.S. will arrange to have this clothing thoroughly aired and packed in sacks before handing it over to Salvage.

Divisional Laundry officer will collect from Salvage Coy. such under-clothing as is serviceable and fit for re-issue and will pass it through the Thresh Disinfector.

APPENDIX 5.

To accompany 11th. Division Order No. 105.
MEDICAL ARRANGEMENTS.

1. **LOCATION OF MEDICAL POSTS.**

    A. **Regimental Aid Posts.**

        C.5.c.4.3.   RED FARM.

        C.4.b.15.40.   COMEDY FARM.

    B. **Divisional Collecting Post.**

        C.10.c.2.6.   MINTY FARM.

    C. **Advanced Dressing Station.**

        C.19.c.4.1.   ESSEX FARM.

    D. **Corps Main Dressing Station.**

        A.23.c.2.9.

    E. **Corps Walking Wounded Collecting Post.**

        H.3.d.5.8.

2. **SCHEME OF EVACUATION.**

    A.   All sick and wounded who are able to walk, will be sent to the Divisional Collecting Post, from where they will be directed along sign-posted routes to ESSEX FARM. From there they will be conveyed to the Corps Walking Wounded Collecting Posts in motor lorries or busses.

    B.   All other sick and wounded will be conveyed by Regimental Stretcher Bearers to Regimental Aid Posts from whence they will be taken to the Advanced Dressing Station by hand-carriages by R.A.M.C. bearers assisted by light railways and motor ambulances where possible.

    C.   Sick and Wounded from Advanced Dressing Station will be conveyed to Corps Main Dressing Station in Motor Ambulance cars under Corps arrangements.

3. **RESERVE STRETCHER BEARERS.**

        The 33rd. Infantry Brigade will detail two companies (total strength 200 O.R.) to act as Stretcher Bearers.
        They will be placed at the disposal of the A.D.M.S. but will remain in their camp (MURAT CAMP) until required.
        The officer in charge of the party will report to A.D.M.S. at Advanced Dressing Station ESSEX FARM, C.19.c.4.1, for orders at Zero plus 4 hours.
        This party will only be used if the R.A.M.C. Bearers cannot cope with the clearing of the Battlefield.

APPENDIX 6.

(To accompany 11th Division Order No.105).

INTER-COMMUNICATION.

Advanced Divl. H.Q. Signal Office will be at dug-out No.15 in CANAL BANK at C.19.c.25.35.

32nd Brigade Forward Station will be at FERDINAND FARM.

WIRELESS.

Wireless sets will be installed at Bde. H.Q. (CANE Trench) and near RED FARM (C.5.c.1.2).
Sets will work to each other and to Corps Directing Station (C.25.d.0.6).

AMPLIFIERS & POWER BUZZERS.

Amplifiers and Power Buzzers will be installed at:

    Brigade H.Q.   (CANE Trench).
    Near RED FARM. (C.5.c.1.2).
    HON BULGARE.   (C.5.c.8.8).
    HAANIXBEEK FARM.
    Batt. H.Q.   (U.29.c.2.3).

None of these sets will move before Zero plus 6 hours, if conditions are then suitable U.29.c.2.3. set will move to RAT HOUSE.

When this set is working, <u>and not before</u>, the HAANIXBEEK set may move to BULOW FARM.

AEROPLANES.

Divl. Dropping Station will be at B.24.d.85.30.

VISUAL.

Divl. Visual Stations will be at   C.19.c.5.5. Call A.V.
                                     & C.14.b.5.3. Call K.V.
Both stations will be permanently manned and will receive or send forwards or rearwards.

BALLOONS.

All Infantry Battalions will work to Balloons if necessary.
Advanced Divl. Visual Station will also work to Balloon.

DOGS.

Two dogs will be available at Bde. H.Q. for message carrying rearwards.

CABLE ROUTES.

Lineman posts are established as far forward as :-
    Left Route - C.5.a.1.7a Call L.I.
    Right "   - C.5.c.80.85. " R.H.
Routes will be continued as far as RAT HOUSE and BULOW FARM before Zero hour if possible.

PIGEONS.

Pigeons will be issued to all units from IRISH FARM.
1 Pair of Pigeons each will be issued to 2 selected companies of each Battn. for release only on capture of objective.
2 Pairs will be available for each Battn. for general purposes.
4 Pairs will be available for Bde. H.Q.
2 Pairs will be available for Advd. Bde. H.Q.
2 Pairs will be available for F.O.O. work to each R.F.A. Bde.

APPENDIX 7.

(To accompany 11th. Division Order No. 105).

LIAISON ARRANGEMENTS.

1. The 32nd. Brigade will attack as follows :-

Left Battalion.	Right Battalion.
8th.Duke of Wellington's Regt.	9th.West Yorkshire Regt.
O.C., Lt.Col. G.H.WEDGWOOD.	O.C.,Lt.Col. F.P.WORSLEY, D.S.O.

One Company of the 5th.Yorkshire Regt. will hold the posts on the extreme left of the Brigade Front, forming a pivot to the left flank of the attack, and this Company will capture WHITE HOUSE and establish touch with 115th. Inf. Bde.

2. The following Officers of the 11th. Division are detailed for Liaison Work :-

(a) With XVIII Corps - Capt.C.B.MAY, 6th.Border Regt.

(b) With 48th. Division. - Major F.TOUNSEND, 9th.W.YorksRegt.

3. The G.O.C. 32nd. Brigade will arrange for Liaison with 144th. Inf. Bde. on his right and the 115th. Inf. Bde. on his left.

4. The G.O.C., 34th. Brigade will detail 2 Officers to proceed to the Divisional Collecting Post, MINTY FARM, so as to arrive there at Zero for the purpose of interrogating lightly wounded Officers and men.

These Officers will be provided with a number of special question forms, and should be provided with two runners each for communicating with Divisional Headquarters on the West Canal Bank in C.19.c.

SECRET.   11th. Division No. G.S. 509.

TO:-.....................

  ....

1.   Reference 11th. Division Order No. 105 dated 25/8/17, the following amendments will be made :-

  (a)   Para 6, Delete 1st. four lines and substitute :-

        " On a date to be communicated later the 58th.
        " Division, after relieving 48th. Division
        " will resume the latters normal Boundary
        " (shown Dotted Yellow on Map) and will relieve
        " all troops of the 11th. Division South of
        " the normal Boundary ".

  (b)   Para 14 :-

        (i) For "Zero plus 40 minutes".
            read "Zero plus 55 minutes".

        (ii) At end of para add :-

            "No troops will fire at low flying
            "aeroplanes on Zero day except the
            "Lewis or Vickers Gun detachments,
            "specially detailed for that purpose".

2.   ACKNOWLEDGE.

                                    signature Major,
26th. August 1917.   General Staff, 11th. Division

Copies to all recipients of 11th.Div. Order No. 105.

S E C R E T.   11th. Division No. G.S. 507.

To:-..................

   ....

   Herewith Appendix 7, (Liaison Arrangements) to
accompany 11th. Division Order No. 105.
   ACKNOWLEDGE.

                                    [signature] Major,
26th. August 1917.   General Staff, 11th. Division.

Copies to all recipients of D.O. 105.

S E C R E T.   11th. Division No. G.S. 490.

To:-..................

....

Herewith Appendix 6, "INTER-COMMUNICATION"

to 11th. Division Order No. 105.

ACKNOWLEDGE.

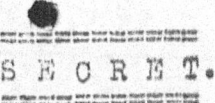
                                                             Major,

25th. August 1917.   General Staff, 11th. Division.

SECRET.   11th. Division No. G.S. 500.

To:- H.E. Div

   Herewith / copies of diagram to accompany
Appendix 6 (Inter-communication) to 11th. Division
Order No. 105.

                                       A C T White
                                       Capt   Major,
25th. August 1917.   General Staff, 11th. Division.

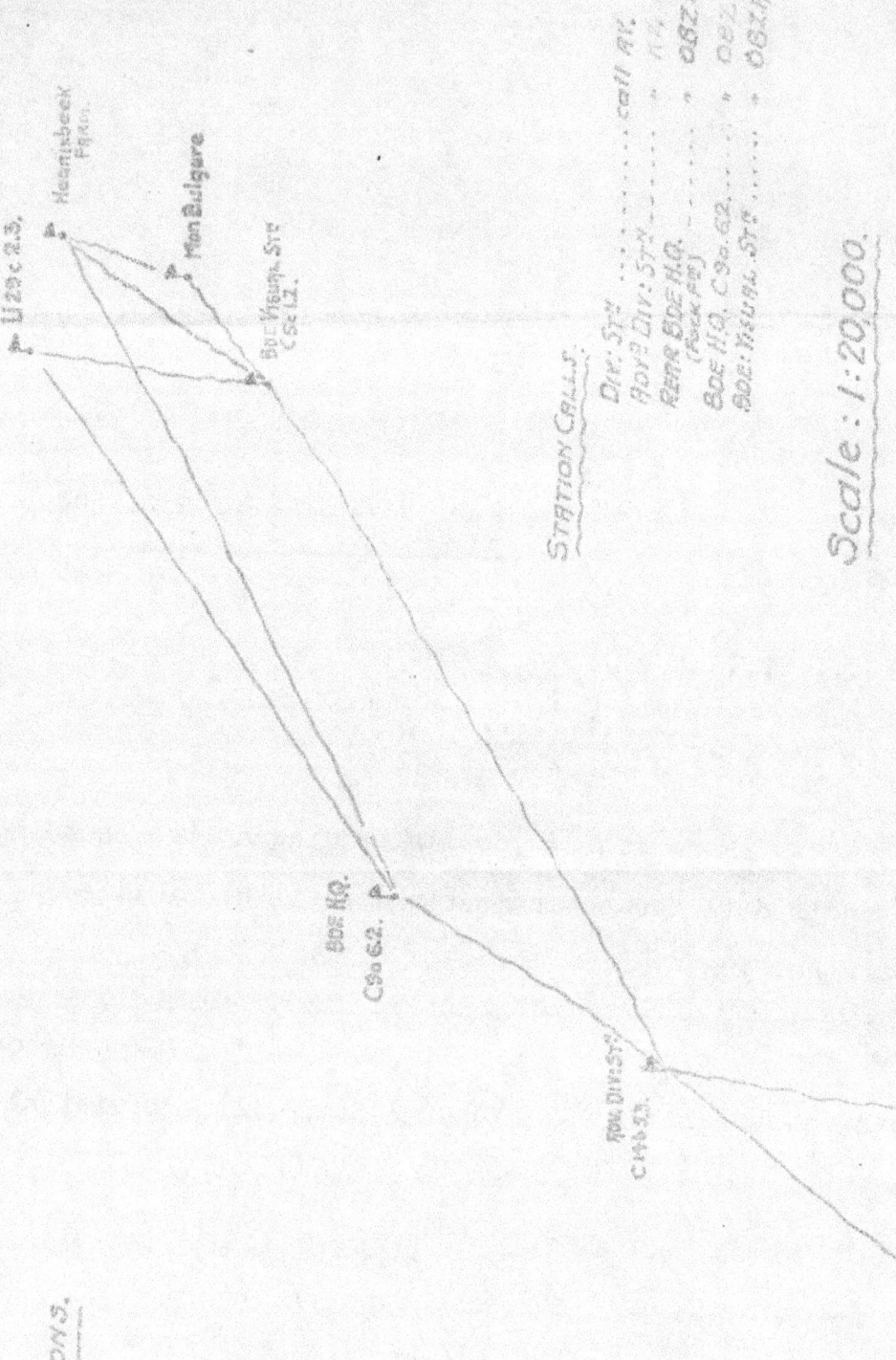

Amplifier & Power Buzzer Communications.
All Stations can send both ways.

Scale 1:20,000.

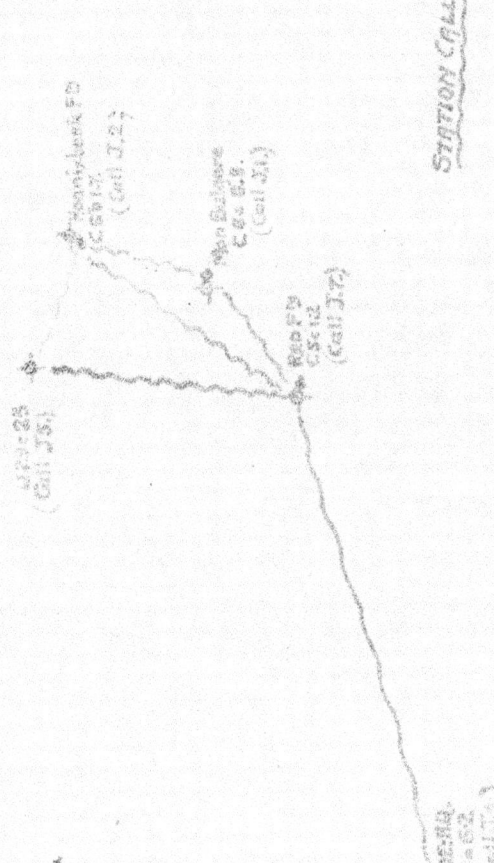

Station Calls
U 29 c 23 — call J.5.
Nieuwbreck Fm " J.2
Mon Bulgare " J.6
vtRoe Farm. " J.7
B.3E H.Q " J.4

WIRELESS COMMUNICATIONS

All Stations can send both ways.

STATION CALLS

Corps Directing	Call YB.
Bde. H.Q.	" DX.
Reg F9	" UX.

Scale 1:20,000.

- "Reg F9" C9.a.13. W
- Bde H.Q. C9.a.52.
- Corps Directing C25.d.a.6. W

- SECRET -

POELCAPPELLE — To Accompany 11th Div: Order No. 105. — EDITION 1.

TRENCHES CORRECTED FROM INFORMATION
RECEIVED UP TO 3-8-17.

Scale 1:10,000

Present Front Line

11th Div:

48th Div:

SECRET. 11th. Division No. G.S. 469.

To:- .......H.P.D Dvr...........

| G.O.C. |
| G.S.O. 1 |
| G.S.O. 2 |
| G.S.O. 3 |

11th. Division Order No. 104 dated 22/8/17, para. 1 (a), and G.S. No. 449 dated 23/8/17, are amended in accordance with attached Table.

Please acknowledge.

23rd. August 1917.

J.M.R. Harrison, Major,
General Staff, 11th. Division.

To all recipients of D.O. 104.

TABLE TO ACCOMPANY 11th Division Order No. 104.

Serial No.	Unit.	Date.	From.	To.	Route.	Remarks.
1.	2 Bns. 32nd Brigade.	Night 24th/25th August.	MURAT CAMP.	SUPPORT.	Under orders of G.O.C. 32nd Brigade.	In relief of 2 Bttns. 33rd Bde. Come under orders of G.O.C. 33rd Brigade.
2.	2 Bns. 33rd Brigade.	Night 24th/25th August.	SUPPORT.	CANAL BANK.	Under orders of G.O.C. 33rd Bde.	Remain under orders of G.O.C. 33rd Bde.
3.	2 Bns. 32nd Brigade.	Night 24th/25th August.	CANAL BANK.	MURAT CAMP.	Under orders of G.O.C. 32nd Bde.	
4.	32nd Bde. H.Q.	Night 25th/26th Augt.	MURAT CAMP.	CANE POST.		G.O.C. 32nd Bde. takes over Command of Line.
5.	33rd Bde. H.Q.	Night 25th/26th Augt.	CANE POST.	TROIS TOURS CHATEAU.		
6.	2 Bns. 32nd Brigade.	Night 26th/27th Augt.	MURAT CAMP.	LINE.	Under orders of G.O.C. 32nd Bde.	
7.	2 Bns. 33rd Brigade.	Night 26th/27th Augt.	LINE	MURAT CAMP.	Under orders of G.O.C. 33rd Bde.	

S E C R E T.

To:— ....

11th. Division No. G.S. 509.

1. Reference 11th. Division Order No. 105 dated 25/8/17, the following amendments will be made :—

(a) Para 6, Delete 1st. four lines and substitute :—

"On a date to be communicated later the 58th.
"Division, after relieving 48th. Division
"will resume the latters normal Boundary
"(shown Dotted Yellow on Map) and will relieve
"all troops of the 11th. Division South of
"the normal Boundary".

(b) Para 14 :—

(i) For "Zero plus 40 minutes".
read "Zero plus 55 minutes".

(ii) At end of para add :—

"No troops will fire at low flying
"aeroplanes on Zero day except the
"Lewis or Vickers Gun detachments,
"specially detailed for that purpose".

2. ACKNOWLEDGE.

26th. August 1917.

R. Harrison Major,
General Staff, 11th. Division

Copies to all recipients of 11th.Div. Order No. 105.

SECRET.

Recd. 9.30 PM

11th. Division No. G.S. 483.

32nd. Inf. Bde.
33rd. "   "
C.R.A.
XVIII Corps.
XVIII Corps H.A.
38th. Division.
48th. Division.

1. The XVIII Corps H.A. have been asked to bombard the following enemy strong points and suspected M.G. emplacements to-morrow 26th. inst. between 8 a.m. and 8 p.m.

   1. FLORA COT.
   2. Selected strong points in PHEASANT TRENCH.
   3. Strong points in KANGAROO TRENCH at U.30.b.70.95 - U.24.d.8.0 and U.24.d.60.15.
   4. Suspected M.G. emplacements at U.30.b.48.95, U.24.d.3.4 and U.24.d.2.5.
   5. PHEASANT FARM.
   6. Huts at U.24.c.95.00 and U.24.c.72.00.
   7. WHITE HOUSE.

2. The posts held by the 11th. Division at U.30.a.3.7, U.30.a.4.8, U.30.a.6.9 will be withdrawn during the night 25th/26th. and the positions re-occupied after the bombardment, on the night 26th/27th., with the exception of the post at U.30.a.6.9 which will not be re-occupied till after Zero, as the Barrage will pass through this point.

3. ACKNOWLEDGE.

J. X. Coleridge
Lieut. Colonel,
General Staff, 11th. Division.

25th. August 1917.

MACHINE GUN PROGRAMME.

1. During the attack by the 11th. Division on the GREEN LINE, the Machine Guns will assist by forming a M.G. Barrage vide Table 1, and attached tracing.

2. The approximate positions of the guns and the barrage lines will be as shown on attached tracing.

3. The 16 guns forming the barrage will be organised into a group consisting of two batteries, each of eight guns; batteries are allotted the letters "b" and "c".

4. O.C., 32nd. M.G. Company will be in command of the group.

5. Watches will be synchronized and the Zero hour communicated to O.C. 32nd. M.G. Company by the 33rd. Brigade.

6. The remaining eight guns of the 32nd. M.G. Company will remain under the direct orders of the G.O.C., 33rd. Brigade.

7. The guns forming the barrage will move into their barrage positions under the orders of the O.C., 32nd. M.G. Company.

TABLE 1.

Battery.	Personnel.	Task.	Rate of Fire.	Remarks.
b.	32nd. M.G. Coy. }	Zero, open fire on BLUE barrage lines.	1000 rounds per hour.	Battery Commanders will take the necessary precautions to prevent hitting men moving near the guns.
c.	33rd. M.G. Coy. }	0 plus 42 minutes, increase rate of fire on BLUE barrage lines.	3000 rounds per hour.	
		0 plus 58 minutes lift to RED barrage lines.	"	
		0 plus 1 hr.45 minutes cease fire except on receipt of an S.O.S. Call, when fire will be intensive on RED barrage lines.		

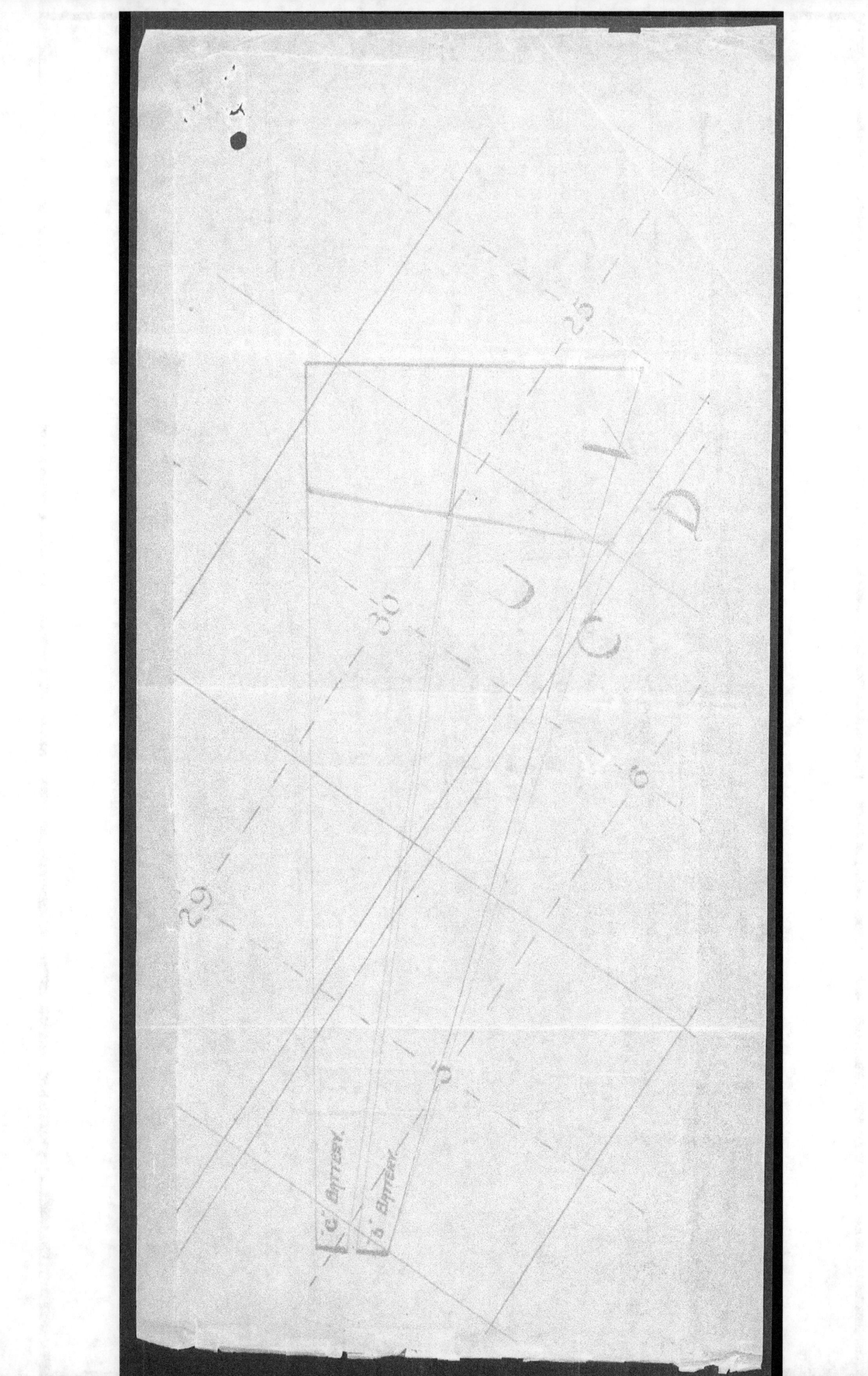

SECRET.

To:- 18th Corps G

11th. Division No.G.S.432.

XVIII CORPS. "O."
No. GS 66/84/17
Date 21.8.17

Reference Para. 6 of 11th. Division Order No. 103, of the 20th. inst. Herewith Programme of Machine Gun co-operation.

ACKNOWLEDGE. *done*

J.M.R. Harrison. Major,

21st. August 1917.   General Staff, 11th. Division.

SECRET.   11th. Division No, G.S. 374.

To:- XVIII Corps

Herewith 1 copies 11th. Division Instructions
No. 9.
     Please acknowledge receipt.

                                   J.M.R. Harrison
                                        Major.

17th. August, 1917.   General Staff, 11th. Division.

S E C R E T.

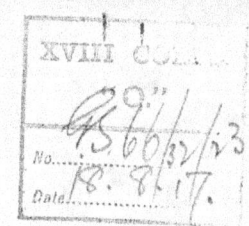

11th. DIVISION INSTRUCTIONS NO. 9.

GENERAL.

1. By the morning of the 18th. August the 33rd. Brigade will have relieved the 34th. Brigade in the Left Sector of the XVIII Corps front, and the Division will then be disposed as detailed in the Table attached to 11th. Division Order No. 100.

METHOD OF HOLDING THE LINE.

2. (a) The 33rd. Brigade will at first hold the sector.

(b) The consolidation and wiring of existing line will be pressed on with vigour, and it will be straightened out and re-organised without delay.

(c) The Front line will be lightly held and the troops disposed in depth. Should the enemy enter our lines he will be immediately counter-attacked by special troops detailed for the purpose.

(d) The Front will be protected by artillery and machine gun barrages, especial attention being given to the DELTA HOUSE - WHITE HOUSE and the POELCAPPELLE - ST. JULIEN ROADS along which the enemy are most likely to counter attack. The flanks of the barrages should be so arranged that they over-lap those of Divisions on either flank.

(e) The closest touch will be maintained with adjoining Units of Flanking Divisions, and a plan showing defensive arrangements submitted.

HOSTILE MACHINE GUNS & SNIPERS.

3. Every effort will be made to check the activity of hostile machine guns and snipers, who may be located in the neighbourhood of our lines. Plans must be made for the capture of machine gun posts and snipers must be counter-sniped or stalked. On no account is the enemy to be permitted to gain the upper hand in this direction, otherwise his moral will be increased to the detriment of ours.

FUTURE OPERATIONS.

4. On a date and at an hour to be detailed later the 11th. Division in conjunction with the Division on our Right will capture those parts of the RED DOTTED LINE not taken yesterday; and with this end in view the following preparations will be made without delay.

A. Positions likely to be held by the enemy, such as :-

1. The COCKCROFT.
2. Gun emplacements C.6.a.2.7.
3. Gun emplacements U.30.c.3.7.
4. RAT HOUSE enclosure.
5. Gun emplacement U.29.b.9.3.
6. House at C.6.a.6.5.
7. BULOW FARM.

will be reconnoitred and occupied if found vacated.

/If.....

- 2 -

If occupied by the enemy plans will at once be made for their capture. It has been found, that the concrete emplacements constructed by the enemy in this area are practically shell-proof against even the largest shells, so that the guns must not be expected to demolish them. Resort must be made, therefore, to other means. The entrance to the building must be screened by :-

(1) Smoke (either from shells or smoke bombs),

(2) Frequent bursts of shrapnel.

(3) Rapid L.T.M. fire.

(4) Machine and Lewis Gun fire.

Number (1) is designed to blind the enemy; Nos. (2), (3) and (4) are designed to force the enemy to keep inside the building until the attacking platoons are close enough to rush the building when the covering fire lifts.

B. On these positions being captured a line as parallel as possible to the RED DOTTED LINE will be taken up as the Divisional Front Line to enable an attack to be made on the RED DOTTED LINE in conjunction with the Division on our right.

WORKS. 5. The C.R.E. will press on work on communications East of the Corps Control; and Infantry parties will be allotted him when required from the supporting Brigade.

J. D. Coleridge
Lieut. Colonel,
General Staff, 11th. Division.

17th. August 1917.

"C" Form (Original). Army Form C. 2123.
(In books of 50's in duplicate.)

MESSAGES AND SIGNALS. No. of Message...........

Prefix....... Code....... Words.......	Received	Sent, or sent out	Office Stamp.
£ s. d.	From................	At............m.	
Charges to collect	By................	To............	
Service Instructions.		By............	

Handed in at......O L R............Office............m. Received......9........m.

TO **48 Div**

*Sender's Number	Day of Month	In reply to Number	A A A
G013	28		

The whole of ~~Octave~~ 11th Div Order

No 106 comes into force aaa

Acknowledge

G.B. 548

G373

FROM
PLACE & TIME 11th Div.

* This line should be erased if not required.
Wt. 432—M437 500,000 Pads. H W V 5 16 Forms C. 2123.

SECRET. WAR DIARY APPENDIX 2 n.

Copy No. 22

PROVISIONAL: To be brought into force
by a wire from D.H.Q.

11th. Division Order No. 106.

27th August 1917.

Reference 1/20,000 Map
Sheet 28 N.W.

1. The 51st. Division will relieve the 11th. Division in the line on the night 29th/30th. August up to the original Southern Boundary.
   The 58th. Division (relieving 48th. Division) will relieve the 11th. Division on the night 29th/30th. August in that portion of the line from D.1.a.6.2 to C.6.b.9.6.

2. Moves will take place in accordance with the attached Table.

   On the completion of moves:-
   The 11th. Division will be concentrated in the OOSTHOEK Area with Divisional H.Q. at "X" Camp (A.16.c.2.3).

3. All details of Relief will be arranged direct between Brigadiers concerned, and command will pass on completion of reliefs.

4. All special maps, trench stores, aeroplane photographs, dumps etc., will be handed over to the Relieving Units. G.O.C., 32nd. Brigade will have a map prepared showing exact dispositions of troops holding the line and in immediate support.

5. The C.E., XVIII Corps will issue orders as regards moves, accommodation and work of Field Companies R.E. and 6th. E. Yorks Regt.(Pioneers).

6. The D.D.M.S. (through A.D.M.S., 11th. Division) will issue orders as to the reliefs of Medical Units.

7. On completion of relief, the command of the Field Artillery covering the Divisional Sector will pass to the C.R.A., 51st. Division.

8. All Units not mentioned in this order will move under the orders of the A.A. & Q.M.G.
   Salvage and Burial parties will remain behind.

9. The Command of the Divisional Sector will pass to the G.O.C. 51st. Division at 11 a.m. on the 30th. August, at which hour D.H.Q. will close at BORDER CAMP, and reopen at "X" Camp, A.16.c.2.3.

10. ACKNOWLEDGE.

J. B. Coleridge
Lieut. Colonel,
General Staff, 11th. Division.

Issued at 10.0 a.m.

Distribution P.T.O.

Distribution.

Copy No.	1.	A.D.C. for G.O.C.
	2.	C.R.A.
	3.	C.R.E.
	4.	32nd. Inf. Bde.
	5.	33rd. " "
	6.	34th. " "
	7.	6th. E. Yorks Regt.
	8.	"Q"
	9.	Signals.
	10.	A.D.M.S.
	11.	A.P.M.
	12.	Train.
	13.	XVIII Corps "G".
	14.	XVIII Corps "Q"
	15.	XVIII Corps R.A.
	16.	XVIII Corps H.A.
	17.	38th. Division.
	18.	48th. Division.
	19.	51st. Division.
	20.	58th. Division.
	21.	Area Commdt. CANAL BANK.
	22-23	War Diary.
	24-25.	File.

Movement Table to Accompany 11th.Division Order No. 106.

Serial No.	Unit.	Date.	From.	To.	Route.	Remarks.
1.	33rd.Brigade.	Aug. 29th.	MURAT CAMP & CANAL BANK.	BRAKE CAMP.	BRIELEN-DAWSONS CORNER-HOSPITAL FARM.	March to be completed by 10 a.m.
2.	154th.Brigade.	-do-	ST.JAN TER BIEZEN.	MURAT CAMP.	POPERINGHE-VLAMERTINGHE-Road.= VLAMERTINGHE-BRIELEN Road.	To be clear of VLAMERTINGHE-POPERINGHE Road by 10 a.m.
3.	152nd.Brigade.	-do-	ST.JAN TER BIEZEN.	CANAL BANK.	By train to REIGERSBURG.	One train in morning. One train in afternoon.
4.	152nd.Brigade.	Night 29/30th.	CANAL BANK.	Front Line.	Under Bde.Orders.	In relief of 32nd. Brigade.
5.	32nd.Brigade.	-do-	Front Line.	CANAL BANK.	-do-	On relief by 152nd. Brigade.
6.	153rd.Brigade.	Aug.30th.	ST.JAN TER BIEZEN.	SIEGE CAMP.	By train to REIGERSBURG.	

/7.....

2.

Serial No.	Unit.	Date.	From.	To.	Route.	Remarks.
7.	34th.Brigade.	Aug.30th.	SIEGE CAMP.	DIRTY BUCKET CAMP.	Via HOSPITAL FARM.	March to be completed by 10 a.m.
8.	32nd.Brigade.	-do-	CANAL BANK.	POPERINGHE (2 Battns) and BROWNE CAMP.	By Train to HOPOUTRE. Entrain REIGERSBURG.	By trains which bring up 153rd.Bde. (Serial 6). Details of trains to be arranged by "Q".
9.	11th.Div.H.Q.	-do-	BORDER CAMP.	"X" Camp A.16.c.2.3.	Via MILITARY ROAD.	Close at BORDER CAMP at 11 a.m.

N.B.   Attention is called to 11th. Division No. G.S. 791 dated 7/7/17 (Intervals on March).

SECRET.   11th. Division No. G.S. 505.

To:- a... G.S. Div...
    ....

11th. Divisional Headquarters close at BORDER CAMP at 11 a.m. 27/8/17 and re-open at WEST CANAL Bank (C.19.c.3.2) at the same hour.

Rear Headquarters will remain at BORDER CAMP.

                                    [signed] Major,
26th. August 1917.   General Staff, 11th. Division.

To all recipients of D.O. 105.

SECRET.   Copy No. 17

11th. Division Order No. 107.
                                                           26th. August 1917.

Reference 1/10,000
POELCAPPELLE Map.

1.   Reference 11th. Division Order No. 105 para. 16.
            1 Battalion 33rd. Brigade will move from the
CANAL BANK so as to arrive at a point to be selected
by G.O.C., 32nd. Brigade at Zero plus 4 hours and
35 minutes, when it will come under orders of G.O.C.
32nd. Brigade and be in close support.

2.   The O.C., selected Battalion or his representatives
will report to the G.O.C., 32nd. Brigade at 10 a.m.
to-morrow to receive instructions as to where the
Battalion will be accommodated.

3.   The Battalion will be prepared to remain in
position until further orders, and will be rationed
by 33rd. Brigade.

4.   ACKNOWLEDGE.
                                    T. D. Coleridge Lieut. Colonel,
Issued at 7:30 P.m.   General Staff, 11th. Division.

Copy No. 1. A.D.C. for G.O.C.
        2. C.R.A.
        3. C.R.E.
        4. 32nd. Inf. Bde.
        5. 33rd. "   "
        6 34th. "   "
        7. "Q"
        8. Signals.
        9. A.D.M.S.
       10. A.P.M.
       11. XVIII Corps "G"
       12. 38th. Division.
       13. 48th. Division.
       14. 51st. Division.
       15. 58th. Division.
    16-17 War Diary.
    18-19. File.

SECRET

recd 10.5 PM KH
29/9/17

11th. Division No. G.S. 894.

To:— 48th Divn

G.O.C.
G.S.O. 1
G.S.O. 2
G.S.O. 3

Herewith   copies 11th. Division Instructions No. 11.

Please acknowledge receipt. → G.C.838.

J. D. Coleridge   Lieut.Colonel,
29th. September 1917.   General Staff, 11th. Division.

Distribution as per 11th. Division Order No. 114.

SECRET.

11th. Division Instructions No. 11.

(Reference Special Map issued to Commanders).

1. **GENERAL.** On dates and at hours to be notified later the Second and Fifth Armies will continue the offensive.
The 48th. Division will attack on the right and the 4th. Division on the left of the 11th. Division.

2. **ROLE OF THE 11th. DIVISION.** (a) The tasks given to the 11th. Division will be the capture of the RED DOTTED and the RED LINES, and the GREEN DOTTED and GREEN LINES.

   (b) **Attack on the RED DOTTED and RED LINES.**

   The 34th. Brigade will attack on the Right, the 33rd. Brigade on the Left.
   The 32nd. Brigade will be training in the HOUTKERQUE Area.
   The boundary between these Brigades will be as shown on the map, East of the STEENBEEK it runs as under :-

   On STEENBEEK at C.5.a.15.10.

   On LANGEMARCK ROAD at U.29.d.80.15.

   On ST. JULIEN-) at U.30.b.90.35.
   POELCAPPELLE Rd.)

   Near RETOUR X Roads. at V.19.d.27.20.

   S.E. of POELCAPPELLE CHURCH at V.20.c.10.84.

3. **CONCENTRATION.** Details regarding the concentration of the 33rd. and 34th. Brigades, and the move of the 32nd. Brigade to the HOUTKERQUE Area will be found in 11th. Division Order No. 114.

4. **HOSTILE ATTITUDE.** The enemy forces opposite the Divisional Sector are distributed in depth, one Battalion holding a system of organised shell holes in the front line, a second Battalion in close support and the third in reserve.
   In the event of an advance by us a counter-attack would be delivered within a very short space of time by elements of the counter-attacking Division now situated in the WESTROOSBEKE AREA.
   This attack may be expected to develop from two to three hours after Zero.
   The enemy is making far less use of his concrete dug-outs, as in several instances the occupants have all been knocked out by direct hits. The men now consider themselves safer in shell holes.

5. **FORMING UP.** The forming up areas must be very carefully reconnoitred. Constant patrols must ensure that there are no enemy posts or removable obstacles between the forming up positions and the lines on which our barrage comes down at Zero. This barrage line will be 150 yds. in front of the forming up positions.

/2........

- 2 -

6. ATTACK FORMATIONS.

The area over which the attack will take place does not appear to contain many concrete buildings except in POELCAPPELLE, but there are a number of derelict trenches which would no doubt afford cover for the enemy. Definite, complete, and distinct units must, therefore, be detailed to engage unexpected areas which may have been consolidated by the enemy and converted into strong points.

Attacking troops will make every effort to follow the barrage as closely as possible.

7. CONSOLIDATION.

The objectives, once gained will be consolidated by definite, complete, and distinct units disposed in depth.

The R.E. will assist in the construction of especially important localities.

8. ARTILLERY.

(a) The attack will be supported by the Right and Left Groups 11th. Division Artillery, consisting of :-

RIGHT GROUP. 58th., 256th., 77th.(Army) and 93rd. (Army) Brigades R.F.A.

LEFT GROUP. 59th., 255th., 34th.(Army) and 298th. (Army) Brigades R.F.A.

STRENGTH. 144 Eighteen Pounders.
40 4.5" Howitzers.

(b) Harassing fire and special treatment of enemy's communications will be carried out from now up to Z day.

(c) Strong points will be dealt with by the Heavy Artillery, but the general terrain will not be destroyed.

(d) The Divisional Artillery will carry out each day short concentrated barrages, varying in intensity, rate and locality.

(e) Barrages for the support of the actual attack will be formed in depth, especial attention being paid to localities from which rifle and machine gun fire could be directed by the enemy through the Creeping barrage.

9. MACHINE GUNS.

The attack will be supported by a Machine Gun barrage of 32 guns from positions about 300 yards in rear of PHEASANT TRENCH, details of which will be issued later.

It is hoped that an extra M.G. Company will be attached to the Division for these operations, in which case all the Machine Guns of the attacking Brigades will remain under the direct orders of their respective G.O's C. Orders on this point will be issued later.

/10......

- 3 -

10. LIGHT TRENCH MORTARS.

As suggested in paras. 4 and 6 above, the enemy will probably be found occupying shell holes rather than concrete buildings.

To deal with this probability and to thicken up the earlier stages of the Artillery barrage, Brigadiers Commanding will arrange to emplace a number of L.T.M's close to the forming up places; these will open a rapid fire at Zero and which will be continued up to Zero plus 3 minutes. Efforts will also be made to push forward one or two Mortars after the attacking troops to assist them in dealing with any opposition which may be encountered from concrete buildings in and around POELCAPPELLE.

11. GAS.

To further demoralise the enemy opposing the Division, gas will be discharged (wind and circumstances permitting) towards POELCAPPELLE during the night immediately preceding Zero.

12. TANKS.

Tanks will co-operate with the Division in the attack - details will be issued later.

13. INTERCOMMUNICATION.

(a) The head of the buried cable route will be at MAISON BULGARE.

(b) Forward communications will be organised on the plan adopted by the Division during the recent operations.

14. DUMPS.

Especially detailed working parties from the 33rd. and 34th. Brigades will establish dumps of S.A.A., Water, etc., at SNIPE HOUSE and BULOW FARM respectively prior to Zero.

15. ROLE OF 32nd. BRIGADE.

Attack on the GREEN and GREEN DOTTED LINES.

(a) The 32nd. Brigade will carry out this attack supported by portions of 33rd. and 34th. Brigades.

Details for this attack will be issued later.

(b) The boundaries between the 11th. Division and Flanking Divisions will be as shown on the Special Map already issued.

16. DIVISIONAL HEADQUARTERS.

11th. Division Battle Headquarters will be on the CANAL BANK C.19.c.1.2.

J.D. Coleridge
Lieut.Colonel,
General Staff, 11th. Division.

29th. September 1917.

SECRET

Scheme A

11th DIV: DIAGRAM No.17B.

"Z"+1 / Z+2 NIGHT. (AFTER RELIEF.)

— 200ˣ — ✕ — 3500ˣ — ✕ — 1800ˣ — ✕ — 800ˣ — ✕ — 800ˣ —

○ DATT. BOMBT (OPR
32ND BDE.

○ SIEGE (O)"A
2 BTZ.N 33RD BDE:

TRENCH (O)"A
2 BAT.LN 34 BDE:

2 BAT.LNS 34RD BDE:

2 BAT.LNS 33RD BDE:

1 BAT.LN 51ST DIV:

1 BAT.LN 51ST DIV:

2 BAT.LNS 51ST DIV:

CANAL DE L'YSER......
OLD BATTLE LINE ......
BLACK LINE
RIVER STEENBECK......
PRESENT FRONT

NOTE:—
ALL POSITIONS SHOWN ARE MERELY APPROXIMATE. EXACT DISPOSITIONS WILL DEPEND ON THE CIRCUMSTANCES AT THE TIME.

SECRET.

Scheme A.

1ST DIV: DIAGRAM Nº 17: Z + 2 DAY (AFTER RELIEF)

```
                2000'           3500'              1500'                 500'
---                                                                                       3BAT 4TH 5TH DIV:
                                                                                                                    ........ HINDENBURG RD
                                                                                                                    LANGEMARCK RD
                                                                                          1BAT 4TH 5TH DIV:
                                                                                                                    ........ R. STEENBEEK


                                                 1BAT 5TH DIV:
                                                                                                                    BRICK LINE
                                                                                                                    OLD BRITISH FRONT LINE

         □ SLEEP/AMP
         3BAT 4TH
         33RD BDE:
 □ DUTY
 BUCKET (AMP)
 3BAT 4TH 32 BDE:                                 1BAT 4TH 32ND BDE:    1BAT 4TH 33RD BDE:
                                        FARM
                                        COVER □                                                                     NEW BRITISH FRONT LINE
```

NOTE.-
34TH BDE. SCHOOL CAMP
ST JANSTER BIEZEN.

- NOTE -
ALL POSITIONS SHOWN ARE MERELY
APPROXIMATE. EXACT DISPOSITIONS
WILL DEPEND ON THE CIRCUMSTANCES
AT THE TIME.

SECRET.

DISPOSITIONS OF 33RD INFANTRY BDE AT 8 A.M.

AUG ST 20TH 1917.

XVIII Corps

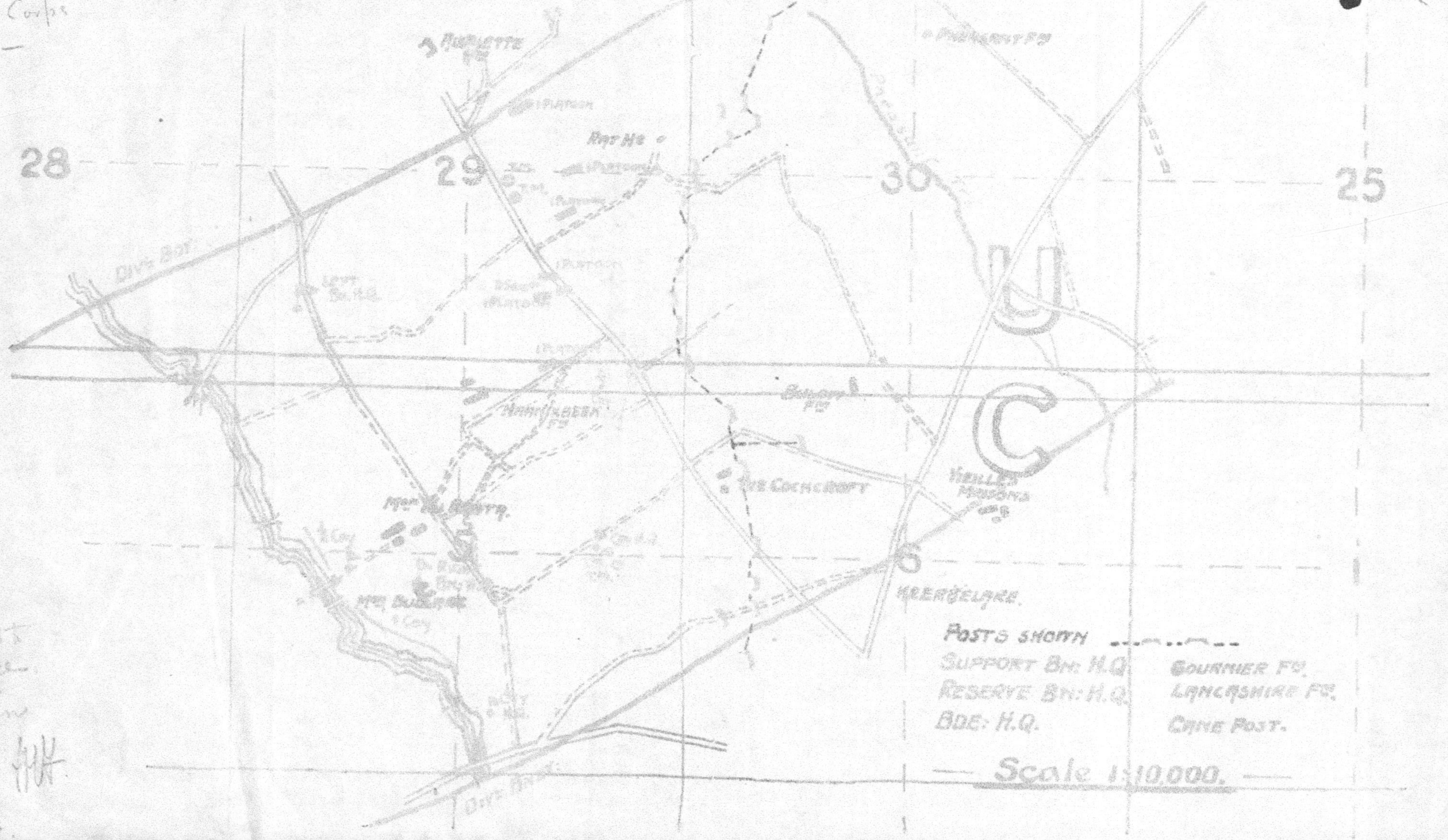

IA.

==========
S E C R E T.
==========

XVIII Corps.

11th. Division No. G.S, 394.

> XVIII CORPS.
> "O."
> No. 9566/94
> Date 22.8.17

Herewith map showing dispositions of 33rd. Brigade at 6 p.m. on 19th. August 1917.

18th. August 1917.

Major General,
Commanding 11th. Division.

POELCAPPELLE

EDITION I.

1:10,000

TRENCHES CORRECTED FROM INFORMATION RECEIVED UP TO 3.8.17.

Disposition of 33 Bde: 6pm 19th Aug.

Support Batt^n
Bn.H.Q^rs Gournier F^m
1 Coy. - C.9d.65 - C.10c.55.
1 Coy. - C.9d.95,80 - C.10c.39.
1 Coy. - C.9b.43 - C.9b.47.
1 Coy at (Gnr R^v) - C.9a.75,99.

Reserve Batt^n
Bn: H.Q. Lancashire F^m
Bn: located in old British & German Front Line in C.4&C.15.

L.T.M.B.
2 Guns U.29 Central.
2 Guns moving to-night to Mon Bulgare for purpose of bombarding Mon D'Hibou. Position will be notified later.

MACHINE GUN BARRAGE
16 GUNS

7TH S. STAFFS

1 Coy 1 Coy 1 Coy 1 Coy 1 Coy

NOTE: Towns shown Green are in defensive positions.

S E C R E T   11th Division No. G.S.470.

XVIII Corps.
51st Division.
58th Division.
48th Division.

Herewith Map showing dispositions of

33rd Brigade.

Please acknowledge.

23rd August, 1917.

Major General,
Commanding 11th Division.

SECRET.

11th. Division No. G.S. 483.

32nd. Inf. Bde.
33rd. "   "
C.R.A.
XVIII Corps.
XVIII Corps H.A.
38th. Division.
48th. Division.

XVIII CORPS.
"O."
No. GS66/103
Date 26.8.17

1. The XVIII Corps H.A. have been asked to bombard the following enemy strong points and suspected M.G. emplacements to-morrow 26th. inst. between 8 a.m. and 8 p.m.

   1. FLORA COT.
   2. Selected strong points in PHEASANT TRENCH.
   3. Strong points in KANGAROO TRENCH at U.30.b.70.95 - U.24.d.8.0 and U.24.d.60.15.
   4. Suspected M.G. emplacements at U.30.b.48.95, U.24.d.3.4 and U.24.d.2.3.
   5. PHEASANT FARM.
   6. Huts at U.24.c.95.00 and U.24.c.72.00.
   7. WHITE HOUSE.

2. The posts held by the 11th. Division at U.30.a.3.7, U.30.a.4.8, U.30.a.6.9 will be withdrawn during the night 25th/26th. and the positions re-occupied after the bombardment, on the night 26th/27th., with the exception of the post at U.30.a.6.9 which will not be re-occupied till after Zero, as the Barrage will pass through this point.

3. ACKNOWLEDGE.

J. B. Coleridge
Lieut.Colonel,
General Staff, 11th. Division.

25th. August 1917.

WAR DIARY.

WEEKLY OPERATION REPORTS.

APPENDIX 5.

War Diary

11th. Division No.G.A. 231.

11th. Division Weekly Operation Report

For period 10 a.m. 8th. August to noon 10th. August.

1. GENERAL.

The general policy of the Division has been :-

(a) To reconnoitre the strength and dispositions of the enemy.

(b) To advance the line of posts beyond the STEENBEEK so as to allow room for an attacking Brigade to form up across the STEENBEEK and attack the LANGEMARCK LINE.

(c) To prepare for an attack on the LANGEMARCK LINE by the making of roads and tracks for a concentration, the formation of dumps etc.

The enemy attitude has been passive on this sector during this period. Enemy patrols have advanced towards our posts, but have never taken the offensive when discovered.

No prisoners have been taken ; one officer is missing, apparently having missed his way when visiting posts, and fallen into enemy hands.

2. OPERATIONS.

8th. inst. (a) Infantry. Confined to patrolling.

(b) Artillery. The artillery under Divisional Command fired 14,888 rounds during the last 24 hours (including 255 gas shells). The COCKCROFT, BULOW FARM, RAT HOUSE, Buildings at C.5.a. & b. and 29.d. and road in this area were bombarded; open spaces in the same area were sprinkled with shrapnel and H.E.

9th. inst. (a) Infantry. NIL.

(b) Artillery. The Artillery under Divisional Command fired 7,680 rounds during the past 24 hours including 125 gas and Lachrymatory shells.
The targets were those indicated in the Summary dated 8th. Ground observation was maintained during the day. One N.F. target was fired on in response to aerial call.

10th.inst. The line of posts was advanced during the night to include MAISON BULGARE and MAISON DU RASTA. No further details are yet to hand.

3. MACHINE GUNS. in the Divisional Sector were employed in indirect fire at nights. Enemy machine gun fire was light and principally from the left of the Divisional Sector.

4. There was no Trench Mortar activity on either side.

5. PATROLS.
8th/9th. A patrol from Right Battalion reconnoitred MON DU RASTA and found three farm buildings. These were brick buildings reinforced with concrete inside and had been knocked about. The buildings on the further side were in ruins. The first building was found to be unoccupied. The patrols returned before entering the other two owing to shell fire. The ground between MON DU RASTA and the STEENBEEK was found to be swampy.

/ 9th/10th......

9th/10th.
Patrols found MAISON BULGARE and MAISON DU RASTA unoccupied. An enemy post was located 50 yards East of MAISON BULGARE. Wire which was partly cut, was found at C.5.a.3.5. No enemy patrols were seen but white Very lights were fired from trees at U.29.c.1.2 and C.5.a.5.9.

7. AIRCRAFT.
Enemy aircraft have on four occasions flown over our forward area. Once in a formation.
Our Vickers and Lewis Guns fire has made them return on two occasions.

8. No reliefs of Battalions have taken place since the line was taken over.

9. WORK DONE BY R.E.

(i) Duck-board Tracks.
 (a) Via CANE AVENUE which has been cleared out and on up to FRANCOIS FARM.

 (b) HURST PARK - REGINA CROSS following the line of Tramway. This is complete up to about C.10.d.2.8.

(ii) Roads.
 (a) KEMPTON PARK - GOURNIER FARM ROAD, this is passable for guns up to C.9.d.0.3.

 (b) KEMPTON PARK - HURST PARK, passable for guns about as far as ENGLISH TREES.

(iii) Dugouts. Parties employed in cleaning out dugouts in CANE TRENCH, CANISTER TRENCH and CANNON TRENCH.

10. CASUALTIES.

Noon 7/8/17 to noon 9/8/17.

Killed.		Wounded.		Missing.	
O.	O.R.	O.	O.R.	O.	O.R.
-	6	2	57	1	-

Captain.
General Staff, 11th. Division.

SECRET.   11th. Division No. G.S. 364.

11th. Division Weekly Operation Report

For Period 10 a.m. 11th. August to 8 a.m. 16th. August.

1. GENERAL.

   The general policy of the Division has been
   - (a) Location of enemy posts etc.,
   - (b) Advancing our posts so as to obtain room on the North-east of the STEENBEEK for forming up.
   - (c) Establishing forward Brigade Dumps.
   - (d) Improvement of roads etc. in forward Area.

2. OPERATIONS. Infantry.

   10th. In conjunction with the 59th. Inf. Bde. on our left the posts of our left Battalions were advanced at 4.15 a.m. under cover of a barrage.
   The intention was to establish posts on a line approximately C.5.a.35.55 - A.3.7 - U.29.c.20.25 - C.10.3.5 - U.28.d.90.45 - d.75.55., but on account of strong resistance on the left and enfilade fire from "Knoll 12", the final line ran almost straight C.5.a.4.4 to U.28.d.4.3.

   11th. The two Battalions in the line (9th.W.Yorkshire Regt. and 8th. Duke of Wellington Regt) were relieved by the 6th. York and Lancs. Regt. and the 6th. Yorkshire Regt. respectively on right and left.

   12th. In order to enable our heavy artillery to fire during the following day at the dugouts in U.29.c. the posts of our left battalion were withdrawn before dawn to a position 300 yards to the rear.
   An attack by the enemy at 1.15 a.m. on our post at C.5.d.1.3 was temporarily successful, but he was immediately counter attacked and driven off, suffering several casualties.

   13th. At 4 a.m. in conjunction with the 59th. Inf. Bde. on our left the posts of our left battalion were again advanced, the intention being to pass the posts they had occupied on the 12th. and go forward to the objective attempted on the 11th.
   Several platoons were, however, met by strong resistance from the block-houses at U.29.c.08.33 and C.5.a.25.75, and suffered severe casualties.
   While these platoons were digging in the remainder pushed on and losing touch, were partially surrounded by the enemy, They suffered such heavy casualties, that they were driven back.
   The final positions of the posts were approximately on the line C.5.a.3.4 - C.5.a.1.6 - U.28.d.5.3.

   14th.   Nil.

   15th. The 34th. Brigade moved to positions of assembly for attack on morning of 16th.

   Artillery.

   11th. The artillery under Divisional Command fired 15,412 rds. during the last 24 hours including 150 lethal and lachrymatory shells. The targets were WHITE HOUSE, RAT HOUSE, BULOW FM, the COCKCROFT, HAANEBEEK FM, and the dugouts and tracks in this area.

   12th. The Artillery under Divisional Command fired 8,929 rounds during the last 24 hours, including 250 gas and lachrymatory shells, and replied to 4 zone calls. The targets were RAT HOUSE, BULOW FARM, the COCKCROFT, House C.5.a.6.5, Dump C.6.b.18.49 and the roads in that area.

/13th...

- 2 -

13th. Divisional Artillery fired 9362 rounds during the past 24 hours including 2 N.F. calls. Targets were those given for the 12th., with the addition of the bank of the STROOMBEEK.

14th. 23,108 rounds were fired including 4 N.F. calls.
The targets were those as for the 13th., with the addition of the wire in front of PHEASANT TRENCH.

15th. 11,249 rounds were fired during the past 24 hours, including 8649 rounds for practice barrage, at HAANIXBEEK FM, RAT HOUSE, the COCKCROFT. Dump U.30.d.54.61, Dugouts U.30.d. 63.53, C.6.a.25.40, C.6.a.55.57, C.6.a.2.7, gun pit C.5.a.66.59 and tracks and roads in this area.

16th. The Artillery under Divisional Command fired 60,533 rounds.

3. MACHINE GUNS.
The 32nd. M.G. Company has been holding the line with 10 guns in support of Infantry and 6 guns in reserve at Coy. H.Q. CANE AVENUE. Very little indirect firing was carried out owing to the movement of large numbers of working and carrying parties in front of the guns.

4. LIGHT TRENCH MORTARS.
88 rounds were fired during the period. The chief targets were U.29.c.75.32 and C.5.a.28.82.

5. PATROLS. Patrols were sent out on the nights 7th/8th. 12th/13th. and 13th/14th.
A considerable amount of information was received about dugouts etc., in "No man's Land", and several enemy posts were encountered.

6. AIRCRAFT.
Both ours and the enemy's have been very active. Our reconnaissance machines making several flights low down over enemy trenches, in spite of hostile fire.

7. RELIEFS. The 32nd. Brigade was relieved by the 34th. Brigade in the line on 14th/15th. August.

8. WORK DONE BY R.E. & PIONEER BATTALION.
(i) Duck-board Tracks.
  (a) Via CANE AVENUE which has been cut and completed up to FRANCOIS FM.
  (b) From HURST PARK and completed to road South of FERDINAND FARM about C.4.d.8.3.
(ii) Roads and Tracks.
  (a) KEMPTON PARK - GOURNIER FARM completed and made passable for guns.
  (b) KEMPTON PARK - HURST PARK completed and made passable for guns. This road has been continued towards BOCHCASTEL along the CANNON TRENCH and is passable for about 150 yards beyond.
Work commenced at Zero plus 2 hours on carrying forward roads and tracks. Little progress made owing to heavy shell fire.
(iii) Dug-outs. Parties employed on cleaning out dugouts and in CANE TRENCH, CANNISTER TRENCH and CANNON TRENCH.

9. CASUALTIES. Noon 9/8/17 to Noon 15/8/17.

Killed.		Wounded.		Missing.	
O.	O.R.	O.	O.R.	O.	O.R.
1	71	17	303		69

E.Westcott Lieut
for. Captain,

General Staff, 11th. Division.

11th. Division No. G.S. 473.

11th. DIVISION WEEKLY OPERATION REPORT

From 8 a.m. 17/8/17 to 8 a.m. 24/8/17.

(In continuation of G.S. 377 dated 17/8/17).

1. GENERAL.

Our operations during the week have resulted in an advance to two successive lines of posts, whose positions were principally determined by the necessity of guarding the flank of the Division on our left, without leaving our own right flank exposed, through the fact that the Division on the right did not on either occasion reach its objectives.

The enemy's resistance on the Divisional front has not been serious; prisoners captured stated that their orders were to hold a line of posts in shell-holes, and if attacked retire to the LANGEMARCK Line. It may be expected that his resistance will stiffen when this line is approached.

The enemy defence has been based on the strength of a number of concrete structures, placed checkerwise and designed to break the unity of our attack. In the attack of the 19th. and 22nd. one or more of these structures were isolated by fire and attacked by Infantry in conjunction with Tanks; this method appears successful, but has not been tried on a larger scale by this Division, and is moreover entirely dependant on the state of the ground.

2. OPERATIONS.

August 17th. The day August 17th. was spent in consolidation of the positions gained on the previous day. During the night 17th/18th. the 33rd. Infantry Brigade relieved the 34th. Infantry Brigade in the line.

Before the relief the line was advanced about 150 yards, RAT HOUSE being taken and a post established just S. of WHITE HOUSE.

The 9th. Sherwood Foresters relieved the 5th. Dorsets and 9th. Lancs. Fusiliers in the left sub-sector and the 7th. S. Staffs. Regt. relieved the 11th. Manchester Regt. and the 8th. Northd. Fusiliers in the right sub-sector on the line U.30.b.6.8. - U.30.b.0.4 - U.29.d.9.5.

The 6th. Border Regt. was in support and the 6th. Lincoln Regt. (in the old British and German front line) in Reserve.

During the night patrols established that the enemy held the COCKCROFT and posts in front of the LANGEMARCK - WINNIPEG ROAD.

August 18th. The line gained was consolidated. Systematic sniping was carried out and the enemy rifle fire was silenced.

August 19th. In conjunction with the Division on our right, at 9.30 a.m. the line was advanced by the 7th. S. Staffs. who constructed posts in a line U.30.c.0.2. U.6.a.2.7. C.6.a.50.85. C.6.a.2.4, C.6.a.50.05 - C.6.c.3.9, C.6.c.50.75, C.6.c.25.55., and captured the COCKCROFT. There was no serious resistance, and casualties were very slight. The Tanks allotted to the Division did not reach their objective, but unquestionably had great moral effect on the enemy.

Patrols again located enemy posts.

/August 20th....

August 20th. There were no Infantry operations today.
During the night 20th/21st. the enemy rushed our post at U.30.a.60.90 inflicting some casualties. The post was immediately re-established and strengthened.

August 21st. Infantry operations were confined to patrols. BULOW FARM was found to be occupied and working parties were discovered by our patrols.

August 22nd. At 4.15 a.m. we attacked and captured the GREEN LINE and established ourselves E. of BULOW FARM on a line U.30.a.2.5, U.30.a.4.1, U.30.c.6.6, U.30.d.05.00, U.6.b.08.40.

The enemy offered no resistance; our casualties were slight. 7 Prisoners and two M.G's were taken. A number of the enemy were killed by our barrage. About 6 p.m. a party of 80 enemy who were relieving on the front of the Division on our right were dispersed by our fire. Many were killed or wounded.

August 23rd, and night Aug.23rd/24th.

Operations were confined to patrolling and consolidation of the posts gained. About 2 a.m. 23rd. a party of enemy tried to rush our advanced post in front of WHITE HOUSE, but were dispersed by our Lewis Gun fire.

3. ARTILLERY.
(a) Our Own. Our 18-pdrs. continued their harassing fire on enemy communications, tracks and roads. 4.5" and 6" Hows. bombarded enemy Strong Points, Houses, M.G. emplacements and trenches. Harassing fire was carried out between the front and support lines of the LANGEMARCK - GHELUVELT Line and also along all tracks as far as POELCAPPELLE. The LEKKERBOTERBEEK Valley, and the KANGAROO AVENUE, ROSE STREET Area received special attention.

4.5" and 6" Howitzers bombarded all trenches in the Divisional area as far back as a line V.19 central - V.26.a.0.0. Our Hows. were used to knock the covering or camouflage off suspected concrete dugouts. If these were found to be strong, Hows. of heavier calibre engaged these targets. Organised shell-holes and weak dugouts were dealt with by 4.5" Howitzers.

On the 19th. our Infantry advanced their posts in co-operation with the Tanks.

A smoke barrage was put down on the high ground near PHEASANT FARM, ROSE HOUSE, and along the line as far as VIEILLES MAISONS.

(b) Enemy Artillery. P.T.O.

4. MACHINE GUNS. (a) Our Own.
Aug.17-19th.

Eight guns of the 34th. M.G. Company in defensive positions in the line, 16 guns of 33rd. M.G. Company in barrage positions to fire an S.O.S. 33rd. M.G. Company moved to MURAT CAMP.

Aug.20th. The 32nd. M.G. Company relieved the 34th. M.G. Coy. and half 33rd. M.G. Coy. 34th. M.G. Coy. returned to SIEGE CAMP and the eight guns of 33rd.M.G. Company to the CANAL BANK.

/Aug. 21st...

Aug. 21st.   Six guns of the 32nd. M.G. Company in defensive positions East of the STEENBEEK, eight in barrage positions West of it with eight of 33rd. M.G. Company.

Aug. 22nd.   16 guns in barrage positions fired a barrage.

(b) Enemy M.G's.
Enemy machine guns have been located at a number of concrete emplacements and have been successively silenced by our artillery.

5. **LIGHT TRENCH MORTARS.**   NIL.

6. **PATROLS.**
Patrols were sent out each night and succeeded in discovering the enemy occupation of strong points, as mentioned in para. 2. It was the intention to occupy such tactical points of importance as were not held, or were lightly held by the enemy.

No enemy patrols were encountered.

7. **AIRCRAFT.**
The week has been one of considerable activity in aircraft. Enemy aeroplanes have flown low over our front lines on several occasions, firing on our posts. Registration by artillery targets has been done by enemy aircraft, who signalled by dropping Very lights in the daytime and by lamp signals at night.

On the whole our aircraft have been more in evidence over the front line than the enemy's machines.

8. **MOVEMENTS & RELIEFS.**
On night 17th/18th. 33rd. Brigade relieved 34th. Brigade in the line.
On night 19th/20th. 6th. Lincoln Regt. relieved 7th. S. Staffs. Regt. in the right Sector, the 7th. S. Staffs. being in Brigade Reserve.
On night 20th/21st. Border Regt. relieved 9th. Sherwood Foresters in left Sector, the latter becoming Brigade Support.

10. **CASUALTIES.**

	KILLED.		WOUNDED.		MISSING.	
	O.	O.R.	O.	O.R.	O.	O.R.
	3	44	17	341	-	-

* (b) Enemy Artillery.
On the 22nd. the Artillery put down a heavy barrage to assist the Infantry in advancing their posts. This was successfully done. From noon 21st. - 4 a.m. 22nd. the enemy concentrated on our batteries causing many casualties and a great deal of damage. This was the heaviest fire the enemy has brought to bear on our batteries since operations in this sector commenced.

a c T White. Capt. for. Major Genl.
Commanding 11th. Divn.

SECRET.   11th. Division No. G.S. 579.

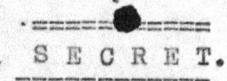

11th. DIVISION WEEKLY OPERATION REPORT.

From 8 a.m. August 24th. to 8 a.m. August 31st.

(In continuation of G.S. 473 dated 24/8/17.)

1. GENERAL.

The following operations have taken place during the past week :-

(1)   Active reconnaissance of the enemy's positions by night patrols.
(2)   Extension of accommodation for attacking troops in shell holes, posts and dugouts to facilitate "jumping-off".
(3)   An attack on PHEASANT TRENCH, VIEILLES MAISONS, and FLORA COTTAGE.

As regards (1), the enemy's dispositions and method of holding the line were established. Fortified shell holes were found about 20 yards apart and some 25 yards in front of PHEASANT TRENCH, these, PHEASANT TRENCH and VIEILLES MAISONS were found to be held.

As regards (2), this was completed by the 33rd. Brigade by the night 26th/27th. August.

The attack was carried out by the 32nd. Brigade on August 27th. VIEILLES MAISONS were captured but PHEASANT TRENCH was only reached by isolated parties.

The heavy rain for 24 hours before the attack and the already sodden nature of the ground hampered the advance. The fact that the enemy's concrete emplacements were not sufficiently destroyed by our shell fire enabled his machine guns to harass the attacking troops without interruption during operations. As a result, the assault on PHEASANT TRENCH did not succeed. The line was re-organised on the 28th. and was handed over to the 51st. Division on August 30th.

2. OPERATIONS.

August 24th.   Nil.   During the night 24th/25th. patrols were sent out -
(a)   To find out whether VIEILLES MAISONS and PHEASANT TRENCH were held by the enemy.
(b)   to occupy any points of tactical importance vacated or lightly held by the enemy.

(i)   Patrol from U.30.a.5.7 found the ground round the LEKKERBOTERBEEK broken; single strands of wire were seen in front of PHEASANT TRENCH and 20 to 30 of the enemy were seen moving about on the parapet of the trench.

(ii)   Patrol from U.30.a.3.4 found the enemy holding shell-holes and posts about 20 yards in front of the trench and 15 - 20 yards apart.

(iii)   Patrol from U.30.a.2.4 saw movement in PHEASANT TRENCH.

(iv)   A patrol from right battalion was fired at by machine gun from VIEILLES MAISONS.

/August 25th..

- 2 -

August 25th.

A patrol from the left battalion reported ground N. of the LEKKERBOTERBEEK badly cut up by shell fire, and water-logged, making movement difficult.

August 26th.

The weather was extremely wet and windy.

A smoke barrage was put up at 4.40 a.m. from posts at BULOW FARM and C.6.a.85.00, but the strength of the wind spoilt the effect.

During the night August 26th/27th. the 32nd. Infantry Brigade moved up to positions of assembly for attack, dug during the previous two days by the 33rd. Infantry Brigade. The condition of the ground made movement difficult, but the assembly was completed by 3 a.m. The attacking troops (9th. West Yorkshire Regt. on the right and 8th. Duke of Wellington's Regt. plus 1 Coy. 6th. Yorkshire Regt. on the left) were disposed in shell-holes (camouflaged), newly dug posts and in one or two small concrete buildings (BULOW FARM, RAT HOUSE, etc.)

August 27th.

The morning was wet and cloudy, but in order to avoid being seen by low flying enemy aeroplanes, the troops remained hidden, and were unmolested. At 1.55 p.m. the attacking battalions, in conjunction with the Divisions on either flank, assaulted PHEASANT TRENCH, moving straight out of their cover in small columns, and deploying, while the artillery barrage rested on PHEASANT TRENCH.

At several points on the Divisional front, isolated parties reached PHEASANT TRENCH, one platoon went on to its objective, and began to dig in about U.30.a.75.75.

Throughout the advance our troops suffered heavy casualties from Rifle and M.G. fire. The enemy was in force and fought well, FLORA COT and PHEASANT FARM appearing to be centres of resistance. It also appears that the enemy put up a defensive barrage of indirect M.G. fire.

VIEILLES MAISONS was reached, and the first building captured, and the enemy prevented entrance to the remaining 2 buildings by machine gun and rifle fire.

Within 8 minutes of the opening of our barrage the enemy put up a barrage consisting chiefly of 5.9 H.E. on the LANGEMARCK - WINNIPEG Road and in the area between that and MON BULGAR. There was also a considerable amount of promiscuous shelling in the area forward of the line VARNA FARM - ADAMS FARM, 5.9 and 4.2 Hows. being chiefly responsible. This activity was continued till 10 p.m. and had completely died down by 11 p.m.

The night 27th/28th. was spent in gaining touch between parties in the line, and with Units on the flanks.

August 28th.

Some enemy rifle fire was directed on our posts in the morning but was beaten down by our sniping.

During the night a fresh platoon of the 6th. York & Lancs. Regt. was sent up to take the remaining buildings of VIEILLES MAISONS, but it was found that the enemy had evacuated them under cover of dark.

/August 29th.....

August 29th.

The enemy's artillery fire which had been abnormally low during the 28th. rose to normal again today.

During the night 29th/30th. the 32nd. Infantry Brigade was relieved in the line by the 152nd. Infantry Brigade, relief being completed by 3 a.m.

The line handed over was -

VIEILLES MAISONS (inclusive)
  C.6.b.2.6.
BULOW FARM (inclusive)
  U.30.c.6.8.
  U.30.a.4.6.
  U.30.a.4.8
  U.30.a.1.9.

Posts on our right or left respectively were :-

58th. Division - 7th. London Regt. at C.6.b.5.1.
38th. Division - S.Wales Borderers.at U.24.c.15.15.

August 30th.

At 11 a.m. the command of the Sector passed from G.O.C., 11th. Division to G.O.C., 51st. Division.

3. ARTILLERY.

At 1.55 p.m. on the 27th. the artillery put down a barrage to assist the Infantry in advancing their line.

During the period under review the 18-pdrs. carried out harassing fire on all roads, tracks and trenches between the Langemarck front and support lines, also on the roads and tracks as far back as the S.W. end of POELCAPPELLE. 4.5" Howitzers bombarded enemy machine gun emplacements, and strong points, also assisted the 18-pdrs. in their harassing schemes. They were also used to knock the camouflage off supposed concrete dug-outs, which if found to be made of concrete were taken on by 9.2, 12 inch or 15 inch.Hows.

During this period, 113,910 rounds were fired.

Enemy counter battery work was not so heavy as during the previous week, although on the morning of the 30th. there was a concentration of all calibres up to 11 inch. on our positions near MORTELDJE EST.

At 10 a.m. on the 30th. the command of Artillery on the Divisional front was handed over to the C.RA. 51st. Division.

4. MACHINE GUNS.

August 24th & 25th.

Six guns of the 32nd. M.G. Company held defensive positions East of the STEENBEEK, two were in reserve in CANE Trench. Eight guns of the 32nd. M.G. Company and eight guns of the 33rd. M.G. Company were in barrage positions West of the STEENBEEK ready to put down a protective barrage on receipt of an S.O.S. call.

August 25th. & 26th.

The remaining eight guns of the 33rd. M.G. Company relieved the eight guns of the 32nd. M.G. Company West of the STEENBEEK. 16 guns of the 34th. M.G. Company moved into barrage positions West of the STEENBEEK.

/August 27th......

- 4 -

August 27th.

At 1.55 p.m. the guns of the 33rd. and 34th. M.G. Companies, to assist the attack of the 32nd. Infantry Brigade opened fire for eight minutes on the Blue barrage lines, as in Appendix to 11th. Division Order No. 105, and then lifted back to the Red barrage lines at the rate of 100 yards in eight minutes, and remained there until 3.15 p.m. when they ceased fire.

6.55 p.m. fire was re-opened on Red barrage lines until 7.40 p.m. After 7.40 p.m. guns remained ready to open a protective barrage at once on the same lines on receipt of an S.O.S. About 190,000 rounds were fired during the day. The guns were in telephonic communication with the Company Commanders, and the D.M.G.O. the whole time.

Eight guns of the 32nd. M.G. Company advanced slightly with the Infantry and took up defensive positions as follows :-

      One at   C.5.d.7.9.
      Two at the COCKCROFT.
      One at   U.29.d.90.05.
      One at   U.29.d.8.7.
      Two at   RAT HOUSE.

One gun and team were destroyed by shell-fire while advancing.

August 28th.

At dusk the guns of the 33rd. M.G. Company were withdrawn to MURAT CAMP.

August 29th.

Shortly after dawn the guns of the 34th. M.G. Company were withdrawn to SIEGE CAMP.

Night 29th/30th.

The 32nd. M.G. Company were relieved by the 152 M.G. Company and returned to POPERINGHE.

5. LIGHT TRENCH MORTARS.

The 32nd. L.T.M. Battery assisted the advance on the 27th. by fire on WHITE HOUSE. A detailed account is not yet to hand.

6. AIRCRAFT.

The weather has been unfavourable for aircraft activity during the period under review.

7. RELIEFS. See Table attached.

8. CASUALTIES.

Killed.		Wounded.	
O.	O.R.	O.	O.R.
8	100	14	400
(approx).		(approx).	

J.D. Coleridge Lt. Col.
for Major General,
Commanding 11th. Division.

31st. August 1917.

Date.	Bn. Relieving.	From.	To.	Bn. Relieved.	To.
23rd/24th.	9th.S.Foresters.	Support.	Line.	6th.Lincoln Regt.	Support.
24th/25th.	7th.S.Staffs.Regt.	—do—	—do—	6th.Border Regt.	—do—
25th/26th.	6th.York & Lancs. Regt. 6th.Yorks Regt.	MURAT CAMP.	Support.	8th.Lincoln Regt. 6th.Border Regt.	CANAL BANK.
	9th.W.Yorks Regt. 8th.W.Riding Regt.	CANAL BANK.	MURAT CAMP.		
26th/27th.	9th.W.Yorks Regt. 8th.W.Riding Regt.	MURAT CAMP.	Line.	9th.S.Foresters. 7th.S.Staffs Regt.	MURAT CAMP.
27th/28th.			——N I L——		
29th.	154th.Brigade.	ST.JAN TER BIEZEN.	MURAT CAMP.	33rd. Brigade.	BRAKE CAMP.
29th/30th.	152nd.Brigade.	—do—	Line.	32nd. Brigade.	POPERINGHE.
30th.	153rd.Brigade.	—do—	SIEGE CAMP.	34th. Brigade.	DIRTY BUCKET CAMP.

APPENDIX 1.

LOCATION RETURNS.

S E C R E T.   30/9/17.   11th. Division No. G.S. 921.

11th. DIVISION.

Location of Units at 8 a.m. Oct. 1st. 1917.

```
34th. Inf. Bde. H.Q.,   )
34th. M.G. Coy.         )
9th. Lancs. Fus.        )   DIRTY BUCKET CAMP.
11th. Manchester Regt.  )
```

No. 2 Company Train.   A.28.c.6.6.

OTHERWISE NO CHANGE.

SECRET   11th. Division No. G.S. 884.

Amendment to Location Return dated 28/9/17.

       9th. W. Yorks Regt.   Line. Right Subsector.
       6th. Yorkshire Regt.   In Reserve.
       8th. D. of Wellingtons R. Line. Left Subsector.
       6th. York & Lancs. Regt. In Support.

S E C R E T.   28th. Sept. 1917.   11th. Division No. G.S. 883.

11th. DIVISION.

Location of Units at 8 a.m. Sept. 29th. 1917.

    34th. L.T.M.B.   CANAL BANK.

    67th. Field Company.   B.30.b.3.4.

OTHERWISE NO CHANGE.

27/9/17.   11th. Division No. G.S. 866.

11th. DIVISION.

Location of Units at 8 a.m. 28/9/17.

NO CHANGE.

S E C R E T.   26/9/17.   11th. Division No. G.S. 851.

11th. DIVISION.

Location of Units at 8 a.m. September 27th. 1917.

9th. W. Yorks Regt. H.Q.   CANAL BANK.

8th. Duke of Well. R,H.Q. GOURNIER FARM.

OTHERWISE NO CHANGE.

SECRET.   25th. Sept. 1917.   11th. Division No. G.S.830.

11th. DIVISION.

Location of Units at 8 a.m. Sept. 26th. 1917.

Divisional Headquarters.   BORDER CAMP. A.30.b.2.2.

C.R.E. 11th. Division.   BORDER CAMP.

C.R.A., 11th. Division.   BORDER CAMP.

A.D.M.S., 11th. Division.   BORDER CAMP.

A.P.M., 11th. Division.   BORDER CAMP.

D.A.D.V.S., 11th. Divn.   BORDER CAMP.

35th. Field Ambulance.   MINTY FARM. C.10.c.1.5.

6th. E. Yorks Regt. (Pioneers) H.Q.   GHENT COTTAGES. BRIELEN.

9th. Lancs. Fusiliers.   D.8.c.1.4.

67th. Field Company. R.E.   B.30.b.2.4.
68th.   "   "   CANAL BANK.
86th.   "   "   C.25.a.7.4 (CANAL BANK).

OTHERWISE NO CHANGE.

SECRET.   24/9/1917.   11th. Division No. G.S. 819.

11th. DIVISION.

Location of Units at 8 a.m. September 25th. 1917.

Divisional Headquarters. WORMHOUDT. Moving to BORDER CAMP. A.30.b.2.3.

32nd. Infantry Brigade. HQ. CANE POST. (Sheet 28. C.9.a.6.3.)
  9th. W. Yorkshire Regt.   In support.
  6th. Yorkshire   Regt.   Line. Left Sub-sector.
  8th. W. Riding   Regt.   In Reserve.
  6th. York & Lancs. Regt.   Line. Right Sub-sector.
  32nd. M.G. Company.   FERDINAND FARM.
  32nd. T.M. Battery.   CANAL BANK.

33rd. Infantry Brigade. H.Q.   E.15.c.2.2.
  6th. Lincoln Regt.   E.25.b.6.4.
  6th. Border Regt.   E.27.a.2.1.
  7th. S. Staffs. Regt.   E.26.b.8.9.
  9th. S. Foresters.   E.19.b.1.5.
  33rd. M.G. Company.   E.25.c.0.9.
  33rd. T.M. Battery.   E.26.b.8.5.

34th. Infantry Brigade. H.Q.   D.7.c.5.1.
  8th. Northd. Fusiliers.   D.19.c.7.0.
  9th. Lancs. Fusiliers.   D.8.c.1.4. - Moving to CANAL BANK on 25t
  5th. Dorset Regt.   D.18.c.2.4.
  11th. Manchester Regt.   D.16.c.1.9.
  34th. M.G. Company.   D.15.a.3.5.
  34th. T.M. Battery.   D.30.a.5.5

6th. E. Yorks Regt.(Pioneers)   CANAL BANK. C.19.c.2.3.

C.R.E. 11th. Division.   POPERINGHE. Moving to BORDER CAMP.
  67th. Field Company.   A.28.central.
  68th.   "   "   A.35.a.4.1.
  86th.   "   "   A.28.b.7.0.

C.R.A., 11th. Division.   WORMHOUDT. Moving to BORDER CAMP.
  58th. F.A.B.   B.29.d.80.97.
  59th. "   C.14.c.2.3.
  11th. D.A.C.   B.30.c.8.5.
  11th. D.T.M.O.   B.28.a.2.3.

A.D.M.S., 11th. Division.   WORMHOUDT. Moving to BORDER CAMP.
  33rd. Field Ambulance.   Adv. Dressing Stn. ESSEX FARM. C.19.c.4.1.
  34th.   "   "   D.17.c.8.7.
  35th.   "   "   ESSEX FARM. C.19.c.4.1.

A.P.M., 11th. Division.   WORMHOUDT. Moving to BORDER CAMP.

D.A.D.O.S., 11th. Division.   A.22.d.6.5

11th. Divisional Train. H.Q.   L.4.b.6.3.
  No. 1 Company.   A.31.b.6.4.
  No. 2   "   F.29.c.3.6.
  No. 3   "   F.27.b.9.4.
  No. 4   "   D.17.d.0.0.

11th. Divisional Supply Column. F.21.c.7.6.

D.A.D.V.S., 11th. Division   WORMHOUDT. Moving to BORDER CAMP.
  22nd. Mobile Vet. Section.   A.28.a.8.9.

11th. Divisional Laundry.   A.22.d.6.5 and 40 Rue de Furness,
                                                           POPERINGHE.

SECRET   22nd September, 1917.   11th Div. No. G.S. 795.

11th DIVISION.

LOCATION of Units at 8 a.m. September, 23rd, 1917.

NO . CHANGE.

War Diary

SECRET. 20th. September, 1917. 11th. Division No. G.S.781

11th. DIVISION.

Location of Units at 8 a.m. on 21st. September, 1917.

NO CHANGE.

****

SECRET.   18th. September, 1917.   11th. Division No.G.S.771.

11th. DIVISION.

Location of Units at 8 a.m. 20th. September, 1917.

Divisional Headquarters.	WORMHOUDT.
C.R.A., 11th. Division.	WORMHOUDT.
C.R.E., 11th. Division.	POPERINGHE.
A.D.M.S., 11th. Division.	WORMHOUDT.
A.P.M., 11th. Division.	WORMHOUDT.
D.A.D.V.S., 11th. Division.	WORMHOUDT.

OTHERWISE NO CHANGE.

```
===============
S E C R E T.                    18th September, 1917,    11th Division No G.S
===============                 ------------------                         758.
                                                                    ---------------
```

11th. DIVISION.

Location of Units at 8am September 19th 1917.

```
Div. H.Q.  "G" Branch.  )
           "Q" Branch.  )
                        )
C.R.A.                  )   Moving to WORMHOUDT 19/9/17.
A.D.M.S.                )
A.P.M.                  )
D.A.D.V.S.              )

C.R.E. 11th Division.       Moving to POPERINGHE 19/9/17.

34th Infantry Brigade H.Q. read D.7.c.5.1.
```

OTHERWISE NO CHANGE.

S E C R E T. 17th. September, 1917. 11th. Division No.G.S.749
11th. DIVISION.

Note.
Ref. Sheet 27 *
Ref. Sheet 28 ø

Location of Units at 8 a.m. September 18th., 1917.

Divisional Headquarters.	"G" Branch. D.17.d.0.0.	*
	"Q" Branch. POPERINGHE.	ø
32nd. Infantry Brigade.	H.Q. 6 Rue des POTS. POPERINGHE.	ø
9th. West Yorkshire Regt.	36 Rue des PRETRES	"
6th. Yorkshire Regt.	10 " " "	"
8th. West Riding Regt.	64 Rue des YPRES	"
6th. York & Lancs. Regt.	33 Rue des BRUGES	"
32nd. M.G. Coy.	1 Rue des POTS	"
32nd. L.T.M.B.	1 " " "	"
33rd. Infantry Brigade.	H.Q. E.15.c.2.2.	*
6th. Lincoln Regt.	E.25.b.6.4.	*
6th. Border Regt.	E.27.a.2.1.	*
7th. S. Staffs. Regt.	E.26.b.8.9.	*
9th. Sherwood Foresters.	E.19.b.1.5.	*
33rd. M.G. Coy.	E.25.c.0.9.	*
33rd. L.T.M.B.	E.26.a.2.5.	*
34th. Infantry Brigade.	H.Q. D.7.c.5.7.	*
8th. North'd Fusiliers.	D.19.c.7.0.	*
9th. Lancashire Fusiliers.	D.8.c.1.4.	*
5th. Dorset Regt.	D.18.c.2.4.	*
11th. Manchester Regt.	D.16.c.1.9.	*
34th. M.G. Coy.	D.15.a.3.5.	*
34th. L.T.M.B.	D.20.b.6.3.	*
6th. E. Yorks. Regt. (Pioneers)	CANAL BANK C.19.c.2.3.	ø
C.R.E., 11th. Division.	"X" Camp. A.16.c.2.3.	ø
67th. Field Coy. R.E.	A.28. central.	ø
68th. " " "	A.23.a.4.1.	ø
86th. " " "	A.28.b.7.0.	ø
C.R.A., 11th. Division.	"X" Camp. A.16.c.2.3.	ø
58th. Bde. R.F.A.	B.29.d.80.97.	ø
59th. " "	C.14.c.2.3.	ø
11th. D.A.C.	B.20.c.8.5.	ø
11th. D.T.M.O.	B.28.a.2.3.	ø
A.D.M.S., 11th. Division.	POPERINGHE.	ø
33rd. Field Ambulance.	A.23.c.8.9.	ø
34th. " "	D.17.c.8.7.	*
35th. " "	L'EBBE FARM. F.29.d.5.9.	*
A.P.M., 11th. Division.	POPERINGHE.	ø
D.A.D.O.S., 11th. Division.	A.22.d.6.5.	ø
11th. Divisional Train.	H.Q. L.4.b.6.3.	*
No. 1 Company.	A.21.b.6.4.	ø
No. 2. "	F.29.c.3.6.	*
No. 3. "	F.27.b.9.4.	*
No. 4. "	D.29.d.5.3.	
11th. Divisional Supply Column.	F.21.c.7.6.	*
D.A.D.V.S., 11th. Division.	POPERINGHE.	ø
22nd. Mobile Vet. Section.	A.28.a.8.9.	ø
11th. Divisional Laundry.	A.22.d.6.5. & 40 Rue des FURNES POPERINGHE.	

11th Division No. G.S. 738.

16th September, 1917.

11th Division.

Location of Units at 8 a.m. September, 17th, 1917.

NO CHANGE.

11th Division.   11th Div. No G.S.734.

Location of Units at 8 a.m 16th Sept. 1917.

NO CHANGE.

War Diary

11th Division.   **11th Div. No G S 719.**

14/9/17.

Location of Units at 8 a.m. 15th Sept. 1917.
===

NO CHANGE.

War Diaries

11th Division No. G.S. 711.

11th DIVISION.

Location of Units at 8 a.m. September 14th.

NO CHANGE.

War Diary

SECRET   12th September, 1917.   11th Div. No. 696.
G.S.

Location of Units at 8 a.m. September 13th.

33rd Infantry Brigade H.Q.	E.15.c.2.2.
6th Lincoln Regt.	E.25.b.6.4.
33rd L.T.M. Battery.	E.26.c.2.5.
No. 3 Coy. Train.	F.27.b.9.4.
No. 4 Coy. Train.	D.29.d.5.3.

OTHERWISE NO CHANGE.

11th DIVISION.

Note.
Ref. Sheet 27 *
Ref. Sheet 28 ∅

Location of Units at 8 a.m. September 12th.

Divisional Headquarters.	"G" Branch. D.17.d.0.0.	*
	"Q" Branch. POPERINGHE	∅
32nd Infantry Brigade.	H.Q. 6 Rue. des POTS, POPERINGHE	∅
9th West Yorkshire Regt.	36 Rue. des PRETRES	"
6th Yorkshire Regt.	10 " " "	"
8th West Riding Regt.	64 Rue des YPRES	"
6th York & Lancs. Regt.	35 Rue des BRUGES	"
32nd M.G. Coy.	1 Rue des POTS	"
32nd L.T.M. Btty.	1 " " "	"
33rd Infantry Brigade.	H.Q. E.21.a.1.0.	*
6th Lincoln Regt.	E.25.b.7.6.	*
6th Border Regt.	E.E.27.a.8.1.	*
7th S. Staffs. Regt.	E.26.b.8.9.	*
8th Sherwood Foresters.	E.19.b.1.5.	*
33rd M.G. Coy.	E.25.c.0.9.	*
33rd L.T.M. Btty.	E.26.c.2.6.	*
34th Infantry Brigade.	H.Q. D.7.c.5.1.	*
8th North'd Fusiliers.	D.19.c.7.0.	*
9th Lancashire Fusiliers.	D.8.c.1.4.	*
5th Dorset Regt.	D.18.c.2.4.	*
11th Manchester Regt.	D.16.c.1.9.	*
34th M.G. Coy.	D.15.a.3.5.	*
34th L.T.M. Btty.	D.20.b.6.3.	*
6th E. Yorks Regt. (Pioneers)	CANAL BANK. C.19.c.2.3.	∅
C.R.E. 11th Division.	"X" Camp. A.16.c.2.3.	∅
67th Field Coy. R.E.	A.28. central.	∅
68th " " "	A.23.a.4.1.	∅
86th " " "	A.28.b.7.0.	∅
C.R.A. 11th Division.	"X" Camp. A.16.c.2.3.	∅
58th Bde. R.F.A.	B.29.d.80.97.	∅
59th " "	C.14.c.2.3.	∅
11th D.A.C.	B.30.c.8.5.	∅
11th D.T.M.O.	B.28.a.8.3.	∅
A.D.M.S. 11th Division.	POPERINGHE.	∅
33rd Field Ambulance.	A.23.c.2.9.	∅
34th " "	D.17.c.8.7.	*
35th " "	L'EBBE FARM. F.29.d.5.9.	*
A.P.M. 11th Division.	POPERINGHE.	∅
D.A.D.O.S. 11th Division.	A.22.d.6.5.	∅
11th Divisional Train.	H.Q. L.4.b.6.3.	*
No. 1 Company.	A.21.b.6.4.	∅
Nos. 2 & 3 Coys.	F.29.c.3.6.	*
No. 4 Coy.	F.27.b.9.4.	*
11th Divisional Supply Column.	F.21.c.7.6.	*
D.A.D.V.S. 11th Division.	POPERINGHE.	∅
22nd Mob. Vet. Section.	A.28.a.8.9.	
11th Divl. Laundry.	A.22.d.6.5. & 40 Rue des FURNES POPERINGHE	∅

S E C R E T   10th September 1917.   11th Division No. G.S. 676

11th DIVISION.   NOTE.
                                       Ref. Sheet 27. *
                                       Ref. Sheet 28 ∅

Location of Units at 8 a.m. September 11th.

Divisional Headquarters	"G" Branch.	WATOU * Moving to D.17.d.0.0 *
	"Q" "	WATOU * Moving to POPERINGHE.

32nd Infantry Brigade.	H.Q.	6th Rue des Pots POPERINGHE.
9th West Yorkshire Regt.		36 Rue des Pretres "
6th Yorkshire Regt.		10 Rue des Pretres "
8th West Riding Regt.		64 Rue des Ypres "
6th York & Lancaster Regt.		33 Rue des Bruges "
32nd M.G. Coy.		1 Rue des Pots "
32nd L.T.M. Btty.		1 Rue des Pots. "

33rd Infantry Brigade.	H.Q.	L.9.b.9.5. * Moving to HOUTKERQUE Area
6th Lincoln Regt.		TAY CAMP L.15.b.6.4 * " "
6th Border Regt.		CLYDE CAMP.L.9.b.6.3 * " "
7th S. Stafford Regt.		ESK CAMP. L.9.b.2.4 * " "
9th Sherwood Foresters.		FORTH CAMP L.15.b.9.1.* " "
33rd Machine Gun Coy.		" " " * " "
33rd L.T.M. Btty.		L.15.b.8.6. * " "

34th Infantry Brigade.	H.Q.	)
8th North'd Fusiliers.		)
9th Lancashire Fusiliers.		)
5th Dorset Regt.		) NOUVEAU MONDE Area.
11th Manchester Regt.		)
34th Machine Gun Coy.		)
34th L.T.M. Btty.		)

6th E. Yorks Regt. (Pioneers)	A.30.a.1.1. ∅

C.R.E. 11th Division.	"X" Camp. A.16.c.2.3 ∅
67th Field Company.	CANAL BANK. ∅
68th " "	ISLY FARM. ∅
86th " "	CANAL BANK. ∅

C.R.A. 11th Division.	WATOU. Moving to "X" Camp. A.16.c.2.3
58th Bde. R.F.A.	B.29.d.80.97. ∅
59th Bde. R.F.A.	C.14.c.2.3. ∅
11th D.A.C.	B.20.c.8.5. ∅
11th D.T.M.B.	B.28.a.2.3.

A.D.M.S. 11th Division.	WATOU. Moving to POPERINGHE.
33rd Field Ambulance.	A.23.c.2.9. ∅
34th " "	L.15.b.8.2. Moving to D.17.c.8.7. *
35th " "	L'EBBE FARM F.29.d.5.9. *

A.P.M. 11th Division.	WATOU. Moving to POPERINGHE.
D.A.D.O.S. 11th Division.	A.22.d.6.5. ∅
11th Divisional Train. H.Q.	L.4.b.6.3. *
No. 1 Company.	A.31.b.6.4. ∅
Nos 2 & 3 Coys.	F.29.c.3.6. *
No. 4 Company.	F.27.b.9.4. *

11th Divisional Supply Column.	F.21.c.7.6. *

D.A.D.V.S. 11th Division.	WATOU. Moving to POPERINGHE.
22nd Mobile Vet. Section.	A.28.a.8.9. ∅

11th Divl. Laundry.	A.22.d.6.5. & 40 Rue des Furnes
	POPERINGHE.

War Diary

SECRET 10th September 1917.   11th Division No. G.S. 670

11th DIVISION.

NOTE.
Ref. Sheet 27. *
Ref. Sheet 28. ∅

Location of Units at 8 a.m. September 11th.

Divisional Headquarters "G" Branch.	WATOU * Moving to D.17.d.0.0 *
"Q" "	WATOU * Moving to POPERINGHE.
32nd Infantry Brigade. H.Q.	6th Rue des Pots. POPERINGHE.
9th West Yorkshire Regt.	36 Rue des Pretres "
6th Yorkshire Regt.	10 Rue des Pretres "
8th West Riding Regt.	64 Rue des Ypres "
6th York & Lancaster Regt.	33 Rue des Bruges "
32nd M.G. Coy.	1 Rue des Pots. "
32nd L.T.M. Btty.	1 Rue des Pots. "
33rd Infantry Brigade. H.Q.	L.9.b.9.5. * Moving to HOUTKERQUE Area
6th Lincoln Regt.	TAY CAMP L.15.b.6.4 * " "
6th Border Regt.	CLYDE CAMP.L.9.b.6.3 * " "
7th S. Stafford Regt.	ESK CAMP. L.9.b.2.4 * " "
9th Sherwood Foresters.	FORTH CAMP L.15.b.9.1.* " "
33rd Machine Gun Coy.	
33rd L.T.M. Btty.	L.15.b.8.6. * " "
34th Infantry Brigade. H.Q.	⎫
8th North'd Fusiliers.	⎬
9th Lancashire Fusiliers.	⎬ Moving to
5th Dorset Regt.	⎬ NOUVEAU MONDE Area.
11th Manchester Regt.	⎬
34th Machine Gun Coy.	⎬
34th L.T.M. Btty.	⎭
6th E. Yorks Regt. (Pioneers)	CANAL BANK C.19.c.2.3.
C.R.E. 11th Division.	"X" Camp. A.16.c.2.3 ∅
67th Field Company.	A.28.central. ∅
68th " "	A.23.a.4.1. ∅
86th " "	A.28.b.7.0. ∅
C.R.A. 11th Division.	WATOU. Moving to "X" Camp. A.16.c.2.3
58th Bde. R.F.A.	B.29.d.80.97. ∅
59th Bde. R.F.A.	C.14.c.2.3. ∅
11th D.A.C.	B.20.c.8.5.
11th D.T.M.B.	B.28.a.2.5.
A.D.M.S. 11th Division.	WATOU. Moving to POPERINGHE.
33rd Field Ambulance.	A.23.c.2.9. ∅
34th " "	L.15.b.8.2. Moving to D.17.c.8.7. *
35th " "	L'EBBE FARM F.29.d.5.9. *
A.P.M. 11th Division.	WATOU. Moving to POPERINGHE.
D.A.D.O.S. 11th Division.	A.22.d.6.5. ∅
11th Divisional Train. H.Q.	L.4.b.6.3. *
No. 1 Company.	A.31.b.6.4. ∅
Nos 2 & 3 Coys.	F.29.c.3.6. *
No. 4 Company.	F.27.b.9.4. *
11th Divisional Supply Column.	F.21.c.7.8. *
D.A.D.V.S. 11th Division.	WATOU. Moving to POPERINGHE.
22nd Mobile Vet. Section.	A.28.a.8.9. ∅
11th Divl. Laundry.	A.22.d.6.5. & 40 Rue des Furnes POPERINGHE.

War Diary

SECRET.   9th. September, 1917.   11th Division No. G.S. 671.

11th. DIVISION.

Location of Units at 8 a.m. September, 1917.

NO CHANGE.

War Diary

8th September, 1917.

11th Division No. G.S.669.

11th Division.

Location of Units at 8 a.m. 9th Sept. 1917.

NO CHANGE.

War Diary

```
==========       ==========================       =========================
S E C R E T       7th September 1917.             11th Div. No. G.S.664
==========       ==========================       =========================
```

11th DIVISION.

Location of Units at 8 a.m. Sept. 8th. 1917

32nd Infantry Brigade. H.Q.	6 Rue des Pots, POPERINGHE.
9th West Yorkshire Regt.	36 Rue des Pretres, "
6th Yorkshire Regt.	10 Rue des Pretres, "
8th West Riding Regt.	64 Rue des Ypres, "
6th York & Lancaster Regt.	33 Rue des Bruges, "
32nd Machine Gun Co.	1 Rue des Pots, "
32nd L.T.M.Bty.	1 Rue des Pots, "
33rd Infantry Brigade H.Q.	L.9.b.9.5.
6th Lincoln Regt.	TAY CAMP L.15.b.4.6.
6th Border Regt.	CLYDE CAMP L.9.b.3.3.
7th S.Staffs Regt.	ESK CAMP L.9.b.2.4.
9th Sherwood Foresters.	FORTH CAMP L.15.b.9.1.
33rd Machine Gun Co.	" " "
33rd L.T.M.Bty.	L.15.b.8.6.
68th Field Co. R.E.	ISLY FARM.
11th Division Laundry.	A.22.d.6.5. & 40 Rue des Furnes POPERINGHE.

Otherwise no change.

War Diary

===========   ===========
S E C R E T   6th Spetember, 1917.   11th Div. No. G.S.655.
===========   ===========

11th Division.

NOTE
Ref. Sheet 27 *
Ref. Sheet 28 ∅

Location of Units at 8 a.m. Sept. 7th.

Divisional Headquarters.   WATOH *

32nd Infantry Brigade.   H.Q.   6 Rue des Pots. POPERINGHE   ∅
  9th W. Yorkshire Regt.   )
  6th Yorkshire Regt.   )
  8th W. Riding Regt.   )   POPERINGHE.   ∅
  6th York & Lancs. Regt.   )
  32nd M.G. Company.   )
  32nd L.T.M. Battery.   )

33rd Infantry Brigade.   H.Q.   L.9.b.8.4.   *
  8th Lincoln Regt.   )
  6th Border Regt.   )
  7th S. Stafford Regt.   )   WATOU Area.   *
  9th Sherwood Foretsres.   )
  33rd M.G. Company.   )
  33rd L.T.M. Battery.   )

34th Infantry Brigade.   H.Q.   L.13. central.   *
  8th North'd Fusiliers.   L.7.d.7.3.   *
  9th Lancs. Fusiliers.   L.8.c.6.6.   *
  5th Dorset Regt.   L.14.b.8.4.   *
  11th Manchester Regt.   L.13.c.4.4.   *
  34th M.G. Company.   K.12.d.7.8.   *
  34th L.T.M. Battery.   L.1.d.4.3.   *

6th E. Yorks Regt. (Pioneers).   A.30.a.1.1.   ∅

C.R.E. 11th Division.
  67th Field Company R.E.   "X" Camp. A.16.c.2.3.   ∅
  68th Field Company R.E.   CANAL BANK.   ∅
  86th Field Company R.E.   B.29.d.8.9.   ∅
                                           CANAL BANK.

C.R.A. 11th Division.   WATOU
  58th F.A.B.   B.29.d.80.97   ∅
  59th F.A.B.   C.14.c.2.3.   ∅
  D.A.C.   B.20.c.8.5.   ∅
  D.T.M.O.   B.28.a.2.3.   ∅

A.D.M.S. 11th Division.   WATOU   *
  33rd Field Amb.   A.23.c.2.9.   ∅
  34th Field Amb.   L.15.b.8.2.   *
  35th Field Amb.   L'EBBE FARM F.29.d.5.9. *

A.P.M. 11th Division.   WATOU.   *

D.A.D.O.S. 11th Division.   A.22.d.6.5.   ∅

11th Divisional Train.   H.Q.   L.4.b.6.3.   *
  No. 1 Company.   A.21.b.6.4.   ∅
  Nos. 2 & 3 Companies.   F.29.c.3.6.   *
  No. 4 Company.   F.27.b.9.4.   *

11th Divisional Supply Column.   E.29.b.5.2.   *

D.A.D.V.S. 11th Division.   WATOU.   *
  22nd Mob. Vet. Section.   A.28.a.8.9.   ∅

War diary

SECRET. 5th. Sept. 1917.   11th Division No.G.S. 646.

11th. DIVISION.

Location of Units at 8 a.m.   6th Sept. 1917.

Divisional Headquarters.   WATOU.

OTHERWISE NO CHANGE.

War Diary

SECRET.

4th. Sept. 1917.   11th. Division No. G.S. 654.

11th. DIVISION.

Location of Units at 8 a.m. 5th. Sept. 1917.

Divisional Headquarters.   Moving to WATOU on 5th. inst.

33rd. Infantry Brigade.   H.Q. L.9.b.8.4.
   6th. Lincoln Regt.   )
   6th. Border Regt.   )
   7th. S. Staffs Regt.   )
   9th. S. Foresters.   )
   33rd. M.G. Company.   ) WATOU Area.
   33rd. T.M. Battery.   )

34th. Infantry Brigade. H.Q.   L.13. central.
   8th. Northd. Fusiliers.   L.7.a.9.6.
   9th. Lancs. Fusiliers.   L.8.c.6.6.
   5th. Dorset Regt.   L.14.b.8.4.
   11th. Manchester Regt.   L.13.c.4.4.
   34th. M.G. Company.   K.12.d.7.8.
   34th. T.M. Battery.   L.1.d.4.3.

59th. Brigade R.F.A.   C.14.c.2.3.

34th. Field Ambulance.   L.15.b.8.2.

11th. Divisional Train. H.Q.   L.4.b.6.3.

OTHERWISE NO CHANGE.

War Diary

SECRET.   3rd. September 1917.   11th. Division No. G.S. 622.

11th. DIVISION.

Location of units at 8 a.m. September 4th. 1917.

Divisional Headquarters.	"X" Camp. A.16.c.2.3.

32nd. Infantry Brigade.   H.Q. 6 Rue des Pots, POPERINGHE.
   9th. W. Yorkshire Regt.   )
   6th. Yorkshire Regt.   )
   8th. W. Riding Regt.   )
   6th. York & Lancs. Regt.   )   POPERINGHE.
   32nd. M.G. Company.   )
   32nd. T.M. Battery   )

33rd. Infantry Brigade.   H.Q.   BRAKE CAMP.
   6th. Lincoln Regt.   )
   6th. Border Regt.   )
   7th. S. Staffs Regt.   )
   9th. S. Foresters.   )   -do-   Moving to WATOU on 4th.inst.
   33rd. M.G. Company.   )
   33rd. T.M. Battery.   )

34th. Infantry Brigade.   H.Q.   DIRTY BUCKET CAMP.
   8th. Northd. Fusiliers.   )
   9th. Lancs. Fusiliers.   )
   5th. Dorset Regt.   )
   11th. Manchester Regt.   )   -do-   Moving to WATOU on 4th.
   34th. M.G. Company.   )
   34th. T.M. Battery.   )

6th. E. Yorks Regt. (Pioneers).   A.30.a.1.1.

C.R.E., 11th. Division.   "X" Camp. A.16.c.2.3.
   67th. Field Company   CANAL BANK.
   68th. "   "   B.29.d.8.9.
   86th. "   "   CANAL BANK.

C.R.A., 11th. Division.   "X" Camp A.16.c.2.3.
   58th. F.A.B.   B.29.d.80.97.
   59th. "   B.28.a.6.1.
   D.A.C.   B.20.c.8.5.
   D.T.M.O.   B.28.a.2.3.

A.D.M.S., 11th. Division.   "X" Camp. A.16.c.2.3.
   33rd. Field Ambulance.   A.23.c.8.9.   Sheet 28.
   34th.   "   "   GWENT FARM. A.28.a.20.65.   " 28
   35th.   "   "   L'EBBE FARM. F.29.d.5.9.   " 27

A.P.M., 11th. Division.   "X" Camp. A.16.c.2.3.

D.A.D.O.S., 11th. Division.   A.22.d.6.5.

11th. Divisional Train,   H.Q.   A.28.c.7.7.
   No. 1 Company.   A.21.b.6.4.
   Nos. 2 and 3 Coys.   F.29.c.3.6.
   No. 4 Company.   F.27.b.9.4.

11th. Divisional Supply Column.   E.29.b.5.2.

D.A.D.V.S., 11th. Division.   "X" Camp. A.16.c.2.3.
   32nd. Mobile Vet. Section.   A.28.a.8.9.

War Diary.

2nd. September 1917.

11th. Division No. G.S. 608.

11th. DIVISION.

Location of Units at 8 a.m. September 3rd.

NO CHANGE.

War Diary

S E C R E T.   1/9/1917.   11th. Division No. G.S. 597.

11th. DIVISION.

Location of Units at 8 a.m. September 2nd. 1917.

```
11th. Divisional Train.  H.Q.   L.4.b.6.3.   Sheet 27.
     No. 1 Company.             A.21.b.6.4.  Sheet 28.
     No. 2 Company.             F.29.c.3.6.  Sheet 27.
     No. 3 Company.             F.29.c.3.6.     "
     No. 4 Company.             B.27.b.9.1.     "

22nd. Mobile Vet. Section.      A.28.a.8.9.  Sheet 28.
```

OTHERWISE NO CHANGE.

APPENDIX 2.

OPERATION ORDERS.

SECRET.   11th. Division No. G.S. 543.

To:- 48th Division

Recd. 8.15am
(29th)

AMENDMENT TO 11th. DIVISION ORDER No.106.

1.   Reference 11th. Division Order No. 106, para. 9.

   Delete lines 3 and 4 and substitute :-

   " 11th. Div. Hd.Qrs. will close at CANAL BANK
   " West (C.19.c.) at 11 a.m. 30th. inst. and
   " re-open at "X" Camp the same hour.

   " 11th. Div. Rear Hd.Qrs. will close at BORDER
   " CAMP at 2 p.m. 29th. inst. and re-open at
   " "X" Camp at the same hour".

2.   Reference Movement Table to accompany 11th. Division

   Order No. 106, Serial No. 8, column 5 :-

   Delete "(2 Battns) and BROWNE CAMP".

3.   ACKNOWLEDGE.

                                                    Major,
28th. August 1917.   General Staff, 11th. Division.

WAR DIARY

S E C R E T.   Copy No. 17

11th Division Order No. 109.

Reference 1/80,000 Map.
Sheet 27 N.E.   9th September, 1917.

1. The 33rd. and 34th. Infantry Brigades will move on September 11th. by road from the WATOU Area to the HOUTKERQUE and LE NOUVEAU MONDE Areas respectively in accordance with attached table.

2. (a) 11th Division H.Q. (less "A" Echelon "G" branch) will move from WATOU to POPERINGHE on the 11th. inst. under orders of the A.A. & Q.M.G. To be clear of WATOU by 3 p.m.

    (b) 11th Division H.Q. ("A" Echelon) will close at WATOU at 3 p.m. 11th. inst and re-open at D.17.d.0.0. at the same hour.

3. A C K N O W L E D G E.

Issued at 3 p.m.

J.M.R. Harrison, Major.,
for A.A.
General Staff, 11th Division.

```
Copy No.  1.  A.D.C. for G.O.C.
          2.  C.R.A.
          3.  C.R.E.
          4.  32nd. Inf. Bde.
          5.  33rd.  "    "   ......(Map attached).
          6.  34th.  "    "   ......(Map attached).
          7.  "Q"
          8.  Signals.
          9.  A.D.M.S.
         10.  A.P.M.
         11.  XVIII Corps "G"
         12.  XVIII Corps "Q"
         13.  Vth. Corps "Q"
         14.  48th. Divn.
         15.  51st. Divn.
         16.  58th. Divn.
    17 & 18.  War Diary.
    19 & 20.  File.
```

TABLE TO ACCOMPANY 11th. DIVISION ORDER No. 189.

Serial No.	Unit.	Date.	From.	To.	Route.	Remarks.
1.	34th. Inf. Bde.	11th. Sept.	WATOU Area.	LE NOUVEAU MONDE Area.	No Restriction.	Tail to be clear of S.E. and S. line through WATOU by 10 a.m.
2.	33rd. Inf. Bde.	11th. Sept.	WATOU Area.	HOUTKERQUE Area.	No Restrictions.	Head not to cross N. and S. line through WATOU before 10 a.m.
3.	34th. Fld. Ambulance.	11th. Sept.	WATOU Area.	D.17.c.8.7.	Under orders of 33rd. Bde.	To move under orders of G.O.C. 33rd. Bde. Comes under orders of G.O.C. 34th. Bde. on arrival at destination.

NOTE. (a) Usual intervals to be kept.
(b) There will be no 10 minutes halts in either WATOU or HOUTKERQUE.

SECRET.   Copy No. 17

11th. Division Order No. 108.   3rd. Sept. 1917.

Reference Maps 1/40,000
   Sheets 27 & 28.

1.   The 33rd. and 34th. Infantry Brigades (with
transport) will move to-morrow, 4th. September, by
march route to WATOU Area, in accordance with the
attached Table.

2.   The 34th. Field Ambulance will march with
and under the orders of G.O.C., 33rd. Infantry Brigade.

3.   Brigades will occupy billeting areas arranged
to-day with Area Commandant, WATOU.

4.   Divisional Headquarters will close at "X" Camp,
A.16.c.2.3, at 12 noon on 5th. September and will
re-open at WATOU at the same hour.

5.   ACKNOWLEDGE.

Issued at 9/1 m   for Lieut. Colonel,
                                   General Staff, 11th. Division.

Copy No. 1 A.D.C. for G.O.C.
         2 C.R.A.
         3 C.R.E.
         4 32nd. Inf. Bde.
         5 33rd. "   "
         6 34th. "   "
         7 "Q"
         8 Signals.
         9 A.D.M.S.
        10 A.P.M.
        11 XVIII Corps "G"
        12 XVIII Corps "Q"
        13 48th. Division.
        14 51st. Division.
        15 58th. Division.
     16-17 War Diary.
     18-19 File.

TABLE TO ACCOMPANY 11th.DIVISION ORDER No. 108.

Serial No.	Unit.	Date.	From.	To.	Route.	Remarks.
1.	34th.Inf.Bde.	4th.Sept.	DIRTY BUCKET CAMP.	WATOU Area.	CHEMIN MILITAIRE — ELVERDINGHE — POPERINGHE Road — SWITCH Road North of POPERINGHE — ST. JAN TER BIEZEN.	Tail of column to be clear of road junction L.4.b.7.3 by 9 a.m.
2.	33rd.Inf.Bde. with 34th Fd. Amb. attached.	4th.Sept.	BRAKE CAMP.	WATOU Area.	CHEMIN MILITAIRE — ELVERDINGHE — POPERINGHE Road — SWITCH Road North of POPERINGHE — L.5.a.3.0.	Tail of column to be clear of POPERINGHE - PROVEN Road by 11 a.m. Not to reach L.5.a.3.0 before 9 a.m.

ADMINISTRATIVE INSTRUCTIONS No. 83.

(Reference to 11th Divn. Order No.109 dated 9/9/17.)

Secret

1. The following Offices will close at WATOU at 3 p.m. 11th instant and will re-open at POPERINGHE at the same hour.

   A & Q. - A.D.M.S. - D.A.D.V.S. - A.P.M. - Camp Commandant.

2. C.R.A. and Signal Coy. Training school will move to X Camp to be clear of WATOU by 3 p.m. 11th instant.

   D.A.D.O.S. and M.V.S. will remain in their present locations.

                                           Lieut. Colonel.
10/9/17.   A.A. & Q.M.G., 11th Division.

A.D.C. for G.O.C.	"G".	V Corps.
C.R.A.	Signals.	48th Division.
C.R.E.	A.D.M.S.	51st Division.
32nd Bde.	A.P.M.	58th Division.
33rd Bde.	XVIII Corps "G".	War Diary.
34th Bde.	XVIII Corps "Q".	File.

SECRET

11th Division No. G.S. 741.

16th September, 1917.

G.O.R.A.
C.R.E.
A.D.M.S.
Signals.
"Q" 11th Div.
XVIII Corps
48th Div.
} for information.

G.O.C.	
G.S.O.1	
G.S.O.2	
G.S.O.3	

11th Division WARNING ORDER.

1. All details of 11th Division Headquarters now at POPERINGHE and "X" Camp, A.I".o.G.S. will move to-morrow the 17th. Instant. to WORMHOUDT.

2. Orders reference move of "A" Echelon D.H.Q. ("Q" Branch) from D.17.d.0.0. will be issued later.

3. WORMHOUDT will not be available until 1 p.m.

4. All details will be clear of POPERINGHE and "X" Camp by 5 p.m.

5. "Q" 11th Division will make all arrangements as to transport.

6. ACKNOWLEDGE.

Lieut-Colonel,
General Staff, 11th Division.

Issued at 12 noon.

SECRET   Copy No. 20

11th Division Order No. 110.

18th September, 1917

1.   All details of 11th Division Headquarters now at POPERINGHE, "X" Camp A.16.c.2.3., and D.17.d.0.0. will move to-morrow 19th instant to WORMHOUDT, except those details for whom special arrangements have been made by A.A. & Q.M.G.

2.   All details will be clear of POPERINGHE and "X" Camp by 3 p.m.

3.   "Q" 11th Division will make all arrangements as to transport.

4.   "G" Branch will close at D.17.d.0.0. at 4 p.m. and Divisional Headquarters will reopen at the same hour at WORMHOUDT.

5.   ACKNOWLEDGE.

Issued at 3-40 p.m.   [signature] Maj for. Lieut-Colonel,
                                                   General Staff. 11th Division.

Copy No. 1.   A.D.C. for G.O.C.
        2.   C.R.A.
        3.   C.R.E.
        4.   32nd Inf. Bde.
        5.   33rd Inf. Bde.
        6.   34th Inf. Bde.
        7.   6th E. Yorks Regt.
        8.   Signals.
        9.   "Q"
        10.   A.D.M.S.
        11.   A.P.M.
        12.   D.A.D.O.S.
        13.   Train.
        14.   XVIII Corps "G"
        15.   XVIII Corps "Q"
        16   18th Division.
        17.   48th Division.
        18.   51st Division.
        19.   58th Division.
    20 & 21. War Diary.
    22 & 23. File.

War Diary

SECRET

11th Division No. G.S. 789.

WARNING ORDER.

21st. Sept. 1917

(Provisional)

1. The 11th Division will probably relieve the 51st Division in the Left Sector of the XVIIIth Corps front on night 24th/25th September.

2. The following is the probable course of events :-

   (a) Morning 24th: Two Battalions of both 33rd and 34th Inf. Brigades will proceed by train to BRIELEN and will remain the day at MURAT CAMP.

   (b) Day 24th: Two Battalions of both 33rd and 34th Inf. Brigades will march to ST JAN TER BIEZEN. (liable to amendment).

   (c) Night 24/25th: Troops mentioned in para 2 (a) will relieve 1 Brigade 51st Division in the Line.

   H.Q. 33rd Inf. Brigade.   CANE POST.

   H.Q. 34th Inf. Brigade.   GOURNIER FARM.

   Details regarding relief will follow.

   (d) Day 25th: Troops mentioned in para 2 (b) will march to SIEGE CAMP.

   (e) Day 25th: 32nd Inf. Brigade will march from POPERINGHE to NOUVEAU MONDE AREA.

   H.Q. D.7.c.5.1.

   (f) Day 25th: Divisional Headquarters to BORDER CAMP.

3. The 33rd and 34th Infantry Brigades will remain in the Line for about 8 days for the purpose of studying local conditions. They will probably be relieved about the 2nd October and will return to their present locations, while the 32nd Brigade moves to ROAD CAMP, ST JAN TER BIEZEN.

4. Details regarding Machine Gun Companies, T.M. Batteries and Administrative matters follow.

5. ACKNOWLEDGE.

J. D. Coleridge
Lieut-Colonel,
General Staff. 11th Division.

Issued at... 6.p.m...

Distribution as under :
COPY			
1	A.D.C. for G.O.C.	7	6th E. Yorks R.
2	C.R.A.	8	Signals
3	C.R.E.	9	"Q"
4	32nd Inf. Bde.	10	A.D.M.S.
5	33rd Inf. Bde.	11	A.P.M.
6	34th Inf. Bde.	12	D.A.D.Q.S.
		13	Train.
14 & 15	War Diary.
16 & 17	File.
18	51st. Division.

War Diary

=========
S E C R E T
=========
11th Division No. G.S. 922.

To _____

Reference 11th Division Order No. 111. dated 22nd September, 1917.

1. One Battalion 34th Brigade referred to in para 2. (e) will not move as therein mentioned, but will remain in their present billets.

2. All references to the move of the above mentioned Battalion are hereby cancelled.

3. ACKNOWLEDGE.

Head Qrs. 11th Division.
24th September, 1917.

J. D. Coleridge
— Lieut-Colonel,
Gen. Staff. 11th Division.

To all recipients of D.O. 111.

SECRET.   Copy No. 21.

                        11th. Division Order No. 111.   22nd. Sept. 1917.

Ref. 1/40,000 Map
Sheet 28.

1.   The 11th. Division will relieve the 51st. Division in the Left Sector of the XVIII Corps front on the night 24th/25th. September.

2. (a)   The 32nd. Infantry Brigade will relieve the 152nd. Infantry Brigade in the line on the night 24th/25th. Sept.

   (b)   Details of relief will be arranged direct between Brigadiers concerned.

   (c)   Command will pass to G.O.C., 32nd. Infantry Brigade on completion of relief.

   (d)   The necessary moves will be carried out in accordance with attached table.

   (e)   One Battalion 34th. Infantry Brigade will proceed by bus on September 25th. to CANAL BANK, there to work under orders of "Q" 11th. Division but, to be tactically under the orders of G.O.C., 32nd. Infantry Brigade. (Details of bus move and move of Battn. transport to be arranged by "Q".

See 11th Div. No. G.S. 922. of 24.9.17.

3.   The C.E., XVIII Corps will issue orders regarding moves, accommodation and work of the Field Coys. R.E. and Pioneer Battalion.

4.   The 32nd. Infantry Brigade will detail an officer, not below the rank of Lieutenant to take over the duties of Forward Area Commandant from an officer of the 51st. Division at GWENT COTTAGES (B.28.b.75.95) on the BRIELEN - ELVERDINGHE ROAD at 8 a.m. on 25th. September.
            The 32nd. Infantry Brigade will also detail one Sergeant, one other N.C.O. and 6 men to report to this officer and come under his orders.

5.   Provisional Order issued under No. G.S. 789 dated 21st. September to Divisional Units is cancelled.
            The 33rd. and 34th. Infantry Brigades will remain in their present areas until further orders.

6.   Units not mentioned in this order will move under orders of the A.A. & Q.M.G.

7.   Divisional Headquarters will close at WORMHOUDT at 9.30 a.m. on 25th. inst. and re-open at BORDER CAMP same hour, at which time, the G.O.C. 11th. Division will assume command of the Left Sector of the Corps Front, and the G.O.C., R.A. 11th. Division will take over command of the Field Artillery covering this Sector.

8.   ACKNOWLEDGE.   J. D. Coleridge Lieut. Colonel,
                                                      General Staff, 11th. Division.
Issued at 7.45 p.m.

For distribution

Distribution.

Copy No.		
1.	A.D.C. for G.O.C.	
2.	32nd. Inf. Bde.	
3.	33rd. " "	
4.	34th. " "	
5.	C.R.A.	
6.	C.R.E.	
7.	"Q"	
8.	A.D.M.S.	
9.	Signals.	
10.	Train.	
11.	A.P.M.	
12.	XVIII Corps "G"	
13.	XVIII Corps "Q"	
14.	XVIII Corps R.A.	
15	18th. Division.	
16.	48th. Division.	
17.	51st. Division.	
18.	58th. Division.	
19.	Area Commdt. WORMHOUDT.	
20.	CANAL BANK Commdt.	
21-22.	War Diary.	
23-24.	File.	

TABLE TO ACCOMPANY 11th.DIVISION ORDER No.111.

Serial No.	Unit.	Date.	From.	To.	Route.	Remarks.
1.	32nd.Inf.Bde.	24th.Sept.	POPERINGHE.	CANAL BANK.	Personnel by Rail. Transport by POPERINGHE - VLAMERTINGHE and VLAMERTINGHE - BRIELEN ROAD.	Entrain POPERINGHE. Detrain BRIELEN. (Details of trains from "Q.") 200 yards between transport of Units. Move to be completed by 10 a.m. Troops on arrival at the CANAL BANK will come under orders of G.O.C., 51st. Division.
2.	32nd. Inf.Bde.	Night 24th/25th. September.	CANAL BANK.	Front Line.	-	Under arrangements to be made direct between Brigadiers concerned.
3.	Brigade 51st. Division.	-do-	Front Line.	SIEGE CAMP.	-	

SECRET   Copy No. 5

11th Division Order No. 118.

1. To assist the advance of the 58th Division, and to repel counter-attacks, four guns of the 32nd M.G. Coy. will barrage the road in D.2. from YORK FARM to WELLINGTON FARM, from positions already constructed about U.29.d.90.45.

2. Times of the barrage, and date and hour of Zero will be notified later.

3. Guns must be in position and all arrangements completed for firing by 12 midnight night of the 25th/26th inst.

4. These four guns will remain in position ready to open fire on their barrage lines on receipt of an S.O.S. call until 8 p.m. on Zero plus 1 day.

5. The remaining guns of the 32nd M.G. Coy. holding defensive positions in the line, will be prepared to take immediate advantage of any targets offered.

6. On the 27th inst. eight guns and teams of the 34th M.G. Coy. will move to the CANAL BANK, and come under the orders of the G.O.C. 32nd Inf. Brigade.

7. Details of move will be arranged by "Q"

8. ACKNOWLEDGE.

Issued at 7 p.m.

Lieut-Colonel,
General Staff.11th Division.

Copy No. 1. 32nd Inf. Bde.
        2. 34th Inf. Bde.
        3. "Q"
     4 & 5. War Diary.
     6 & 7. File.
        8. 33 Bde (for information)

SECRET.

11th. Division No. G.S. 860.

32nd. Inf. Bde.

G.O.C.
G.S.O. 1
G.S.O. 2
G.S.O. 3

Reference this office letter G.S. 809 of 23/9/17, para. 3 (b), the following extract from XVIII Corps Order No. 78 of 26/9/17 is forwarded for information and necessary action :-

"On the night Sept. 28th/29th. 11th. Division will hand over to the 48th. Division that portion of their Div. Sector to the South East of the DOTTED BROWN LINE (VIEILLES MAISONS - South of BAVAROISE HOUSE - thence along LEKKERBOTERBEEK). This DOTTED BROWN LINE will then become the inter-Divisional boundary"

All arrangements for handing over will be made direct by G.O.C., 32nd. Inf. Bde. with G.O.C., 145th. Inf. Bde., and completion reported by wire to 11th. Div. H.Q.

ACKNOWLEDGE.

Lieut. Colonel,
27th. September 1917.   General Staff, 11th. Division.

Copy to 48th. Division
and all recipients of
11th. Div. Instrns. No. 10.

SECRET.   Copy No.......

11th. Division Order No. 113.

28th. Sept. 1917.

Reference PILCKEM & POELCAPPELLE
1/10,000 Special Maps
& Sheet 27 1/20,000.

1. Gas will be discharged on a date and at an hour to be notified later, from 200 Projectors on the Divisional Front, emplaced about U.30.a.5.6.

2. **OBJECTIVES.**
   RETOUR CROSS ROADS & DELTA HOUSE and the road and ground between them.

3. The discharge will be combined with an Artillery bombardment on the same targets.

4. The wind limits will be from W.N.W. through W. to S.E.

5. The personnel of 'Z' Special Company R.E. on receipt of orders from 11th. Division H.Q. will carry out the operation, will proceed at an appropriate time to the projectors and will discharge the gas unless :-

    (i) The wind prove unfavourable at the selected hour.

    (ii) Tactical developements or some other reason make the discharge inadvisable.

6. If Gas is to be discharged, Priority wires will be sent by O.C., 'Z' Special Company R.E. from Left Brigade H.Q. at Zero minus 9 hours to :-

    (1) C.R.A., 11th. Division.

    (2) 33rd. and 34th. Brigade H.Q.

    (3) Divisions on either Flank.

    The following code phrase will be used :-

    "FRESH MEAT NOT AVAILABLE"

7. O.C., 'Z' Company will be at VARNA FARM on the night of the discharge.

8. All troops will be warned and there will be a stringent gas alert after 6 p.m. on night 30th. September, by which time some gas bombs will have been installed.

9. "Q" 11th. Division will arrange for transport of gas apparatus up to a point about U.28.d.9.2 beginning night 29th/30th. September.

/10.......

- 2 -

10. (a) The 32nd. Brigade will supply the necessary carrying parties nightly commencing with the night of 29th/30th.

    (b) Personnel of 'Z' Special Company R.E. will emplace the Projectors and load them.

11. 'Z' Special Coy. R.E., H.Q. is at GODEWAERSVELDE (Sheet 27. R.7.b.1.6).

12. ACKNOWLEDGE.

Issued at..2.p.m...

J. D. Coleridge Lieut.Colonel,
General Staff, 11th. Division.

Copy No. 1 A.D.C. for G.O.C.
     2. O.R.A.
     3. C.R.E.
     4. 32nd. Inf. Bde.
     5. 33rd.   "   "
     6. 34th.   "   "
     7. 6th. E. Yorks Regt.
     8. Signals.
     9. "Q"
    10. A.D.M.S.
    11. Train.
    12. 'Z' Special Coy. R.E.
    13. 4th. Division.
    14. 48th. Division.
    15. XIV Corps.
    16. XVIII Corps.
  17-18. War Diary.
  19-20. File.

SECRET.   Copy No. 19

11th. Division Order No. 114.
                                                          26th. Sept. 1917.

Reference Maps 1/10,000 POELCAPPELLE)
                              POLCKEM.)
              1/40,000 Sheet 28.

1.   The 33rd. and 34th. Brigades will relieve the 32nd. Brigade in the line in accordance with the attached Table.

2.   All details of relief will be arranged between the B.G's C. concerned.

3.   The Artillery, R.E., Pioneers and 32nd. M.G. Coy. will remain in action.

4.   Especial attention is drawn to the "embussing and debussing routine" issued as an Appendix to this order.

5. (a) On completion of relief G.O.C. 34th. Brigade assumes command of the Right Sector, and G.O.C., 33rd. Brigade of the Left Sector.

   (b) Headquarters will be as under :-

        32nd. Brigade.   HOUTKERQUE.

        33rd. Brigade.   VARNA FARM.

        34th. Brigade Advd.   MAISON BULGARE.

         "   "   Rear.   CANE POST.

        Right Artillery Group.   MACDONALD'S FARM.

        Left Artillery Group.   CANE POST.

6.   Administrative instructions will be issued later.

7.   ACKNOWLEDGE.

Issued at 9 a.m.   J. D. Coleridge
                                   Lieut. Colonel,
                              General Staff, 11th. Division.

Copy No. 1 A.D.C. for G.O.C.   Copy No. 11. A.P.M.
        2. C.R.A.   12. XVIII Corps "G"
        3. C.R.E.   13.   "   "   "Q"
        4. 32nd. Inf. Bde.   14.   "   "   R.A.
        5. 33rd. "   "   15. 4th. Division.
        6. 34th. "   "   16. 48th. Division.
        7. "Q".
        8. A.D.M.S.   17. CANAL BANK Cmmdt.
        9. Signals.   18-19 War Diary.
       10. Train.   20-21 File.

Movement Table to accompany 11th. Division Order No. 114.

Serial No.	Unit.	Date.	From.	Via.	To.	Remarks.
1.	33rd. Brigade less 2 Battalions.	Oct. 1st.	HOUTKERQUE.	VLAMERTINGHE.	SIEGE CAMP.	(a) Busses for 1750. Embus at 9 a.m. (b) Route march from VLAMERTINGHE to SIEGE CAMP.
2.	34th. Brigade less 2 Battalions.	Oct. 1st.	NOUVEAU-MONDE Area.	VLAMERTINGHE.	DIRTY BUCKET CAMP.	(a) Busses for 1750. Embus at 9 a.m. (b) Route march from VLAMERTINGHE to DIRTY BUCKET CAMP.
3.	1 Bn. 33rd. Bde. 33rd. M.G. Coy.	Oct. 2nd.	SIEGE CAMP.		CANAL BANK.	To arrive on CANAL BANK at 9.30 a.m. Under orders of G.O.C. 32nd. Brigade.
4.	1 Bn. 34th. Bde. 34th. M.G. Coy.	Oct. 2nd.	DIRTY BUCKET CAMP.		CANAL BANK.	To arrive on CANAL BANK at 10 a.m. Under orders of G.O.C. 32nd. Brigade.
5.	2 Bns. 33rd. Bde.	Oct. 2nd.	HOUTKERQUE.	VLAMERTINGHE.	SIEGE CAMP.	As in Serial No. 1.
6.	2 Bns. 34th. Bde.	Oct. 2nd.	NOUVEAU-MONDE Area.	VLAMERTINGHE.	DIRTY BUCKET CAMP.	As in Serial No. 2.
7.	2 Bns. 32nd. Bde.	Oct. 2nd.	CANAL BANK.	VLAMERTINGHE.	HOUTKERQUE.	(a) To be clear of CANAL BANK by 9.15 a.m. (b) Proceed by route march to VLAMERTINGHE and bivouac there. (c) Proceed in busses used by 33rd. Bde. Bns. to HOUTKERQUE.

- 2 -

Serial No.	Unit.	Date.	From.	Via.	To.	Remarks.
8.	1 Bn. 34th. Bde. 34th. M.G. Coy.	Night 2nd./3rd. Oct.	CANAL BANK.		Line.	Relief of Right Sector of Divnl. Front.
9.	1 Bn. 33rd. Bde. 33rd. M.G. Coy.	Night 2nd./3rd. Oct.	CANAL BANK.		Line.	Relief of Left Sector of Divnl. Front.
10.	1 Bn. 33rd. Bde.	Night 2nd./3rd. Oct.	SIEGE CAMP.		Support positions and CANAL BANK.	Relief of Left Sector of Divnl. Front.
11.	32nd. Brigade less 2 Bns. and 32nd. M.G. Coy.	Night 2nd./3rd. Oct.	Line.	CANAL BANK and VLAMERTINGHE.	HOUTKERQUE.	(a) After relief rest on CANAL BANK until 11 a.m. (b) Proceed by route march to VLAMERTINGHE. (c) Embus at 2.30 p.m. on 3rd. Oct.
12.	32nd. M.G. Coy.	Night 2nd./3rd. Oct.	Line.		To positions to be pointed out by D.M.G.O.	
13.	1 Br. 34th. Bde.	Oct. 3rd.	DIRTY BUCKET CAMP.		CANAL BANK.	To arrive CANAL BANK at 11 a.m.
14.	2 Bns. 34th. Bde.	Oct. 3rd.	DIRTY BUCKET CAMP.		SIEGE CAMP.	

NOTE: Troops of the 33rd. and 34th. Brigades employed on making dumps will rejoin their Units at SIEGE and DIRTY BUCKET CAMPS on completion of their various duties.

APPENDIX TO 11th. DIVISION ORDER No. 114.

EMBUSSING AND DEBUSSING ROUTINE.

1. (a)   Each bus will hold 25 men and personnel will be told off into parties of 25 before arriving at the embussing point.

   (b)   Immediately on arrival at the debussing point, Companies will march off independently as soon as formed up.

   It is most important that there should be no delay in marching off, so that busses can move away from debussing point and thus prevent congestion of traffic.

   (c)   In the forward area at least 200 yards will be maintained between Companies.

   (d)   An Officer of the Army bus Park will call at each Brigade H.Q. on the day previous to the move in order to arrange details.

   (e)   A Staff Officer of the Brigade concerned will be present at the embussing and at the debussing point to superintend arrangements on the spot.

2.   Transport will march on the same day as that on which the unit to which it belongs moves, route ST. JAN TER BIEZEN - SWITCH Road, N. of POPERINGHE and vice versa.

3. (a)   Busses for moving 33rd. Brigade will assemble with head of column at HOUTKERQUE CHURCH.

   (b)   Busses for moving 34th. Brigade will assemble with tail of column just clear of HERZEELE on the HOUTKERQUE - HERZEELE Road.

*****

War Diary

SECRET.

11th. Division Order No. 115.

Copy No. 11

30th. Sept. 1917.

Reference POELCAPPELLE Map 1/10,000

1. At 3 p.m. to-morrow the Heavy Artillery of both XIVth. and XVIII Corps will bombard the following points in front of the Divisional Sector :-

   V.25.d.55.84)
   V.25.d.40.82)
   V.25.d.30.78)

   U.24.d.90.00)
   U.30.b.80.95)
   U.24.d.65.00)
   U.24.d.35.32)
   U.24.d.25.61)

2. The G.O.C., 32nd. Brigade will arrange to withdraw all posts situated within 300 yards of the points to be bombarded on the night 30th.Sept./1st.Oct. The posts will be re-occupied on 1st. October after dark.

3. The D.M.G.O. will arrange for the 32nd. M.G. Company to fire on these points at uncertain intervals during the bombardment.

4. ACKNOWLEDGE.

Issued at 11-0 am

J. D. Coleridge
Lieut. Colonel,
General Staff, 11th. Division.

Copy No. 1 G.O.C.
2. C.R.A.
3. 32nd. Inf. Bde.
4. "Q"
5. D.M.G.O.
6. 48th. Division.
7. 4th. Division.
8. XVIII Corps."Q".
9.   "   "   H.A.
10-11 War Diary.
12-13 File.

11th. Division No. G.S. 940.

To:—............

....

Reference Revised Movement Table issued with

D.O. 114, Serial 17, Columns 6 and 7,

For "CANAL BANK"

read "MURAT Shelters".

ACKNOWLEDGE.

A.J.Bowne,

Major,

1st. October 1917.   General Staff, 11th. Division.

Copies to all recipients of D.O. 114.

War Diary

SECRET. 11th. Division No. G.S. 910.

TO:-.....................

....

Movement Table issued with Divisional Order No. 114 is cancelled, and the attached Table substituted. Please acknowledge receipt.

J.D. Coleridge Lieut. Colonel,
30th. September 1917. General Staff, 11th. Division.

Copies to all recipients of D.O. 114.

MOVEMENT TABLE TO ACCOMPANY 11th. DIVISION ORDER NO 114.

Serial No.	Unit.	Date.	From.	Via.	To.	Remarks.
1.	33rd. Brigade less 2 Bns.	Oct. 1st.	HOUTKERQUE.	VLAMERTINGHE.	SIEGE CAMP.	(a) Busses for 1250. Embus at 9 a.m. (b) Route march from VLAMERTINGHE to SIEGE CAMP.
2.	34th. Brigade less 1 Bn.	Oct. 1st.	NOUVEAU MONDE Area.	VLAMERTINGHE.	DIRTY BUCKET CAMP.	(a) Busses for 1750. Embus at 9 a.m. (b) Route march from VLAMERTINGHE to DIRTY BUCKET CAMP.
3.	1 Coy. 53rd. Bde.	Oct. 2nd.	(a) SIEGE CAMP or (b) CANAL BANK from dump parties.		CANE TRENCH.	To arrive at CANE TRENCH by 8 a.m. and come under orders of G.O.C., 32nd. Brigade.
4.	1 Coy. 34th. Bde.	Oct. 2nd.	(a) DIRTY BUCKET CAMP or (b) CANAL BANK from dump parties.		CANE TRENCH.	As in Serial No. 3.
5.	1 Bn. 33rd. Bde. 33rd. M.G. Coy.	Oct. 2nd.	SIEGE CAMP.		CANAL BANK.	To arrive on CANAL BANK at 9.30 a.m. and to come under orders of G.O.C. 32nd. Brigade.
6.	1 Coy. 33rd. Bde.	Oct. 2nd.	SIEGE CAMP.		MURAT Shelters.	To arrive at MURAT shelters at 9.30 a.m. and to come under orders of G.O.C. 32nd. Brigade.

Serial No.	Unit.	Date.	From.	Via.	To.	Remarks.
7.	1 Bn. 34th. Bde. 34th. M.G. Coy.	Oct. 2nd.	DIRTY BUCKET CAMP.		CANAL BANK.	As in Serial No. 5 but to arrive on CANAL BANK at 10 a.m.
8.	1 Coy, 34th. Bde.	Oct. 2nd.	DIRTY BUCKET CAMP.		MURAT Shelters	As in Serial No. 6 but to arrive at MURAT Shelters at 10 a.m.
9.	2 Bns. 33rd.Bde. less Dump parties.	Oct. 2nd.	HOUTKERQUE.	VLAMERTINGHE.	SIEGE CAMP.	As in Serial No. 1.
10.	2 Bns. 34th. Bde. less Dump parties.	Oct. 2nd.	NOUVEAU MONDE AREA.	VLAMERTINGHE.	DIRTY BUCKET CAMP.	As in Serial No. 2.
11.	2 Bns. 32nd. Bde. less 2 Coys.	Oct. 2nd.	CANAL BANK AND GANT TRENCH.	VLAMERTINGHE.	HOUTKERQUE.	(a) To be clear of C..L BANK by 9.15 a.m. (b) Proceed by route march to VLAM... and bivouac ther... (c) Proceed in bus... by 33rd. Brigade to HOUTKERQUE.
12.	(a) 1 Bn.33rd.Bde. (b) 33rd.M.G.Coy. (c) 1 Coy. 33rd.Bde.	Night Oct. 2nd/3rd.	CANAL BANK AND MURAT Shelters.		Line.	Relief of Left Sector of Divisional Front.
13.	(a) 1 Bn. 34th. Bde. 34th.M.G.Coy. (b) 1 Coy. 34th.Bde.	Night Oct. 2nd/3rd.	CANAL BANK & MURAT Shelters.		Line.	Relief of Right Sector of Divisional Front.
14.	32nd. Brigade less 6 Coys. and 32nd.M.G.Coy.	Night Oct. 2nd/3rd.	Line.	CANAL BANK MURAT Shelters and VLAMERTINGHE.	HOUTKERQUE.	(a) After relief rest on CANAL BANK and MURAT Shelters until 11 a.m. (b) Proceed by route march to VLAMERTINGHE. (c) Embus at 2.30 p.m. Oct. 3rd.

- 3 -

Serial No.	Unit.	Date.	From.	Via.	To.	Remarks.
15.	33nd.M.G.Coy.	Night Oct.2nd/3rd.	Line.		Positions to be pointed out by D.M.G.O.	
16.	1 Bn. 33rd.Bde. less 1 Coy. (or Bn. less 2 Coys. provided Bn. has provided Coy. for Serial No. 3).	Oct.3rd.	SIEGE CAMP.		CANAL BANK.	To arrive on CANAL BANK at 11 a.m.
17.	1 Bn.34th. Bde. less 1 Coy. (or 1 Bn. less 2 Coys. provided that Bn. has provided Coy. for Serial No. 4).	Oct. 3rd.	DIRTY BUCKET CAMP.		CANAL BANK. MURAT Shelters	To arrive on CANAL BANK at 11.30 a.m. MURAT Shelters
18.	2 Bns. 34th.Bde. (less Dump Parties)	Oct. 3rd.	DIRTY BUCKET CAMP.		SIEGE CAMP.	

NOTES: Units of the 33rd. and 34th. Brigades which have been employed on making Dumps, or have been furnishing troops for Serial Nos. 3 and 4, until relieved on Oct. 3rd. under Brigade arrangements (provided men from Dump Parties have been taken for this latter duty) will rejoin their Brigades on completion of these duties.

S E C R E T.   11th. Division No. G.S. 962.

33rd. Inf. Bde.
34th. "   "
C.R.A.
C.R.E.
'Z' Special Coy. R.E.

Ref. Map POELCAPPELLE 1/10,000, Edition. 3.

       Reference 11th. Division Order No. 113.

       If the wind is favourable, gas will be projected against DELTA HOUSE and RETOUR CROSS ROADS, both on the ST.JULIEN - POELCAPPELLE Road in V 19.c. at 9.45 p.m. to-night.

3rd.October 1917.

J. D. Coleridge Lieut.Col.,
General Staff,11th.Division.

Copies to XVIII Corps.
       4th. Division.
       48th. Division.

SECRET. 11th. Division No. G.S. 923.

G.O.C., H.A.

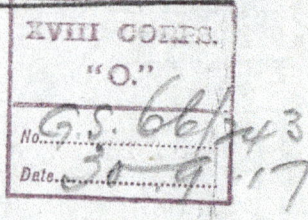

In accordance with XVIII Corps wire G. 628. of 28th. September, herewith list of strong points to be bombarded between now and next attack, please.

U.24.d.25.61.- U.24.d.35.32
U.24.d.65.00- U.30.b.80.95 - U.24.d.90.00.

V.19.b.60.35   Concrete.
V.19.b.38.20   "
V.20.a.35.00   "
V.14.c.15.20   "
V.20.a.05.65   "
V.19.a.62.13   "
V.19.c.8.5   "
V.19.b.5.1   "
V.19.b.60.25   "
V.19.b.45.00   "
V.19.d.35.95   "
V.19.a.7.6 (FERDAN HOUSE)
V.19.b.05.95.

Areas :- Concrete emplacements etc., in area.-

V.20.a.05 - V.20.a.5.8.
V.14.c.1.2 - V.14.c.5.3.
V.19.b.6.7 - V.19.b.9.4.
V.19.b.8.8 - V.20.a.0.5.

Area covered by concrete emplacements between junction of roads at V.19.b.5.1.

TWEED HOUSE.
MEBU at V.19.c.65.10
TERRIER FARM.
Shell holes at V.26.a.10.95.
BEEK HOUSES.
OXFORD HOUSES.
GLOSTER FARM.
Shell holes at V.20.c.8.4.
Shell holes at V.20.c.3.7.

Major,
30th. September 1917. General Staff, 11th. Division.

Copy to XVIII Corps.

SECRET.

APPENDIX 3.

MISCELLANEOUS.

SECRET.

11th. Division No. G.S. 549.

To:-..............

....

CONFERENCE.

1. The G.O.C. will hold a Conference on the 2nd. September during the afternoon (hour to be detailed later).

2. The following will attend :-

    C.R.A. and Staff Officer.

    3 B.G's Commanding Inf. Bdes. and 1 Staff Offr. each.

    A.A. & Q.M.G.

    A.D.M.S.

    C.R.E.

    O.C., Signal Company.

    D.M.G.O.

3. The following points will be discussed :-

    (a) Method of dealing with concrete strong points.

    (b) System of patrolling.

    (c) Are the formations now in use suitable for the present phase of Operations ?

    (d) Are any alterations in the Artillery or M.G. barrages necessary ?
    What should be the pace of their advance in ordinary weather ?

    (e) Is any improvement in means of inter-communication possible ?

    (f) Should any alteration be made in the equipment worn by men in the attack ? Especial attention being given to the following points :-

        (i) Number of bombs, etc. carried.
        (ii) Amount of S.A.A. carried.
        (iii) Carriage of a second water bottle, should it contain tea ?

    (g) The advisibility of having a second 2nd. in Command during operations, one would remain in the Transport lines, and the other would assist the C.O. during the battle.

/(h).....

- 2 -

    (h) Provision of Brigade Burying Parties.

    (i) Programme of Training to be carried out during 3 weeks Division will probably be out of the line.

4.   Commanders should hold Conferences before the 2nd. September and discuss the above points, and any others which may occur, with their subordinate commanders.
    Decisions arrived at will be brought before the Conference on the 2nd. September.

J. D. Coleridge Lieut.Colonel,

29th. August 1917.   General Staff, 11th. Division.

=============
S E C R E T.   11th. Division No. G.S. 624.
=============

C.R.A.
32nd. Inf. Bde.
33rd. "   "
34th. "   "
C.R.E.
"Q"
A.D.M.S.
Signals.
D.M.G.O.

PART I

At a Conference held at 11th. Division H.Q. on 2/9/1917, the following points were discussed :-

1. Method of Dealing with Concrete Strong Points.

2. What modifications should be made in our existing formations and methods in the attack - if any ?

3. Should any alterations be made in existing Artillery and Machine Gun Barrages ?

The decisions arrived at are detailed in the attached notes.

T. D. Coleridge
Lieut. Colonel,
3rd. September 1917.   General Staff, 11th. Division.

NOTES ON THE OPERATIONS.

(A) GENERAL.

The experiences gained during the late operations go to prove that the defensive methods now adopted by the enemy will necessitate modifications in our attack formations and methods.

In the first place the system of waves which we have used with success against lines of trenches, cannot be easily manoeuvred against the present German system of defence.

Secondly the "concrete pill boxes" drive wedges into the advancing lines and break up our formations.

Thirdly, the linear formation is very difficult to maintain in the water-logged, shell-hole pitted terrain over which we are at present operating.

(B) METHOD OF DEALING WITH CONCRETE STRONG POINTS.

1. All concrete strong points located within 200 yards of our front line should be captured before an advance on a large scale is carried out. Once captured, they must be occupied, the garrisons becoming outposts and covering the forming up of the attacking columns.

2. Concrete strong points situated within 200 yards of our front line, being so close, ▆▆▆ it should be possible to know all about them and their exact location. The reduction of each point should therefore, be carried out methodically.

    To begin with, thorough reconnaissance for the purpose of locating the enemy's dispositions and the position of the loopholes in the concrete strong points must be made. This done, the concrete strong points should either be rushed at night without artillery support, or attacked under a barrage. Again, the garrison might be treated to gas shelling combined with shrapnel and smoke on several occasions (which would cause the men to take shelter in the concrete strong point and to put on their gas helmets), and no attack follow. On the occasion of the attack, the shrapnel and smoke shelling would be used but no gas when it would be hoped that the enemy, having been drilled to gas, would take his usual precautions and in consequence be caught at a disadvantage.

    Experience goes to prove, that the garrisons of these concrete strong points are inclined to surrender when the attacking parties begin to work round towards the rear of the buildings. It is suggested, therefore, that platoons detailed for attacks on isolated concrete strong points should converge on the objective with the hope of getting behind them, and that direct attacks should be avoided, machine or Lewis guns should be sufficient to engage loopholes which fire to the front or slightly to a flank.

3. In the event of a large operation being ordered, the position of some of the concrete strong points in the area will be known and some unknown.

    (a) For the capture of the known strong points, special parties must be detailed beforehand, the sole objective of these parties will be the capture and consolidation of the individual strong point for which they have been detailed.

/As to ......

As to the method to be employed for the capture of these strong points during a large operation, it is suggested that the attacking parties should act as described in para. 2 above, i.e., work round the flanks and take the strong point in the rear. In addition, the artillery barrage should be especially thick round the strong points, so as to deal with any machine guns the enemy may attempt to bring out of the shelters. Further, a box barrage might be placed round the strong point, this would admit of the troops on either side of the strong point moving past it, while giving the defenders the impression that the barrage has not yet passed them. The actual attackers of the strong point would remain just outside the "box barrage" ready to rush in directly it lifted.

(b) As before stated, some unknown strong points are certain to occur in the area attacked over; for their reduction parties must be told off previously and kept in hand until called upon to act. No especial barrage can be arranged for such strong points, and the attacking parties must act rapidly under local Commanders as circumstances dictate.

(C) FORMATIONS SUGGESTED FOR LARGE OPERATIONS.

1. One or two lines of widely extended skirmishers who will deal with the garrisons of shell holes, pass by "concrete strong points" and move straight on after the barrage to the objective.

2. Directly behind the skirmishers will come the platoons specially detailed for the reduction of

(a) the known strong points,
(b) the unknown strong points.

3. Following the especial platoons will be the remainder of the attacking troops, who will take no notice of the concrete strong points, but will follow the skirmishers on to the objective.

(NOTE: Nos. 2 and 3 will move in small columns, probably in single file).

(D) FURTHER POINTS.

1. It is considered, that the creeping artillery barrage should move as follows :-

(a) In good weather - 100 yards in 5 or 6 minutes.
(b) In bad weather - 100 yards in 8 minutes.

2. It is considered that better value would be procured from machine gun barrages if fire was concentrated on important points, and not distributed along the front.

3. It was found, that the Division suffered heavy casualties during the time that the men were waiting during the advance for other flanking units to come into line with them. It is recognised, that there must be pauses during an advance, but it is suggested that every effort should be made to ensure that adjoining Divisions be given advances of equal length, and that all halts and fresh starts be made at the same hours.

/4.....

4. The initial barrage falls as a rule, 200 yards in advance of where the Infantry forms up. During the late operations, cases have occurred, when small bodies of the enemy have been hiding within 200 yards of the assembling infantry and hence inside the barrage, and have inflicted losses on the Infantry directly the advance started. One Battalion (5th. Dorsets) dealt with this effectively by sending out Lewis guns in advance of the forming up place - stokes mortars might also be used.

5. In trench to trench attacks, fire action by the advancing Infantry was deprecated, and its one and only duty was to reach the objective on the heels of the barrage. In the new circumstances, which have now arisen, when hostile infantry in small groups may be met with at any moment during an advance, our leading infantry must be constantly ready to use their rifles and bring fire to bear on isolated hostile groups which have escaped the barrage.

6. It is considered that advances should not be too long - e.g. A penetration of 500 yards depth one day, followed by a similar penetration shortly afterwards, is more likely to succeed than an attempt to penetrate 1000 yards on one day.

SECRET.   11th. Division No. G.S. 625.

To:,....................

....

PART II.

The following is the result of a Conference held at 11th. Division H.Q. on 2nd. September 1917, for the discussion of various points :-

4. SYSTEM OF PATROLLING.

It was decided :-

(a)   That reliable reports could not be expected from patrols unless the patrols were commanded by an officer.

(b)   That definite orders as to the objective, time and route of each patrol must be laid down. Patrol reports must be written on a regular form.

(c)   That ordinary patrols should be carried out by companies in the line; but important patrols should be carried out by Regimental Scouts (who should be especially trained) under selected officers.

Brigadiers were requested to give the matter of training Regimental Scouts particular attention.

5. IS ANY IMPROVEMENT IN THE MEANS OF INTERCOMMUNICATION POSSIBLE ?

(a)   It was stated, that the Divisional Intercommunication Scheme, based on S.S. 148 had not given satisfactory results in all cases, and that telephonic communication had been spoilt on numerous occasions by line men interrupting conversations etc. It was pointed out, that the scheme tended to combine the whole of the Divisional resources and means of intercommunication and was in the end saving in personnel and material, and that many of the faults complained of were due to the inexperience of the personnel, which would, it was hoped, be improved by training.

(b)   Brigadiers were requested to draw their Commanding Officers' attention to the numerous methods of communication available, and to impress on them that runners should only be used when other means had failed. During the late operations, practically no use was made of Power Buzzers and wireless, though these were in working order.

(c)   During the operations, signal rockets were not sufficiently used, and O.C., 11th. Signals was directed to organise courses of instruction in the use of Signal rockets during the period the Division is at rest.

(d) The pigeon baskets at present in use are difficult to carry and are conspicuous.
O.C., 11th. Signals was directed to arrange for all pigeon baskets to be painted some dark colour, and fit them up so that pigeon men could carry them on their backs.

(e) The importance of properly caring for pigeons was emphasized.

6. EQUIPMENT TO BE CARRIED - SHOULD ANY ALTERATIONS BE MADE ?

(a) The general impression was that the present arrangements are satisfactory, Brigadiers being at liberty to make minor changes to suit local conditions.

(b) Now the cool weather was approaching, a second water bottle was not considered a vital necessity, if carried the second bottle should contain tea.

(c) The YUKON Pack is considered good for long carrys and when the ground is dry. For short carrys, and when the ground is wet, it is not recommended. Every man carrying a load on a YUKON Pack is to be provided with a stick under Divisional arrangements.

7. EXTRA 2nd. IN COMMAND.
The advisability of having a second 2nd. in Command during operations to assist the Commanding Officer was discussed, and it was left to Brigadiers to appoint one should they deem it necessary.

8. BURYING PARTIES.
Brigadiers were requested to organise Brigade Burying parties while they were in the line, and to impress on all ranks the importance of burying all dead bodies found near the lines, not only for sanitary reasons but for moral also.

9. BATTALION STRETCHER BEARERS etc.

(a) The A.D.M.S. drew attention to the fact, that work done by Battalion Stretcher Bearers varied considerably; some units doing well in this respect and others extremely badly. The G.O.C. requested Brigadiers to give this matter particular attention, and to instruct Commanding Officers to select good men as stretcher bearers and to insist on Battalion Medical Officers exacting the maximum amount of work from these men.

(b) Care should be taken, that the number of wounded reported should not be exaggerated. It is common for the medical authorities to receive frequent reports of many men being wounded. In response, stretcher bearers are sent to clear the places where the wounded are supposed to be and as often as not, no wounded, or very few, are found.

10. TRAINING ETC.

(a) In conclusion, the G.O.C. indicated on an especial map, issued to all concerned, the course operations were likely to take during the next few weeks, and the probable part to be played by the Division. Brigadiers were requested to organise training on the lines indicated.

(b) Night operations are to be practised.

3rd. September 1917.

J. D. Coleridge
Lieut. Colonel,
General Staff, 11th. Division.

War Diary

To:-............   11th. Division No. G.S. 905.

....

Reference 11th. Division Instructions No. 11, Para. 2 (b), co-ordinate V.20.c.10.13 should read V.20.c.10.87.

A C T White Capt for

Lieut. Colonel,
29th. September 1917.   General Staff, 11th. Division.

Copies to all recipients of Instrns. No. 11.

SECRET.   11th. Division No. G.S. 609.

11th. DIVISION INSTRUCTIONS No. 10.

PRELIMINARY INSTRUCTIONS.

GENERAL. 1. By the morning of the 25th. September the 11th. Division will have relieved the 51st. Division in the Left Sector of the XVIIIth. Corps front.

METHOD OF HOLDING THE LINE. 2. The 32nd. Brigade will hold the Line with 1 Battalion of the 34th. Brigade located in the CANAL BANK in Support.
   The front system will be lightly held, and especial bodies of troops will be detailed for immediate counter-attack. The G.O.C. 32nd. Brigade will submit a plan for the defence of the Sector.

FUTURE OPERATIONS. 3. The following is the probable course of future events.

(a) On an early date to be detailed later the Division on our right in conjunction with the Corps on its right will carry out an attack for the purpose of gaining the high ground near AVIATIK FARM. The 11th. Division will not take part in this attack, but there will be a bombardment and a Chinese attack on our front, of which details will be issued to the 32nd. Brigade.

(b) On the day succeeding this attack the Division will probably hand over to the Division on its right that portion of the front which lies between D.1.b.6.3 and U.25.d.2.6.

(c) On a date which has been communicated verbally to all concerned the 34th. Brigade on the right and the 33rd. Brigade on the Left will take over the Divisional front from the 32nd. Brigade preparatory to carrying out the operations discussed at Divisional H.Q. on 23rd. instant.

ROLE OF THE 32nd. BRIGADE. 4. The 32nd. Brigade will assist in preparing for the operations mentioned in para. 1 (c) above as follows:-

(a) Occupy MALTA HOUSE and straighten the front line so that it will run from U.25.a.4.0 to U.30.b.7.9.

(b) Complete cable "bury" from FERDINAND FARM to MAISON BULGARE

(c) Establish dumps for the 34th. and 33rd. Brigades as far forward as possible. 11th. Division "Q" will arrange all details and the attached Battalion of the 34th. Brigade (vide para. 2 above) will be employed for the work.

23rd. September 1917.

T.D. Coleridge Lieut.Colonel,
General Staff, 11th. Division.

Distribution.
============

32nd. Inf. Bde.
33rd. "   "
34th. "   "
C.R.A.
C.R.E.
A.D.M.S.
"Q".
Signals.
6th. E. Yorks Regt.

SECRET.

11th. Division No. G.S. 860.

32nd. Inf. Bde.

Reference this office letter G.S. 809 of 23/9/17, para. 3 (b), the following extract from XVIII Corps Order No. 78 of 26/9/17 is forwarded for information and necessary action :-

" On the night Sept. 28th/29th. 11th. Division will hand over to the 48th. Division that portion of their Div. Sector to the South East of the DOTTED BROWN LINE (VIEILLES MAISONS - South of BAVAROISE HOUSE - thence along LEKKERBOTERBEEK). This DOTTED BROWN LINE will then become the inter-Divisional boundary"

All arrangements for handing over will be made direct by G.O.C., 32nd. Inf. Bde. with G.O.C., 145th. Inf. Bde., and completion reported by wire to 11th. Div. H.Q.

ACKNOWLEDGE.

[signature]

Lieut. Colonel,

27th. September 1917. General Staff, 11th. Division.

Copy to 48th. Division
and all recipients of
11th. Div. Instrns. No. 10.

SECRET.

11th. Division No. G.S. 894.

To:—........................

....

  Herewith   copies 11th. Division Instructions

No. 11.

  Please acknowledge receipt.

T. X. Coleridge Lieut.Colonel,

29th. September 1917.   General Staff, 11th. Division.

Distribution as per 11th. Division Order No. 114.

S E C R E T.

11th. Division Instructions No. 11.

(Reference Special Map issued to Commanders).

1. GENERAL. On dates and at hours to be notified later the Second and Fifth Armies will continue the offensive.
The 48th. Division will attack on the right and the 4th. Division on the left of the 11th. Division.

2. ROLE OF THE 11th. DIVISION.
(a) The tasks given to the 11th. Division will be the capture of the RED DOTTED and the RED LINES, and the GREEN DOTTED and GREEN LINES.

(b) Attack on the RED DOTTED and RED LINES.

The 34th. Brigade will attack on the Right, the 33rd. Brigade on the Left.
The 32nd. Brigade will be training in the HOUTKERQUE Area.
The boundary between these Brigades will be as shown on the map, East of the STEENBEEK it runs as under :-

On STEENBEEK at C.5.a.15.10.

On LANGEMARCK ROAD at U.29.d.80.15.

On ST.JULIEN-
POELCAPPELLE Rd.) at U.30.b.90.35.

Near RETOUR X Roads. at V.19.b.27.20.

S.E. of POELCAPPELLE CHURCH at V.20.c.10.15.

3. CONCENTRATION. Details regarding the concentration of the 33rd. and 34th. Brigades, and the move of the 32nd. Brigade to the HOUTKERQUE Area will be found in 11th. Division Order No. 114.

4. HOSTILE ATTITUDE. The enemy forces opposite the Divisional Sector are distributed in depth, one Battalion holding a system of organised shell holes in the front line, a second Battalion in close support and the third in reserve.
In the event of an advance by us a counter-attack would be delivered within a very short space of time by elements of the counter-attacking Division now situated in the WESTROOSBEKE AREA.
This attack may be expected to develop from two to three hours after Zero.
The enemy is making far less use of his concrete dug-outs, as in several instances the occupants have all been knocked out by direct hits. The men now consider themselves safer in shell holes.

5. FORMING UP. The forming up areas must be very carefully reconnoitred. Constant patrols must ensure that there are no enemy posts or removable obstacles between the forming up positions and the lines on which our barrage comes down at Zero. This barrage line will be 150 yds. in front of the forming up positions.

/6........

- 2 -

6. **ATTACK FORMATIONS.**

The area over which the attack will take place does not appear to contain many concrete buildings except in POELCAPPELLE, but there are a number of derelict trenches which would no doubt afford cover for the enemy. Definite, complete, and distinct units must, therefore, be detailed to engage unexpected areas which may have been consolidated by the enemy and converted into strong points.

Attacking troops will make every effort to follow the barrage as closely as possible.

7. **CONSOLIDATION.**

The objectives, once gained will be consolidated by definite, complete, and distinct units disposed in depth.

The R.E. will assist in the construction of especially important localities.

8. **ARTILLERY.**

(a) The attack will be supported by the Right and Left Groups 11th. Division Artillery, consisting of :-

RIGHT GROUP. 58th., 256th., 77th.(Army) and 93rd. (Army) Brigades R.F.A.

LEFT GROUP.   59th., 255th., 34th.(Army) and 298th. (Army) Brigades R.F.A.

STRENGTH.   144 Eighteen Pounders.
              48 4.5" Howitzers.

(b) Harassing fire and special treatment of enemy's communications will be carried out from now up to Z day.

(c) Strong points will be dealt with by the Heavy Artillery, but the general terrain will not be destroyed.

(d) The Divisional Artillery will carry out each day short concentrated barrages, varying in intensity, rate and locality.

(e) Barrages for the support of the actual attack will be formed in depth, especial attention being paid to localities from which rifle and machine gun fire could be directed by the enemy through the Creeping barrage.

9. **MACHINE GUNS.**

The attack will be supported by a Machine Gun barrage of 32 guns from positions about 200 yards in rear of PHEASANT TRENCH, details of which will be issued later.

It is hoped that an extra M.G. Company will be attached to the Division for these operations, in which case all the Machine Guns of the attacking Brigades will remain under the direct orders of their respective G.O's C. Orders on this point will be issued later.

/10......

- 3 -

10. **LIGHT TRENCH MORTARS.** As suggested in paras. 4 and 6 above, the enemy will probably be found occupying shell holes rather than concrete buildings.

    To deal with this probability and to thicken up the earlier stages of the Artillery barrage, Brigadiers Commanding will arrange to emplace a number of L.T.M's close to the forming up places; these will open a rapid fire at Zero and which will be continued up to Zero plus 3 minutes. Efforts will also be made to push forward one or two Mortars after the attacking troops to assist them in dealing with any opposition which may be encountered from concrete buildings in and around POELCAPPELLE.

11. **GAS.** To further demoralise the enemy opposing the Division, gas will be discharged (wind and circumstances permitting) towards POELCAPPELLE during the night immediately preceding Zero.

12. **TANKS.** Tanks will co-operate with the Division in the attack - details will be issued later.

13. **INTERCOMMUNICATION.** (a) The head of the buried cable route will be at MAISON BULGARE.

    (b) Forward communications will be organised on the plan adopted by the Division during the recent operations.

14. **DUMPS.** Especially detailed working parties from the 33rd. and 34th. Brigades will establish dumps of S.A.A., Water, etc., at SNIPE HOUSE and BULOW FARM respectively prior to Zero.

15. **ROLE OF 32nd. BRIGADE.** <u>Attack on the GREEN and GREEN DOTTED LINES.</u>

    (a) The 32nd. Brigade will carry out this attack supported by portions of 33rd. and 34th. Brigades.
    Details for this attack will be issued later.

    (b) The boundaries between the 11th. Division and Flanking Divisions will be as shown on the Special Map already issued.

16. **DIVISIONAL HEADQUARTERS.** 11th. Division Battle Headquarters will be on the CANAL BANK C.19.c.1.2.

J.D. Coleridge
Lieut.Colonel,
General Staff, 11th. Division.

29th.September 1917.

APPENDIX 4.

11th DIVISION INTELLIGENCE SUMMARIES.

11th. Division Intelligence Summary No. 1.

For 24 hours ending 6 p.m. 25th. Sept. 1917.

NOT TO BE TAKEN BEYOND BATTALION OR BATTERY
HEADQUARTERS.

1. OUR OPERATIONS.
   (a) Infantry. 32nd. Inf. Bde. relieved the 152nd. Inf. Bde. in the line.

   (b) Artillery. The artillery under Divisional Command fired 1807 rounds during the past 24 hours, the targets being the banks of LEKKERBOTERBEEK in V.26.a & b. POELCAPPELLE, MEUNIER HOUSE, GLOSTER FARM, OXFORD HOUSE, COUNTY CROSS ROADS, TRACAS FARM.

2. ENEMY OPERATIONS.
   (a) Infantry. Intermittent sniping during the night from shell holes behind BEER TRENCH and from KANGAROO TRENCH.

   (b) Artillery. Hostile fire was normal during the day. The following places were those most heavily shelled :-

Time.	No. of Rds.	Calibre.	Area shelled.	Direction.
6 - 6.10 p.m.	250	5.9	C.11.b., C.12.a.	POELCAPPELLE
6.20 - 6.35.	150	5.9 / 8"	C.5.	"
6.25 - 6.40	100	4.2 / 5.9	V.30.a., C.6.b.) ST.JULIEN. C.9.)	
6.40	150	77 mm.	Front line.	
7.5 - 7.11	130	4.2 / 77 mm.	C.5.	V.20. b. and c.
8.30	100	Various.	C.5.	POELCAPPELLE
12 - 12.15 am.	160	"	C.5.	"

At 10.30 a.m. on the line NEW HOUSES, PHEASANT FARM, WHITE HOUSE & on ALOUETTE FARM, enemy put down a light and short barrage; observers report that each gun seemed to fire only two shots.

(c) Machine guns. A machine gun at U.24 central fired intermittently during the night at targets near BULOW FARM and RAT HOUSE.

3. ENEMY SIGNALS etc.
   During the night the enemy sent up the usual Very lights and also rockets which burst into two red stars; most of these were sent up from about TWEED HOUSE.

4. AIRCRAFT. Enemy aeroplanes were very active both yesterday and today.

/A flight of..

- 2 -

      A flight of 8 Albatross Scouts flew over our forward areas several times during the morning. At 10.40 a.m. a reconnaissance E.A. dropped a white light over GOURNIER FARM; this was followed by light shelling (4.2 Hows, which made good shooting.)

      At 3 p.m. a flight of 9 R.E.A. flew over KITCHENERS WOOD apparently spotting for two 8" Hows. firing into the area of the Division on our right. They were chased away by our machines.

5. PATROLS.   NIL.

                                          A.C.White
                                              Captain,

                       General Staff, 11th. Division.

11th. Division Intelligence Summary No. 2.   SECRET.

For 24 hours ending 6 p.m. September 26th.

1. OUR OPERATIONS.
    (a) Infantry. The units in the line assisted the attack of the Division on our right by working dummy figures (i.e. a camouflage attack).
    (b) Artillery. The Artillery under Divisional Command fired 26,790 rounds during the past 24 hours of which the majority were fired in the camouflage attack of this morning.

2. ENEMY OPERATIONS.
    (a) Infantry. Confined to slight sniping.
    (b) Artillery. At Zero plus 6 minutes this morning, the enemy shelled RAT HOUSE and the STEENBEEK VALLEY.
        At 6.10 a.m. he put down a fairly heavy barrage on the LANGEMARCK-WINNEPEG ROAD and scattered fire on the STEENBEEK and the road in C.14.b. This lasted until 6.40 a.m. The same was shelled intermittently the whole morning; by 11 a.m. shelling had fallen to normal. At 11.30 a.m. the LANGEMARCK-WINNEPEG ROAD was barraged by 4.2 and 5.9's.
    (c) Machine Guns.
        The machine gun firing from U.24.central was active on the tracks from SNIPE HOUSE to PHEASANT FARM during the night.
        Another fired from V.26.d.25.70 on to our posts at V.25.d.1.3.

3. ENEMY MOVEMENT.
        Throughout the period the enemy has been seen moving about in V.25.a.b. & d., many hits being claimed by our men.
        A Party of about 40 Germans with tools, was seen to deploy in front of YORK FARM and were dispersed by our rifle and Lewis Gun fire.

4. ENEMY SIGNALS etc.
        Very lights were normal. The enemy was seen to send up white lights bursting into two red stars when his artillery fire fell on his own post.

5. AIRCRAFT. Was more active than usual on both sides. Today our planes appeared to have complete mastery though yesterday evening 5 R.E.A. flew over our forward areas.
        At 1.30 a.m. an R.E.A. got over our lines and after firing Tracer bullets promiscuously over our forward areas flew over the area of the Division on our right dropping 5 white lights.

6. GENERAL.   3 p.m.   7 E.A. dropped bombs near RACECOURSE FARM.
                6.10 p.m. 10 bombs dropped on HIGH COMMAND REDOUBT.
                9.15 p.m. Enemy dump at a T.B. 860 from FYSH FARM.
                10.15 p.m. "   "   "   "   74° "   "   "
        HINDENBURG FARM positions (A/255) were bombed at 8 p.m.

                                            A.C.T. White.
                                            ――――――― Captain,
                                            General Staff, 11th. Division.

Appendix to 11th. Division Intelligence Summary No. 2.

Map. Ref. Sheet POELCAPPELLE 1/10,000.

REPORT ON GROUND IN FRONT OF PRESENT FRONT LINE
EXTENDING FROM :- U.30.d.85.92 to U.24.d.30.52.

GROUND. Dry, but absolutely torn up by shell fire.
It is very flat.

TRENCHES.

STROOM TRENCH. Absolutely destroyed.

BEER TRENCH. Can be recognised but badly damaged and would give little cover.

C.T.- running from BEER TRENCH to point V.25.a.8.3 - has about 6 shelters but these afford little cover from shell fire.

CHURCH TRENCH. Parts of it quite good and was partly consolidated by our men.

Trench at U.30.b.7.7 to V.25.a.2.9.- Absolutely destroyed.

KANGAROO TRENCH. Can be recognised but destroyed for fighting purposes.

NOTE: No other trenches existed.

LANDMARKS.

MALTA HOUSE. In ruins and gives no cover.

DELTA HOUSE. In ruins and gives no cover.

ROSE HOUSE. In ruins and gives no cover.

These houses can just be recognised.

POELCAPPELLE-ST. JULIEN ROAD.
Very much torn up but can be easily recognised.

TREES at Point U.24.d.6.7 - Can be recognised.

CONCRETE STRUCTURES - Are all destroyed.
A "Pill Box" at Point V.19.c.8.5 is occupied by the enemy and appears to be intact.

FIELD OF FIRE - From the LEKKERBOTERBEEK to DELTA HOUSE there is a poor Field of fire as the ground slopes away with a slight ridge immediately in front.
On the left of ROSE HOUSE there is a very good field of fire.

(Sd). F.W. MESTON, 2/Lieut.
I.O., 4th. Bn. Gordon Hdrs.

Examination of Aeroplane photographs taken on 25th. September shows the following :-

7. AE. 824.   Concrete structures are still intact at :-

   V.19.d.55.95.

   V.19.b.10.10

   V.19.b.40.00

   V.19.b.55.25

   V.19.a.6.1.

7. AE. 827.   GLOSTER FARM nearly destroyed but track still leads towards it.
   There appear to be fortified shell holes at V.20.c.15.25.

   828.   ROSE STREET in V.19.c. is in fairly good condition.

   835.   Shews our line of posts near BAVAROISE HOUSE.
   A line of fortified shell holes faces our line from V.25.d.20.95 to V.25.d.50.85.

   836.   A structure at BEEK HOUSES (V.20.d.05.00) is still standing and appears to be concreted.

   835.   Building at V.25.d.25.75 appears not to exist; there is a mound or camouflaged emplacement at V.25.d.30.77.

Appendix to 11th. Division Intelligence Summary No. 2.

FIELD COMPANY R.E.

Report on (1) POELCAPPELLE ROAD bridge over LEKKERBOTERBEEK at U.30.d.64.95.
(2) State of POELCAPPELLE ROAD.

(1) ROAD BRIDGE.

Brick Culvert.
Span 10'
Width 36'

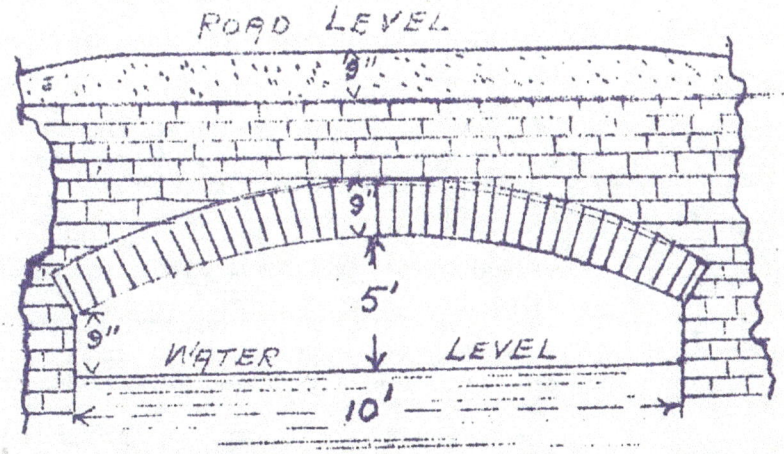

Arch 5" thick at crown and 2' extra in 4 courses of brickwork plus 9" of road metal. All in good condition. This Bridge will take Tanks.

(2) POELCAPPELLE ROAD.
Only oak tree felled across road between TRAINGLE FARM and C.6.b.2.6 and road in excellent condition. Tree is close to two derelict tanks within 30 yards of TRIANGLE FARM.
19 trees felled across road between C.6.b.2.6 and the bridge as below.

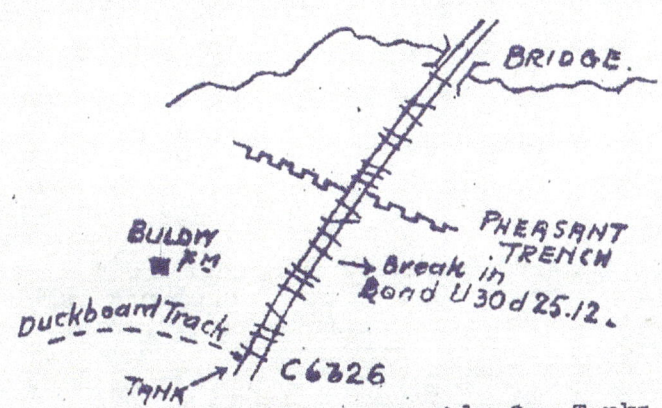

Road would be passable for Tanks up to bridge when trees are removed except in one place at U.30.d.25.82 where there is a 10' gap caused by a line of shell holes.

War Diary

SECRET.

11th. Division Intelligence Summary No. 3.

For 24 hours ending 6 p.m. 28th. September 1917.

1. **OUR OWN OPERATIONS.**
   (a) <u>Infantry</u>. Confined to patrolling and sniping.

   (b) <u>Artillery</u>. The Artillery under Divisional Command fired 7,533 rounds.   The targets were POELCAPPELLE CHURCH and the approaches and open ground near POELCAPPELLE-LEKKER-BOTERBEEK Valley, Roads and tracks in V.19., V.20., V.25., V.26.,
   9.45 Trench Mortars fired 64 rounds at targets between our front lines and road junction V.19.b.4.1.

   (c) <u>Machine Guns</u>.
   In reply to S.O.S. our barrage guns fired 11,000 rounds.
   During the night 5,000 rounds indirect were fired on RETOUR & COUNTY CROSS ROADS, the LEKKERBOTERBEEK, and the Cross Roads at V.26.a.0.9.
   On an S.O.S. going up on the front of the Division on our right at 6 a.m. 3,000 rounds were fired on WINCHESTER FARM - WELLINGTON HOUSE Road.

2. **ENEMY OPERATIONS.**
   (a) <u>Infantry</u>. Slight sniping from vicinity of D.1.b.6.6.

   (b) <u>Artillery</u>. Hostile fire has been normal during the period under review. Our front was not shelled as much as usual, but the support line and the Steenbeek received the greater portion of enemy fire.
   The enemy carried out an organised harassing programme on our roads and tracks West of the Steenbeek.
   Enemy anti-aircraft guns were very active.
   The following places were those most heavily shelled :-

Time.	Number of rounds.	Calibre.	Area Shelled.	Direction.
12 noon to 3.30 a.m.	250	5.9/4.2.	Area C.4.c.	POELCAPPELLE.
12 noon.	400	15 cm.	Area C.9.b.	
1 p.m. to 5.30 p.m.	350	5.9/4.2.	Areas, LANGEMARCK Road, Cockcroft, VIEILLES MAISONS, PHEASANT TRENCH, ST. JULIEN ROAD, KITCHENERS WOOD, Steenbeek and Poelcappelle Road.	R. of POEL-CAPPELLE T.B.30°, 40° from VIEILLES MAISONS.
1.25 p.m. to 2.35 p.m.	200	10.5/77/ 15 cm.	RUDOLPH FARM and Supports in U.29.b. and U.30.a.	PAASCHENDALE.
2.50 to 6 p.m.	500	5.9/8"	Areas C.10.d., C.11.c. 16.b. 17.a.	Gravenstafel Group.
5.30 p.m.	250	5.9.	Sundown Farm Area C.10.c. & d.	

/5.55 p.m.

- 2 -

Time.	Number of rounds.	Calibre.	Area shelled.	Direction.
5.55 p.m.	200	77/10.5 cm.	RAT HOUSE,-BULOW FARM,LANGEMARCK Line.	
6 p.m.	200	5.9	U.30.a.9.9.to U.30.d.2.9.	
6.4 p.m. to 7.20 p.m.	250	Various.	Support line of Division.	
8.30 p.m. to M.N.	300	5.9/8"	MORTELDJE and neighbourhood.	
6.45 p.m. to 11.30 p.m.	300	8"/5.9	Areas C.16.a. & c. Boundary Road and Light Railway in C.15.	
8 p.m. to 11 p.m.	200	10.5/15 cm.	Military Road, Bridge across Steenbeek Rd. 5 Chemins Est. to Steenbeek.	
10 p.m. to 3 a.m.	100	10.5 cm.	Areas C.3, U.27.d. and C.9.a. & b.	

(c) Machine Guns.

The gun at U.24 d.2.8 was again firing during the night sweeping the ground round the posts of our left battalion.

3. ENEMY DEFENCES.

A party of about 70 men was seen by one of our patrols to be working at D.2.a.0.4.

4. ENEMY MOVEMENTS. From 3 to 5 p.m. on the 27th. men wearing redcross brassards were seen looking for wounded in U.19.c. A party of two men carrying a stretcher preceded by a man carrying a large red cross flag, left their area and went towards POELCAPPELLE.

Two enemy seen near OXFORD HOUSES. They ran along track in V.26.b. towards the LEKKERBOTERBEEK.

On our heavies opening fire on MEUNIER HOUSE at 3.25 p.m. three enemy ran out and disappeared 200 yards to the south.

5. AIRCRAFT.

Our aeroplanes were very active all day, keeping the enemy over his own lines.

E.A. were active during the night.

2 E.A. fell in flames near MON DU HIBOU at 6 p.m. 5.35 p.m. One E.A. brought down over PHEASANT FARM.

During the night E.A. bombed back areas until 2 a.m. Several E.A. were up early this morning, a flight of four patrolling our lines at 9 a.m. at a height of 500 feet.

6. BALLOONS. An enemy balloon signalling in morse code was up during the night at a true bearing of 76° from BULOW FARM.

/7......

7. ROCKETS.

Golden rain rockets were sent up by the enemy during our S.O.S. An E.A. dropped a silver rain rocket over POELCAPPELLE during this time.

8. GENERAL.

It is probable that the S.O.S. fired on by our batteries was caused by the enemy sending up our S.O.S. Signals.

for Captain,
General Staff, 11th. Division.

S E C R E T.

11th. Division Intelligence Summary No. 3.

For 24 hours ending 6 p.m. 28th. September 1917.

1. OUR OWN OPERATIONS.
   (a) Infantry.   Confined to patrolling and sniping.
   (b) Artillery. The Artillery under Divisional Command fired 7,533 rounds.   The targets were POELCAPPELLE CHURCH and the approaches and open ground near POELCAPPELLE-LEKKER-BOTERBEEK Valley, Roads and tracks in V.19., V.20., V.25., V.26.,
          9.45 Trench Mortars fired 64 rounds at targets between our front lines and road junction V.19.b.4.1.
   (c) Machine Guns.
          In reply to S.O.S. our barrage guns fired 11,000 rounds.
          During the night 5,000 rounds indirect were fired on RETOUR & COUNTY CROSS ROADS, the LEKKERBOTERBEEK, and the Cross Roads at V.26.a.0.9.
          On an S.O.S. going up on the front of the Division on our right at 6 a.m. 3,000 rounds were fired on WINCHESTER FARM -WELLINGTON HOUSE Road.

2. ENEMY OPERATIONS.
   (a) Infantry.   Slight sniping from vicinity of D.1.b.6.6.
   (b) Artillery. Hostile fire has been normal during the period under review. Our front was not shelled as much as usual, but the support line and the Steenbeek received the greater portion of enemy fire.
          The enemy carried out an organised harassing programme on our roads and tracks West of the Steenbeek.
          Enemy anti-aircraft guns were very active.
          The following places were those most heavily shelled :-

Time.	Number of rounds.	Calibre.	Area Shelled.	Direction.
12 noon to 3.30 a.m.	250	5.9/4.2.	Area C.4.c.	POELCAPPELLE.
12 noon.	400	15 cm.	Area C.9.b.	
1 p.m. to 5.30 p.m.	350	5.9/4.2.	Areas, LANGEMARCK Road, Cockcroft, VIEILLES MAISONS, PHEASANT TRENCH, ST. JULIEN ROAD, KITCHENERS WOOD, Steenbeek and Poelcappelle Road.	R. of POEL-CAPPELLE T.B.30°,40° from VIEILLES MAISONS.
1.25 p.m. to 2.35 p.m.	200	10.5/77/ 15 cm.	RUDOLPH FARM and Supports in U.29.b. and U.30.a.	PAASCHENDALE.
3.50 to 6 p.m.	500	5.9/8"	Areas C.10.d., C.11.c. 16.b. 17.a.	Graven-stafel Group.
5.30 p.m.	250	8"/5.9	Sandown Farm Area and C.10.c. & d.	

/5.55 p.m.

- 2 -

Time.	Number of rounds.	Calibre.	Area shelled.	Direction.
5.55 p.m.	200	77/10.5 cm.	RAT HOUSE,-BULOW FARM,LANGEMARCK Line.	
6 p.m.	200	5.9	U.30.a.9.9. to U.30.d.2.9.	
6.4 p.m. to 7.30 p.m.	250	Various.	Support line of Division.	
8.30 p.m. to M.N.	300	5.9/8"	MORTELDJE and neighbourhood. Areas 0.16.a. & c.	
6.45 p.m. to 11.30 p.m.	300	8"/5.9	Boundary Road and Light Railway in 0.15.	
8 p.m. to 11 p.m.	200	10.5/15 cm.	Military Road, Bridge across Steenbeek Rd. 5 Chemins Est. to Steenbeek.	
10 p.m. to 3 a.m.	100	10.5 cm.	Areas O.3, U.27.d. and O.9.a. & b.	

(c) <u>Machine Guns.</u> The gun at U.24.d.2.8 was again firing during the night sweeping the ground round the posts of our left battalion.

3. <u>ENEMY DEFENCES.</u> A party of about 70 men was seen by one of our patrols to be working at D.2.a.0.4.

4. <u>ENEMY MOVEMENTS.</u> From 3 to 5 p.m. on the 27th. men wearing redcross brassards were seen looking for wounded in U.19.c. A party of two men carrying a stretcher preceded by a man carrying a large red cross flag, left their area and went towards POELCAPPELLE.
   Two enemy seen near OXFORD HOUSES. They ran along track in V.26.b. towards the LEKKERBOTERBEEK.
   On our heavies opening fire on MEUNIER HOUSE at 3.25 p.m. three enemy ran out and disappeared 200 yards to the south.

5. <u>AIRCRAFT.</u> Our aeroplanes were very active all day, keeping the enemy over his own lines.
   E.A. were active during the night.
   2 E.A. fell in flames near MON DU HIBOU at 6 p.m.
   3.35 p.m. One E.A. brought down over PHEASANT FARM.
   During the night E.A. bombed back areas until 2 a.m.
   Several E.A. were up early this morning, a flight of four patrolling our lines at 9 a.m. at a height of 500 feet.

6. <u>BALLOONS.</u> An enemy balloon signalling in morse code was up during the night at a true bearing of 76° from BULOW FARM.

/7......

7. **ROCKETS.** Golden rain rockets were sent up by the enemy during our S.O.S. An E.A. dropped a silver rain rocket over POELCAPPELLE during this time.

8. **GENERAL.** It is probable that the S.O.S. fired on by our batteries was caused by the enemy sending up our S.O.S. Signals.

for Captain,
General Staff, 11th. Division.

11th. Division Intelligence Summary No. 4.

For 24 hours ending Noon September 29th.

1. OUR OWN OPERATIONS.
   (a) **Infantry.** Confined to patrolling and an inter-battalion relief, the former being much hampered by gas shelling.

   (b) **Artillery.** The artillery under Divisional Command fired 2,170 rounds during the past 24 hours. Short harassing barrages were placed on KANGAROO AVENUE, the roads, tracks and avenues of approach in V.19., 20, 25 & 26.

   (c) **Machine Guns.** During the night 3,000 rounds (indirect fire) were fired on COUNTY X, RETOUR CROSS Roads, and up the LEKKERBOTERBEEK Valley.

2. ENEMY OPERATIONS.
   (a) **Infantry.** Occasional sniping.

   (b) **Artillery.** Enemy artillery has been below normal during the last 24 hours. Considerable activity was noticed from 10 a.m. to 1 p.m. in C.10. Battery positions in C.10.c. also in C.3.d. and C.4.a. were subjected to gas shelling. During this shelling a new type of shell was fired. This is a 5.9 or 8" shell containing 1/3 phosgene and 2/3 high explosive. This makes a considerable crater; it is sometimes mixed with the ordinary gas shell.

   The Steenbeek Valley, Iron Cross and the Langemarck Winnipeg Road were fairly heavily shelled at times.

   A heavy howitzer shelled C.16.a. or C.22.a. between 9. and 9.30 p.m. 15 rounds being fired.

   The following places were those most heavily shelled :-

Time.	No. of rounds.	Calibre.	Area shelled.	Direction.
12 noon - 6 p.m.	250	4.2/5.9	Areas C.10.b. & d and C.9.b.	
12 noon - 1 p.m.	100	"	Steenbeek Valley and Langemarck Road.	Poelcappelle.
1 p.m. - 2 p.m.	200	5.9	C.10.b.	
6.20 p.m.	100	4.2/5.9	Areas C.5.d. Regina, Cross, C.6.b. & D.1.c.	Paaschendale.
8 p.m. - 9 p.m.	100	4.2	Area between Steenbeek and Langemarck Farm.	
4 a.m.	300	4.2 and 5.9.	Areas C.10.c. & d and C.9.	Poelcappelle.
10.30 - 12.30 p.m.	2000	77 and heavier calibre.	C.15.b.c & d.	
11.30 p.m. to 4 a.m.	100	4.2 77 mm	C.10 and C.16.	

- 2 -

Time.	No. of rounds.	Calibre.	Area shelled.	Direction.
12.15 a.m. - 3 a.m.	200	All calibres.	C.10.c.	
4.30 a.m. - 6.30 a.m.	200	4.2/77	Between Langemarck and Steenbeek.	
9 am. - 12 noon	100	5.9	East of Steenbeek 5 Chemins Est. and Pilckem Road in C.14.	
11 a.m. - 11.40 a.m.	150	4.2	O.P. at VIEILLES MAISONS.	Paaschendale

3. PATROLS went out on both battalion fronts, but owing to gas shelling during the hours detailed for patrolling, were unable to proceed. Gas shelling so near the enemy line is noteworthy as the wind was S.W. at this time.

4. MOVEMENT.
The enemy has shown himself in the line U.30.b.7.6 to V.25.a.1.4 and at 8 p.m. a wood-saw was heard at work on the former.

5. ENEMY SIGNALS ETC.
On the enemy's dropping several short rounds on KANGAROO TRENCH on the night 27th/28th. no signal was sent up. Two rockets went up at 10.45 a.m. each bursting into 2 White lights. No result was observed.

6. AIRCRAFT.
Our aircraft was very active.
During the last few days enemy flights have been few and far between. E.A. crossed our lines as follows :-

1 at 2 p.m.   2 at 4.30 p.m.
2 at 3 p.m.   1 at 6.50 p.m.
1 at 3.30 p.m.

An enemy balloon (T.B. 43° from U.28.d.68.22 and $37\frac{1}{2}°$ from C.5.a.5.2) was signalling at 6.50 p.m. - VERKEHR ODER TRUPPEN BEREITSTELLUNG GESEHEN - mixed with some code signals, was read from CANE POST.

7. GENERAL. The use of incendiary shell by the enemy on our forward positions is noticeably on increasing.

A.C.T. White. Captain,
General Staff, 11th. Division.

War Diary

11th. Division Intelligence Summary No. 5.

24 Hours ending noon 30th. September 1917.

1. OUR OWN OPERATIONS.
   (a) Infantry.   Between 9.30 and 11.30 p.m. our Lewis gunners and riflemen fired at the enemy who appeared to be carrying out a relief opposite the front of our left battalion.

   (b) Artillery.   The Artillery under Divisional Command fired 4,141 rounds, including 1144 gas shells, during the last 24 hours. The targets being the trenches, consolidated shell holes and roads on the Divisional front.

   (c) Machine Guns.   Indirect fire was maintained during the night on usual targets.

2. ENEMY OPERATIONS.
   (a) Infantry.   Usual occasional sniping.

   (b) Artillery.   Enemy fire has been slightly above normal during the past 24 hours. The Steenbeek Valley, Langemarck-Winnipeg Road and the 5 Chemins Est.-Hindenburg Farm area received most attention.
                        Most of the shelling came from N.E. and E. of POELCAPPELLE. Some of this was gas.
                        The following places were those most heavily shelled :-

Time.	No. of rounds.	Calibre.	Area Shelled.	Direction.
12 noon.	150	4.2/5.9	Area C.6.a. & c.	POELCAPPELLE.
3 - 5 p.m.	200	15 cm.	C.10.c.5.7	"
7 p.m.	100	4.2	Kliest Fm. and area C.9.b. & d.	"
12 m.n.	100	4.2	Road from BOCH-CASTEL to Steenbeek.	T.B.40°,50° fr. C.15.c. 73.1
10.30 p.m. 4.30 a.m.	200	4.2	C.10.c. & d. and C.9.d.	50% gas.
4 - 5 a.m.	100	10.5	Au Bon Gité Area.	Paaschendale
9.30 - 11.30)	1000	10.5	C.15.b. & d.	
10.30 a.m.	150	77/10.5	Area between Steenbeek and Road in C.4.b.	Poelcappelle.

   (c) Machine Guns.   No enemy M.G's reported to be firing.

   (d) Trench Mortars. A heavy T.M. was reported to have been active to the S.W. of PHEASANT FM. The majority of the bombs failed to explode.

3. ENEMY SIGNALS & LIGHTS.   At 7 p.m. several white parachute lights were observed to float upwards from the enemy's lines, possibly to determine the direction of the wind. "Very" lights were sent up from V.25.a.2.4.

/4........

- 2 -

4. **AIRCRAFT.**
   (a) *Aeroplanes.* Enemy aeroplanes were unusually active between 4 and 8 p.m. as many as 24 being counted at one time. Albatross scouts attempting to fly low over our posts were driven off by our A.A. Lewis Gun fire.
   (b) 7 Balloons were seen up to-day.

5. **PATROLS.** A patrol reports an enemy post at U.24.d.3.4. The wire here is in a bad state and can be passed.
   A patrol of the left Battalion reports enemy posts at V.25.a.2.7 and V.25.a.2.4 and U.30.b.85.55.

6. **GENERAL.** The following report has been made by the Right Battalion :-
   Report on the junction of the LEKKERBOTERBEEK with the STROOMBEEK.

   The LEKKERBOTERBEEK presents no obstacle to an advance. It is more a series of small pools than a stream. Most of them could be jumped and troops could pass between them.

   There is no water to speak of at the immediate junction of the streams, but about 40 or 50 yards south of the junction, shells have made quite considerable pools in the stream - even these could be got round.

   It must be remembered that rain has not fallen for some considerable time and that a heavy fall would soon make a marsh of this area. It would seem to be a wise measure to have some light bridging material (long bridged duck-boards) at BULOW FARM ready for such an emergency as rain.

7. **EXTRACTS FROM OTHER SUMMARIES.**

   (a) <u>Division on Right.</u>
   A patrol from the left Battalion located an enemy working party at D.1.b.8.4. The patrol was fired on by riflemen from YORK FARM.
   A second patrol reports that the road leading to YORK FARM is too badly cut up to be passable. This patrol was also fired on from YORK FARM.

   <u>Hostile Machine Guns.</u>
   The following locations are reported :-

   D.2.c.1.4.
   D.2.c.40.45 (concrete structure)
   D.2.c.75.15.
   V.26.b.65.40 (concrete structure).

   (b) <u>Division on Left.</u>
   Patrols report enemy advanced post 25 to 30 strong near U.24.d.05.80. Patrol which reached about U.24.a.9.5 was fired on at short range. Enemy post also found in KANGAROO Trench to North of RICE HOUSE.

   <u>Machine Guns.</u> Two machine guns fired intermittently throughout the night from vicinity of U.24.a.40.65.

   A.C.T.White
   ———————— Captain,

   General Staff, 11th. Division.

APPENDIX 3.

DIVISIONAL INSTRUCTIONS

and

MISCELLANEOUS.

APPENDIX 3a

To:-................   11th. Division No. G.S. 168.

     ....   S E C R E T

The following points were raised at a Conference held at XVIIIth. Corps Headquarters yesterday. As they are of general interest and refer to the present fighting they are published for information.

1. ENEMY TACTICS.
   (a)   The 39th. Division, on entering the LANGEMARCK LINE (in C.12. and D.7) on the 31st. July found the actual trench empty. About 100 yards in rear, however, there was a line of dug-outs full of hostile troops. These tactics will no doubt be repeated.

   (b)   The enemy made use of the concrete shelters erected by him all over the battlefield as strong points and pivots of resistance. Rifle bombs were found most effective for dealing with these, as they caused the enemy's Infantrymen to run for safety inside the concrete shelter, where they were surrounded and captured.
            Every man therefore, should carry a Rifle bomb rod in addition to a Mills Bomb, when engaged in an attack on a position known to contain a number of these concrete shelters.

2. INITIATIVE.
            On the 31st. July, a number of hostile aircraft flew over a position which was in course of consolidation by a company of the 51st. Division. Noting this the company Commander on his own initiative stopped work and moved forward 100 yards or so and begun digging in in a new position. This action was immediately justified as, shortly afterwards the hostile artillery began a bombardment of the original position which was frequently struck, while the company digging in in front suffered no casualties.

3. INTER-COMMUNICATION.
            Throughout the battle on the 31st. intercommunication was extremely difficult, owing no doubt, to bad weather and heavy ground. On several occasions, however, pigeon messages were sent in and gave valuable information. It appears, however, that insufficient pigeons were used.

4. FLARES.
   On the 31st very few flares were lighted in the GREEN LINE. Every man proceeding into action should carry a flare.

5. INFORMATION FROM WOUNDED.
            Some excellent information was received from slightly wounded officers and men. It is intended to detail a special officer to interrogate wounded at Dressing Stations during the next battle. A form of question paper is about to be produced.

6. DUCK-BOARD TRACKS. etc.
            Very great difficulty has been experienced in carrying up supplies, ammunition etc., owing to the deplorable state of the ground and the lack of tracks. The provision of duck-board tracks, therefore, is all-important.

- 2 -

Another pair will be constructed if time permits, & the weather makes it necessary.

While the Division is in the line one "up" and one "down" duck boarded track will be constructed in the Divisional Sector. The C.R.E. has the matter in hand, and infantry working parties will be placed at his disposal so as to ensure rapid construction of these tracks. It is hoped that a lorry road and the light Railway will reach ADMIRAL'S ROAD by the 10th instant.

7. SITUATION REPORTS.

Great difficulty has been experienced during the late operations in obtaining information as to the situation of the troops. All subordinate commanders should write situation reports, if possible, & make use of the maps on the back of the special message form when doing so. The approximate position of the Headquarters of the Officer writing these reports should be shown on the map.

8. HOLDING THE LINE.

The main defence of the line is performed by the Artillery and Machine Gun barrages. Few infantry, therefore, are necessary for holding the line, and in view of the forthcoming operations men should be nursed and economised as far as possible.

9. MODEL.

A model of the ground over which the Division is likely to operate in the near future is in course of construction at A.30. central. and will it is hoped be completed about the 10th instant.

10. ENEMY'S ATTITUDE.

Our patrols cross the STEENBEEK every night at will, there are no enemy in MON DU RASTA and MON BULGARE; and the nearest hostile infantry appear to be about HAANIXBEEK FARM, but this too is uncertain. Patrols proceeding North West of U.89.c.2.8. however, are invariably fired on and the assumption is that the enemy is digging in round about LANGEMARK.

H.Q. 11th Division.
5th August, 1917.

J. D. Coleridge
Lieut-Colonel,
General Staff. 11th Division.

APPENDIX 3 G

S E C R E T. 11th. Division No. G.S. 196.

C.R.A.
C.R.E.
32nd. Inf. Bde.
33rd. "   "
34th. "   "
6th. E. Yorks Regt.
"Q".
A.D.M.S.
Signals.

        Herewith copy copies 11th. Division Instructions

No. 5, (General Staff).

        Please acknowledge receipt.

J.M.R. Harrison

                                    Major,
7th. August, 1917.   General Staff, 11th. Division.

11th. DIVISION INSTRUCTIONS NO. 5.

(General Staff).

GENERAL. 1. By the morning of the 8th. August the 11th. Division will have relieved the 51st. Division in the Left Sector of the XVIIIth. Corps front and will be disposed as detailed in 11th. Division Order No. 94.

METHOD OF HOLDING THE LINE. 2. The 32nd. Brigade will hold the front system with 2 Battalions North of the BLACK LINE inclusive and 2 Battalions in the CANAL BANK.

The front line will be lightly held and the troops disposed in depth.. Should the enemy enter our lines he will be counter attacked at once by special troops detailed for the purpose.

It should be borne in mind, that our powerful artillery is the chief factor in the defence, and that a few Infantry in possession of Vickers and Lewis Guns should, with the help of the Artillery, as detailed in 11th. D.A. Order No. 54 be able to repel all hostile attacks.

The closest touch will be maintained with adjoining units of flanking Divisions, and a plan showing defensive arrangements submitted.

FUTURE OPERATIONS. 3. On a date, and at an hour to be detailed later, a general advance will be made for the purpose of capturing the LANGEMARCK LINE.

The final objective allotted to the 11th. Division is approximately the line C.6.b.9.7 - PHEASANT FARM V.30.b.05.55 - WHITE HOUSE V.24.c.5.1 (inclusive).

The 34th. Infantry Brigade is detailed for this task. The 145th. Infantry Brigade (48th. Division) will attack on the Right.

The 20th. Division will attack on the Left.

Maps showing detailed objectives, boundaries, Artillery and Machine gun barrages will be issued later.

PLAN. 4. The G.O.C., 34th. Infantry Brigade will draw up a plan for the attack to be delivered by his Brigade.

ROLE OF THE 32nd. INF. BRIGADE. 5. The 32nd. Infantry Brigade will assist in the preparations for the attack as follows :-

(a) Vigorously patrol the Right bank of the STEENBEEK, and establish a superiority in "NO MAN'S LAND", so as to ensure that troops of the 34th. Brigade will have sufficient space, at least 300 yards in depth, to enable them to "form up" unmolested.

(b) Commence cutting the wire along the East bank of the STEENBEEK, so that it will form no obstacle to an advance. The wire must be carefully cut so as not to attract attention, and the posts will be left standing.

/(c).......

(c) Establish dumps of Rations, S.A.A., Bombs, etc., in the neighbourhood of FERDINAND and COMEDY FARMS, so as to shorten the "carry" for the 34th. Infantry Brigade during the action.

(d) Construct the "duck-board" tracks on the lines laid down in Instructions No. 6.

RELIEFS. 6. The 34th. Infantry Brigade will relieve the 32nd. Infantry Brigade in the line 36 hours before Zero.

APPENIX 3c.

=============
S E C R E T.
=============

11th. Division No. G.S. 195.

32nd. Inf. Bde.
33rd. "   "
34th. "   "
C.R.A.
C.R.E.
"Q".
Signals.
A.D.M.S.
6th. E. Yorks Regt.

      Herewith   copies 11th. Division Instructions
No. 6, "R.E. INSTRUCTIONS".

      Please acknowledge receipt.

                                    J.M.R. Harrison, Major,

7th. August, 1917.   General Staff, 11th. Division.

11th. DIVISION INSTRUCTIONS No. 6.   S E C R E T.

R.E. INSTRUCTIONS.

In view of future operations which it is hoped will take place at a very early date, it is most important that every effort should be made to push forward communications. Maps have been issued showing proposed roads and tracks. In addition it is proposed to push forward duck-board tracks to be available in case of wet weather.

Approximate lines for these duck-board tracks are as under :-

(a) HURST PARK towards FERDINAND FARM.

(b) BELOW FARM - GOURNIER FARM towards FRANCOIS FARM.

(c) 5 CHEMINS ESTAMINET to RUDOLPHE FARM.

The 86th. Field Company are in charge of the Right half of the front Brigade area forward of the BLACK LINE including HURST PARK ROAD and duck-board track (a).

The 67th. Field Company are in charge of the left half of the front Brigade area forward of the BLACK LINE including marking out of the over-land track and duck-board track (b).

The 68th. Field Company are in charge of the area behind the BLACK LINE including the BELOW FARM - GOURNIER FARM ROAD and the KEMPTON PARK to BELOW FARM - GOURNIER FARM ROAD.

Every effort must be made to improve dug-out accommodation and water supply in these areas.

The 86th. and 67th. Field Companies will endeavour to repair the existing bridges over the STEENBEKE.
Light foot-bridges to supplement the existing bridges are being made in the Corps Park.

The 6th. E. Yorks Regt. (Pioneers) will be employed on the MORTELDJE ESTAMINET - HURST PARK ROAD.

The 51st. Division Pioneers will work on the roads and tracks in rear of the old front line and also on the track and duck-board track up to BELOW FARM.

The C.E., XVIII Corps has undertaken to make the duck-board track (c) with the 179th. Tunnelling Company as soon as the buried cable is completed.

APPENDIX 3d.

ARTILLERY AND INFANTRY
CABLE COMMUNICATION SCHEME.   SECRET.

The following notes are in amplification of 11th. Division Instructions No. 2, Appendix "A", "INTER-COMMUNICATIONS"

(1) <u>Distribution of Units.</u>

The Right Artillery Group will consist of :-

Group Commander - O.C., 58th. Brigade R.F.A.

    58th. Brigade R.F.A.
    256th.   "   "
    282nd.(Army) Brigade R.F.A.

The Left Artillery Group will consist of :-

Group Commander - O.C., 59th. Brigade R.F.A.

    59th. Brigade R.F.A.
    77th. (Army) Brigade R.F.A.
    255th. Brigade R.F.A.

(2) <u>Personnel.</u>

(a)   O.C., 58th. Brigade R.F.A. will furnish the Artillery Cable Officer for the Right Main Route.
O.C., 59th. Brigade R.F.A. will furnish the A.C.O. for the Left Main Route.
Each A.C.O. will work under the direction of the Signalling Officer of his own Artillery Brigade.
These Signalling Officers (i.e., Lieut. MAGUIRE 58th. Brigade R.F.A. and Lieut. YOUNG, 59th. Bde.R.F.A.) will control the organising of the personnel, and the general scheme for laying the Main Routes, the A.C.O. will merely lay the cables.
Once the main routes have been layed by the A.C.O's (directed by the Artillery Group H.Q. Signals Officers), the Signal Officer of the Infantry Brigade concerned will take over the responsibility for running the system.
Artillery and Infantry Brigade Signal Officers must work in conjunction.
When selecting an officer to perform the duties of A.C.O. it must be borne in mind that :-

(i) The success of the scheme depends largely on the A.C.O.
(ii) Technical Signal knowledge is desirable, but not essential.
(iii) Courage, cunning, energy, good eye for country, and an appreciation of the tactical situation are essential.

(b) <u>Personnel Available.</u>

For Right Main Route.

58th. Brigade R.F.A.   Signalling Officer and
        Artillery Cable Officer.
        8 Linemen.
        2 Men for Test Boxes.

/256th......

- 3 -

256th. Brigade R.F.A.	8 Linemen. 2 men for Test Boxes.
282nd. Brigade R.F.A.	8 Linemen. 2 men for Test Boxes.
34th. Infantry Brigade.	8 Linemen. 2 men for Test Boxes.
33rd. Infantry Brigade.	4 Linemen. 4 men for Test Boxes.

      TOTAL: 1 Signalling Officer.
              1 A.C.O.
              36 Linemen.
              12 men for Test Boxes.

For Left Main Route.

59th. Brigade R.F.A.	Signalling Officer, and Artillery Cable Officer. 8 Linemen. 2 men for Test Boxes.
77th. Brigade R.F.A.	8 Linemen. 2 men for Test Boxes.
255th. Brigade R.F.A.	8 Linemen. 2 men for Test Boxes.
34th. Infantry Brigade.	8 Linemen. 2 men for Test Boxes.
32nd. Infantry Brigade.	4 Linemen. 4 men for Test Boxes.

      TOTAL: 1 Signalling Officer.
              1 A.C.O.
              36 Linemen.
              12 men for Test Boxes.

(3)   In addition the following personnel will work under the Signals officer of the Infantry Brigade concerned :-

    56th. Brigade R.F.A.)
    59th.   "   ") Each Brigade - 2 men
    77th.   "   ")
    255th. "   ") to assist in the
    256th. "   ")
    282nd. "   ") manning of Test Boxes.

    This personnel will at first work under Signals Officer 34th. Infantry Brigade, and subsequently will come under Signals Officers of 32nd. and 34th. Brigades according to the areas in which they may be working.

/4..........

(4)   When laying out lines between Cable Head or First Linesman Post (as the case may be) and the line of Battalion Headquarters, the working parties of the Infantry Brigade Signals Officer will accompany the A.M.O's Party.

The A.C.O. will select the "dug-outs" for Linesman Posts.

The Infantry Brigade working party will provide and carry the test boards and connect the lines to them, as far as Battalion Headquarters only.

(N.B.   This situation arises when Battalion H.Q. are moving forward faster than the cable is being laid, or when the A.C.O. starts laying his main route in rear of Battalion H.Q.)

(5) Date of Inauguration of the Scheme.

On the night August 7th/8th. the 11th. Division will relieve the 51st. Division in the Line, and as soon as O.C., Signal Company has taken over the existing communications and adapted them to 11th. Division Scheme, the parties detailed in para 8 (b) will start functioning.

This will allow of the personnel and system being a running concern before any offensive operation is undertaken.

The actual date will be ordered by General Staff, 11th. Division and Signal Officers of 58th. and 59th. Brigades R.F.A. will then inform Signal Officers of Artillery and Infantry Brigades when and where the requisite personnel are to join.

It is probable that there will not be scope for the employment of all the personnel before an advance is made; if such is the case personnel should be employed in relays so that they may all gain experience in the general scheme and their own particular duties.

(6) Equipment.

O.C., 11th. Div. Signal Company has arranged with Signal Officers of Artillery and Infantry Brigades as to the distribution of telephone equipment etc.

(7) Responsibilities.

Reference " Artillery and Infantry Cable Communication Scheme, Para.3 A. Lines 19 and 20".

It has now been decided that the Artillery Cable Officer will lay forward all the <u>original</u> lines;

i.e., In each Main Route.

3 Artillery Lines.
8 Infantry Lines.
1 Test Line.

/More......

- 4 -

More satisfactory results will be obtained by one Officer laying all the lines, and the allotment of Infantry Personnel to A.C.O's parties has been made on this account.

The Artillery Cable Officers will be responsible solely for the laying of the lines, which must be pushed as far forward as possible; upon the Infantry Brigade Signalling Officers will devolve the responsibility for installing the Test Boxes and Duplicating the Infantry Lines, and for the general supervision of the Mains, once they have been layed.

Duplicate lines for Artillery Brigades will be layed under Artillery Brigade arrangements and will follow existing Main Routes.

War Diary   APPENDIX 3.e.

SECRET.   11th. Division No. G.S. 226.

To:-..................

....

    Herewith   copies 11th. Division Instructions for the Offensive No. 7, "ANTI-AIRCRAFT PRECAUTIONS".
Please acknowledge receipt.

                                         Lieut. Colonel,
9th. August 1917.   General Staff, 11th. Division.

SECRET.

11th. Division Instructions for the Offensive No. 7.

ANTI-AIRCRAFT PRECAUTIONS.

1. From experience gained in recent operations and from captured German documents, it is the evident intention of the enemy to make even more use of the low flying aeroplane than he has already done.

2. It is not possible for our aeroplanes or A.A. guns to deal successfully with low flying aeroplanes. The only defence against them is rifle, Lewis and Vickers Machine Gun fire.

3. With this end in view Lewis guns on pole mountings will be disposed in 3 echelons.

   (a) <u>1st. Echelon.</u>
   About 500 yards in rear of our front line; one gun to every 500 yards of front.

   (b) <u>2nd. Echelon.</u>
   About 1500 yards in rear of our front line; one gun to every 500 yards.

   (c) <u>3rd. Echelon.</u>
   About the line of the Field Artillery. One Lewis Gun per F.A. Brigade.

4. As regards para. 3 above :-

   (a) <u>1st. Echelon.</u>
   The 34th. Brigade will detail 3 Lewis guns, with crews, from the battalions detailed to capture the GREEN LINE for this duty. These guns will be placed in position West of the LANGEMARCK - GHELUVELT Road, after the GREEN LINE is taken. Light pole mountings for this purpose will be issued to the 34th. Brigade previous to Zero.

   (b) <u>2nd. Echelon.</u>
   The 32nd. Brigade will detail 3 Lewis guns with crews from the Brigade for this duty. The guns will be placed in position along the Old BLACK LINE without delay and remain in action until relieved.

   (c) <u>3rd. Echelon.</u>
   The 6th. East Yorks (Pioneers) will place 3 Lewis Guns at the disposal of the C.R.A., who will place these guns in convenient positions in the neighbourhood of F.A. Brigades in the line. These guns will be manned by Artillery men.

   Light pole mountings will be issued as soon as available for (b) and (c), until which time extemporized mountings must be used.

5. During the forthcoming operations, it is not proposed to move the 2nd. and 3rd. Echelons. The 1st. Echelon will be moved if found too far back to adequately protect our positions on the final objective.

APPENDIX 3f.

SECRET.   11th. Division No. G.S. 232.

To:-................

    ....

    Herewith   copies of 11th. Division Instructions for the Offensive No. 8, "CO-OPERATION OF INFANTRY WITH TANKS". Please acknowledge receipt.

10th. August, 1917.

Major,
General Staff, 11th. Division.

SECRET.

11th. Division Instructions for the Offensive No. 6.

CO-OPERATION OF INFANTRY WITH TANKS.

1. Infantry should not bunch together near Tanks as the latter are likely to draw fire.

2. Infantry will not wait for Tanks should the latter be delayed by bad ground, but will push on as close to the barrage as possible.

3. The following points should be borne in mind :-

   (a) Tanks although ditched, and unable to move forward, can often assist in the reduction of strong points, by means of their Lewis Guns manned by their crews.

   (b) Tanks carry pigeons, which are available for carrying back valuable information to Divisional Headquarters.

   (c) Tanks are detailed to assist the Infantry in taking certain definite objectives as far as the state of the ground allows, they will not be directed on new objectives until the original ones are captured.

4. It has been arranged that the following Tank to Infantry Calls will be used for the forthcoming operations:-

   GREEN DISC.................. Wire cut.

   RED   " .... Wire uncut.

   RED.   )
   GREEN) " .... Objective reached.

   RED   )
   RED   ) " .... Enemy counter-attacking
   GREEN.)

   RED   )
   RED   ) " .... Out of action.
   RED   )

   RED   )
   WHITE) " ....Enemy is in dug-outs.
   RED.   )

   The following Infantry to Tank Signal may be used :-

   Helmets waved   Tanks wanted
   on bayonets ....   to help Infantry.

Forwarded as arranged.

SECRET.

War Diary   APPENDIX 3g.

11th. Division No. G.S. 847.

FORMING UP 34th. INFANTRY BRIGADE.

REFERENCE PLAN.
1. The attached large scale plan depicts, (1) a suggested assembly formation for your Brigade at ZERO, and (2) the approximate position of footbridges across the STEENBEEK.

GENERAL.
2. It has been noted that the enemy puts down a barrage daily about dawn on the FERDINAND FARM – COMEDY FARM ROAD and creeps backwards towards the BLACK LINE. It is all important, therefore, that assembling troops should be N.E. of the FERDINAND FARM – COMEDY FARM ROAD before 3.30 a.m. in event of a ZERO being about dawn.

FRONTAGES.
3. The front to be attacked by your Brigade is approximately 1,300 yards or 650 yards to a Battalion, (in event of 2 Battalions attacking in line) or approximately 160 yards per Company, provided all four companies are deployed in 4 lines. (i.e. 2 waves).

COMPASS BEARINGS.
4. The true bearing of the centre line of advance is about 56°.
Troops on the right of this line would, therefore, have to be aligned on a line bearing 146° (true); while those on the left would have to be aligned on a line bearing 326° (true).
Troops formed on these lines would have their front approximately parallel to the GREEN and RED DOTTED LINES.

METHOD FOR FORMING UP.
5. The following method for forming up is suggested:-

A. **1st. Line.** At a selected hour previous to ZERO, 8 selected officers or N.C.O's would move out along the centre line on a true bearing of 56°. Four would proceed 180 yards from the STEENBEEK and four 110 yards. On arrival 2 would turn outwards at each halting place, and then proceed to march in opposite directions, those on the right on a bearing of 146° (true), and those on the left on a bearing of 326° (true). Fatigue men accompanying these officers would place discs 40- 120 200 - 280 - 360 - 440 - 520 - and 600 yards from the centre line. This would give 2 lines of discs at 80 yards interval and 40 yards distance; if time permits tapes will be laid to connect up these discs on Y/Z night and thus greatly facilitate assembly.

At the hour of assembly the troops would be marched up in small columns until the tapes or discs were reached, and then wheeled into line with the centre of the front line of each platoon on a disc.

Each disc should be marked with the number of the platoon it is proposed to form on it.

It should be noted (1) that the right of the front line of the right battalion is at Road junction at C.5.d.25.10, (2) that the rear line of the right centre of the right battalion is on the bank of the STEENBEEK (3) that the left centre of the front line of the right battalion skirts the South western face of the MON DU RASTA enclosure, (4) that the right centre of the front line of the left battalion passes through a building at C.5.a.15.75 (5) that the centre of the rear line of the left battalion touches the STEENBEEK (6) and that the left of the Left Battalion will have to be slightly refused so as to be clear of the barrage which is drawn back on our left flank.

/B........

B. <u>2nd. Line.</u> The method of preparing the forming up ground would be the same, but it is suggested, that the troops halt in small platoon columns ready to cross the STEENBEEK directly the barrage commences.

Points to notice are :-

(1) That the RED FARM is near the centre of the rear line of the Right Battalion.

(2) That the centre of the front line touches the STEENBEEK, as does the left of the front line of the left battalion.

BRIDGES. 6. Every effort will be made to place 16 light foot-bridges in positions convenient for the passage of the troops across the STEENBEEK before ZERO. Bridges should be numbered from 1 to 16, and platoons will be definitely told off to definite bridges.

T. D. Coleridge
Lieut. Colonel,

10th. August, 1917. General Staff, 11th. Division.

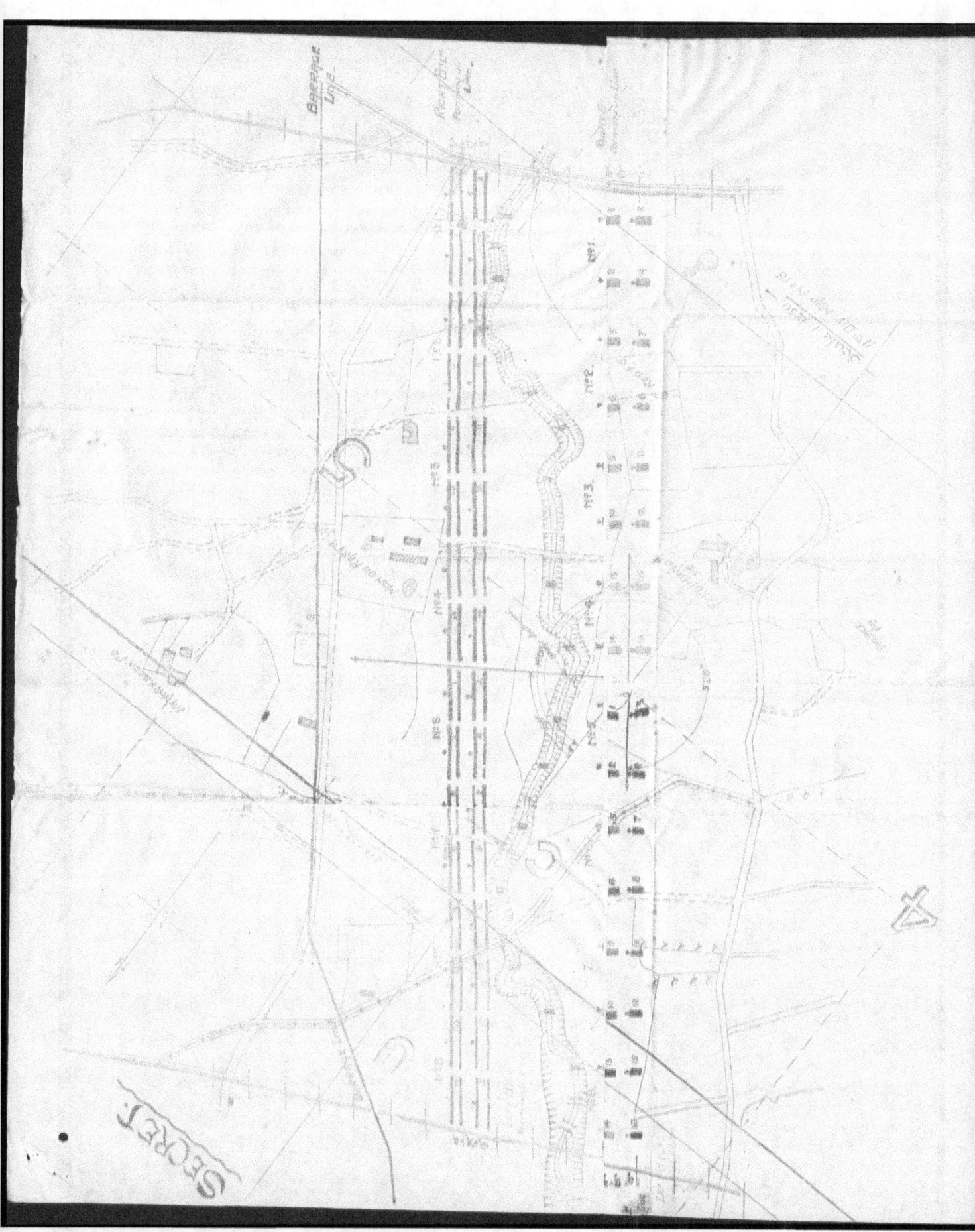

APPENDIX 31.

S E C R E T.   11th. Division No. G.S. 374.

TO:- War Diary

        Herewith   copies 11th. Division Instructions
No. 9.
        Please acknowledge receipt.

JMR Harrison
Major.

17th. August, 1917.   General Staff, 11th. Division.

S E C R E T.

11th. DIVISION INSTRUCTIONS NO. 9.

GENERAL. 1. By the morning of the 18th. August the 33rd. Brigade will have relieved the 34th. Brigade in the Left Sector of the XVIII Corps front, and the Division will then be disposed as detailed in the Table attached to 11th. Division Order No. 100.

METHOD OF HOLDING THE LINE.

2.(a) The 33rd. Brigade will at first hold the sector.

(b) The consolidation and wiring of existing line will be pressed on with vigour, and it will be straightened out and re-organised without delay.

(c) The Front line will be lightly held and the troops disposed in depth. Should the enemy enter our lines he will be immediately counter-attacked by special troops detailed for the purpose.

(d) The Front will be protected by artillery and machine gun barrages, especial attention being given to the DELTA HOUSE - WHITE HOUSE and the POELCAPPELLE - ST. JULIEN ROADS along which the enemy are most likely to counter attack. The flanks of the barrages should be so arranged that they over-lap those of Divisions on either flank.

(e) The closest touch will be maintained with adjoining Units of Flanking Divisions, and a plan showing defensive arrangements submitted.

HOSTILE MACHINE GUNS & SNIPERS. 3. Every effort will be made to check the activity of hostile machine guns and snipers, who may be located in the neighbourhood of our lines. Plans must be made for the capture of machine gun posts and snipers must be counter-sniped or stalked. On no account is the enemy to be permitted to gain the upper hand in this direction, otherwise his moral will be increased to the detriment of ours.

FUTURE OPERATIONS. 4. On a date and at an hour to be detailed later the 11th. Division in conjunction with the Division on our Right will capture those parts of the RED DOTTED LINE not taken yesterday; and with this end in view the following preparations will be made without delay.

A. Positions likely to be held by the enemy, such as :-

    1. The COCKCROFT.
    2. Gun emplacements C.6.a.2.7.
    3. Gun emplacements U.30.c.3.7.
    4. RAT HOUSE enclosure.
    5. Gun emplacement U.29.b.9.3.
    6. House at C.6.a.6.5.
    7. BULOW FARM.

will be reconnoitred and occupied if found vacated.

/If.....

- 2 -

If occupied by the enemy plans will at once be made for their capture. It has been found, that the concrete emplacements constructed by the enemy in this area are practically shell-proof against even the largest shells, so that the guns must not be expected to demolish them. Resort must be made, therefore, to other means. The entrance to the building must be screened by :-

(1) Smoke (either from shells or smoke bombs).

(2) Frequent bursts of shrapnel.

(3) Rapid L.T.M. fire.

(4) Machine and Lewis Gun fire.

Number (1) is designed to blind the enemy; Nos. (2), (3) and (4) are designed to force the enemy to keep inside the building until the attacking platoons are close enough to rush the building when the covering fire lifts.

B. On these positions being captured a line as parallel as possible to the RED DOTTED LINE will be taken up as the Divisional Front Line to enable an attack to be made on the RED DOTTED LINE in conjunction with the Division on our right.

WORKS. 5. The C.R.E. will press on work on communications East of the Corps Control; and Infantry parties will be allotted him when required from the supporting Brigade.

J. D. Coleridge
Lieut. Colonel,
General Staff, 11th. Division.

17th. August 1917.

SECRET.   11th. Division No. G.S. 415.

To:- ....

    ....

The following alterations will be made in Appendix "A", 11th. Division Instructions No. 8, "ARTILLERY & INFANTRY CABLE COMMUNICATION SCHEME", as a result of experience gained in the recent operations.

---

1. Main Routes only will be laid, for the construction of which the party detailed below will be responsible.

2. Lines to the number of 6 pairs will be run and maintained to Battalion H.Q. At all times lines numbered 1, 2 and 5 will be for the use of the Artillery, 3 and 4 for the use of the Infantry, and 6 a lineman pilot.
   Should the Battalion H.Q. move forward, Main routes will be continued up to the new H.Q.

3. Infantry Brigade Signal Officers will be responsible for keeping this route as far forward as necessary and will select the points to which it will run.
   Before definitely fixing these points he will discuss the route to be taken with the Artillery Group Signal Officers.

4. "Lineman Posts" will be established as laid down in Appendix "A".

5. Rations and stores will be supplied by Divisional Signal Company who will be responsible for the distribution.

6. Personnel required :-

   1 Man (good lineman) per R.F.A. Battery.
   4 Men ("   "   ) per Infantry Battalion.
   8 Men ("   "   ) per Infantry Brigade Section.

   This party will only be used to lay the main routes, maintain the same and man test dug-outs.
   All men not employed forward will live at D.H.Q. Camp, an Officer of the Divnl. Signal Company will be at the Camp, and will superintend sending out parties, rations etc., and will arrange reliefs approximately every two days.
   The party will be permanently attached to Divnl. Signal Company and will move with them.

/7.......

- 2 -

7.   The Divisional Artillery will detail two N.C.O's (Signallers) and the 33rd. and 34th. Inf. Bdes. each one N.C.O. (Signaller) to report to Signal Camp B.29.d.5.1 by 12 noon to-morrow 21st. inst.for duty with this party.

8.   This revised scheme will come into force at midnight 20th/21st. August. Lieut.PRENDERGAST will be the representative of the Divnl. Signal Company with his Headquarters at Dug-out 218 CANAL BANK.

20th. August 1917.

J.M.R. Harrison.
Major,
General Staff, 11th. Division.

War Diary APPENDIX 3i

SPECIAL ORDER OF THE DAY.

1. Though no great success was obtained on 27th. August, the G.O.C. is well aware that this was in no way due to any want of good fighting on the part of the troops, and wishes to thank the 32nd. Infantry Brigade for the gallantry they showed under heavy Machine Gun fire, and under weather conditions that made movement most difficult.

    The capture of VIEILLES MAISONS is an important success which will much help future operations.

    The G.O.C. also congratulates the 33rd. Infantry Brigade on the well-planned operations by which our line was advanced 1,000 yards during the time they held the Divisional Front.

2. The G.O.C. wishes to particularly thank the Artillery on the Divisional Front, including the 11th. Divisional Artillery, the 51st. Divisional Artillery, 77th. A.F.A. Brigade and 282nd. A.F.A. Brigade, for the very gallant manner in which they have done their duty during the three weeks that the 11th. Division has been in the line. In spite of long continuance in the line, very hard work, and many casualties, they have well sustained the high reputation of their Regiment.

29th. August, 1917.

J. D. Coleridge
Lieut. Colonel,
General Staff, 11th. Division.

 War Diary. APPENDIX 3.j

S E C R E T.

XVIII, CORPS LEFT SECTOR.

Handing Over Report.

Reference Special Maps
attached: No. 20. Roads and Tracks.
           No. 21. Dispositions and O.P's.
           No. 22. Inter-communications.

---

1. **ENEMY ATTITUDE.**

   (a)   Unless attacked the attitude of the hostile infantry is one of passive defence. There is some sniping and machine gun fire but little else - Patrols are seldom met with.

   (b)   Between 17th. and 27th. very little opposition was made to our advances. The COCKCROFT and BULOW FARM were given up practically wihtout a fight, but on the 27th. the enemy fought very well, especially in PHEASANT TRENCH between U.30.b.0.0 and U.30.a.8.3, and at PHEASANT FARM where there were 4 machine guns in action at one time.

   (c)   PHEASANT FARM is no doubt of great value to the enemy as from it he can command the whole of the ground East and West of the STEENBEEK, and he will, it is certain fight hard for its retention.
        Excellent views of PHEASANT FARM can be obtained from near MAISON BULGARE C.6.b.2.1 and near RAT HOUSE U.29.b.8.4. An Artillery F.O.O. who was 2 hours in PHEASANT TRENCH during the 27th. states that there appear to be 2 concrete buildings at PHEASANT FARM, in which the enemy sheltered his men and machine guns during the barrage. Directly the barrage passed over the FARM, however, the enemy left the buildings and manned small trenches or shell holes etc., about U.30.b.1.6 and 00.65, and poured fire into our advancing Infantry who were floundering about in the mud about U.30.a.Central.

   (d)   The hostile Artillery is formidable and its action is somewhat as detailed below.

       1.   Concentrated shoots on certain battery areas. There are no half-hearted measures about these shoots, some 10 to 12 batteries (105 mm. 150 mm. and heavier) take part and the area is thoroughly pounded for 2 or 3 hours, our guns and personnel being subjected to an unpleasant ordeal.

       2.   Night firing on battery positions and lines of approach is frequent, often combined with Gas shelling.

       3.   The enemy evidently still expects dawn attacks, as nearly every morning from 4 to 5.30 a.m. he brings down barrages on the following lines :-

          (a) The WINNIPEG - LANGEMARCK Road.
          (b) The STEENBEEK Valley.

   (e)   From about 5.30 to 8.30 a.m. daily, the enemy is as a rule very quiet, and there is practically no fire. Parties working West of the STEENBEEK are not, as a rule interfered with.

/2.........

- 2 -

2. **OUR POSITION.**

    (a)   As long as PHEASANT TRENCH & PHEASANT FARM are in the enemy's hands, we have the worst of the position, but it is believed that no concrete strong points now remain between our lines and PHEASANT TRENCH.

    (b)   Two Battalions should be ample for holding the line, but it should be borne in mind that heavily laden men take 2½ to 3 hours to reach the front line from the CANAL Bank. The question, therefore, arises as to whether another Battalion should not be located in and about the old British Front Line and the crest of the PILKEM RIDGE as far East as GOURNIER FARM.

3. **GROUND CONDITIONS.**

    The whole area is water-logged and pitted with shell-holes filled with water, in consequence, at the present time, movement across country is practically impossible.

4. **DUGOUT ACCOMMODATION ON THE CORPS FRONT.**

    The are reported to be 117 old German concrete shelters in the area between the old German Front Line and the STEENBEEK; of these, 19 have been destroyed by shell fire, but 98 are either inhabited or can be made so after pumping, draining and cleaning. The Corps is taking up this matter and a "Dug-out Town Major" is about to be appointed whose duties will be to allot accommodation and keep the shelters in proper order.

    East of the STEENBEEK there are a number of concrete shelters in the Divisional Area. Details will be handed over by G.O.C., 32nd. Brigade to G.O.C., 152nd. Brigade.

5. **COMMUNICATIONS.**

    (a)   For Roads and Tracks see Map 20.

    (b)   The policy has been to concentrate labour on the Road GOURNIER FARM - VARNA FARM - MILITARY ROAD, in preference to that running from HURST PARK towards REGINA CROSS which is over heavily shelled ground.

    (c)   Duck-boarded tracks are as shewn on map 21.
    Especially detailed parties are necessary to keep these tracks in repair, especially the Northern track from CINQ CHEMINS ESTAMINET and CANE AVENUE. The centre track to GOURNIER FARM is excellent.

    (d)   The fair weather tracks are useless at the present.

    (e)   The tramway is making good progress.

6. **OBSERVATION POSTS.**
    The best O.P's are as shewn on Maps 20 and 21.

7. **INTERCOMMUNICATION.**
    For means of intercommunication see Map 22.

8. **ADMINISTRATIVE ARRANGEMENTS.**
    An Administrative Map will be handed over by "Q".

9. **GENERAL.**   A further advance depends on -

    1. Improvement in weather and ground.

    2. The forward move of the Artillery.

/As regards...

As regards (1), it is suggested that the present bad weather will much delay the improvement of conditions and that as regards (2), forward artillery positions are difficult to find as long as the conditions remain in their present state and the enemy holds the high ground to the South and East.

J. D. Coleridge

30th. August 1917.

Lieut.Colonel,
General Staff, 11th. Division.

APPENDIX 6.

11th DIVISION.

REPORT ON OPERATIONS.

8th to 30th August, 1917.

11th. DIVISION.
REPORT ON OPERATIONS – 8th. to 30th. August 1917.

INDEX.

Order of Battle.

Action of 32nd. Brigade 8th-15th. August, Paras 1 - 8

Action of 34th. Brigade 15th-17th. August, " 9 - 12

Action of 33rd. Brigade 17th-26th. August, " 12 - 20

Action of 32nd. Brigade 26th-30th. August, " 21 - 28

Attitude of the Enemy 8th-30th. August, para. 29

Notes on the Operations 8th-30th. August, " 30

List of Appendices. " 31

APPENDICES.

Artillery Report.	No. 1.
Machine Gun Report.	No. 2.
R.E. Report.	No. 3.
Report on Administrative Arrangements.	No. 4.
Report on Medical Arrangements.	No. 5.
Report on Inter-communication.	No. 6.
Table showing number of Casualties.	No. 7.
Table showing Prisoners and War Material captured.	No. 8.

MAPS.

Dispositions taken over from 51st. Division. No. 1.

Progress made between 8th. and 30th. August. No. 2.

Dispositions handed over to 51st. Division. No. 3.

11th. DIVISION
ORDER OF BATTLE.

Commander.   Col.(temp.Maj-Genl) H.R.DAVIES, C.B.

G.S.O. 1.   Bt.Lt.Col. J.F.S.D.COLERIDGE, D.S.O. p.s.c.

A.A. & Q.M.G.   Bt.Lt.Col. W.F.L.GORDON, D.S.O.

DIVISIONAL ARTILLERY.

Commander.   Lt.Col.(temp.Brig-Genl) J.W.F.LAMONT,
                                                       C.M.G., D.S.O.

58th. Bde. R.F.A.   Lt.Col. O.de L.WINTER, C.M.G, D.S.O.
59th. " "   Major(temp.Lt.Col.) A.F.THOMSON, D.S.O.
* 77th. Army F.A. Bde.   Lt.Col. T.M.ARCHDALE, D.S.O.
* 282nd. " " "   Lt.Col. A.F.PRECHTEL, D.S.O.(T.F.)
* 255th.Bde. R.F.A.)51st.   Lt.Col. M.M.DUNCAN, C.M.G. (T.F.)
* 256th. " ")Div.   Major (temp.Lt.Col) L.M.DYSON, D.S.O.
11th. D.A.C.   Temp.Maj.(act.Lt.Col.) F.S.EVANS, D.S.O.
* 51st. D.A.C.   Lt.Col. G.McL. ROBERTSON, (T.F.)

                            * Attached.

Commanding Divisional Engineers. Bt.Lt.Col.F.A.K. WHITE,
      67th., 68th., & 86th. Field Companies. R.E.

32nd. Infantry Brigade.

Commander.   Bt.Lt.Col.(temp.Brig-Genl) T.H.F. PRICE,
                                                       D.S.O.

9th. West Yorkshire R.   Bt.Major (temp.Lt.Col) F.T.WORSLEY, D.S.O.
6th. Yorkshire Regt.   Major,(temp.Lt.Col.)   C.R.WHITE.
8th. West Riding Regt.   Major (temp.Lt.Col.) G.H.WEDGWOOD.
6th. York & Lancs. R.   Major (temp.Lt.Col.)   H.E. LAVER.

33rd. Infantry Brigade.

Commander.   Bt.Col.(temp.Brig-Genl) A.C.DALY, p.s.c.

6th. Lincoln Regt.   Temp.Lt.Col.   G.H. GATER, D.S.O.
6th. Border Regt.   Temp.Major(act.Lt.Col.) A.E.SOUTHERN.
7th. S. Staffs Regt.   Captain (act.Lt.Col.) W.N.CARTER, D.S.O.,
                                                                       M.C.
9th Sherwood Foresters   Major (temp.Lt.Col.) W.B.THORNTON, D.S.O.

34th. Infantry Brigade.

Commander.   Bt.Lt.Col.(temp.Brig-Genl.) B.G.CLAY, D.S.O.

8th. Northd. Fus.   Captain (temp.Lt.Col.) V.T.R.FORD,
9th. Lancs. Fus.   Major (temp.Lt.Col.) V.B.THURSTON.
5th. Dorset Regt.   Lt.Col. C.C. HANNAY.
11th. Manchester Regt.   Bt.Lt.Col.Sir T.D.JACKSON, Bart. M.V.O.,
                                                                       D.S.O.

6th.E.Yorks Regt.(Pnrs).Major (temp.Lt.Col).M.C.COWPER, D.S.O.

Commanding Divnl.Train. Lt.Col. F.H. LEATHER.

A.D.M.S.   Bt.Col.(temp.col.) D.D.SHANAHAN, D.S.O.
33rd. Field Ambulance.   Capt. (temp.Lt.Col.) J.D.BOWIE, D.S.O.
34th. " "   Major (temp.Lt.Col.) M.J.FAWCETT, D.S.O.
35th. " "   Major (temp.Lt.Col.) W.M.B.SPARKES, D.S.O.

11th. DIVISION.

Report on Operations from 8th. to 30th. August 1917.

1. On the night 7th/8th. August, the 32nd. Brigade (11th. Division) relieved the 154th. Brigade (51st. Division) in the left Sector of the XVIIIth. Corps front. The dispositions taken over were as shown on Map 1.
   The 9th. West Yorkshire Regt. held the right Sub-sector.
   The 8th. West Riding Regt. held the left Sub-sector.
   The 6th. Yorks and 6th. York & Lancaster Regt. were in Brigade Reserve in the CANAL BANK.
   The 34th. Brigade was located at HIMLY CAMP, and the 33rd. Brigade at DIRTY BUCKET CAMP.

2. The tasks allotted to the 32nd. Brigade were :-
   (a) To accurately locate the positions of the enemy's forward posts.
   (b) To advance our forward posts so as to admit of troops having sufficient space for forming up N.E. of the STEENBEEK.
   (c) To establish forward dumps of rations, stores, S.A.A. etc.
   (d) To improve communications.

3. On the night 9th./10th. MAISON BULGARE and MAISON DU PASTA were occupied without opposition, and our posts advanced N.E. of the STEENBEEK as much as 150 yards in the centre, and 50 yards on either flank.

4. On the night of 10th/11th. the 8th. West Riding Regt. in conjunction with the 59th. Brigade on the left attempted to advance their forward posts to a line running C.5.a.35.65 – U.29.c.20.25 – U.29.d.75.55. The advance was carried out under a barrage but the enemy made a stout resistance, especially about a concrete building at U.29.c.09.55 and "Knoll 19" whence heavy enfilade M.G. fire was brought to bear. The result being that the objectives were not gained and the final line ran from C.5.a.4.4 to the STEENBEEK at U.29.d.4.5.

5. On the night 11th/12th. the 9th. West Yorkshire Regt. was relieved by the 6th. York & Lancaster Regt. and the 8th. West Riding Regt. by the 6th. Yorkshire Regt. in the front line.

6. On the night 12th/13th. in order to enable the heavy artillery to bombard strong points in U.29.c. during the 13th., the posts occupied by the left Battalion (6th.Yorks) across the STEENBEEK were withdrawn. At 1.15 a.m. on the 13th. the enemy attacked our post at C.5.d.1.5 but was driven off.

7. On the night 13th/14th. in conjunction with the 59th. Brigade on the left the 6th. Yorks attempted to advance their posts to the line indicated in Para. 4 above. The advance was made at 4 a.m. under a barrage, two companies being employed. The enemy again fought stubbornly, especially at the strong points U.29.c.09.55 and C.5.a.35.75 and we made but little progress, eventually establishing a line C.5.a.3.4 – C.5.a.1.6 – U.29.d.5.5.

8. On the night of the 14th/15th. the 34th. Brigade relieved the 32nd. Brigade in the line, the 8th. Northd. Fusiliers on the right and the 5th. Dorset Regt. on the left taking over the front line shown RED on Map 1.

/2........

- 2 -

9. It had been previously decided, that the Fifth Army should capture GHELUVELT - LANGEMARCK LINE on the 16th. inst. The objectives and boundaries allotted to the 11th. Division were as shoewn on Map No. 2., that is ;

    1st. Objective - Line of the WINNIPEG - LANGEMARCK Road.
    2nd. Objective - GHELUVELT - LANGEMARCK LINE and an outpost line beyond it including PHEASANT FARM & WHITE HOUSE.

The 34th. Brigade was detailed to carry out the attack on the 11th. Division front with two Battalions 33rd. Brigade in close support.

It was decided, that the 8th. Northd. Fusiliers on the Right and the 5th. Dorset Regt. on the left should attack the 1st. Objective, and that the 11th. Manchester Regt. on the Right and the 9th. Lancs. Fusiliers on the left should pass through them and capture the 2nd. Objective.

There was to be a pause of one hour and 55 minutes on the 1st. Objective and of 30 minutes on the GHELUVELT - LANGEMARCK LINE. Zero hour was to be 4.45 a.m. and the attack was to be carried out under Artillery and Machine Gun barrages which were to advance at the rate of 100 yards in 5 minutes. Tanks did not co-operate owing to the state of the ground.

10. The 15th. passed quietly, and by midnight 15th/16th. the Division was disposed as under :-

(a) 34th. Brigade in Line.   (8th. Northd. Fusiliers (Right)
                                (5th. Dorset Regt. (Left).

    Approaching   (11th. Manchester Regt. (Right)
    STEENBEEK   (9th. Lancs. Fusiliers. (Left).
              H.Q.   FOCH FARM.

(b) 33rd. Brigade in CANAL (7th. S. Staffs. Regt.) In close
                   BANK. (9th Sherwood Foresters.) support.

    At SIEGE CAMP.   6th. Border Regt.

    With C.R.E.   (2 Companies 8th. Lincoln Regt.
                  (less 1 Platoon.

    With 33rd. M.G.Co. 1 Platoon 8th. Lincoln Regt.

    Carrying Parties. 2 Companies 6th. Lincoln Regt.

(c) 32nd. Brigade.   DIRTY BUCKET CAMP.

(d) The Artillery, Field companies, and 6th. E. Yorks Regt. (Pioneers) were in action.

(e) H.Q., 11th. Division "X" Camp.
    Advanced Report Centre, GORDON TERRACE, CANAL BANK.

11. The following is a detailed report on the action of the 34th. Brigade during the 16th/17th.

(a) Approach March.

The approach march of the 11th. Manchesters and the 9th. Lancs. Fusiliers from the CANAL Bank to the STEENBEEK was carried out successfully and with only a few casualties. By 3 a.m. on the 17th. the whole Brigade was assembled near the STEENBEEK, and formed up ready to advance.

/(b).......

- 2 -

(b) <u>Forming Up.</u>

In order to carry out the attack it was necessary for the Brigade to form up astride the STEENBEEK.

The original plan was for the two leading Battalions (8th. Northd. Fusiliers on the Right and 5th. Dorset Regt. on the Left) who had gone into the line on the night of 14th/15th. and were holding posts East of the STEENBEEK to close up behind these posts and be all formed up East of the STEENBEEK. But, owing to the partial failure of previous attempts by the 32nd. Brigade, and by the Division on our left to drive back the enemy advanced posts, only the two leading companies of the 5th. Dorset Regt. were able to form up East of the STEENBEEK, and, therefore, their supporting companies lined up on the West side. The 8th. Northd. Fusiliers formed up on the East side without much difficulty. Behind these leading battalions, the two rear battalions (11th. Manchester Regt. on the Right and the 9th. Lancashire Fusiliers on the Left) were formed up West of the STEENBEEK.

To carry out the operation of forming up, the Intelligence Officers of each battalions with a specially selected party laid out tapes. This difficult operation was successfully accomplished, as a daylight inspection subsequently proved, and all the battalions formed up as planned, though a patrol of the enemy from near BON GITE noticed and bombed the tape of 8th. Northd. Fusiliers, and one of the supporting platoons of 5th. Dorset Regt. was thrown into confusion by a shell, which caused 8 casualties and for a considerable time lost touch with the leading platoons.

(c) <u>Zero to Zero plus 5 minutes.</u>

During the period from Zero to Zero plus 5 minutes, while the leading battalions were closing up to the barrage and the supporting battalions were pushing up to and across the STEENBEEK, the 11th. Manchester Regt. (Right Support battalion) suffered heavy losses from the enemy shell fire. In fact, 8 out of their 12 Company Officers became casualties when only just across the STEENBEEK. The 9th. Lancashire Fusiliers (Left Support Battalion) on the other hand met with no casualties from the enemy barrage, which came down on the STEENBEEK on our Right; thus catching 11th. Manchester Regt. but then ran N.W. to about CONNEDY FARM, thereby missing 9th. Lancs. Fusiliers.

At Zero plus 5 minutes, (4.50 a.m.) the barrage moved forward followed closely by the leading battalions.

(d) <u>Action of 8th. Northd. Fusiliers.</u>

The troubles of the 8th. Northd. Fusiliers commenced soon after the advance began. It would appear that the left companies of the 145th. Brigade on the Right encountered heavy opposition directly after Zero, with the result that they made slow progress and thus the right flank of the 8th. Northd. Fusiliers became exposed to heavy machine gun fire. Both company commanders of the leading and supporting Right companies were killed, and there were other Officer casualties. In addition, the enemy sheltering in his concrete shelters was undisturbed by our barrage and fired through it at our advancing Infantry.

/At 5 a.m........

At 5 a.m. Lieut. CHEESEWRIGHT was Commanding both the Right Companies, and Sergt. BARLOW the two left companies of the 8th. Northd. Fusiliers. The first obstacle met with was a series of snipers' posts arranged in three lines parallel to and about 100 yards in front of the gun positions at C.5.d.6.7. These held in all about 100 men, who were nearly all killed. The gun positions at C.5.d.6.5, then held up the Right companies and by the time 2/Lieut. CHEESEWRIGHT had captured this strong point by putting Lewis Guns on both flanks, bombarding with Rifle grenades and rushing the position, the barrage had already passed beyond the first objective to its protective line. Sergt. BARLOW, Commanding the two Companies on the Left had difficulty in over-coming the blockhouse at C.5.d.6.9 and thereby also lost the barrage. He, however, pushed on with the Left front company and dug in 100 yards East of LANGEMARCK Road with his left on Cemetery at C.5.b.6.8. Owing to the heavy fire from MON DU HIBOU and the TRIANGLE on the exposed Right flank the Right Companies who had suffered very heavily were unable to advance past the line C.5.d.6.7 - C.5.d.6.9, where they remained and dug in facing Eastwards.

(e) <u>Action of the 5th. Dorsets.</u>
Meanwhile on the left, the 5th. Dorset Regt. had advanced without much difficulty. As the Commanding Officer suspected strong points at the start between his men and the barrage, he had ordered the two leading companies to push out Lewis Gun posts to assist the advance at Zero hour up to the barrage. This proved a most wise and necessary step and materially assisted the advance, the garrisons of the posts being rushed and dealt with, under the fire of the Lewis Guns. Touch was kept througout the advance with the Brigade on the left, but the party detailed on the Right for liaison with 8th. Northd. Fusiliers failed to make touch and another party at once detailed also failed. The LANGEMARCK Road was reached up to time and consolidation began at once on both sides of the road. The Right leading Company finding their Right exposed, at once seized the huts at U.29.d.9.2 and took prisoners from there. This Company refused its flank back to the LANGEMARCK Road, while the Right Support company, seeing the position on the Right, made a defensive flank, to South side of HANNIXBEEK FARM - a fine bit of tactical work. Within an hour all the posts were well on their way to completion, having been well sited and giving good mutual support. This Battalion did excellent work, not only were all objectives gained, but in addition 2 -4.2" Hows., 2 M.G's and about 150 prisoners were captured.

(f) <u>Action of the 11th. Manchesters.</u>
The 11th. Manchester Regt., which was detailed to pass through the 8th. Northd. Fusiliers and to advance on to the 2nd. Objective, had suffered heavily immediately after Zero, especially among Officers; in fact, only 3 company Officers remained when their advance began.

The advance from the STEENBEEK to the LANGEMARCK Road was greatly hampered throughout by heavy fire from MON DU HIBOU and the TRIANGLE, and in consequence, when the Battalion reached the LANGEMARCK ROAD the barrage had already started off towards the 2nd. Objective.

/The. COCKCROFT...

The COCKCROFT however, was found to be unoccupied, and the advancing troops passed through it. On emerging, the Right leading Company came under heavy machine gun fire from the Right flank, and the O.C. Company (Lieut.FALCONER), finding no troops of the Right Brigade near at hand determined to make a left-handed detour which he hoped would enable him to cross the danger zone, and make it possible for him to continue his advance on to the 2nd. Objective. The Commanding Officer of the Battalion, seeing this movement himself, and not understanding the cause, sent a runner to Lieut. FALCONER with an order to keep to his right. At the same time he ordered Captain BLEAKLEY, Commanding the Right Support Company to go up and fill the gap on the Right. He shortly afterwards received a message from Captain BLEAKLEY from the work at C.5.d.8.9 stating that he could not get on on the right flank, owing to heavy fire from the direction of MON DU HIBOU. The C.O. then went to the spot himself to ascertain the exact position of affairs and found Captain BLEAKLEY'S report was correct. MON DU HIBOU had not been captured by the 145th. Brigade and heavy, enfilade machine gun fire was being poured into our right flank from there. The C.O. therefore ordered Captain BLEAKLEY to stay where he was and to form a defensive flank. Meanwhile, Lieut. FALCONER, on receiving the order from his C.O. swung back towards the right and captured the work at C.5.a.55.50 with 40 prisoners; his company then came under heavy fire from BULOW FARM and the Right front, and having only a few men left, Lieut. FALCONER decided to withdraw to a more defensible position which he did.

The Left leading Company, supported by 2 platoons crossed the BANGHMARCK Road on the left, and advanced until they arrived about U.30.c.5.4 where they came under heavy flanking fire from BULOW FARM and finding both flanks unsupported they began to fall back. The Battalion Commander seeing this retrograde movement sent his Adjutant to rally them, occupy the huts at U.30.d.90.35, form a defensive flank, and join up with the 9th. Lancs. Fusiliers on their left. This was done and the positions were held until the Brigade was relieved.

(g) Action of the 9th. Lancs. Fusiliers.

On the left, the 9th. Lancs. Fusiliers passed through the 5th. Dorset Regt. on the GREEN LINE and went forward with the barrage at the right time. The advance went well till the Right Company came under heavy enfilade fire from BULOW FARM and also from the work on their front at U.30.c.2.8. At this point, Captain GRAINGER, Commanding the Right leading Company was killed and the Company after holding on for a time eventually fell back in line with the 11th. Manchester Regt. about the huts at U.29.d.90.35.

Meanwhile, the Left leading Company pushed on, and, though one platoon lost 18 men going from RAT HOUSE to PHEASANT TRENCH, their objective was gained. The Left Support Company had closed up owing to the losses of its leading Company and reached the trench almost at the same time, but extending more to the Right. Touch had been lost with the Right Companies when they were held up. Lieut. HAYES, now commanding the two Left Companies, hoping the Right Companies might have reached the trench more to the right, sent a bombing party down the trench hoping that they would regain touch. This party never came back. Two patrols sent to the right also never returned, but a third patrol located the enemy in PHEASANT TRENCH at U.30.a.80.50. Lieut. HAYES therefore established a block at U.30.a.25.85, the trench from that point to U.30.a.80.50 being flooded.

/In the meantime...

In the meantime 2/Lieut. GOSS, whose platoon had been
detailed to take WHITE HOUSE, occupied this point;
subsequently he was heavily shelled, 6 of his platoon being
killed and he himself being wounded. It was then agreed
with the Right Company of the Right Battalion (K.S.L.I.)
of 60th. Brigade to withdraw and hold 2 posts 50 yards
West of WHITE HOUSE, which was visited by patrols period-
ically and never re-occupied by the enemy. Throughout
2/Lieut. INGLIS kept touch with the Brigade on our left,
and Lieut. HAYES refused his Right Flank to get touch with
the Right Companies, the line running from PHEASANT TRENCH
West of RAT HOUSE and then joining up with 11th. Manchester
Regt. on the LEKKERBOTERBEEK at U.29.d.99.45.

(h) Subsequent Events.

The above outlines the position during the
night of 16th/17th. On Z plus 1 day it was decided RAT
HOUSE must be occupied to straighten the line at that
point to strengthen the defensive flank. 9th. Lancs.
Fusiliers were ordered to carry out this minor operation.
After dusk, Lieut. HAYES sent out a patrol which reported
RAT HOUSE unoccupied by the enemy, but snipers in the COPSE
East of it. A platoon then advanced in extended order,
occupied RAT HOUSE and passing on mopped up and killed 6
enemy snipers who were scattered in shell holes in the
COPSE East of RAT HOUSE. New posts were then dug so
that the line ran from WHITE HOUSE, which was again occupied
without opposition, through PHEASANT TRENCH at U.30.a.5.8,
2.7, 1.4, 0.1., U.29.d.9.9., 9.7 to the Battalion boundary
on the LEKKERBOTERBEEK at U.29.d.99.45. This line was
handed over to 33rd. Brigade on relief on night 17th/18th.

The 20th. Division also dug a defensive line
from the salient in PHEASANT TRENCH at U23.d.9.0 due South.
The 5th. Dorset Regt. therefore dug a post about U.29.b.88.
55 to join up the existing post at U.29.b.8.4 to the
Divisional boundary at U.29.b.8.7. This post was dug about
3'6" deep before relief and was then handed over to the
relieving Company of the 9th. Sherwood Foresters.

(i) Action by the 54th. M.G. Company.

O.C., 54th. Machine Gun Company had 4 guns
detailed for the consolidation of the GREEN LINE and four
for the consolidation of the RED LINE. These guns crossed
the STEENBEEK about 6.45 a.m. The guns detailed to help the
Right got into action to try and assist the attack when
held up, and remained in position there, one being subsequently knocked out. On the left the two guns helping the
consolidation of the 5th. Dorset Regt. got into position
about 8.5 a.m. while the two detailed to help the 9th.
Lancs. Fusiliers moved on and finding the Right of 9th.
Lancs. Fusiliers was held up came into action behind RAT
HOUSE to protect the right flank. About 4 p.m. these guns
withdrew and took up positions in front of the LANGEMARCK
Road on the line of the Dorset forward posts.

/(j).......

- 7 -

(j) **Action by the 54th. L.T.M.Battery.**

O.C., 54th. L.T.M.Battery detailed two guns to assist each flank. The two guns on the Right advanced behind 8th. Northd. Fusiliers to C.8.d.8.9 and the Infantry being held up, a gun was got into action and with one man holding it between his legs, 2/Lieut. JONES fired at the COCKCROFT and continued till M.G. firing from the COCKCROFT ceased. No ammunition was left. The carriers were either wounded or had gone forward with the Infantry, and it was therefore decided to go into Reserve. The two guns on the left crossed the STEENBEEK behind the 5th. Dorset Regt. but were not called on during the advance to the LANGEMARCK ROAD. Following on behind the 9th. Lancs. Fusiliers they reached a position about 100 yards West of RAT HOUSE, but the position of our troops being uncertain, were unable to fire from there. They withdrew later and took up a position near one of the 5th. Dorset Regt. posts, where they remained till the relief.

(k) **Inter-communication.**

Communications during operations were difficult, owing to the heavy shell fire that the enemy kept up on the rising ground of the STEENBEEK. As soon as lines were laid across that area they were immediately cut. But great credit is due to the 5th. Dorset Regt. who got continual messages back to Brigade H.Q. from the very outset, mostly by runner.

(l) **Casualties.**

Casualties were heavy in three out of the four battalions, all three losing very severely in officers, but 8th. Northd. Fusiliers casualties were the heaviest of all, and the loss of all their four Company Commanders very soon after Zero was a great handicap to them. Details as to casualties will be found in Appendix 7.

(m) **Action by the 52nd. Brigade.**

Throughout the 16th. and the 17th. the 6th. Lincolns were employed on various works - i.e., under the C.R.E. and for the provision of carrying parties; these duties were carried out in a thoroughly efficient manner.

As regards the remainder of the Brigade on the 16th. :-

1. 6.45 a.m.   H.Q. moved to FOCH FARM.
   7th. S. Staffords arrived in immediate support of the 54th. Brigade near HORTULUS ESTAMINET.
   6th. Borders arrived on the Canal Bank from SIEGE CAMP.

2. 7.45 a.m. 9th Sherwood Foresters arrived LANCASHIRE FARM.

3. 9.15 a.m.   7th. S. Staffords arrived on line MINTY FARM - GOURNIER FARM with H.Q. across the STEENBEEK in close touch with the 54th. Brigade.
   9th Sherwood Foresters in CANE TRENCH with H.Q. at GOURNIER FARM.

4. 9.30 a.m.   3 Coys. 7th. S.Staffords ordered across the STEENBEEK to support the 54th. Brigade whose right flank was in difficulties; before they arrived however, the 54th.Brigade had managed to form a defensive flank as described above.

/9.15 a.m....

- 8 -

      5.   5.15 p.m.   2 Companies 6th. Borders arrived about
                              MINTY FARM.

      6.   7.30 p.m.   Remaining Company 7th. S.Staffords
                              joined the Battalion East of the
                              STEENBECK.

                              From this hour onwards there was no
change in the situation until the Brigade relieved the
34th. Brigade in the line on the night of the 17th/18th.
when the 7th. South Staffords took over the Right Sub-
sector and the 9th Sherwood Foresters the Left. The 8th.
Borders were located in CANE TRENCH, and the 6th.
Lincolns formed the Brigade Reserve about LANCASHIRE
FARM.

  (n)   The line handed over by the 34th. Brigade to
the 33rd. Brigade is shown in   BROWN   on Map No. 2.

12. (a)   On the morning of the 18th. inst. the Infantry of the
Division was disposed as under :-

        33rd. Brigade - D Line - 7th. S.Staffords on Right.
                                  9th Sherwood Foresters on Left.

                      CANE TRENCH 6th. Borders.

                      LANCASHIRE)
                      FARM.   ) 6th. Lincolns.

                      H.Q.   FOCH FARM (moving to CANE
                                     POST C.9.a.6.3).

        32nd. Brigade - 2 Battalions - CANAL BANK.
                          Brigade less 2 Battalions MURAT CAMP.

        34th. Brigade - SIROM CAMP.

  (b)   The task allotted to the 33rd. Brigade while it was in
the line, was to advance the line so as to establish a
jumping off place suitable for an attack on and parallel to
PHEASANT TRENCH.

  (c)   During the day it was arranged that in conjunction with
the Division on the right our line should be improved by the
capture of the following places on the morning of the 19th.

        (i) The COCKCROFT.
        (ii) GUN PITS at C.8.a.2.2.
        (iii) CONCRETE SHELTERS at C.8.a.80.85.

        The attack was to be primarily a Tank enterprise, the
Infantry action being guided by the progress made by the Tanks.
Two Tanks were allotted to the 11th. Division, and 3 Platoons
of the 7th. South Staffords were detailed to occupy the points
mentioned above. The movement of the Tanks was to be screened
by an Artillery smoke barrage.

13. Events of the 19th. inst.
  (a)   The Tanks left their forming up places near ST.JULIEN
at 4.45 a.m. and proceeded to move on their objectives. Rapid
and striking successes were gained on the Right, several enemy
strong points, including MAISON DU HIBOU were reduced, and a
great moral effect was caused, the enemy, in many cases
surrendering on the approach of the Tanks.

                                                               /(b)......

- 9 -

(b) As regards the action on the 11th. Division front.
The Tanks first became visible at 5.50 a.m.
At 6.30 a.m. one of the Tanks detailed to the 11th. Division front was seen on the WINNIPEG - LANGEMARCK Road, it was then obscured by smoke but at 7.40 a.m. it again became discernible out of action by the side of the road about 50 yards from the COCKCROFT. As the Tank was incapable of further movement, the Infantry advance was carried on without it and by 10.30 a.m. all objectives were gained. The enemy made very little resistance and the only fire noticeable was from BULOW FARM, where a considerable number of the enemy were collected. There appears to be no doubt, that the enemy were greatly demoralised by the action of the Tanks, and fled on their approach. The result being that some very useful ground was gained at a small cost.

(c) The front line now held is shown as Red on Map 2.

14. **Events of the 20th.**
The 20th. passed quietly as far as the Infantry action was concerned, but the hostile artillery was more active than usual, especially in the neighbourhood of the STEENBEEK.
The 6th. Lincolns and the 6th. Borders relieved the 7th. S.Staffords and the 9th. Sherwood Foresters in the line on the night of the 20th/21st.

15. **Events of the 21st.**
(a) At 5.30 a.m. on the 21st. the enemy rushed a small post at U.30.a.8.9, inflicting several casualties. Before daylight however, the post was re-established and the garrison strengthened.

(b) The day was again quiet from an Infantry point of view. A patrol found BULOW FARM occupied by the enemy.

(c) From 9.15 a.m. to 12 noon the hostile artillery concentrated on our battery positions in C.14, 15, 20 and 21 and subjected the area to a very heavy bombardment (for details see Appendix 1).

(d) During the day, plans were made to advance our line East of BULOW FARM in conjunction with the Division on the right. Two tanks were detailed to assist the 11th.Division

16. **Events of the 22nd.**
(a) **Method of Attack.**
The advance was carried out by the 6th. Lincoln Regt. on the right and 6th. Border Regt. on the left.
The 6th. Lincoln Regt. advanced on a two Company front, the 6th. Border Regt. on a one Company front.

(b) **Action of the 6th. Borders.**
The 6th. Border Regt. on the left advanced in touch with the 6th. Lincoln Regt. and gained their objective without any delay. This was a perfectly straightforward operation and practically no opposition was encountered.
All the orders issued, and arrangements made by O.C., 6th. Border Regt. at a very short notice and under very difficult circumstances, were, however, excellent.

(c) **Action of the 6th. Lincolns.**
It is necessary to go into the dispositions of O.C., 6th. Lincoln Regt. in detail as the important movements were on this flank.

Assaulting Companies.

"D" Company - Capt. SUTHERLAND M.C., on Right.
"B" Company - Capt. JONES on Left.

/Positions of....

Positions of above companies by 4.50 a.m. before the assault.

"D" Coy. on Right - 200 Yards N.E. of LANGEMARCK Road with its right at C.6.a.6.8 and left immediately in advance of the COCKCROFT. Formation - 2 lines - 2 platoons in each line; platoons and sections ready to advance in artillery formation.

"B" Company on Left. - Had a much shorter front. 2 Platoons in line of posts from COCKCROFT to Nutments. 1 Officer and 2 platoons told off in 4 parties of 10 each to be formed up in vicinity of the advanced post at Dugouts (C.6.a.6.8). The special role of these parties was to capture of BULOW FARM. The remaining 2 platoons were to go forward in the same formation as "B" Coy. H.Q. of "B" and "C" Coys. were at COCKCROFT.

"A" Coy. (Capt. HOWIE, M.C.) was in support to "B" and "D" Coys. in the vicinity of NUTMENTS and CEMETERY (C.5.b.9.8).

"C" Coy. (Capt. BOWE) in Battalion Reserve dug in E. of STRAWBERK behind Battalion H.Q.

Narrative.

At Zero, the assaulting Companies moved forward as close to the barrage as possible, ready to follow it up at Z plus 40.

"B" Coy. on the left advanced close under the barrage. As the Coy. approached BULOW FARM about 14 Germans ran out. 9 of these were taken prisoners, of which 4 were killed by bullets and shell fire on the way back to Battalion H.Q. There were a good many dead Germans in the vicinity of BULOW FARM.

At about 6.40 a.m. "B" Coy. was digging in on its objectives and flares were lit. Captain SUTHERLAND then went to the right to see what had happened to "D" Coy. He found that the right of "B" Coy. was exposed and that "D" Coy. was not up on their flank. Captain SUTHERLAND immediately took a section and a Lewis gun from a platoon of "A" Coy. (in support) and stationed them on the right flank of "B" Coy. and facing VIEILLES MAISONS. He then went over to "D" Coy. and found the situation was not satisfactory. The men were leaderless, the 2 subaltern officers who led the assault, together with 5 Sergts., having become casualties, almost at once.

As the troops of the 48th. Division on the right were in difficulties and were making slow progress, Captain SUTHERLAND immediately sent for Captain JONES (at the COCKCROFT) and these two officers then led "D" Coy. forward and placed the men in line with, and on the right of "B" Coy. i.e., from S.E. of BULOW FARM to Cross Roads at C.6.b.05.45. This position was then consolidated. To make doubly sure, Captain SUTHERLAND then returned to the Support Coy. ("A") and brought up 1½ platoons from there. With these men, Captain SUTHERLAND formed a defensive flank from Cross Roads at C.6.b.05.45 to Cross Roads at C.6.c.80.65, digging in about 50 to 100 yards W. of POELCAPPELLE Road. Captain SUTHERLAND then returned to his company and went round his posts. He found them all dug in and the position secure. The time would then be about 7.40 a.m. In the meantime, the place where "D" Coy. was digging in was very swampy and one post was, in consequence, pushed out to about C.6.b.1.9½., where it was very much exposed and subjected to all kinds of fire. Captain JONES went out to visit this post and could not get back owing to snipers. Whilst he was there a shell landed in the post - wounded Captain JONES and two men. Captain JONES was unfortunately killed by a shell whilst trying to get back to the Dressing Station. Captain SUTHERLAND then assumed command of both companies.

/That night

- 11 -

That night, the Commanding Officer relieved "D" Company by "A" Company (Capt. HOWIS). "D" Company was put in support and placed under Capt. HOWIS'S orders, and a platoon of "C" Company under an officer was sent up that night to reinforce the supporting Company.

The enemy were very active and aggressive on the right flank and it was most fortunate that a good officer like Captain SUTHERLAND was on the spot, and it was entirely due to his initiative and quick appreciation of the situation that the flank was so well secured.

(d) <u>Comments on Smoke Barrage.</u>

The morning of the operation was a very misty one and consequently it is difficult to report very accurately on the efficacy of the smoke barrage put up by our artillery. As far as could be judged, it was good, and combined with shrapnel barrage would have formed a satisfactory screen.

(e) <u>Action of Tanks.</u>

The action of the Tanks - DRACULA (Male) and DEVIL (Female) as far as can be ascertained from officers who were on the spot, was as follows :-
(The mist and smoke made it difficult to observe the movements with great accuracy).

By Zero DRACULA, which was leading, had reached the junction of the ST. JULIEN - POELCAPPELLE and WINNIPEG - LANGEMARCK Roads, with DEVIL close behind. They advanced with the Infantry, but on getting to within 150 yards of the track leaving POELCAPPEL Road for BULOW FARM at C.8.b.15.85, found the road blocked by fallen trees and were unable to proceed any further. They were then about level with VIEILLES MAISONS upon which they opened fire for a short time. They then came back towards home. During their homeward journey, a direct hit was observed on DEVIL. This shell is reported to have killed the brakesman and wounded the gunners. 2/Lieut. LAWRIE commanding the tank then got out and commenced to bandage up the wounded man, when a second shell arrived and killed both him and the wounded man. Nothing further was seen of the Tank DRACULA until the evening when it was located on the West side of the POELCAPPELLE Road about C.8.c.9.8.

(f) <u>Notes.</u>

1. Eight Germans of 125th. I.R. were taken prisoners in a small earth dugout about 50 yards West of BULOW FARM during the attack. 2 of these were killed by German snipers and 2 by German shells while crossing "No Man's Land".
On the evening of August 22nd. another prisoner, belong to 23rd. R.I.R. was captured in "No Man's Land".

2. As soon as our barrage reached PHEASANT TRENCH a number of the enemy ran back from it. Some hours later, when they realised that our advance had stopped, they came back and re-occupied it.

3. 2 Machine guns were captured at BULOW FARM and brought back to Battalion H.Q.

17. <u>Events of the 23rd.</u>
(a) <u>Future Policy.</u>

On the 23rd., it was decided that on the 27th. the 32nd. Brigade would attack PHEASANT TRENCH by day, and establish posts beyond it and PHEASANT FARM. The 33rd. Brigade was, therefore, ordered to -

(1) Reconnoitre PHEASANT TRENCH & VIEILLES MAISONS and occupy them should they be found unoccupied.

/(ii)...

(11) Enlarge all existing posts so as to give sufficient forming up space for the 2 Battalions of the 32nd. Brigade destined to carry out the attack.

(b) **Orders issued by the 33rd. Brigade.**

On the afternoon of the 23rd. August, the following orders were issued to O.C., 6th. Lincoln Regt. (Right Battalion in the line) and O.C., 8th. Border Regt. (Left Battalion in the line) and 9th. Sherwood Foresters, (Battalion in Support) to the following effect :-

(1) To send out patrols to ascertain whether the enemy had vacated PHEASANT TRENCH and VIEILLES MAISONS.

(2) Should both PHEASANT TRENCH and VIEILLES MAISONS be found vacated, to occupy them, but not to occupy them PHEASANT TRENCH if the enemy had not vacated VIEILLES MAISONS..

(3) Should PHEASANT TRENCH be found to be still in possession of the enemy, but VIEILLES MAISONS vacated by him, the latter would be occupied by O.C., 6th. Lincolns patrols.

(4) 9th. Sherwood Foresters to relieve 6th. Lincoln Regt. as soon as the latter's patrols had established themselves on the new line.

(c) **Action of Patrols.**

Between 9.30 p.m. and 10.0 p.m. on the night of 23rd/24th. August, patrols were sent forward with the following results:-

(1) A machine gun position was located at VANCOUVER (C.8.d.2.3). These guns opened fire on our patrols.

(2) When within 80 yards of VIEILLES MAISONS, our patrol came under Machine gun fire from that place.

(3) Very lights were seen being sent up from about U.30.d.25.70, and our patrol advancing towards that point, found that the lights were coming from a point about 20 yards in front of PHEASANT TRENCH, and located a post approximately U.30.d.20.70. This post was watched by our patrol for a considerable time to make sure that it was a fixed post and not a patrol. 8 shots were fired at our patrol from PHEASANT TRENCH in that vicinity.

(4) A working party of about 20 to 25 Germans was observed about U.30.central apparently repairing the parapet.

(5) When within 40 yards of PHEASANT TRENCH, our patrol saw a party of enemy near PHEASANT TRENCH in U.30.a. apparently going round their posts. They were seen to visit 4 posts within a distance of 50 yards. They stopped and talked for about 2 minutes at each post. On moving further forward, our patrol came across some wire and located 5 parties of the enemy in shell holes in front of the trench. A considerable number of the enemy were seen by this patrol on their right. Very lights were seen to be fired from a point about 70 yards East of PHEASANT TRENCH.

(6) Three or four of the enemy were seen moving in PHEASANT TRENCH just to the right of PHEASANT FM. Very lights were sent up from behind PHEASANT FARM.

(7) The reconnaissances proved, that the enemy was occupying VIEILLES MAISONS, PHEASANT TRENCH and PHEASANT FARM.

-13-

(d) Relief.
On the return of the patrols, whose doings are recorded above, the 6th. Lincolns were relieved in the right of the line by the 9th Sherwood Foresters and proceeded to CANE TRENCH.

(e) Raid.
During the night a hostile attack on our post near WHITE HOUSE was driven off.

18. Events of the 24th.
(a) General. The day was uneventful, but good work was done in enlarging posts and making them suitable for forming up.

(b) Reliefs. During the night of the 24th/25th. the 7th. South Staffords relieved the 6th. Borders in the left sub-sector.

The 6th. Borders and 7th. South Staffords marched to the CANAL BANK, and the 8th. Yorks and 6th. York and Lancaster Regts. moved to CANE TRENCH and the vicinity of LANCASHIRE FARM respectively.

19. Events of the 25th.
The day passed without incident, and forming up places were further improved. In the evening the G.O.C., 32nd. Brigade moved his H.Q. to CANE POST and took over command of the line while H.Q., 33rd. Brigade moved to TROIS TOURS CHATEAU.

20. Events of the 26th.
(a) Relief. This was another quiet day. During the night of 26th/27th. the 9th. West Yorkshire Regt. on the right and the 8th. West Riding Regt. on the left took over the line from the 9th Sherwood Foresters and the 7th. South Staffords, who moved to MURAT CAMP.

Despite the weather being very wet and stormy, the relief went off without hitch, the troops of the 32nd. Brigade finding the forming up places dug for them by the 33rd. Brigade satisfactory in every way. The assembly was completed by 3.50 a.m. on the 27th.

(b) Work done by 33rd. Brigade.
Map No. 2 shows the advance made by the 33rd. Brigade between the 17th. and 26th. August. This was most satisfactory and reflects credit on all concerned, especially when it is remembered, that the Brigade held the whole of the XVIII Corps front for a fortnight in July, during a period when heavy bombardments (including gas shelling) were of frequent occurrence and casualties in consequence heavy.

21. Plan for the 27th.
The plan for the 27th. was as outlined in para 17 (a) above and Zero hour was fixed for 1.55 p.m. For objectives See; Map 3.

22. Dispositions at Zero on the 27th.
(a) 32nd. Brigade.
The assembly of the Brigade was in no way interfered with, and the troops suffered no losses in their forming up places, although they were in position from 3.50 a.m. to 1.55 p.m. It is therefore, probable that they were not detected by the enemy; the dull and stormy weather had no doubt much to do with this, but in any case the assembly was well organised and reflects creditably on all concerned.

/At Zero....

- 14 -

At Zero, the troops were disposed as under :-

9th. West Yorkshire Regt.
In assembly posts on the right sector.
Battalion Headquarters at MAISON BULGAR, with an advanced Headquarters in a concrete dugout near the COCKCROFT.

8th. Duke of Wellington's Regt.
In assembly posts on the left sector.
Battalion Headquarters in a concrete dugout at U.29.c.1.5 with an advanced Headquarters in a concrete dugout between RAT HOUSE and the LANGEMARCK - WINNIPEG ROAD.

8th. York & Lancaster Regt.
One company near MAISON BULGAR.
" " " MAISON DU RASTA.
" " " HURST PARK.
" " " CANISTER TRENCH.
Battalion Headquarters at GOURNIER FARM.

6th. Yorkshire Regt.
One Company in assembly posts on the extreme left of the Brigade Sector.
One Company in trenches and dug-outs behind RAT HOUSE.
Two Companies in CANE AVENUE.
Battalion Headquarters RUDOLPHE FARM.

32nd Machine Gun Company.
8 guns in forward positions to support a forward move with the attack.
These were distributed :-
2 Vickers Guns near the COCKCROFT.
2 " " " HANNIXBEEK FARM.
2 " " " RAT HOUSE.
2 " " covering the valley of the LEKKERBOTER BEEK.
8 guns in Reserve on the CANAL BANK.
Headquarters in CANE TRENCH.

32nd L.T.M. Battery.
2 Mortars at C.6.a.6.5.
2 " " U.30.a.2.5.
4 " in Reserve in MACDONALDS' WOOD.

(b) **33rd Brigade.**

33rd Machine Gun Coy. in position West of the STEENBEEK for Barrage work.

6th Border Regt.) In CANAL BANK in close support
6th Lincoln Regt.) of the 32nd Brigade.

7th South Staffords Regt.)
9th Sherwood Foresters.) MURAT CAMP.
33rd L.T.M. Battery.)

H.Q. 33rd Brigade. TROIS TOURS CHATEAU.

(c) 34th Machine Gun Coy. In position West of the STEENBEEK for Barrage work.

34th Brigade less) SIEGE CAMP.
34th M.G. Coy.)

/(d).........

- 15 -

    (d) R.A., R.E. and Pioneers in action.

    (e) Battle H.Q., 11th. Division at CANAL BANK near Bridge 4.

23. <u>Fighting Strength of the 32nd. Brigade.</u>

    The approximate strengths at which units went into battle were as follows :-

9th. West Yorkshire Regt.	15 Off.	530 O.R.
6th. Yorkshire Regt.	16 "	540 "
8th D. of Wellingtons. Regt.	16 "	540 "
6th. York & Lancs. Regt.	16 "	600 "

Companies were organised on a 3 platoon basis.

24. <u>Narrative of Events on 27th.</u>

    (a) <u>Our Barrage.</u>
        Our barrage appeared thin in the centre of the Brigade front (over PHEASANT FARM) and nowhere really thick, due probably to the fact that a very few of the shells burst on graze. The actual line of the barrage is reported to have been very indefinite.

    (b) <u>Enemy action on our attack commencing.</u>
        The hostile barrage was put down 8 to 10 minutes after our own. Light at first, but gradually becoming very heavy on a line BULOW FARM - RAT HOUSE, and in patches further to the rear, especially near MAISON BULGAR.
        Hostile machine gun fire, however, commenced almost at once - from PHEASANT TRENCH, PHEASANT FARM, positions on either flank of the Brigade, and from behind our barrage.
        A Machine gun firing from the centre of PHEASANT TRENCH and one from the roof of PHEASANT FARM appeared to be unaffected by our barrage.
        Owing to the good visibility at the time the advance commenced, and to the fact that there was no dust and very little smoke from the barrage, the enemy were able to see exactly in what strength we were attacking.

    (c) <u>Our action immediately after Zero.</u>
        The attacking Infantry were seen to leave their assembly posts at Zero and to be advancing well in spite of the very heavy ground, and the rain which began to fall soon after 2 p.m. and continued steadily the whole afternoon and evening.

    (d) <u>Action of the 9th. West Yorkshire Regt.</u>
        The troops advanced to the line VIEILLES MAISONS - U.30.central as close to the line of the barrage as possible.
        The 144th. Infantry Brigade appeared to be advancing well on the right, and the Duke of Wellington's on the left.
        Shortly after the advance started the front lines came under heavy M.G. and rifle fire from PHEASANT TRENCH to their front and VANCOUVER and HUBNER TRENCH in C.6.d. on their right and right rear.
        Zero plus 30 min:- The lines continued to advance slowly but owing to the flooded state of the ground, and the men slipping and falling in the mud, rifles and Lewis guns became choked and the advance was checked. The enemy had a great advantage over us as they were

/moving......

- 16 -

moving in a duck-boarded trench and their rifles and machine guns were not affected by the weather.

The barrage, not being as heavy as had been anticipated, for the reasons already stated, the enemy was enabled to use both machine gun and rifle fire to a greater extent than normally would have been the case.

Meanwhile the right company was in difficulties opposite VIEILLES MAISONS. They seized the nearest concrete building but owing to heavy losses and enfilade M.G. fire from the right, were unable to make further progress. Two platoons of 8th. York & Lancaster Regt. were sent up to reinforce the 9th. West Yorkshire Regt. but were also unable to make further progress.

Fortunately the building in VIEILLES MAISONS which had been seized, commanded the entrances to the 2 other buildings in the group of houses, and this fact no doubt caused the enemy to vacate these two buildings on the night 28th/29th.

The troops who took the first building worked round either flank, and directly the enemy found their line of retreat menaced they left the building and attempted to escape, practically all were accounted for.

A few isolated parties of the 9th. West Yorkshire Regt. succeeded in getting to PHEASANT TRENCH and beyond. These parties got through near the POELCAPPELLE Road, and at about C.6.b.9.6, but were obliged to withdraw owing to their being isolated and to heavy flanking M.G. fire.

(e) Action of the 8th. Duke of Wellington's Regt.

The enemy opened heavy rifle and machine gun fire, especially from the right front, as soon as the advance commenced. The fire appeared to come chiefly from PHEASANT FARM and PHEASANT TRENCH from U.30.central - U.30.a.7.6. Our barrage did not appear to be sufficiently thick in the centre of the Brigade front to stop this fire. A M.G. was seen firing from the roof of the right hand concrete building of PHEASANT FARM, but could not be silenced.

The right front company of the Battalion was unable to reach its objective on account of this M.G. fire. The company in second line reinforced and endeavoured to carry it on, but made no progress and was forced to consolidate on a line 60 yards in front of our original position.

One platoon, however, of the second line company under Sergt. KEYWOOD managed to cross the PHEASANT TRENCH near the LEKKERBOTERBEEK and started consolidating S.E. of PHEASANT FARM. Finding himself isolated and having only 4 men left, Sergt. KEYWOOD was obliged to fall back after maintaining his position for 2 hours.

The left Company of the Battalion reached PHEASANT TRENCH and occupied it as far south as U.30.a.5.7, and the second company moved up prepared to go through to the final objective. It was found, however, impossible to advance any further owing to the very heavy M.G. and rifle fire.

Owing to the losses and to the bad state of the ground there were large gaps in the line. These were filled by "B" Company of the 8th. Yorkshire Regt. touch being established throughout the line and on both flanks.

/(f)....

- 17 -

(f) Action of the 8th. Yorkshire Regt.
"A" Company. One platoon of this company advanced on WHITE HOUSE; found it unoccupied and dug themselves in on the E. side of the house. They were, however, forced to retire owing to the heavy artillery fire, and finally occupied, with the remainder of the company, the posts originally held before the commencement of the operations.

At 8.50 p.m. owing to touch not being continuous in the Duke of Wellington's line, "B" Company was ordered up to fill the gaps in the line and establish touch throughout.

At 9.15 p.m. a third company was sent to Battalion Headquarters, 8th. Duke of Wellington's Regt. to be used for the purposes of counter-attack or emergency.

The remaining company of the 8th. Yorkshire Regt. was employed on carrying.

(g) Action of the 8th. York & Lancaster Regt.
At 3.40 p.m. one company near MAISON DU HASTA was moved to near the COCKCROFT in support of the 9th. West Yorkshire Regt. At the same time the remainder of the Battalion was moved from GOURNIER FARM and vicinity to MAISON BULWAR, where it remained ready to counter attack if necessary.

(h) Action of the 8th. Borders.
At 5.50 p.m. in accordance with instructions, the Battalion moved forward into Support, with 2 Coys. in CANISTER TRENCH. One Coy. in CALEDONIAN AVENUE, one Coy. in CANE TRENCH and Battalion H.Q. at CANE POST.

About 10 p.m. "D" Coy. were ordered to carry rations from HURST PARK to the Battalions of the 32nd. Brigade in the line. They left HURST PARK at 11 p.m. and returned at 3 a.m. Meantime, "B" Coy. had been ordered to move forward and support the Battalion on the left, and re-counter attack in the case of a counter attack.

This company moved off from CANE TRENCH about 2.50 a.m. and occupied support trenches near RAT HOUSE. It remained in support all next day.

(i) Action of the 32nd. L.T.M. Battery.
The guns took up the positions and engaged the targets allotted. 177 rounds were fired, and one enemy M.G. was knocked out. One of our mortars was knocked out by shell fire.

25. Events of the 28th. inst.
(a) The night of the 27th/28th. was very quiet and the hostile artillery fire died down completely by midnight.

(b) During the 28th. the 6th. York & Lancs. Regt. and the 8th. Yorkshire Regt. relieved the 9th. West Yorks and the 8th. W.Riding Regts. in the line, which was organised.

(c) The 8th. Border Regt. performed some very useful carrying work and it was entirely due to their efforts that the troops in the line were supplied with rations and hot tea.

/(d).....

(d)   During the early part of the night 28th/29th.
2 platoons of the 6th. York & Lancaster Regt.
occupied the 2 remaining houses of VIEILLES MAISONS
without opposition, the enemy having been found to
have vacated the position.

26. Events of the 29th.inst.

(a)   The day passed without incident as far as the
front line was concerned.

(b)   The 33rd. Brigade less the 6th. Border Regt.
moved from the CANAL BANK and MURAT CAMP to BRAKE CAMP.

(c)   The 6th.Border Regt. after a rest on the
CANAL BANK joined the remainder of the Brigade at BRAKE
CAMP.

27. Events of the 30th. inst.
(a)   During the night of the 29th/30th. the 152nd.
Brigade of the 51st. Division relieved the 32nd. Brigade
in the line.   The relief was successfully carried out
without casualties.
        On relief the 32nd. Brigade proceeded by train
to POPERINGHE

(b)   The 34th. Brigade marched from SIEGE CAMP to
DIRTY BUCKET CAMP.

(c)   Divisional H.Q. moved from the CANAL BANK
to "X" Camp, and the G.O.C., 11th. Division handed
over the Command of the line to the G.O.C., 51st.
Division, at 11 a.m.

(d)   For dispositions handed over to the 51st.
Division see Map 5.

28. Comments on the Action of the 27th.
        The disappointing results of the day can,
it is considered, be justly attributed to the bad weather
and the state of the ground which handicapped both the
artillery and infantry to a great extent, and prevented
either doing themselves justice.
        After the 9th. West Yorkshire and the 8th.
Duke of Wellington's Regts. had failed it was decided
not to put any more men into action as it was considered
no success was likely to accrue owing to the deplorable
state of the ground.   Hence the 6th. Borders and the
6th. Lincolns who were in close support were not called
upon to fight.

/29.....

- 19 -

29. **ENEMY ATTITUDE DURING PERIOD 8th. to 30th. AUGUST.**

(a) The attitude of the hostile infantry unless attacked is partly defensive. There is some sniping and machine gun fire but little else. Patrols are seldom met with.

(b) It is true, that the enemy gave up the COCKCROFT and BULOW practically without a fight; but any points which he considers valuable, such as the Block House at U.29.c.08.35 guarding the crossing of the STEENBEEK, and PHEASANT FARM, which affords him an excellent observation post, he fights for stubbornly.

(c) During one of our attacks, the enemy's methods are somewhat as follows :-

1. The front line appears to be a line of shell holes (sometimes connected up, more often isolated) held by small troops of Infantry. These are, as a rule dealt with by our Artillery barrages, and our advancing Infantry.

2. Behind the shell hole line comes a series of concrete strong points, which are proof against Artillery unless directly hit by the heaviest shells. During our barrages, the enemy shelters men and machine guns in these strong points; directly the barrage lifts, however, men and guns are brought out, small trenches or shell holes in the neighbourhood are manned, and heavy fire opened on our men who are somewhat disorganised by the Infantry Groups encountered in the shell hole line in front, and by the difficulty of the ground over which they are advancing.
   For instance, on the 27th. 4 machine guns were brought out of PHEASANT FARM as soon as the barrage lifted, and effectually checked our advance.
   In some cases where the concrete strong points were furnished with loop-holes, machine gun fire was brought to bear from them through the barrage on to advancing Infantry.

3. During the actions of the 16th. and 27th. the enemy made much use of long range enfilade machine gun fire, which proved effective against our advancing lines.
   It has also been stated, that the enemy has been making use of long range machine gun barrages similar to our own, but confirmation of this statement is required.

4. No organised counter attack has been experienced by the Division during the period under review, any /hostile counter attacks contemplated were either broken up by our artillery fire, or were confined to long range fire action.

(d) The hostile artillery is formidable and its action has been somewhat as detailed below.

1. Concentrated shoots on certain battery areas. There are no half-hearted measures about these shoots, some 10 to 12 batteries (105 mm. 150 mm. and heavier) take part and the area is thoroughly pounded for 2 or 3 hours, our guns and personnel being subjected to an unpleasant ordeal.

/2....

2. Night firing on battery positions and lines of approach is frequent, often combined with Gas shelling.

3. The enemy evidently expects dawn attacks, as nearly every morning from 4 to 6.30 a.m. he brings down barrages on the following lines (i.e. fixed area barrages).

    (a) The WINNIPEG - LANGEMARCK ROAD.
    (b) The STEENBEEK Valley.

(c) From about 5.30 to 8.30 a.m. daily, the enemy is as a rule very quiet, and there is practically no fire. Parties working East of the STEENBEEK are seldom interfered with.

/30......

30.   NOTES ON THE OPERATIONS.

(A) GENERAL.

The experiences gained during the late operations go to prove that the defensive methods now adopted by the enemy will necessitate modifications in our attack formations and methods.

In the first place the system of waves which we have used with success against lines of trenches, cannot be easily manoeuvred against the present German system of defence.

Secondly the "concrete pill boxes" drive wedges into the advancing lines and break up our formations.

Thirdly, the linear formation is very difficult to maintain in the water-logged, shell-hole pitted terrain over which we are at present operating.

(B) METHOD OF DEALING WITH CONCRETE STRONG POINTS.

1.   All concrete strong points located within 800 yards of our front line should be captured before an advance on a large scale is carried out. Once captured, they must be occupied, the garrisons becoming outposts and covering the forming up of the attacking columns.

2.   Concrete strong points situated within 800 yards of our front line, being so close, it should be possible to know all about them and their exact location. The reduction of each point should therefore, be carried out methodically.
To begin with, thorough reconnaissance for the purpose of locating the enemy's dispositions and the position of the loopholes in the concrete strong points must be made. This done, the concrete strong points should either be rushed at night without artillery support, or attacked under a barrage. Again, the garrison might be treated to gas shelling combined with shrapnel and smoke on several occasions (which would cause the men to take shelter in the concrete strong point and to put on their gas helmets), and no attack follow. On the occasion of the attack, the shrapnel and smoke shelling would be used but no gas when it would be hoped that the enemy, having been drilled to gas, would take his usual precautions and in consequence be caught at a disadvantage.
Experience goes to prove, that the garrisons whom of these concrete strong points are inclined to surrender when the attacking parties begin to work round towards the rear of the buildings. It is suggested, therefore, that platoons detailed for attacks on isolated concrete strong points should converge on the objective with the hope of getting behind them, and that direct attacks should be avoided, machine or Lewis guns should be sufficient to engage loopholes which fire to the front or slightly to a flank.

3.   In the event of a large operation being ordered, the position of some of the concrete strong points in the area will be known and some unknown.

(a)   For the capture of the known strong points, special parties must be detailed beforehand, the sole objective of these parties will be the capture and consolidation of the individual strong point for which they have been detailed.

/As to ......

As to the method to be employed for the capture of these strong points during a large operation, it is suggested that the attacking parties should act as described in para. 2 above, i.e., work round the flanks and take the strong point in the rear. In addition, the artillery barrage should be especially thick round the strong points, so as to deal with any machine guns the enemy may attempt to bring out of the shelters. Further, a box barrage might be placed round the strong point, this would admit of the troops on either side of the strong point moving past it, while giving the defenders the impression that the barrage has not yet passed them. The actual attackers of the strong point would remain just outside the "box barrage" ready to rush in directly it lifted.

(b) As before stated, some unknown strong points are certain to occur in the area attacked over; for their reduction parties must be told off previously and kept inhand until called upon to act. No especial barrage can be arranged for such strong points, and the attacking parties must act rapidly under local Commanders as circumstances dictate.

(C) <u>FORMATIONS SUGGESTED FOR LARGE OPERATIONS.</u>

1. One or two lines of widely extended skirmishers who will deal with the garrisons of shell holes, pass by "concrete strong points" and move straight on after the barrage to the objective.

2. Directly behind the skirmishers will come the platoons specially detailed for the reduction of

(a) the known strong points,
(b) the unknown strong points.

3. Following the especial platoons will be the remainder of the attacking troops, who will take no notice of the concrete strong points, but will follow the skirmishers on to the objective.

(NOTE: Nos. 2 and 3 will move in small columns, probably in single file).

(D) <u>FURTHER POINTS.</u>

1. It is considered, that the creeping artillery barrage should move as follows :-

(a) In good weather - 100 yards in 5 or 6 minutes.
(b) In bad weather - 100 yards in 8 minutes.

2. It is considered that better value would be procured from machine gun barrages if fire was concentrated on important points, and not distributed along the front.

3. It was found, that the Division suffered heavy casualties during the time that the men were waiting during the advance for other flanking units to come into line with them. It is recognised, that there must be pauses during an advance, but it is suggested that every effort should be made to ensure that adjoining Divisions be given advances of equal length, and that all halts and fresh starts be made at the same hours.

/4.....

4. The initial barrage falls as a rule, 200 yards in advance of where the Infantry forms up. During the late operations, cases have occurred, when small bodies of the enemy have been hiding within 200 yards of the assembling infantry and hence inside the barrage, and have inflicted losses on the Infantry directly the advance started. One Battalion (5th. Dorsets) dealt with this effectively by sending out Lewis guns in advance of the forming up place - Stokes mortars might also be used.

5. In trench to trench attacks, fire action by the advancing Infantry was deprecated, and its one and only duty was to reach the objective on the heels of the barrage. In the new circumstances, which have now arisen, when hostile infantry in small groups may be met with at any moment during an advance, our leading infantry must be constantly ready to use their rifles and bring fire to bear on isolated hostile groups which have escaped the barrage.

6. It is considered that advances should not be too long - e.g. A penetration of 500 yards depth one day, followed by a similar penetration shortly afterwards, is more likely to succeed than an attempt to penetrate 1000 yards on one day.

=*=*=*=*=*=*=*=

31. The following Appendices are attached :-

No. 1. Artillery Report.
2. Machine Gun Report.
3. R.E. Report.
4. Report on Administrative Arrangements.
5. Report on Medical Arrangements.
6. Report on Inter-communication.
7. Table showing number of casualties.
8. Table showing Prisoners and War Material captured.

ARTILLERY REPORT.   APPENDIX 1.

RELIEF.

On the night August 7th/8th the 11th Division relieved the 51st Division in the front held by the Left Division XVIIIth Corps, and at 10 a.m. August 8th the C.C.G. R.A. 11th Division assumed Command of the Divisional Artillery covering that front.

GROUPING.

The Divisional Artillery were grouped as follows :-

Right Group.
    Group Commander O.C. 58th Brigade R.F.A.
        (Lt-Col. G. de L'EPEE WINTER, C.M.G., D.S.O., R.F.A.)

        58th Brigade R.F.A.
        255th Brigade R.F.A.   (51st Divisional Artillery).
        232nd (Army) Brigade R.F.A.

Left Group.
    Group Commander O.C. 59th Brigade R.F.A.
        (Lt-Col. A. H. THOMSON, D.S.O., R.F.A.).

        59th Brigade R.F.A.
        77th (A) Brigade R.F.A.
        256th Brigade R.F.A.   (51st Divisional Artillery).

Right Group Headquarters were situated at BRIDE FARM, on the YPRES - BRIELEN Road, and Left Group Headquarters were at CHATEAU TROIS TOURS on the BRIELEN-ELVERDINGHE Road.
        C.C.G. R.A. had his Headquarters at "F" Camp, 2½ miles S.E. of POPERINGHE.
        The 5th Siege Battery .R.G.A. was attached for fire control to Right Group 11th Divisional Artillery.
        The ammunition supply was established on the following lines :-
        The 11th Div. Amm. Column supplied the 58th and 255th Brigades, the 51st Div. Amm. Column supplied the 59th and 256th Brigades.
        The two Army Brigades were supplied by their own Brigade Ammunition Columns.
        All Battery positions were situated in the Divisional Area between THE CANAL and the old German Front Line.

HARASSING FIRE.

At the time of relief the existing policy was to carry out vigorous harassing fire, the daily expenditure of each Group amounting to 5000 rounds 18- Pounders, and 500 rounds 4.5 Howitzers. This policy was continued.

AMMUNITION.

As the supply of ammunition to Battery positions was carried out by Pack animals, this heavy expenditure put a severe strain on Wagon Line and Ammunition Column personnel and horses.
        In addition to replacing the daily expenditure dumps of ammunition at Gun positions had to be brought up to 1000 rounds per 18-Pdr. and 4.5 Howitzer.

/August 9th..........

2.

August 9th.
Early on the morning of August 9th the IInd Corps carried out an operation, and a feint was made at the same hour by XIXth, XVIIIth and XIVth Corps.

The 11th Divisional Artillery forming an attacking Barrage for one hour.

August 10th.
In addition to the normal Harrassing Fire, a bombardment by 4.5 Howitzers of Left Group, was carried out on a House just East of the STEENBEEK which was inconveniencing the Left of the 32nd Infantry Brigade.

(O.C. 77th (Army) Brigade R.F.A. (Lt-Col. T.H. ARCHDALE, D.S.O., P.P.A.) assumed Command of the Left Group.

August 11th.
At dawn the 32nd Infantry Brigade co-operated with the Right of the XIVth Corps in an endeavour to push the front line clear of the STEENBEEK on the Eastern side, and thus give sufficient depth for attacking troops to form up East of the River.

The attack was supported by both Groups of the Divisional Artillery.

This operation was not entirely successful; hostile M.G's held up the attack, and as the XIVth Corps were also unable to get on, no forward line was established.

During this period one hostile Battery was engaged each night with Lethal and Lachrymatory Shell, and on alternate nights one other suitable target was similarily treated.

Owing to the heavy casualties that Batteries had recently suffered from enemy gas shell every effort was made, and every cunning employed to achieve the most effective results with the ammunition available.

August 12th.
A daily programme of Harrassing Fire was issued to Groups in order that the fire of both Groups should be co-ordinated. A systematic sweeping and searching of all ground on the Divisional Front was aimed at.

At 6 p.m. Artillery Order No. 67 was issued; this order dealt with the Artillery support of the attack on the LANGEMARCK-GHELUVELT line.

August 13th.
At 6 a.m. a Practice Barrage was carried out with the object of testing the junction of XVIIIth Corps and XIVth Corps Barrages.

The Barrage on each front only extended 200 yards inside the Boundary.

Similar Barrages were carried out on August 13th to check junction between Barrages of 11th Divisional Artillery and 48th Divisional Artillery, and also between Barrages of Right and Left Groups.

The 585th Brigade moved to positions near HINDENBURG FARM.

August 14th.
The 11th Divisional Artillery supported a second attempt by 32nd Infantry Brigade to establish their Line clear of the STEENBEEK on the Eastern side. This attack was partially successful and secured the necessary area for forming up.

The enemy counter-attacked about 11-00 a.m. but his attack was held off by Barrage Fire.

/The........

The ammunition expenditure for this period of 24 hours was heavy amounting to eighteen thousand 18-Pdr. and five thousand 4.5 Howitzer.

On the night August 14th/15th one 18-Pdr. and one 4.5 How. Battery of 232nd (A) Brigade R.F.A. attempted to move to forward positions near HURST PARK, but owing to the very sodden condition of the ground only succeeded in getting one gun into action - the remainder being stuck close to their original positions.

Hostile Fire had been continuous, though at no time very heavy. The daily casualty list had never been high but there was a steady drain of a few men each day.

August 15th.

60th and 77th Brigades established their Headquarters at LANCASHIRE FARM.

The two Batteries of 232nd Brigade R.F.A. continued their move and with the exception of one or two guns completed it during the night.

During the night August 15th/16th the 4.5 Howitzers of both Groups co-operated in a systematic Gasshell bombardment of hostile Batteries, under the direction of XVIIIth Corps Counter Battery Staff Officer.

August 16th.

At 4-45 a.m. the 34th Infantry Brigade attacked supported by Right and Left Groups 11th Divisional Artillery.

Captain LEWIS (A/58 Battery R.F.A.) was Liaison Officer at Headquarters 34th Infantry Brigade and at each Battalion Headquarters there was also a Liaison Officer.

In each Group one Artillery Officer was responsible for carrying forward the main cable routes. Special parties drawn from the Artillery and Infantry had previously been allotted for laying these lines and for manning the necessary test boxes. performed

Very gallant work was ~~shown~~/by these parties, but owing to heavy casualties and incessant damage to cables by hostile fire, no very satisfactory results were obtained. Lieut. FRASER who was operating on the Right Group front was reported missing and no trace of him has yet been found. Lt. PURVIS of the Left Group was severely wounded in the right arm.

The strength of the Divisional Artillery supporting the attack was :-

Six Artillery Brigades i.e.
108 eighteen pounders
36 4.5 Howitzers.

The ammunition expenditure for this period of 24 hours was .-

47,000 eighteen pounders.
13,400 4.5 Howitzers.

The attack was only partially successful.

In the afternoon enemy concentrations were frequently either seen or reported from other sources.

In all cases Artillery Fire was rapidly turned on to them, and in cases where observation was possible, the results were gratifying.

The enemy Counter-Battery work was not severe, and practically all the Artillery casualties were amongst those employed in the forward area.

The casualties for the day amounted to:-

Lt. D. V. FRASER	Missing.
2/Lt. A. CASTLE.)	
2/Lt. E. CAMPBELL.)	Wounded.
2/Lt. J. M. PURVIS.)	
1 Other Rank.	Killed.
12 Other Ranks.	Wounded.

/At............

At the close of the day's fighting when darkness prevented further observation the Protective Barrage to be used in case of S.O.S. was fixed on PHEASANT TRENCH on Right Boundary to U.30.a.30.75, thence to U.24.c.60.10 to U.24.c.90.50.

In places this line was some considerable distance from our most advanced troops, but as the 48th. Division on our right were in doubt how far forward their posts were situated, it was necessary to push the right of our barrage out to join their left.

A significant feature of the days operations was the pronounced hostile barrage.

In the recent attacks at ARRAS and WYTSCHAETE communications and movements of troops had not been interfered with by any marked barrage, on this occasion communicated with F.O.Os and Liaison Officers were maintained under the greatest difficulties.

A new system of laying forward the main cable Routes had been inaugurated for this operation, but the intensity of the enemy barrage precluded satisfactory results from being obtained by any system other than a "bury".

August 17th.
At dawn all batteries "stood to" in case of a hostile attack, but nothing developed.

During the day several hostile parties were seen and engaged.

Harassing fire continued by day and night, every effort being made to prevent the enemy constructing any new defences.

The 33rd. Infantry Brigade relieved the 38nd. Infantry Brigade in the line.

August 18th.
Harassing fire continued.

August 19th.
The 33rd. Infantry Brigade assisted by "G" Battn. Tank Corps, attacked the COCKCROFT, co-operating with 48th. Division who were carrying out a similar operation against strong points on their front.

The Artillery co-operated by forming x smoke barrages to mask all high ground from which the enemy could view the movement of the Tanks, and also standing barrages of shrapnel and H.E. on trenches and works occupied by the enemy.

The allotment of Smoke-shell was inadequate for the task, and the Smoke barrage was accordingly thickened up in places with Lachrymatory shell and H.E.

The actual 18-pdr. smoke barrages worked out at only one round per 30 yards on barrage line per minute; although this was considered thinner than authorities on smoke barrages direct, the results appear to have been satisfactory.

The result of the operation was most successful, the COCKCROFT being occupied, and the enemy garrison routed.

August 20th.
Harassing fire continued, but no operations carried out.

/August 21st.....

August 21st.

The noticeable feature of the day was a most marked concentration of enemy artillery on battery positions in C.14, 15, 20 and 21.

Guns and howitzers of all calibres were employed.

Fire opened at about 9 a.m. and continued without interruption till noon.

The bombardment was resumed for about two hours in the afternoon, and again about 10 p.m.

Batteries of 58th. Brigade R.F.A. suffered considerably, three officers (including the battery Commander) of A/58 Battery being wounded.

August 22nd.

At dawn the 33rd. Brigade, covered by the fire of both Groups advanced their line with a view to occupying a suitable line for a further advance against PHEASANT TRENCH.

BULOW FARM was included in the day's captures.

Smoke barrages were again used to blind the enemy's observation.

August 23rd. & 24th.

On August 23rd. & 24th. no operations were carried out, harassing fire being still continued.

On August 24th. Headquarters 11th. Divisional Artillery moved to BORDER CAMP.

August 25th.

The enemy repeated his Artillery concentration on battery positions in the neighbourhood of BOUNDARY Road and ADMIRAL'S ROAD, inflicting heavy casualties on 58th. Brigade R.F.A.

August 26th.

Practice barrages were carried out in preparation for the attack on PHEASANT TRENCH which had been ordered for August 27th.

The junction of barrages and Divisional and Group boundaries were tested.

A/58 Battery R.F.A. whose position had been the centre of the enemy's concentrated artillery fire on August 21st. and 25th. were moved forward about 500 yards in position close behind the crest.

August 27th.

Headquarters 11th. Division and 11th. Divisional Artillery were established on the CANAL BANK at 11 a.m.

At 1.55 p.m. the 32nd. Infantry Brigade attacked PHEASANT TRENCH, the 48th. Division on the right carrying out a similar operation.

The attack was supported by both groups; smoke barrages were again employed.

During the attack, the enemy carried out practically no counter-battery work.

The Creeping Barrage was reported to be thin. This can be accounted for by the fact that owing to the very wet state of the ground, no dust was thrown up by shrapnel bullets, and all shell which burst on graze gave no apparent results.

/A better barrage..

A better barrage would probably have been obtained by bursting more than 50% in the air.

An F.O.O. from each group got forward into PHEASANT TRENCH. They were able to give a good account of the action taken by the enemy, but owing to communications breaking down they were not able to direct fire on to points from which the enemy was shooting with rifles and machine guns.

Lt. JENKINS of the 255th. Brigade R.F.A. was the F.O.O. of the Left Group, and Lt. WHEELER, 58th. Brigade R.F.A. was the F.O.O. of the Right Group.

August 28th/29th.
No further operations took place.
Harassing fire being carried out.

August 30th.
G.O.C., R.A. 51st. Division relieved G.O.C., R.A. 11th. Division at 11 a.m.

IMPRESSIONS.

1. The Batteries partaking in these operations came into action on this front at the beginning of July. The majority having come straight from some other "offensive". In some cases a few days rest had been fitted in on the march up.

    Since the middle of July each battery had probably fired an average of over six hundred rounds per day.

    This expenditure entails very heavy work, not only in shooting but also in replenishing.

2. At the beginning of August it became possible to withdraw a certain percentage of the personnel from the batteries for a few days' rest. As the expenditure was not affected by the number of guns out of action, or personnel resting, the work of the gunners in action was increased, proportionately to the number of men being rested.

    A rest house was provided in POPERINGHE, but it is doubtful if the few days' rest spent there materially benefitted the personnel as a whole.

    Wagon line and D.A.C. personnel were working throughout at high pressure.

    A battery, even if it was up to establishement (which it never is) cannot put men out of work altogether.

    To rest one man, is merely to double another man's work.

3. The problem of tracks and roads in wet weather is still unsolved.

    Every assistance in their power was given by the Royal Engineers and Pioneers, but still difficulties were experienced.

    The solution appears to be "more men, more material".

    It is doubtful if the artillery could have kept pace with the advance, had the operations been carried through with the success that was anticipated.

4. An endeavour was made to break down the parochial system of Telephone Communication which is so dear to the heart of every gunner.

    Conditions did not favour the new scheme. Want of training and practice, and an unwonted interference on the part of the enemy militated against the success of the co-operative system.

    Its failure has, it is feared, strengthened the hand of those in favour of "every man for himself".

5. The present slow rate of advance, and the enemy's policy of occupying areas and strong points instead of a definite trench system, must influence the policy of future barrages.

6. Details of ammunition expenditure are attached.

AMMUNITION EXPENDITURE.

From 8th August 1917 to 30th August 1917.

DATE.	4.5" Howitzer.	18-Pounder.	TOTAL.
8th/9th Augt.	1549	5931	7480
9th/10th Augt.	1917	10185	12102
10th/11th Augt.	1991	12681	14672
11th/12th Augt.	1804	7035	8839
12th/13th Augt.	1484	7733	9217
13th/14th Augt.	4731	18132	22663
14th/15th Augt.	1696	9233	10929
15th/16th Augt.	13409	47000	60409
16th/17th Augt.	2979	16917	19896
17th/18th Augt.	1956	7586	9542
18th/19th Augt.	2340	12484	14824
19th/20th Augt.	1376	5598	6974
20th/21st Augt.	1690	5291	6981
21st/22nd Augt.	5891	27372	33263
22nd/23rd Augt.	1253	6824	8077
23rd/24th Augt.	1708	7098	8806
24th/25th Augt.	1080	7708	8788
25th/26th Augt.	1475	6700	8175
26th/27th Augt.	1320	10785	12105
27th/28th Augt.	10577	60049	70626
28th/29th Augt.	1559	5157	6716
TOTAL	63785	297499	361284

APPENDIX 2.

MACHINE GUN SUPPORT.

8th. - 30th. August 1917.

1. During the period 8th. to 15th. when the front line was situated about the STEENBEEK, the 32nd. Machine Gun Coy. was disposed as under :-

   (a) 10 guns in defensive positions.
   (b) 6 guns in Reserve in CANE TRENCH.

   The 33rd. and 34th. Machine Gun Companies remained at rest with their Brigades.

2. During the period 15th. to 30th. the Machine gun policy of the Division was as under :-

   A. *While holding the Line defensively*

   (i) 8 guns have been disposed in depth behind the front line for close defence.

   (ii) 8/16 guns in barrage positions ready to open fire if need be but normally silent.

   (iii) 24/32 guns resting.

   B. *During Offensive Operations.*

   (i) 8 guns were detailed to go forward and support the new positions when gained.

   (ii) 8 guns were kept in Mobile reserve.

   (iii) 32 guns combined with the Artillery and fired regular set barrages.

3. *Plan for the attack on the 16th.*
   For the attack on the LANGEMARCK LINE on the 16th. inst. the machine guns of the Division were allotted as follows :-

   32nd. and 33rd. M.G. Companies to form a M.G. barrage from positions East of the STEENBEEK as shown on tracing attached to Appendix 2 of 11th. Division Order No. 95.
   34th. M.G. Company - 8 guns to go forward behind the Infantry to points previously selected to help to consolidate the line.

   8 guns in Reserve - Four in CANE TRENCH.
   Four in CANAL BANK.

4. *Action of the 32nd. and 33rd. Machine Gun Companies.*
   On the night of the 14th/15th. the guns of the 32nd) M.G.Company ~~were in dug-outs~~ were relieved in defensive positions in the line and moved to dug-outs in the vicinity of their barrage positions which had been reconnoitred previously. On the night of the 15th/16th. the 32nd. and 33rd. M.G. Companies moved into their barrage positions as soon after dark as possible.
   The night was spent in constructing emplacements which had consisted of shell holes with sand-bag platforms on them, and in completing the supply of S.A.A.

/By 4 a.m.....

By 4 a.m. on the morning of the 16th. inst. the guns were in position and laid on their barrage lines.

At Zero plus 30 minutes all guns opened fire. Unfortunately, the enemy barrage was very heavy around the guns, and an enemy aeroplane dropped a light over the positions of the 32nd. M.G.Company, and they were traversed by a 5.9 Howitzer. Two of the guns were blown up and the Officer in charge withdrew the remainder of to their dugouts until the shelling had abated slightly. The tripods were left in position. Shortly afterwards when the hostile shelling had slackened, the teams returned but found that five of their tripods had been blown up. The remainder of the guns got into action again. At 5 p.m. the guns were withdrawn to CANE TRENCH and on the 17th. inst. into MURAT CAMP.

The 33rd. M.G. Company were more fortunate and carried out the whole of their barrages as ordered. Four of their guns were knocked out.

The Companies between them fired 100,000 rounds.

After the barrage was finished the guns remained in their positions to answer any S.O.S. call sent up. No S.O.S. calls were, however, recorded.

The casualties in guns and material were heavy, but the casualties in personnel were not severe.

5. Action of the 34th. Machine Gun Company.

The 34th. Machine Gun Company on the night of the 14th. inst. relieved two guns of the 32nd. Machine Gun Company in the line. These guns were withdrawn the next night.

At Zero hour, the guns were situated as follows:-

Eight in their assembly positions preparatory to advancing.
Four in Reserve in CANE TRENCH.
Four in Reserve in CANAL BANK.

At 5.30 a.m. the eight guns detailed to go forward commenced to advance to positions previously selected; as, however, all the objectives were not captured most of the guns could not take up these positions.

Two guns got into position on the road East of the STEENBEEK near MON DU RASTA, two about U.29.d.8.8, two near RAT HOUSE.

About 4 p.m. some of the posts in front of RAT HOUSE were driven back and the two M.G's in consequence came back slightly.

During the day the guns of the 34th. M.G. Company got several targets consisting of small parties of Germans and inflicted casualties on them.

By 7 p.m. the guns were situated as follows, where they remained until relieved on 20th/21st. by 32nd. Machine Gun Company :-

One at RED FARM.
Two at MON DU RASTA.
One at U.29.d.3.2.
One at C.5.b.8.8.
One at U.29.d.8.3.
One at U.29.b.3.6.
One at U.29.c.7.6.
Four in CANE TRENCH.
Four in CANAL BANK.

The casualties in this company were not severe.

/6......

- 3 -

6. **Dispositions 17th. - 19th.**
   During this period the 3 Companies were disposed as under :-

     32nd. M.G. Coy.   -   At rest.

     33rd. M.G. Coy.   -   8 Guns CANAL BANK.
              8 Guns in barrage positions West of STEENBEEK.

     34th. M.G. Coy.   -   8 guns in barrage positions West of STEENBEEK.
              8 guns in defensive positions in the Line.

7. **Dispositions on the 20th. and 21st.**

     32nd. M.G. Coy.   -   6 guns in defensive positions in the Line.
              2 guns in Mobile Reserve in CANE TRENCH.
              8 guns in barrage positions West of STEENBEEK.

     33rd. M.G. Coy.   -   8 guns in barrage positions West of STEENBEEK.
              8 guns in the CANAL BANK.

     34th. M.G. Coy.   -   At SIEGE CAMP Resting.

8. **Action by 32nd. and half 33rd. M.G. Company on 22nd.**
   To cover the advance of the 33rd. Brigade the 16 guns West of the STEENBEEK opened fire at 4.45 a.m. on the BLUE barrage lines, as shown on tracing attached to the Machine Gun programme issued with 11th. Division Order No. 103. At 5.43 a.m. the guns lifted on to the RED barrage lines and at 6.30 a.m. they ceased fire remaining in positions ready to put down a protective barrage on receipt of an S.O.S. About 30,000 rounds were fired. The guns East of the STEENBEEK were pushed slightly further forward.

9.   The dispositions described in Para. 7 above remained in force until the 25th.

10. **Arrangements for the Attack on the 27th.**
    The remaining eight guns of the 33rd. M.G. Coy. relieved the eight guns of the 32nd. M.G. Company West of the STEENBEEK. 16 guns of the 34th. M.G. Company moved into barrage positions West of the STEENBEEK.

11. **Action by 32nd. M.G. Company on 27th.**
    The eight guns of the 32nd. Machine Gun Company holding defensive positions East of the STEENBEEK had orders to advance after the Infantry and take up defensive positions.
    After the Infantry had passed beyond VIEILLES MAISONS, Lieut. Drunning, thinking that all the houses of VIEILLES MAISONS had been captured went forward to reconnoitre with a Corporal, but both were wounded by rifle fire from the untaken houses. Later on, his two teams under the remaining N.C.O. tried to advance, but owing to heavy rifle and M.G. fire were unable to do so, and three more of the men were hit. The remainder of the two teams then withdrew to the COCKCROFT where they took up defensive positions. The other six teams were unable to advance. By 8 p.m. the guns East of the STEENBEEK were situated as follows :-
      One at C.5.d.7.9.   Two at the COCKCROFT.
      One at U.29.d.90.05. One at U.29.d.8.7.
      Two at RAT HOUSE.

/12.....

- 4 -

12. **Action by 33rd. and 34th. M.G. Companies on 27th.**

    At 1.55 p.m. the guns of the 33rd. and 34th. M.G. Companies, to assist the attack of the 52nd. Infantry Brigade opened fire for eight minutes on the BLUE barrage lines, as in Appendix to 11th. Division Order No. 105, and then lifted back to the RED barrage lines at the rate of 100 yards in eight minutes, and remained there until 3.15 p.m. when they ceased fire.

    6.55 p.m. fire was re-opened on RED barrage lines until 7.40 p.m. After 7.40 p.m. guns remained ready to open a protective barrage at once on the same lines on receipt of an S.O.S. About 190,000 rounds were fired during the day. The guns were in telephonic communication with the Company Commanders, and the D.M.G.O. the whole time, and suffered no casualties.

13. **Events of the 28th.**

    At dusk, the guns of the 33rd. M.G. Company were withdrawn to MURAT CAMP.

14. **Events of the 29th.**

    Shortly after dawn, the guns of the 34th. M.G. Coy. were withdrawn to SIEGE CAMP.

15. **Events of the night 29th/30th.**

    The 32nd. M.G. Company were relieved by the 152nd. M.G. Company and returned to POPERINGHE.

=*=*=*=*=*=*=

APPENDIX S.

R.E. WORK.

1. On taking over from the 51st. Divisional Engineers, work was allotted to Units as follows :-

86th. Field Coy. all R.E. work in the Right forward sub-section.
87th. Field Coy. all R.E. work in the Left forward sub-section.
88th. Field Coy. work in rear sub-section.
8th. East Yorks (Pioneers) Repair and maintenance of road forward from MORTELJAE ESTAMINET.

2. Work was commenced on the 8th. instant and was concentrated on communications as follows in preparation for the attack of the 16th.

(a) Duck-board track from 5 CHEMINS EST. to FRANCOIS FM via CANE AVENUE.
(b) Duckboard track from HURST PARK to FERDINAND FARM.
(c) Fair weather tracks for the purpose of getting guns forward from HURST PARK towards FERDINAND FARM.
(d) -ditto- from C.10.a.3.5 to join MILITARY ROAD at C.4.b.5.0.
(e) The KEMPTON PARK - REGINA CROSS ROAD and KEMPTON PARK - GOUNNIER FARM ROAD.

Work was necessarily slow on these communications for the following reasons :-

Much of the work had to be done at night and was interfered with a good deal by gas shelling; all day work had to be done by very small and scattered parties as shell fire was invariably opened on any large parties working on roads ; owing to the roads in rear being in a very bad condition it was exceedingly difficult to get material anywhere near the work by horsed transport, in consequence of which large carrying parties were required and these were, on several occasions not available.

By the evening of the 15th. the state of these communications was as follows :-

(a) Complete to metalled road S.W. of FERDINAND FARM.
(b) " " FRANCOIS FARM.
(c) Passable to C.10.a.7.3.
(d) " " C.10.a.0.5.
(e) Passable for guns to 150 yards beyond HURST PARK and up to GOUNNIER FARM.

During this period a number of dugouts were cleared out and repaired.
Dumps of material were formed near the STEENBEEK for the repair of bridges and a large number of Infantry Bridges were placed in position on the STEENBEEK.

3. For the attack of the 16th. inst. the following arrangements were made :-

Two sections were detailed for the construction of 4 strong points, two on each flank; the garrisons were to be met on the sites selected and were to assist in consolidation. Two sections were detailed for the repair of bridges over the STEENBEEK. The remainder of R.E's and Pioneers were to continue on communications (c), (d) and (e) as soon after Zero as possible.
The following work was actually carried out :-

- 2 -

1. Consolidation of 3 strong points HASHINBRUK FARM U.29.d.1.9 and C.5.b.8.0. The party told off for the consolidation of the COCKCROFT was unable to reach its objective owing to this point not being held; this party assisted at C.5.b.8.0 where considerable difficulty was experienced in working owing to Machine gun and Rifle fire from MON DU HIBOU.

2. Bridges were repaired and made fit for traffic as follows :-

   MILITARY ROAD BRIDGE.
   BRIDGE "M" C.5.c.4.8.
   "   "N" C.5.c.9.4.

3. Work on tracks and roads (c), (d) and (e) was commenced two hours after Zero.

4. After Zero on the 16th. inst. the Corps had arranged to take over the maintenance and repair of roads up to and including the road from C.2?.a.central (CHEDDAR VILLA) to C.3.d. central (RUDOLPH FARM), consequently work was discontinued on roads (e) (KEMPTON PARK - GOURNIER FARM and BOSICASTEL) and was commenced forward of these two places.

   The BOSICASTEL - REGINA CROSS ROAD had been very heavily shelled and a great deal of work was required on it; it was made passable for pack transport throughout by the morning of the 17th.

   The road from RUDOLPHE FARM forward was made passable for guns as THE INGS by the morning of the 17th. Thereafter, work of improvement, widening, draining, etc., was continued. On the 19th. it was found advisable to withdraw the parties working forward of BOSICASTEL and employ them on the road from MORTELDJE EST. up to BOSICASTEL which was in a very bad condition and required a great deal of maintenance at the southern end.

5. On the 18th. the construction of a tramway starting along-side the light railway at ALGERIAN COT, was commenced; this tramway was to run via HURST PARK towards FERDINAND FARM. Work on it was much hampered by persistent shell fire. By the 23rd. track had been laid to opposite MINTY FARM with spurs in to KEMPTON PARK and MINTY FARM ADV. Dressing Station.

   By the 29th. the track had been laid to C.10.b.0.5 and dump of sleepers and track had been formed at C.10.a.6.1. Work on this job was slow as parties available for work were small and not always available and towards the latter stage there was difficulty in getting up sufficient Decauville track.

6. Construction of Advanced Dressing Station at MINTY FARM was taken in hand on 21st. Two large elephant shelters were erected and covered with reinforced concrete and rails; this job was not quite completed by the 30th. To facilitate the carrying of wounded a double duck-board track was laid from GOURNIER FARM to MINTY FARM.

7. From the 16th. to the 20th. the work of the two Field Coys. in line was devoted to fair weather tracks (c) and (d) and by the 29th. the condition of these tracks was as follows :-

   (c) Passable up to nearly opposite VON WERDER HOUSE.
   (d) Passable from GOURNIER FARM up to C.4.b.6.0.

   Work on these tracks was very difficult as it was all night work and shelling was fairly frequent, especially gas shells.

/3.....

8.   On the 21st. parties on the fair weather tracks were reduced and continuation of duck-board tracks (a) and (b) were taken in hand. By the 23rd. (a) was completed up to MILITARY ROAD.
     By the 26th. duck-board track (b) was complete from FERDINAND FARM via MON DU RASTA BRIDGE up to C.5.a.9.1 and the length from HURST PARK - VON WERDER HOUSE had been doubled.
     Large maintenance parties were required on duck-board tracks owing to damage by shell fire and by their use by pack animals.

9.   Two sections of the 87th. Field Company were told off for construction of strong points on the night of the 27th. after the attack by the 52nd. Brigade but these parties were unable to get forward to sites selected and no work was done.
     The remainder of the R.E's and Pioneers were employed up till the 29th. on which date they were relieved by units of the 51st. Division,
on fair weather track (c) which was completed to C.4.d.9.5.
  "   "   "   (d) "   "   "   and improved
                       to MILITARY ROAD.
(These tracks were eventually of little use owing to the bad weather).
     Road from MORTELDJE EST. to KITCHENERS HOUSE, draining, metalling, widening and slabbing.
     Road from RUDOLPHE FARM - VARNA FARM - CHIEN FARM and thence south along CHIEN FARM - REGINA CROSS ROAD. This road was made passable for guns as far as C.4.b.5.5.

APPENDIX 4.

ADMINISTRATIVE ARRANGEMENTS.

GENERAL.

The operations presented abnormal conditions for the services of maintenance owing to the paucity of roads, the nature of the terrain which was in full view of the enemy as far West as the line Hill 23 - GATWICK PARK, the intersection of the area of operations by the STEENBEEK, and lastly by the absence of water supply East of the YSER CANAL.

To increase these difficulties, the enemy continually put down heavy barrages on the line RUDOLPH FARM - KITCHENERS WOOD, as well as on the STEENBEEK, making the carriage of supplies and ammunitions across this stream very uncertain until the latter phase of the operations.

Reserves dumps consisting of S.A.A., grenades, Rockets, very lights, etc., as well as 8000 Reserve Rations were established at C.19.d.1.1 and C.19.d.4.2 respectively. Fresh water was stored in 400 petrol cans at the ration dump. From these all forward dumps were supplied.

The supply of Artillery ammunition is dealt with in C.R.A. report.

OPERATIONS 16th. August 1917.

DUMPS.

Dumps of ammunition, rations, water and R.E. material were established by 14th. August at FRANCOIS & VON WERDER FARMS for the operations of the 16th. August, a carrying party of 2 coys. 6th. Lincoln Regt. being ready, one company at each farm, to push forward dumps by Zero plus 4 to the East side of the STEENBEEK. This was accomplished, and ammunition, water, rations and R.E. material were established at U.29.c.2.5 within 600 yards of the troops by 9 a.m. The casualties in these carrying parties being 10 killed, 12 wounded, 1 missing.

Guides for the establishment of the dumps were provided by 34th. Brigade.

RATIONS.

The supply was normal, the troops taking part carrying one day's preserved in addition to their iron rations.

WATER.

Each man carried two filled water bottles. Replenishment being from the forward dumps.

TRANSPORT.

Pack transport alone was used, but could get only as far as GOURNIER and MINTY FARMS. This entailed much carrying by YUKON PACK towards the forward dumps which told hard on the troops, the weather being very bad, and the enemy shelling incessant.

ROADS.

Roads were only available for pack from KEMPTON PARK as far as GOURNIER and MINTY FARMS, to which point limbers were feasible. Duckboard tracks to FRANCOIS FARM and VON WERDER FARM.

/OPERATIONS 27th. August....

OPERATIONS 27th. August 1917.

DUMPS.

Dumps were pushed forward and a general dump of ammunition, water, rations and R.E. material was established at C.5.c.4.9 by 33rd. Brigade carrying parties, all being ready by the 26th. August.

In addition, a rear forward dump, was established at FERDINAND FARM on the West bank of the STEENBEEK.

RATIONS.

Supply was normal. Troops taking part carried a good haversack ration in addition to the unexpired and Iron Ration.

WATER.

Troops taking part carried a second water bottle.

TRANSPORT.

Limbers were in use as far as RUDOLPH FARM and HURST PARK, while pack could go as far as FERDINAND FARM, thus reducing man transport to a minimum.

ROADS.

The KEMPTON PARK - GOURNIER FARM Road had advanced as far as CHIEN FARM and was in fairly good condition and was suitable for limbers as far as that point. The KEMPTON PARK - MINTY FARM Road had advanced as far as HURST PARK and was good for limbers as far as that point.

TRAMWAYS.

A Decauville tramway was commenced on the 19th. August to run from ADMIRALS ROAD to FERDINAND FARM. This had reached HURST PARK on the 27th. and although it had not then been taken into use for supply and ammunition work, it proved of the utmost value in the evacuation of the wounded from the collecting station at MINTY FARM, releasing a large number of bearers for further duty of clearing the battlefield.

PRISONERS.

Throughout the whole operations no hitch occurred in the handling of prisoners from the battlefield to the Divisional Cage. No unnecessary escorts were employed.

STRAGGLER POSTS.

Three stragglers were stopped at the posts and were dealt with.

ROAD CONTROLS. Road controls were satisfactory.

CLEARING BATTLEFIELD.

Burial of the dead was carried out expeditiously, cemeteries being formed and all burials carried out in them as far as possible. Equipment was salvaged with good results.

VETERINARY ARRANGEMENTS.

During operations, 74 animal casualties occurred, resulting in 47 deaths. Slightly injured animals were treated in their own lines; serious cases were sent direct to the Mobile Veterinary Section, from where they were evacuated.

ORDNANCE SERVICES.

Replacement and re-equipment were expeditiously carried out under D.A.D.O.S. the arms being overhauled as soon as units came out of the line.

/FINAL......

FINAL.
It is suggested that the principle of employing light tramways should be exploited to a greater degree in the areas taken from the enemy. They are quicker to get into use than roads and are more easily repaired. They reduce the difficulties of maintenance to a minimum and are more than valuable for evacuating the wounded. As a man-power saving institution alone, they should be extensively employed.

APPENDIX 5.

MEDICAL ARRANGEMENTS.

At 7 p.m., 7th. August, 1917, the Advanced Dressing Station, ESSEX FARM (C.19.c.4.1), and the evacuation of wounded from the front, were taken over from the 51st. Division by 34th. and 33rd. Field Ambulances respectively.

The distribution of the personnel of 33rd, 34th., and 35th. Field Ambulances was as follows :-

    33rd. Field Amb.   2 Tent sub-divisions at XVIII Corps Main Dressing Station.
                                     1 Tent sub-division at No. 4 C.C.S.

    35th.   "   "   2 Tent sub-divisions at XVIII Corps Rest Station.
                                     1 Tent sub-division at XVIII Corps Walking Wounded Collecting Post.

Leaving at disposal of A.D.M.S., 11th. Division for the collection, evacuation, and treatment of the wounded :-

    34th. Field Ambulance.
    Bearer Divisions of 33rd. and 35th. Field Ambulances.

Evacuation at this time was by hand carriage from Regimental Aid posts to tramway at 5 CHEMINS ESTAMINET, on the left, and to light railway about C.21.a.4.7 on the right, from which places cases were conveyed to the Advanced Dressing Station by trollies.

On 15th. August, a Divisional Collecting Post and Artillery Aid Post was established at C.15.c.5.1., with accommodation for about 15 stretcher cases.

On 16th. August, Advanced Bearer Posts were pushed up to FRANCOIS FARM (C.4.c.4.4) on the left, and VON WERDER FARM (C.10.b.2.5) on the right, the method of evacuation remaining unchanged.

On 20th. August, CANE POST (C.9.a.6.3) was handed over to 33rd. Infantry Brigade and MINTY FARM (C.10.c.5.1) taken over by A.D.M.S., 11th. Division. Work was commenced on the latter as a Divisional Collecting Post and evacuation was now as follows :-

    By hand carriage from both Flanks, to MINTY FARM, thence by hand carriage to C.15.c.5.1, and thence by light railway to the Advanced Dressing Station, ESSEX FARM.

On 26th. August, Advanced Bearer Posts were established at COMEDY FARM (C.4.b.15.40) on the left, and at RED FARM (C.5.c.4.3) on the right, and a tramway from ADMIRALS ROAD was completed as far as MINTY FARM. Evacuation from MINTY FARM to C.15.c.5.1 was now by tramway instead of hand carriage, but otherwise was unchanged.

At 9 a.m. 30th. August, the relief of personnel at Advanced Dressing Station and RELAY POSTS etc., by personnel of Field Ambulances of 51st. Division was completed.

On 16th and 27th Augt. Wounds were in following proportions:

	SHELL WOUNDS.	BULLET WOUNDS.	VARIOUS.
16th Augt.	81.35	16.05	2.6
27th Augt.	63.4	30.9	5.7

APPENDIX 6.

INTER-COMMUNICATIONS.

Period August 8th. - August 28th. 1917.

1. GENERAL.
   (a) The communications taken over from the 51st. Division were duplicated throughout, and alternative routes put down where necessary.

   (b) Owing to the constant interruptions on the buries through earth faults, and the length of time which it necessarily takes to repair broken buried lines, overland and overhead routes proved more satisfactory than those laid in buries.

   (c) Buried routes were constantly broken because -
      (1) The enemy deliberately shelled the cable trenches.
      (2) There was not time to make the buries more than 6 feet deep which proved insufficient.

   (d) Shallow trenches, one foot by eight inches were used from 15th. inst. onwards for ground lines and gave a certain amount of protection to the cables; these are advocated if it is not intended to bury lines, at least 8 feet deep.

   (e) For the last four days a system of cables on poles (30 yard bays and 4 feet sag) was tried and worked satisfactorily, and although many times broken it was very easy to repair.

2. TELEPHONE & TELEGRAPH COMMUNICATION.
   (a) Divisional Communications to Brigades.
       Signals from the Division to Brigades were maintained throughout, and from the 21st. onwards, although the Brigade Headquarters shifted 3,000 yards forward, speech was good.
       During the action on the 27th. first class speaking was obtainable as far as Brigade Forward Station (FERDINAND FARM), and, when lines held, as far as RAT HOUSE, (Battalion Headquarters).

   (b) From Brigades forward to Battalion and Company H.Q.
       On the 16th., during the period between Zero minus 4 hours and Zero plus 6 hours it was impossible to keep lines through in the left sector of the front, but communication was maintained in the right sector, as far as the Brigade Forward Station. Forward of this nothing held long enough to get a message through owing to the heavy shell fire.
       After Zero plus 6 hours line communication was normal.

3. VISUAL.
       Visual was possible from almost any part of the front by direct observation or by relay. The Divisional Signal Station was open throughout but was not called on to work. Units do not realise sufficiently that this station is there to help them as well as to receive messages for the Division.
       During the fighting on the 16th. and 27th. visual was most unsatisfactory, and, practically useless, owing to smoke etc.

/4......

4. RUNNERS.

Runners were much used and proved satisfactory.

Many messages were sent by this means, however, which might have gone some other way. Greater care is necessary and units should realise that runners are not to be used if other means are available.

5. PIGEONS.

Pigeons were very successful during the early part of the action of the 16th. but proved useless on the 27th. owing to heavy rain.

Pigeons are frequently flown singly instead of in pairs; they are also held too long before being released.

Times of flight were satisfactory when the birds were properly despatched.

6. WIRELESS, AMPLIFIERS and POWER BUZZERS.

Wireless worked throughout on the 16th. intermittently, but on the 27th. continuously.

All Power Buzzers sent over with the advancing Infantry were destroyed by shell fire before they could be set up.

On the 16th. Amplifiers were pushed too far forward and were destroyed by shell fire or else the heavy firing broke the "valves" rendering the sets useless.

On the 27th. Amplifiers were kept at a safe distance from the front (about 500 yards) and worked satisfactorily throughout.

Very few messages were sent by this means, and it seems a great pity to employ so many trained men of this work if no use is made of the sets.

It was clearly proved, during the operations carried out by the Division, that Amplifier and Wireless sets installed at a safe distance from the front will work continuously and give satisfaction, if carried too far forward the whole scheme is upset and the chain of communication broken, also that in fighting of this sort Power Buzzers are useless to the attacking Infantry in the early stages of the fighting, (i.e. they should not go forward until the situation is cleared up and a suitable position found for them).

7. MOUNTED D.R.

These were supplied by Corps Cavalry and were most useful and satisfactory.

8. AEROPLANES.

Aeroplanes worked satisfactorily with Dropping Stations, on the 16th. inst. The weather on the 27th. made flying impossible.

9. BALLOON.

No messages sent; it is doubtful if this form of communication is worth the number of trained personnel necessary for its maintenance.

10. ROCKETS.

Only four were fired during the period under review, two reached the destination required, the other two were not picked up.

Rockets should prove a useful means of communication but practice and organisation are required before it can become satisfactory.

/11......

11. ARTILLERY.

Communications between artillery units was satisfactory throughout, but the liaison lines between the Artillery and Infantry on the 16th. gave a lot of trouble.

12. DIVISIONAL SCHEME. (Based on S.S. 148).

The scheme was satisfactory throughout from an Infantry point of view, but not satisfactory on the 16th. from an Artillery point of view.

The scheme has been revised and will, it is hoped, work satisfactorily in the future as far as advanced Brigade Headquarters or line of Battalion Headquarters.

13. CONCLUSION.

Communications were very difficult throughout, and a very heavy strain was thrown on all.

The results achieved reflect great credit on the personnel of the Divisional Signal Company, and on the Artillery, Brigade, and Battalion Signallers.

APPENDIX 7.

CASUALTIES.

From Noon 7th. to Noon 30th. August 1917.

	KILLED.		WOUNDED.		MISSING.	
	O.	O.R.	O.	O.R.	O.	O.R.
58th. F.A.B.	–	20	7	58	1	–
59th. "	–	4	3	52	–	–
11th. D.A.C.	–	–	–	11	–	–
11th. T.M. Bde.	–	1	–	3	–	–
67th. Field Co. R.E.	–	–	2	11	–	–
68th. " " "	–	2	–	15	–	–
86th. " " "	1	2	–	14	–	–
11th. Sig. Co. H.Q.) and No. 1 Section.)	–	–	1	–	–	–
H.Q., 32nd. Inf. Bde.) & No. 2 Sig. Section.)	–	–	–	1	–	–
9th. W. Yorkshire Regt.	3	68	8	176	–	18
6th. Yorkshire Regt.	1	28	4	129	–	28
8th. W. Riding Regt.	4	56	6	197	1	58
8th. York & Lancs. Regt.	–	14	4	78	–	2
32nd. M.G. Company.	–	7	1	23	–	1
32nd. L.T.M. Battery.	–	–	–	2	–	–
H.Q., 33rd. Inf. Bde.) & No. 3 Sig. Section.)	–	–	–	–	–	–
6th. Lincoln Regt.	2	29	4	78	–	6
6th. Border Regt.	–	16	2	57	–	1
7th. S. Staffs Regt.	–	20	2	78	–	1
9th. S. Foresters.	–	8	1	46	–	–
33rd. M.G. Company.	2	5	2	15	–	–
33rd. L.T.M. Battery.	–	–	–	1	–	–
H.Q., 34th. Inf. Bde.) & No. 4 Sig. Section.)	–	–	–	12	–	1
8th. Northd. Fusiliers.	4	46	6	241	–	28
9th. Lancs. Fusiliers.	1	36	9	192	–	25
5th. Dorset Regt.	–	25	3	117	–	4
11th. Manchester Regt.	4	53	5	185	1	14
34th. M.G. Company.	–	7	–	30	–	1
34th. L.T.M. Battery.	–	1	–	8	–	–
6th. E. Yorks (Pioneers).	–	16	2	46	–	–
11th. Div. Train.	–	–	–	2	–	–
33rd. Field Amb.) 34th. " ") 35th. " ")	–	6	–	40	–	–
	20	470	72	1,898	3	168*

* It is anticipated that the majority of these will be accounted for as killed or wounded.

APPENDIX 8.

PRISONERS ETC. CAPTURED.

Captured from 8th. August. to 30th. August 1917.

PRISONERS OF WAR.

Officers.	Other Ranks.
4	850

WAR MATERIAL.

Machine Guns.	Howitzers. (believed 4.2")
8	2

MAPS 1, 2, & 3.